26th Ibero-American Conference on Software Engineering (CIbSE 2023)

Held online

Montevideo, Uruguay
24-28 April 2023

ISBN: 978-1-7138-7354-9

Printed from e-media with permission by:

Curran Associates, Inc.
57 Morehouse Lane
Red Hook, NY 12571

Some format issues inherent in the e-media version may also appear in this print version.

CIbSE - IberoAmerican Conference on Software Engineering
c/o Luca Cernuzzi
Universidad Católica "Nuestra Seóra de la Asunción",
Campus Universitario, Asunción
Barrio Santa Ana, C.C.1683, C.P. 1364
Asunción - Paraguay

Phone: +595 21 334650
Fax: +595 21 310587

lcernuzz@uca.edu.py

Additional copies of this publication are available from:

Curran Associates, Inc.
57 Morehouse Lane
Red Hook, NY 12571 USA
Phone: 845-758-0400
Fax: 845-758-2633
Email: curran@proceedings.com
Web: www.proceedings.com

Table of Contents

Main Conference

Table of Contents

Doctoral Symposium

CIbSE 2023

XXVI Congreso Iberoamericano en Ingeniería de Software
XXVI Congresso Ibero-Americano en Engenharia de Software
XXVI Ibero-American Conference on Software Engineering
Montevideo, Uruguay, April 24 - 28, 2023

PROGRAM COMMITTEE CHAIRS

Giovanni Giachetti (Universidad Andrés Bello, Chile; Universitat Politècnica de València, Spain)
Breno de França (UNICAMP, Brazil)

DOCTORAL SYMPOSIUM CHAIRS

Sheila Reinehr (Pontifical Catholic University of Paraná (PUCPR), Brazil)
Aurora Vizcaíno (Universidad de Castilla-La Mancha, Spain)

JOURNAL FIRST CHAIRS

Gleison Santos (Universidade Federal do Estado do Rio de Janeiro (Unirio), Brazil)
Ignacio Panach (Universidad de Valencia, Spain)

EIbAIS CHAIRS

Andrea Delgado (Universidad de la República de Uruguay, Uruguay)
Marcos Kalinowski (Pontifical Catholic University of Rio de Janeiro (PUC-Rio), Brazil)

INDUSTRY TALKS CHAIRS

Cecilia Apa (Universidad de la República de Uruguay, Uruguay)
Silvana Moreno (Universidad de la República de Uruguay, Uruguay)

GENERAL CHAIRS

Martín Solari (Universidad ORT, Uruguay)
Diego Vallespir General Chair (Universidad de la República – Pyxis, Uruguay)

PROCEEDINGS CHAIR

Christian Quesada-López (Universidad de Costa Rica, Costa Rica)

Preface

On behalf of the CIbSE 2023 Organizing Committee, we are proud to present the proceedings of the 26th Iberoamerican Conference on Software Engineering (CIbSE 2023). CIbSE has provided a forum to present recent advances in the practices for the engineering of software-intensive systems since 1998. This year the conference was hosted by the Universidad de la República in Montevideo, Uruguay, which was a perfect scenario to make this high-quality event possible.

In a society increasingly relies on software systems for our daily activity (e.g., in communication, finance, healthcare, and transport), the use of adequate engineering practices in the form of methods, processes, and tools throughout the lifecycle of these systems becomes essential to ensure their suitability. In this context, CIbSE is the leading research forum on Software Engineering (SE) in Ibero-America, which promotes high-quality scientific research and, thus, supports the researchers in this community in publishing and discussing their work. In addition, the conference fosters collaboration and cross-fertilization among academics, students, and practitioners from the industry.

Sixty papers were submitted in this edition of the conference. Each submission was reviewed by at least three members of the Program Committee, formed by leading experts. After a careful peer-review process, 18 papers were finally selected (30% acceptance rate). Five distinguished papers were be invited to submit an extended version to the Science of Computer Programming journal, and the best paper received an award certificate. In addition to the 18 original papers, three papers were accepted in the Journal First category, offering an opportunity for the authors to discuss their work with the community as well as to enrich the CIbSE technical program.

CIbSE 2023 hosted the Doctoral Symposium, which aims at bringing together doctoral students working on foundations, techniques, tools, and applications of Software Engineering and giving them the opportunity to present and discuss their research in a constructive and international atmosphere where a board of experts discuss with the students to suggest new perspectives and improvements to the PhD theses. Six ongoing doctorate research projects were presented. Moreover, prof. Guilherme Travassos. (Federal University of Rio de Janeiro, Brazil) presented the keynote "Why, for what, for whom, and how to conduct useful, robust, and reliable Software Engineering research".

CIbSE 2023 also hosted the 6th edition of the Ibero-American School on Software Engineering (EIbAIS). EIbAIS aims at promoting a forum for discussions regarding Software Engineering, its related technologies and theoretical foundations, allowing the participation of practitioners, undergraduate and graduate students, and researchers.

This year, EIbAIS presented four tutorials, discussing general and specific topics of Software Engineering together with cross-fertilization with other technology disciplines:

Data and Big Data Quality in the context of Software Engineering (Adriana Marotta, Universidad de la República, Uruguay), Quantum Software Engineering (Ignacio García-Rodríguez de Guzmán, Universidad de Castilla-La Mancha, Spain), Software Architecture Challenges of ML-Enabled Systems (Ipek Ozkaya, Carnegie Mellon University Software Engineering Institute (SEI)).

CIbSE 2023 included the Industry Talks, which aims at providing the industry and practitioners means to discuss and work together in exploring how Software Engineer processes, methods, techniques, and tools can provide the industry with better solutions. Seven experts from the industry shared their experience with the CIbSE audience.

The conference had two renowned keynote speakers. Ipek Ozkaya (Carnegie Mellon University Software Engineering Institute (SEI)), discussed the opportunities and implications of AI-Augmented Software Development. Ignacio García-Rodríguez de Guzmán (Universidad de Castilla-La Mancha, Spain), presented an interesting sight about the intersection of software engineering practices in the development of future quantic computing applications.

Finally, we would like to thank all people who contributed to make this event possible. The quality of the technical program is a result of the dedication of the members of the Program Committee and additional reviewers. We would also like to thank all members of the organizing committee, authors, keynotes, panelists, instructors, session chairs and all the participants for their collaboration in making CIbSE 2023 a success. We express our gratitude to the CIbSE Steering Committee for their great support, particularly to Marcela Genero and Renata Guizzardi. Finally, we are thankful for the opportunity of serving as chairs for this conference.

Giovanni Giachetti and Breno de França
CIbSE 2023 PC Chairs

Main Conference

PC Chairs

Giovanni Giachetti (Universidad Andrés Bello, Chile; Universitat Politècnica de València, Spain)
Breno de França (UNICAMP, Brazil)

Program Committee

Fernanda Alencar (Universidade Federal de Pernambuco, Brazil)
Leandro Antonelli (LIFIA, Facultad de Informática, UNLP, Argentina)
Joao Araujo (Universidade NOVA de Lisboa, Portugal)
Hernan Astudillo (Universidad Tecnica Federico Santa María, Chile)
Claudia P. Ayala (Universitat Politècnica de Catalunya, Spain)
Clara Ayora (Tree Technology S.A., Spain)
Monalessa Barcellos (UFES, Brazil)
María Cecilia Bastarrica (Universidad de Chile, Chile)
Pablo Becker (GIDIS_Web, Engineering School, UNLPam, Argentina)
David Benavides (University of Seville, Spain)
Regina Braga (UFJF, Brazil)
Antonio Brogi (Università di Pisa, Italy)
Cristina Cachero (Universidad de Alicante, Spain)
Daniel Calegari (Instituto de Computación, Facultad de Ingeniería, Uruguay)
Bruno Cartaxo (IFPE, Brazil)
Juan Pablo Carvallo (Universidad del Azuay, Ecuador)
Carlos Cetina (San Jorge University, Spain)
Nelly Condori-Fernández (Universidad de Santiago de Compostela, Spain)
Heitor Costa (Federal University of Lavras, Brazil)
Jose Antonio Cruz-Lemus (University of Castilla-La Mancha, Spain)
Jose Luis de la Vara (University of Castilla-La Mancha, Spain)
Rafael de Mello (UFRJ, Brazil, Brazil)
Andrea Delgado (Instituto de Computación, Facultad de Ingeniería, Universidad de la República, Uruguay)
Amador Durán Toro (University of Seville, Spain)
Ronnie E. de Souza Santos (Recife Center for Advanced Studies and Systems (CESAR), Brazil)
Maria Claudia Emer (Universidade Tecnologica Federal do Parana, Brazil)
Eduardo Figueiredo (Federal University of Minas Gerais, Brazil)
Efraín R. Fonseca C. (Universidad de las Fuerzas Armadas ESPE, Ecuador)
Awdren Fontão (Federal University of Mato Grosso do Sul, Brazil)
César França (Federal Rural University of Pernambuco - UFRPE, Brazil)
Kelly Garces Pernett (Universidad de los Andes, Colombia)

Felix Garcia (Alarcos Research Group, Information and Systems Department, Escuela Superior de informática, University of Castilla - La Mancha, Spain)
Jesus Garcia-Molina (Universidad de Murcia, Spain)
Alejandra Garrido (LIFIA-Facultad de Informatica-UNLP, Argentina)
Gustavo Gatica (Universidad Andrés Bello, Chile)
Laura González (University of the Republic, Uruguay)
Miguel Goulão (NOVA LINCS, Departamento de Informática, Faculdade de Ciências e Tecnologia, Universidade Nova de Lisboa, Portugal)
Renata Guizzardi (Universidade Federal do Espirito Santo, Brazil)
Graciela Dora Susana Hadad (Universidad Nacional del Oeste, Argentina)
Emilio Insfran (Universitat Politècnica de València, Spain)
Luis Iribarne (University of Almería, Spain)
Clemente Izurieta (Montana State University, United States)
Marcelo Jenkins (University of Costa Rica, Costa Rica)
Marcos Kalinowski (Pontifical Catholic University of Rio de Janeiro (PUC-Rio), Brazil)
Miguel Katrib (Professor, Doctor, Cuba)
Uirá Kulesza (UFRN, Brazil)
Maria Lencastre (Universidade de Pernambuco, Brazil)
Lidia Lopez (Barcelona Supercomputing Center, Spain)
Ivan Machado (UFBA - Federal University of Bahia, Brazil)
Marcelo Martin Marciszack (UTN FRC, Argentina)
Johnny Marques (Instituto Tecnológico de Aeronáutica (ITA), Brazil)
Silverio Martínez-Fernández (Universitat Politècnica de Catalunya - BarcelonaTech, Spain)
Beatriz Marín (Universitat Politècnica de València, Chile)
Santiago Matalonga (University of the West of Scotlannd, United Kingdom)
Gerardo Matturro (Universidad ORT Uruguay, Uruguay)
Marian Moraga (Universidad de Castilla-La Mancha, Spain)
Leonardo Murta (Universidade Federal Fluminense (UFF), Brazil)
Denisse Muñante (ENSIIE & SAMOVAR, France)
Elisa Yumi Nakagawa (University of São Paulo, Brazil)
Vânia Neves (UFF, Brazil)
Toacy Oliveira (COPPE/UFRJ, Brazil)
Luis Olsina (GIDIS_Web, Engineering School, UNLPam, Argentina)
Marc Oriol Hilari (Universitat Politècnica de Catalunya, Spain)
Cristina Palomares (Universitat Politècnica de Catalunya, Spain)
Jose Ignacio Panach Navarrete (Universitat de València, Spain)
Oscar Pastor (Universidad Politécnica de Valencia, Spain)
Ernesto Pimentel (University of Malaga, Spain)
João Pimentel (UFRPE - Universidade Federal Rural de Pernambuco, Brazil)
Claudia Pons (Universidad Nacional de La Plata, Argentina)
Carme Quer (Universitat Politècnica de Catalunya, Spain)
Christian Quesada-López (Universidad de Costa Rica, Costa Rica)
Sheila Reinehr (PucPR, Brazil)
José Fabián Reyes Román (Universitat Politècnica de València, Spain)
Marcela Ridao (INTIA UNICEN, Argentina)

Gustavo Rossi (LIFIA-F. Informatica. UNLP, Argentina)
Marcela Ruiz (Zurich University of Applied Sciences, Switzerland)
Daniela S. Cruzes (NTNU, Norway)
Victor Santander (Universidad Estadual do Oeste do Paraná, Brazil)
Gleison Santos (UNIRIO, Brazil)
Rodrigo Santos (UNIRIO, Brazil)
Carla Silva (Universidade Federal de Pernambuco, Brazil)
Isabel Sofia (Instituto Politécnico de Beja, Portugal)
Martin Solari (Universidad ORT Uruguay, Uruguay)
Simone R. S. Souza (ICMC/USP, Brazil)
Vitor E. Silva Souza (Federal University of Espírito Santo, Brazil, Brazil)
Carla Taramasco (Universidad Andrés Bello, Chile)
Guilherme Travassos (COPPE/UFRJ, Brazil)
Pedro Valderas (Universitat Politècnica de València, Spain)
Diego Vallespir (Facultad de Ingeniería, Universidad de la República, Uruguay)
Davi Viana (Federal University of Maranhão, Brazil)
Jéssyka Vilela (Universidade Federal de Pernambuco, Brazil)

Additional Reviewers

Aboua Ange Kevin N'Da
Leonardo Barcelos
Juan Carlos Moreno

Doctoral Symposium

DS Chairs

Sheila Reinehr (Pontifical Catholic University of Paraná (PUCPR), Brazil)
Aurora Vizcaíno (Universidad de Castilla-La Mancha, Spain)

DS Committee

Andreia Malucelli - Pontifícia Universidade Católica do Paraná - Brazil
Daniel Calegari - Universidad de la República - Uruguay
Edson Oliveira - Universidade Estadual de Maringá - Brazil
Félix García - University of Castilla-La Mancha - Spain
Guilherme Travassos - Universidade Federal do Rio de Janeiro - Brazil
Isabel Britto - Polytechnic Institute of Beja - Portugal
Luca Cernuzzi - Universidad Católica Nuestra Señora de la Asunción - Paraguai
Marcela Genero - University of Castilla-La Mancha - Spain
Oscar Pastor - Universitat Politècnica de València - Spain
Teresa Baldassarre - University of Bari - Italy

Effort Estimation in Agile Software Development: The State of the Practice in Colombia

Diana Gomez[1], Juan Cubillos[1], Jairo Aponte[1], Edwar Rojas[1]

[1]Universidad Nacional de Colombia. Facultad de Ingeniería. Bogotá - Colombia

{dgomezcar, jmcubillosa, jhapontem, edrojasb}@unal.edu.co

Abstract. *Effort estimation is fundamental for developing software projects and critical for their success. This paper focuses on how Colombian agile practitioners perform effort estimates in agile projects. For this purpose, we conducted an exploratory survey study that involved 60 respondents. The main findings are the following: (1) Agile practitioners prefer estimation techniques based on Expert Judgement. (2) Most of the respondents perceive that their estimates have a medium accuracy level. (3) The determining effort drivers are features of the project team and the software to be built. (4) The use of datasets for estimation is not common. (5) Most of the results of related studies are similar to ours, with differences in terms of the roles involved and the techniques used.*

1. Introduction

Software Development Effort Estimation (SDEE) is the process of assessing or predicting the most realistic effort, duration, and cost of a software endeavor [1], [2]. In the software engineering domain, effort estimation and planning are two closely related activities since the first one is essential to carry out the second one [3]. Accurate and precise estimates influence several planning tasks that help complete the project properly, such as creating a detailed schedule, breaking a project down into phases, and prioritizing functionalities for delivery.

Although effort estimation has been widely studied, the iterative nature of agile methods requires specialized estimation techniques [4]. Despite the numerous approaches proposed so far, the effort estimates in Agile Software Development (ASD) are far from perfect and in most cases the tendency is to underestimate the effort required. Requirements, management, and team-related issues are cited as the top causes for large differences between the actual and estimated effort [5].

Expert Judgment techniques have been by far the most common estimation approach used in Agile Effort Estimation (AEE) to predict software development effort. Expert Judgment is the assessment based on the experience of an application area, knowledge field, discipline, or industry, for the activity being performed. Such expertise may be provided by groups or individuals with specific education, knowledge, skills, experience, or training [6]. The most widely used estimation technique in ASD is Planning Poker, which is a variation of Expert Judgment.

A recent update of a Systematic Literature Review (SLR) on effort estimation in ASD summarizes the results of primary studies published from December 2013 to January 2020. The review focuses on 73 papers that provided new evidence for characterizing estimation activities in agile projects. These results confirm that Planning Poker has become the most widely used estimation technique, and it is very closely related to the most frequently used size metric, namely Story Points (SP). Moreover, SP estimate the size and complexity of user stories, which are the main artifacts for specifying user requirements in ASD [5].

The aim of this work is to analyze the current state of the software estimation process for agile software development in Colombia. To the best of our knowledge, there are no similar studies conducted in this region on AEE. Even more important, our interest is to verify the main findings of other studies regarding the effort estimation process in ASD, specifically concerning techniques used, existing problems, and opportunities for improvement.

We collected and analyzed data from five areas of interest: (1) Techniques used to carry out effort estimation; (2) Accuracy level of effort estimation in ASD; (3) Effort predictors used in this process; (4) Datasets, i.e. a collection of information containing estimations from software projects, used to perform effort estimation activities and (5) Differences between our findings and previous studies conducted in other regions. The data collection instrument was an online survey. It allowed us to gather information related to the aforementioned areas of interest, along with the demographic information of people who play various technical and managerial roles in ASD.

The paper is organized as follows. Section 2 presents related work of software development effort estimation on agile contexts. Section 3 describes the research methodology. Section 4 presents the most significant results of the study. Section 5 discusses the principal findings. Threats to validity and conclusions are described in sections 6 and 7, respectively.

2. Related Work

There is extensive literature of effort estimation based on surveys. Most of these studies have been carried out on traditional software development. Molokken and Jorgensen reported studies of this type since 1984 [7]. As traditional software methods are still in used, there are recent publications with the same scope [8], [9]. On the contrary, the literature review indicates that there are few studies, regarding effort estimation on ASD, similar to ours.

The first of them is the research by Usman et al., which validates a previous study by the same authors [10]. In this work of 2014, they surveyed 60 agile practitioners with experience in effort estimation from 16 different countries belonging to the five continents. Results showed that Planning Poker, Analogy, and Expert Judgment are frequently used estimation techniques in ASD, while SP is the most frequently employed size metric. Moreover, the expertise level of the team and prior experience are the most commonly used cost drivers. More than half of the respondents believe that their effort estimates on average are under/overestimated by an error of 25% or more. Finally, they found that most agile teams take into account implementation and testing activities during effort estimation, and it is mostly performed at iteration and release planning levels in ASD.

The second study was carried out in 2018 by Vera et al. [11]. They conducted an empirical study that identified the most frequent approaches to effort estimation in Chilean companies. Their main findings reveal that companies use Expert Judgment mainly due to their inability to count on trustworthy historical data. This inability to record reliable information is usually a consequence of the unplanned human resource sharing performed by the small software companies. It is worth noting that this study included all kinds of software projects.

In 2019, Prokopova et al. [12] conducted a study aimed at analyzing the project estimation process in Czech companies. 91 companies, belonging to six information technology areas were surveyed. They found that the most widely used estimation technique is Expert Judgment with 57% incidence. Overall, 48% of companies report implementation time as a key factor for the estimation. The most common cause (39%) of delivery delays in software projects is the requirements volatility. In general, 54% companies failed to complete a quarter of projects in the estimated timeframe. It is important to note that this study considered both agile and traditional projects.

Regarding effort estimation accuracy levels in ASD, Ramessur et al. [13] analyzed 15 projects in a well-known Mauritanian company and uncovered eighteen factors that influence iterations effort estimation and promote better estimation accuracy levels. These factors mainly refer to stakeholders, team characteristics, code base features, requirements aspects, and managerial factors.

Finally, there are several studies about effort estimation on User Stories [14], [15], [16], [17]. Majchrzak et al. [14] propose factors influencing User Story estimation. Their results show three major factor groups: management, knowledge, and requirements issues. Additionally, there are post-release defect factors that are directly related to inaccurate estimates: demotivation, stress, missing requirements, and inappropriate tests. Abrahamsson et al. [15] propose an ASD method for predicting development effort based on well structured user stories. Mahnič and Hovelja [16] carried out an empirical study using Planning Poker for estimating user stories, whose main finding is the correlation between the expertise of estimators and the estimation accuracy. Haugen [17] shows that the introduction of Planning Poker improves the estimation performance of the team on Extreme Programming (XP) environments.

3. Research Methodology

This work is a survey study that follows the approach suggested by Linaker et al. [18] who define the fundamental activities that must be carried out in studies based on surveys, within the software engineering field.

In 2015, Usman et al. [10] conducted a survey study aimed at validating the results of a previous SLR where ASD practitioners were consulted. Following a similar approach, we identified an SLR performed by Fernandez-Diego et al. [5] that was published just before the beginning of this research. Aside from being a recent SLR, there are several circumstances that make it suitable for our survey design. First, it is an update of an SLR carried out by Usman et al. and published in 2014 [19]. Second, it covered primary studies published between December 2013 and January 2020. Lastly, it keeps the research questions from 2014 SLR which are included in our study.

3.1. Research Questions

The main motivation for our study is to know how Colombian ASD practitioners estimate effort. In the absence of studies in this regard, we consider it pertinent and useful to carry out a survey study that, in the context of agile methods, inquires about the similar aspects investigated by other studies at a global level.

With the above in mind, we selected four research questions from Usman and Fernandez-Diego [19] [5]. We adapted two of them to focus only on effort estimation. We added a fifth question about how the results of our study compare with similar ones in other regions of the world. As a result, through this study, we answer the following research questions:

- RQ1: What techniques have been used to estimate effort in ASD?
- RQ2: What is the accuracy level of effort estimation techniques in ASD?
- RQ3: What effort predictors have been used for effort estimation in ASD?
- RQ4: What are the characteristics of the datasets used for effort estimation in ASD?
- RQ5: Are there significant differences between the results of our study and previous studies conducted in other regions?

3.2. The Survey and the Respondents

An online survey was sent to 146 ASD practitioners from diverse technology areas and regions of the country who have worked on ASD projects performing, among others, software estimation activities.

To determine the target population, we made a list of people who had academic or work relationships with us. In addition, we made sure that all of them were working in companies or departments involved in software development. This approach to select the participants can be classified as "convenience sampling", where the sample is taken from a group of people easy to contact [20].

The survey has 23 questions distributed into five sections. The first section, related to the demographic profile, inquiries about the profession, educational level, age, gender, and software development experience of the respondents. The other sections are all related to software effort estimation and collect information to help answer the research questions. These sections request information regarding techniques, tools, standards, and effort drivers, among others.

The survey was available for three weeks and 60 complete responses were collected. These answers correspond to the 41% of the sample initially planned. The survey was distributed in Spanish and an English version is available online [21].

4. Results

4.1. Demographics

Sixty Colombian ASD practitioners from different regions answered the survey. Geographically, almost all the respondents work in the Andean region of the country, where the most densely populated cities are located.

In respect of *age and education level*, 50% of the respondents are over 36 years old, 45% are between 25 and 35 years old, and 5% of them are under 25. Moreover, more than 90% of them own at least a bachelor's degree and 63% earned a postgraduate degree.

Regarding *roles*, the respondents are mostly developers (46.7%), software designers (18.3%), and business analysts (11.7%). There is minor representation of other roles,

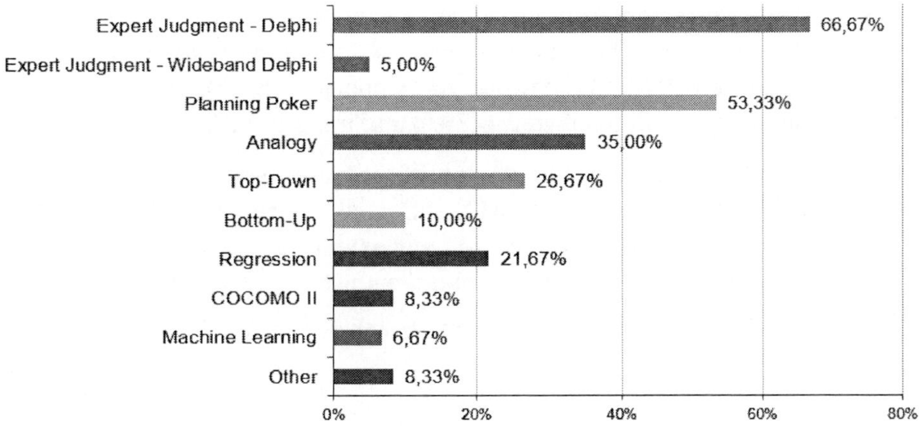

Figure 1. Techniques used for Effort Estimating

such as software architects (5%), scrum masters (5%), project leaders (5%), IT managers (2%), among others.

Regarding the *business area* where they work, most of them are in the information technology (59%) and financial sectors (27%). Other minor areas reported were government and medical and healthcare industries.

Finally, concerning *experience in software engineering*, 81.7% of the respondents reported more than 5 years working in the software industry and regarding *effort estimation experience*, 48.3% of respondents reported more than 5 years of experience, 26.7% have at least 2 years, and 13.3% less than one year doing estimation tasks.

4.2. Effort Estimation

This section presents the survey results grouped by research question.

4.2.1. RQ1: What techniques have been used to estimate effort in ASD?

There are six questions in the survey oriented to answer this research question. First, we asked them about the effort estimation techniques used in their agile projects. The results show that the top 5 techniques used by the respondents are Expert Judgment - Delphi (66.7%), Planning Poker (53.3%), Analogy (35%), Top-Down (26.7%), and Regression (21.7%). Figure 1 shows the results for all effort techniques.

Second, we inquired about agile frameworks used by the respondents. The most used frameworks are Scrum (100%), Kanban (41.7%), Extreme Programming (36,6%), and Test-Driven Development (15%). Other agile methods are used by less than 10% of the respondents, including Lean Software Development, Crystal, Dynamic Systems Development Method (DSDM) and Feature Driven Development (FDD). Frameworks for scaling agile such as SAFe were reported in only a few cases.

Third, we asked at what planning levels the respondents perform the effort estimation. The results indicate that 78.3% of the respondents estimate at the User Story level, 66.7% estimate at project level and 45% estimate at release and iteration level.

Fourth, we inquired about the software lifecycle activities where the respondents performed effort estimation. The most relevant software activities where estimation is performed are development (88.3%), followed by analysis (60%), design (53.3%), testing (51.7%), documentation, maintenance (36.7%), and training (18.3%).

Fifth, we inquired about tools to support the effort estimation process. We found that spreadsheets are the most used (90%), followed by customized tools (20%). Specialized tools for estimation are used to a lesser extent (20% for open source tools and 10% for proprietary ones). 5% of the respondents use no tools and only 3.3% of them use project management or application lifecycle management tools such as Kanban, MS Project or Azure DevOps tools.

Finally, we asked about software measurement units used in agile projects. The most used unit is Story Points (58.3%), followed by Use Case Points (33.3%), Function Points (30%), and Lines of Code (21.7%). A significant percentage of respondents (16.7%) use no unit and some of them reported 'working hours' as an additional measurement unit, even though this one is not defined as a software measurement unit.

4.2.2. RQ2: What is the level of accuracy of effort estimation techniques in ASD?

To answer RQ2, the survey includes three general questions and one specific for the Planning Poker technique.

The results show that the accuracy level is high for 23.3% of the respondents, medium for 53.3%, and low or very low for 11.7% of them. Additionally, 11.7% of the respondents do not have a clear idea about the accuracy of their estimates.

With respect to techniques for measuring the effort estimation accuracy. Most of the respondents (70%) use no technique to calculate the estimation accuracy levels, while 18.3% use variance analysis, 8.3% Prediction at level X or PRED(X), and 8.3% Magnitude of Relative Error (MRE).

Regarding factors affecting accuracy of effort estimation. Results show that the most relevant factors are requirements definition (80%), followed by the size and experience of the project team (58.3%), user involvement (45%), excessive optimism or pessimism (36.7%), project management (35%), and formality of the estimation process (23.3%). Figure 2 shows all factors that somehow influence effort accuracy level.

Table 1. Results of Accuracy Level for Planning Poker

Type of estimation	Accuracy level					
	Very High	High	Medium	Low	Very low	Not Apply
Duration	12%	41%	**44%**	0%	3%	0%
Cost	6%	12%	**56%**	14%	3%	9%
Resources	3%	38%	**45%**	6%	0%	8%

Focused on ASD and considering that Planning Poker is the most used effort estimation technique [10], we formulated questions to find out the accuracy level of duration, cost, and resources estimates. The data collected indicate that 56.6% of the respondents

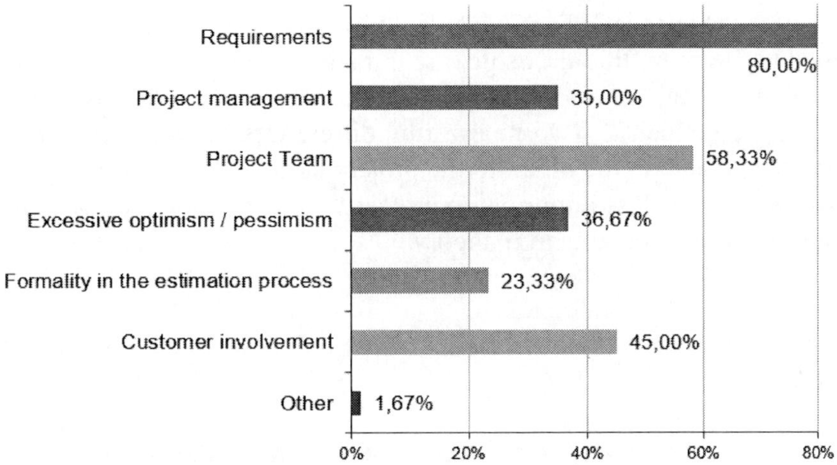

Figure 2. Factors Influencing Effort Accuracy Level

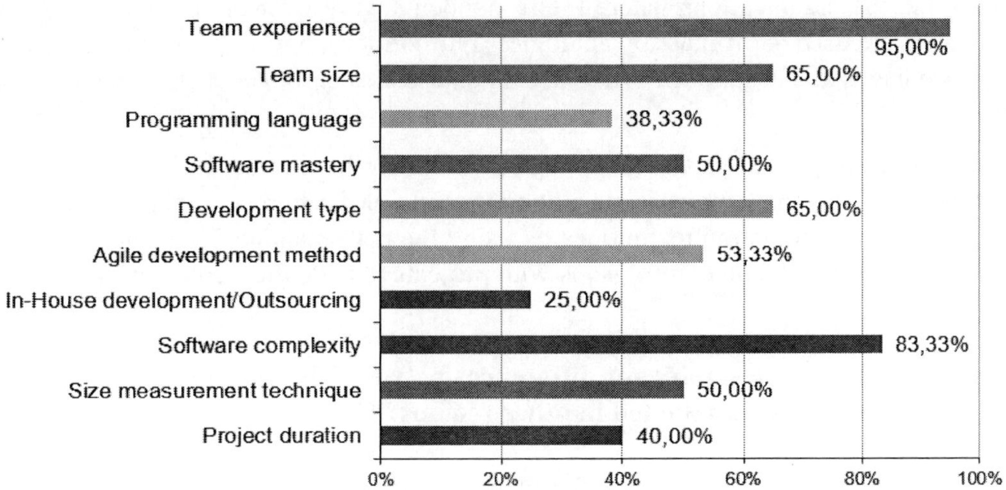

Figure 3. Effort Predictors in ASD

have used Planning Poker as an effort estimation technique. Table 1 shows the results distributed by type of estimation and accuracy where Planning Poker is used.

4.2.3. RQ3: What effort predictors have been used for effort estimation in ASD?

We formulate two questions to know which effort predictors are considered fundamental in ASD. Regarding the perception of the predictors' importance in the effort estimation activities, results show that the team experience is a fundamental factor for almost all of the respondents (95%). The second most selected factor is software complexity (83.3%). The third, fourth, and fifth places in the list are type of development (65%), team size (65%), and agile development method (53.3%), respectively (Figure 3).

Concerning the predictors actually used by the respondents, the resulting list is almost the same. They consider team experience as the main factor (86.7%), followed by software complexity (70%), development type, i.e., new or maintenance (60%), and team size (55%). Other factors are considered but to a lesser extent, including development method (agile or traditional), software domain (business sector), and programming language, among others. The four most important effort predictors are the most used in practice by the respondents. Two noteworthy differences refer, on the one hand, to the agile method used, and on the other, to the project duration. The agile approach adopted by the team seems to be less important in practice, while the project duration turns out to be more important in practice than in theory.

4.2.4. RQ4: What are the characteristics of the datasets used for effort estimation in ASD?

First of all, the most important finding is that the majority of the people surveyed (83.6%) have never made an effort estimate based on project datasets. However, from the responses of people who have used datasets, we identified two characteristics of the datasets used. First, the organizations where the respondents work own these datasets. Second, the datasets are used to estimate by analogies. Furthermore, only 3.6% of the respondents have used licensed datasets, 7.2% free access datasets, and 10.9% datasets owned by the company.

Regarding how the datasets have been used, we found that 12.7% of the respondents use them to make comparisons among projects of the same company, 9.09% apply parametric effort estimation techniques by using the datasets, and 5.4% use the datasets to estimate effort based on comparisons with projects outside their companies.

4.2.5. RQ5: Are there significant differences between the results of this study and previous studies conducted in other regions?

Estimation techniques. In this regard, Usman et al. [10] conclude that Planning Poker and Analogy are the most used techniques in ASD. Vera et al. [11] report Expert Judgment as the main technique for software effort estimation and, in some cases, Expert Judgment combined with Analogy. In our study, Expert Judgment and Planning Poker are the most used techniques for effort estimating. Our study and the one by Usman et al. [10] are entirely comparable, as the respondents chose from the same list of estimation techniques. The comparison with the study by Vera et al. [11] is partial because the list of techniques provided by their survey is unknown. In the study by Prokopova et al. [12], respondents had the option of choosing Expert Judgment and Analogy but not Planning Poker. Therefore, only the results obtained in relation to Expert Judgment are comparable in all studies, as shown in Figure 4.

Effort predictors. Our results point out that the most relevant is team experience, followed by software complexity, and development type (new or maintenance). Ramessur et al. [13] list similar factors affecting the effort estimates and conclude that the prime factors that may affect the estimation accuracy are team experience, technical skills, and requirements complexity.

Estimation Accuracy Level. Our results indicate that the perception of accuracy level of estimates is high for 23.3% of the respondents, medium for 53.3%, and low or very low for 11.7% of them. On the other hand, 11.7% of the respondents do not have a clear idea about the accuracy of their estimates. Usman et al. [10], as many other authors, report a tendency to effort underestimation. They also found that the combination of techniques and Story Points have a positive correlation with estimation accuracy. Vera et al. [11] indicate that almost half of companies overestimate the project effort, independently of the life cycle being used. This happens in some cases because the company uses a multiplier to overestimate projects in order to reduce the endeavor risk. Additionally, companies get no feedback from their estimations, and consequently they do not know the estimations accuracy level.

Prokopova et al. [12] investigate the number of projects that are delivered on time. They found that more than half of the companies (54%) do not finish 25% of their projects within their estimations, which is consistent with the trend identified in the other related studies.

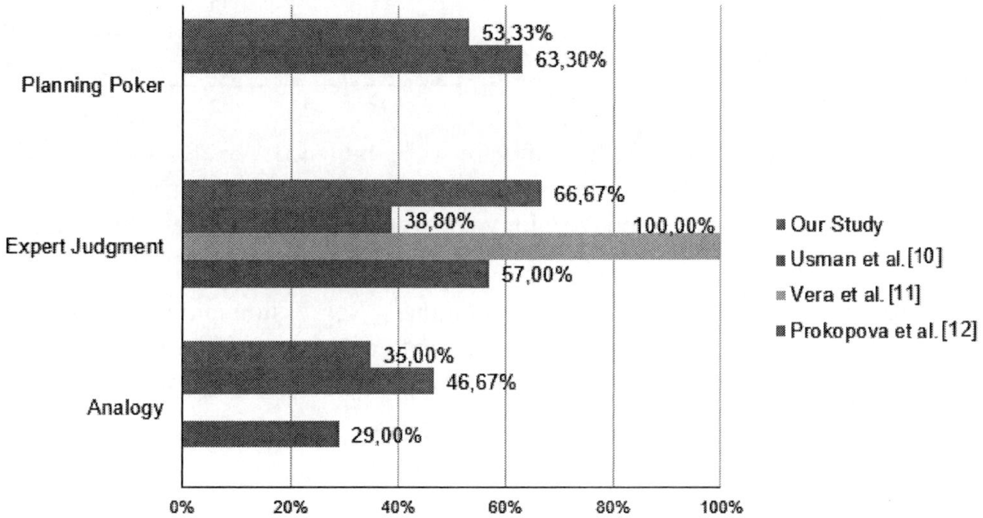

Figure 4. Estimation Techniques in Related Studies

4.3. Correlations

A correlation analysis was performed to identify some of the main interdependencies between significant variables. We used JASP, a free and open-source program for statistical analysis supported by the University of Amsterdam [22]. Most of the variables are nominal categorical with more than two values. Contingency tables, contingency coefficient, and Chi-squared test were used to determine whether there is a statistically significance between selected variables. Table 2 shows the results of the correlation analysis. Our results are similar to the Mahnič and Hovelja in terms of dependencies between respondents experience and effort estimation accuracy level [16].

5. Discussion

5.1. Effort Estimation Techniques

In ASD there is a preference for non-algorithmic techniques because project managers and teams favor approaches that aid collaboration and consensus for the estimation of the

Table 2. Correlations between Significant Variables

Variables	p-value	Contingency Coefficient	Explanation
SWE Experience and SDEE Experience	$p<0.001$	0.653	Significant association (moderate positive correlation) between the Software Engineering Experience and Experience in Software Development Effort Estimation.
SWE Experience and Accuracy Level	$p=0.012$	0.497	Significant association (moderate positive correlation) between the Software Engineering Experience and the Perception about Estimation Accuracy Levels.
SDEE Experience and Accuracy Level	$p<0.001$	0.610	Significant association (moderate positive correlation) between the Software Development Effort Estimation Experience and the perception about Estimation Accuracy Levels.

effort required and/or the size of the software to be built [5]. In this category, Expert Judgment oriented techniques are most commonly used by ASD practitioners. Planning Poker and Delphi are the most used. Analogy and Top-Down techniques are at the second level of use.

In regard to algorithmic estimation techniques, Regression and COCOMO are the most relevant, although they are used to a lesser extent than non-algorithmic techniques. Interestingly, techniques based on function points are not commonly used.

On the other hand, learning-oriented techniques are not sufficiently widespread in agile contexts. Instead of asking for specific techniques, our survey asks only for the use of learning-oriented techniques. Only 6.7% of the respondents have used them for software estimation.

Another important finding is that almost all respondents use at least one estimation technique. This fact suggests that effort estimation is a frequent and valuable process in agile projects.

Regarding estimation accuracy, the perception of respondents of high, average, and low levels of accuracy are 23.3%, 53.3%, and 11,7%, respectively. Moreover, 70% of the respondents use no technique for analyzing the accuracy of their estimates. Among the respondents who analyze accuracy, the most representative technique for measuring it is variance analysis(18.3%). In less than 17% of cases, the techniques used are oriented to measure deviation or error magnitude. The aspects that most influence estimation accuracy are requirements (definition, specification, size, etc.) and team size and experience.

5.2. Predictors for Effort Estimation

The factors that most influence the estimation process can be divided into two main groups: Those related to the team carrying out the software project and those that are connected to the characteristics of the project.

On the one hand, team experience includes aspects such as the technical skills of the members, their maturity as a team, as well as the quantity and quality of their training and the know-how of the team members about the software process to be used. That experience is the most important factor to consider in estimating effort, according to the results. On the other hand, the characteristics of the project have similar relevance. In this category, the complexity of the software to be built is the most significant factor. Another influential factor is whether the project is a new development, maintenance, or enhancement, mainly due to the level of uncertainty involved in each type of development. Lastly, in a third-place of relevance is the software domain, i.e., the targeted subject area of the software to be built.

5.3. Datasets and Tools for Effort Estimation

We found that spreadsheets are the most popular tool for supporting the effort estimation process, possibly due to the ease and flexibility to build models with them. Spreadsheets are suitable for building simple applications to implement effort models such as regression curves based on public or proprietary datasets. The use of proprietary tools is not common perhaps due to the licensing prices of this type of tools.

With respect to datasets, they are rarely used. This can be a strong reason to have low usage rates of parametric and learning-oriented effort techniques. In cases where datasets are used, proprietary datasets stand out, i.e., datasets based on info from previous projects of the company. Finally, datasets are employed mainly for productivity comparison purposes between past and current projects within the organization.

5.4. Planning Level in ASD

The most frequent planning level is User Stories / Requirements / Use Cases (78.3%). Likewise, there are high levels of planning on projects (66.7%), releases (45%), and iterations (45%). This might suggest that there is an interest in ASD for effort predictions at iteration, release, and project level. This in turn would confirm one of the main effort estimation goals in the early stages of the software life cycle: planning, as accurately as possible, the resources required by the software project. It would be interesting to know how planning is performed at the project level, as one of the main characteristics of ASD projects is uncertainty in scope. Lastly, it is worth noting that more than 98% of the people surveyed perform some type of planning. Only one respondent admitted that she makes no planning, at least at the levels considered in the survey.

5.5. Comparison with other Studies

Table 3 shows the summary of related studies, in terms of the characteristics of the data collection processes.

Our results show that almost all surveyed people (88.3%) estimate coding activities, while analysis (60%), design (53.3%), and testing (51.6%) activities are taken into account for effort estimation in similar proportions. This is in line with Usman et al. [10], where coding activities are considered to be the most important for effort estimation (86.67%). However, they found that analysis (43,33%) and design (53,33%) activities are considered for effort estimation in a smaller proportion, while testing activities are the second most important factor.

With respect to factors that can affect effort estimation, they are similar in all cases. Likewise, the relevance assigned to these factors is also similar. Finally, team

Table 3. Characteristics of Related Studies

Study	Instrument	Analysis Unit	Observations
Usman et al. [10]	Survey	Individual	Online questionnaire 60 people surveyed.
Vera et al. [11]	Interview	Company	Semi-structured interview, One person per company 10 people surveyed.
Prokopova et al. [12]	Survey	Company	Questionnaire sent to 91 companies.
Our study	Survey	Individual	Online questionnaire 60 people surveyed.

experience is the most important factor to consider in effort estimation according to our results and related studies [10], [13], [14].

As for estimation accuracy, we used a 5-point scale: very high, high, medium, low, and very low. For the same purpose, Usman et al. [10] use 2 major categories: over-estimated or underestimated to express estimation accuracy. Vera et al. [11] do not report how accurate the effort estimates are, instead, they concluded that the effort is always overestimated due to a multiplying factor that magnifies the estimates. In Prokopova et al. [12], only the percentage of projects not delivered on-time is reported.

6. Threats to Validity

Validity determines how much we can trust that the study findings accurately reflect the reality we want to describe or explain. For the particular case of a survey, many factors can affect that validity and they are discussed in this section, as well as, the actions we took to avoid or mitigate their effects.

External validity. First, the participants were mostly developers or people who play specific roles within software teams such as designers, analysts, architects, or scrum masters. Most of them have more than 5 years of experience in the software industry, with ages ranging from under 25 to over 45 years. Thus, the sample is quite heterogeneous in terms of experience, age, and job role. Second, the vast majority of them are in the Andean region where the largest population and the greatest industrial development of the country are concentrated. Despite the above, the results of our study cannot be fully applied to the entire population. Consequently, it is feasible that a replication of this study yields somewhat different results, in some of the analyzed aspects.

Internal validity. First, to reduce the threat that the subjects may not be competent enough to answer the questionnaire proposed, a list of potential respondents was built to ensure that participants had worked for software companies and had at least basic knowledge of effort estimation. Second, we collected specific demographic information regarding their career to be sure that the answers given by our respondents are reliable and suitable. Third, we conducted a pilot experiment with two graduate students and obtained feedback about the questionnaire itself and the time required to respond.

Construct validity. In this regard, we mitigated the associated threats by designing the questionnaire based on the results of an SLR. In addition, we guaranteed the relevance of each question included by associating it with one of the research questions formulated in this study. Moreover, the questionnaire items were iteratively improved so that we ensure the questions are valid, clear, unambiguous, and bias-free. Lastly, we write an introduction to the survey where we explained the purpose of the study, and clarified the concept of effort estimation.

7. Conclusions

We present a survey study aimed at determining how Colombian ASD practitioners carry out the effort estimation process within agile projects. The designed survey inquires about the effort estimation techniques used, the accuracy of the estimates, the factors that influence the accuracy of the estimates and whether datasets are used to support the estimation processes in any way. The survey was answered by 60 people who play various roles within Colombian software companies. We used convenience sampling and ensured that all participants work in the software industry.

With respect to estimation techniques, the ones based on Expert Judgment are the most frequently used. Within this category, Planning Poker stands out because it is used by more than half of the respondents and its effectiveness is considered medium-high when estimating duration, costs, and resources in ASD projects. Furthermore, the use of parametric techniques is representative (regression, COCOMO, Function Points Analysis). A minority of the respondents report using learning-oriented techniques and the use of proprietary techniques is marginal.

Regarding the agile processes, Scrum has been used by all participants, while Kanban and XP were reported by less than half of the respondents. The predominance of Scrum makes it the typical framework where the application of effort estimation techniques takes place. Moreover, effort estimation occurs primarily within the fine-grained planning process, that is, at the User Story or Use Case level. Data also suggests that estimation results are used, to a lesser extent, in planning iterations, releases, and the entire project. These results are consistent with studies that describe the way agile projects are planned and managed [10].

The respondents also reported that the activities for which effort estimates are carried out are development (90.9%), analysis phase (61.8%), design tasks (58.2%), and software testing work (56.4%).

Regarding software sizing, Story Points and Use Case Points are used to a great extent as units for estimating software size. Approximately, one-third of the surveyed people use Function Points, and LOC to a lesser extent. Additionally, about 20% of the respondents reported that they use no size measurement technique.

As for tooling, the use of specialized software to perform software estimation is not common. This activity is dominated by spreadsheets (90.9%) and, to a lesser extent, by software tools tailored to the needs of each organization, which may be based on spreadsheets.

Estimation accuracy is considered high for a fifth of the surveyed people, average for slightly more than half of them, and low or indeterminate for the rest of the respondents. However, about 71% of the respondents report that a formal accuracy analysis process is not carried out. The use of variability analysis was reported by 20% of them, while MRE and PRED(X) were reported by a small proportion of people. All factors affecting the accuracy of estimates suggested in the survey are recognized as significant.

With respect to effort predictors, the most relevant in order of importance are team experience, software complexity, development type, team size, software domain, and software size measurement technique used.

With respect to datasets, we found that, in most cases, they are not used to support the effort estimation process. This indicates a low level use of parametric or learning-oriented techniques, which require historical data for calculating estimates or training the models. In the few cases where datasets are used, they are mostly public sources or historical data from the organization itself.

The general results suggest that although estimations are performed as an input for project planning, their accuracy is not formally evaluated. In this regard, the majority of respondents simply perceive that their estimates are acceptable or good, but there is no evidence of any effective process that supports such perceptions. We believe that the support of tools that facilitate data capture, as well as its subsequent analysis, could substantially improve the quality of the estimates.

References

[1] M. Chemuturi, 2009.Software Estimation Best Practices Tools & Techniques, Broward-Florida, J. Ross Publishing.

[2] J. Wen, S. Li, Z. Lin, Y. Hu, and C. Huang, "Systematic Literature Review of Machine Learning Based Software Development Effort Estimation Models," Inf. Softw. Technol., vol. 54, no. 1, pp. 41–59, 2012. https://doi.org/10.1016/j.infsof.2011.09.002

[3] A. Trendowicz, 2014, Software Project Effort Estimation. Berlin, Germany, Springer-Verlag.

[4] O. Malgonde and K. Chari, "An Ensemble-Based Model for Predicting Agile Software Development Effort," Empirical. Software. Engineering., vol. 24, no. 2, pp. 1017–1055, 2019. https://doi.org/10.1007/s10664-018-9647-0

[5] M. Fernandez-Diego, E. R. Mendez, F. Gonzalez-Ladron-De-Guevara, S. Abrahao, and E. Insfran, "An Update on Effort Estimation in Agile Software Development: A Systematic Literature Review," IEEE Access, vol. 8, pp. 166768–166800, 2020. https://doi.org/10.1109/ACCESS.2020.3021664

[6] PMI, A Guide to the Project Management Body of Knowledge, 6th ed. Newtown Square, Pennsylvania, USA: Project Management Institute, 2017.

[7] K. Moløkken and M. Jørgensen, "A review of software surveys on software effort estimation," in Proceedings - 2003 International Symposium on Empirical Software Engineering, ISESE 2003, 2003, pp. 223–230.

[8] T. Vera, S. F. Ochoa, and D. Perovich, "Survey of Software Development Effort Estimation Taxonomies," no. March, 2018.

[9] A. Saeed, W. H. Butt, F. Kazmi, and M. Arif, "Survey of software development effort estimation techniques," in ACM International Conference Proceeding Series, 2018, pp. 82–86.

[10] M. Usman, E. Mendes, and J. Börstler, "Effort Estimation in Agile Software Development: A Survey on the State of the Practice," in ACM International Conference Proceeding Series, 2015, vol. 27-29-Apri, p. 10. https://doi.org/10.1145/2745802.2745813

[11] T. Vera, S. F. Ochoa, and D. Perovich, "Understanding the Software Development Effort Estimation in Chilean Small," 2018.

[12] Z. Prokopova, P. Silhavy, and R. Silhavy, Analysis of the Software Project Estimation Process: A Case Study, vol. 984. Springer International Publishing, 2019. https://doi.org/10.1007/978-3-030-19807-744

[13] M. A. Ramessur and S. D. Nagowah, "Factors Affecting Sprint Effort Estimation," Adv. Intell. Syst. Comput., vol. 1089, no. January, pp. 507–518, 2020. https://doi.org/10.1007/978-981-15-1483-8_43

[14] L. Madeyski and M. Majchrzak, "Factors influencing User Story estimations: an industrial interview and a conceptual model," Cent. East. Eur. J. Manag. Econ., vol. 4, no. 4, pp. 261–280, 2016.

[15] P. Abrahamsson, I. Fronza, R. Moser, J. Vlasenko, and W. Pedrycz, "Predicting Development Effort from User Stories," Int. Symp. Empirical Software Engineering. Meas., pp. 400–403, 2011. https://doi.ieeecomputersociety.org/10.1109/ESEM.2011.58

[16] V. Mahnič and T. Hovelja, "On Using Planning Poker for Estimating User Stories," J. Syst. Softw., vol. 85, no. 9, pp. 2086–2095, 2012. https://doi.org/10.1016/j.jss.2012.04.005

[17] N. C. Haugen, "An Empirical Study of Using Planning Poker for User Story Estimation," Proc. - Agil. Conf. 2006, vol. 2006, pp. 23–31, 2006. https://doi.org/10.1109/AGILE.2006.16

[18] J. Linaker, S. M. Sulaman, R. Maiani de Mello and M. Host, "Guidelines for Conducting Surveys in Software Engineering," Department of Computer Science, Lund University, 2015.

[19] M. Usman, E. Mendes, F. Weidt, and R. Britto, "Effort Estimation in Agile Software Development: A systematic literature review," in ACM International Conference Proceeding Series, 2014, pp. 82–91. https://doi.org/10.1145/2639490.2639503

[20] M. Saunders, P. Lewis, and A. Thornhill, Research Methods For Business Students, 8th ed. Pearson Education, 2019.

[21] "Survey Translation" 2022. [Online]. Available: http://it-jmca.com/UN/Paper2/Survey.pdf

[22] JASP Team. (2022). JASP (Version 0.16.4)[Computer software]. Retrieved from https://jasp-stats.org/

What can we learn from surveys on the importance of software development productivity factors?

Magne Jørgensen[1]

[1]Simula Metropolitan Center for Digital Engineering
Oslo, Norway
magnej@simula.no

Abstract: A proper interpretation of survey results on the importance of software development productivity factors requires an understanding of what the responses reflect. To find out more about this, we conducted a survey with 79 experienced software professionals. The strongest connection found was between the high perceived importance of a productivity factor and how frequently the respondents had experienced that a low performance on that factor had caused productivity problems. We argue that it is challenging to interpret survey-based results on the importance of productivity factors. Instead of conducting more surveys on the importance of such factors, we recommend asking directly about previous experiences related to productivity factors and including contextual information that enables proper interpretation of the responses.

1. Introduction

There is no shortage of studies aiming at identifying characteristics of people, processes, and products that influence software productivity. The identified number of such characteristics, often termed productivity factors, is large. As an illustration, the review of productivity factors in (de Barros Sampaio, Barros, de Aquino, e Silva, & de Lemos Meira, 2010) examined thirty-nine productivity factors covered in the research literature, and the review in (Wagner & Ruhe, 2018) reports from a set of studies identifying between and ten and around 250 productivity factors. By introducing a finer level of detail of the productivity factors and extending the scope of addressed contexts, one may argue that the number of productivity factors relevant in at least one context can get as large as desired. For example, the reliability of the power supply is usually not considered to be a productivity factor in software development, but there are contexts where this matters a lot.

Many of the reported studies not only report the existence of these factors but also try to rank them in terms of the importance or strength of influence on productivity. This strong interest in the importance of productivity factors is motivated by their obvious importance. The results may, for example, be used to focus the improvement effort on the factors that affect productivity most. Many of the studies on the relative importance of productivity factors are survey-based. Table 1 displays elements of three such studies, and exemplifies that such surveys vary in the factors included, how they ask about the importance, and whom they ask. While this variance in study designs is likely to affect the results, all studies share the interest in trying to identify the importance of different productivity factors. Notice that the three studies in Table 1 are just meant as illustrations of how surveys on productivity factors are *typically* conducted and motivate the research questions in this paper. We have *not* attempted to conduct a systematic review of studies or to give examples of all variants of surveys on productivity factors.

Table 1: Three examples of surveys on software development productivity factors

Study	(Blackburn, Scudder, & Van Wassenhove, 1996)	(Paiva, Barbosa, Lima Jr, & Albuquerque, 2010)	(Machuca-Villegas, Gasca-Hurtado, Puente, & Tamayo, 2022)
Sampling method for productivity factors	11 factors chosen from «*those that have been identified in the literature*».	Productivitity factors identified in the research literature grouped into 32 factors.	13 social and human factors chosen from 57 productivity factors identified in a literature review.
Formulation of question	*To what extent were the following factors useful in reducing the overall software development time for the project?*[i]	*What is the influence of the factor on software development productivity?*[ii]	Questions of the type: *To improve productivity in software development teams ...* [iii]
Scale points	Not at all helpful ... Very helpful	High positive influence ... High negative influence	Strongly disagree ... Strongly agree
Sampling method - participants	Selection of managers in software-related industries from a list supplied by a leading European management school (98 responses, response rate of 27.3%).	Convenience sample of software professionals from 11 Brazilian companies (77 responses, response and sampling process not reported).	Convenience sample of software professionals, mainly from Columbia (81 responses, unknown response response and sampling process not reported)
Three most important productivity factors	1) Better customer specifications 2) Better programmers of software engineers 3) Improvements in communications between team members	1) Commitment 2) Motivation 3) Consistent requirements	1) Communication 2) Collaboration 3) Commitment

i) The participants were requested to consider a recently completed project. The ranked importance of a factor is based on the median of the mean responses from previous studies in Japan and the US, and the current study with respondents from Europe.
ii) Actual question is not included in the paper, and the one in the table may be inaccurate. The ranked importance of a factor is based on the proportion of responses with "High positive influence".
iii) There were 4-6 questions per productivity factor. The ranked importance is based on the score relative to the maximum possible score for a productivity factor.

The main motivation for initiating the study presented in this paper was the difficulty we had in interpreting results from such surveys on the importance of productivity factors, expemplified by those in Table 1. This difficulty is not only caused by the variation in productivity factors included in the survey, who was asked, and the formulation of the questions. A major part of the problem is related to interpreting what the respondents meant by productivity, what they understood with the different productivity factors, and, in particular, what they meant by "more important" (or "more influential").

To illustrate this type of interpretation problem, assume that an empirical study reports that *psychological safety* is perceived as a more important software development team productivity factor than *developer skill*.[1] We can think of several possible

[1] This is, for example, what is reported in the frequently cited survey and interview-based study on google software development teams, see for example (rework.withgoogle.com/print/guides/5721312655835136/). Unfortunately, the above study is not published or peer-reviewed, and our requests for more information about the study have been conducted remain unanswered, but we suspect that this study has the same challenges as described earlier.

evaluation processes used by the respondents, which may be combined, of this finding, including the following five:

1. The *variation* in psychological safety explains the variation in productivity among the teams very well, and better than the variation in developer skills. This includes a stronger connection between an increase in psychological safety and an increase in productivity, than the corresponding connection for developer skill. As there are neither commonly accepted measures of the level of psychological safety or developer skill, nor of the level of productivity, the strength of such connection may be hard to evaluate for the respondents.
2. A *good* performance in psychological safety has a strong connection with high productivity, and this connection is stronger than with a very good performance in developer skills. There are similar interpretation problems as for the above interpretation, but it may perhaps be easier to think back on teams with high productivity and their main characteristics than trying to identify a general relationship.
3. A *poor* performance in psychological safety has a strong connection with low productivity and this connection is stronger than with a low performance in developer skills. This interpretation is analog to the previous, with similar challenges.
4. The *frequency of experienced productivity problems* caused by low performance in psychological safety is high, and higher than for developer skills.
5. There is a *belief* that psychological safety is important, and that it is more important than developer skills based on sources not related to own experience. This may, for example, include general knowledge about software development and teamwork, opinions of other software developers, and what is a common belief in their professional communities.

It will typically be hard to know which of the above types (or combinations of them), or other types of interpretations are reasonable to assume are in place when responding to questions on the importance of these two productivity factors. It is also possible that the two productivity factors will have different types of interpretations and that different respondents will base their answers on different interpretations. Assume, for example, that a respondent never has experienced anything other than teams with highly skilled developers and never experienced that low developer skill has led to productivity problems. The psychological safety in the teams has, on the other hand, varied a lot, and sometimes (when psychological safety has been low) team members have reported problems too late in the project, which has led to large problems. For this respondent, it may be natural to give psychological safety a high score, and developer skill a much lower score. When, later, experiencing a team with productivity problems due to the low skill of some of the developers, the perceived importance of developer skill may increase substantially and exceed that of psychological safety.

To further complicate this interpretation of the survey-based importance of productivity factors, there may be substantial challenges related to analyzing to what extent a factor, such as increased psychological safety, actually *causes* productivity in a particular team or project, or is just an indicator of a well-composed and skilled team. The interpretation of causal relationships in the teams and projects may consequently easily be affected by prior beliefs on importance, i.e., the type of influences often denoted as "you see it if you believe it" or "confirmation bias" (Chattopadhyay et al., 2022; Jørgensen, 2013; Jørgensen & Papatheocharous, 2015).

The study reported in this paper aims to address some of the above challenges and to guide future attempts to conduct such studies. We do not intend to cover all types of possible interpretations of what the high importance of a productivity factor may mean or all types of potential connections in this paper. The focus is on the following, potentially relevant, interpretations (which are similar to the four first exemplified with psychological safety and developments skill earlier), i.e., to what extent a higher importance of a productivity factor, as experienced by the respondent, is connected with:

1. Larger variation in how well previous projects and teams have performed regarding that productivity factor. This analysis is motivated by that if a respondent has experienced a high degree of variation regarding a productivity factor, assuming that the productivity also varies with that factor, this will lead to a perception of a higher importance of that factor.
2. Better performance in previous projects and teams regarding that productivity factor. The analysis is motivated with that it may be easier to recall a connection between very good performance on a productivity factor and high productivity, than trying to connect the full range of variance as in 1.
3. Poorer performance in previous projects and teams regarding that productivity factor. The analysis is motivated similarly to 2, but with poor performance on a productivity factor and low productivity.
4. A higher frequency of observing low performance on a productivity factor has caused low productivity. This interpretation is similar to 3. but puts a stronger emphasis on that the respondent has actually (believed to have) observed a causal connection between the productivity factor and the productivity.

For productivity factors where none of the above four interpretations give a fit to the responses, a fifth natural interpretation is more likely, i.e., that there is a belief, based on other sources than own experience, that the factor is important. This may be especially relevant if this productivity factor has received a lot of attention in the software development communities as important for high productivity.

The remaining part of the paper is organized as follows. Section 2 describes the study design. Section 3 presents the results. Section 4 discusses the results and concludes.

2. Study Design

The design elements of our survey are described in Table 2 and information about the survey participants is given in Table 3.

Table 2: Design elements of the survey

Study element	Description
Recruitment of the survey participants	We recruited software professionals offering team or project management services on the freelancer marketplace *Upwork.com*. Inclusion criteria to qualify for participating in the survey were experience from at least five teams or projects and good feedback from previous clients (at least 90% success rate). 178 invitations were sent to qualifying software professionals on Upwork.com. Of these, 79 were hired and paid (based on their ordinary hourly payment) for the participation in the survey.
The productivity factors examined	Team productivity factors presented to the survey participants are the following: • Software development competence and skill of the team members • Competence and skill in team management • Domain and business experience of the team members

	• Team autonomy (freedom to choose when and/or how to develop the software) • Psychological safety («The belief that one will not be punished or humiliated for speaking up with ideas questions, concerns, or mistakes, and that the team is safe for interpersonal risk-taking") • Trust between the team members (trust in that all are doing the right things and with the right intentions) • Job satisfaction and well-being of the team members • Use of efficient software development processes and tools (e.g., good use of agile software development practices) • Ability of team members to learn from and/or innovate based on feedback/experience. • Ability of team members to focus and prioritize • Job motivation and enthusiasm of the team members • Communication and collaboration within the team, with management and with clients • Composition of the team (good mix of roles, skills, and personalities within the team) • Interpersonal relationship and emotional intelligence The above team productivity factors are selected from those used in previous surveys, in particular the three reported in Table 1, with an emphasis on the social and human factors reported in (Machuca-Villegas, Hurtado, Puente, & Tamayo, 2021). The selection is not meant to be complete or necessarily represent the most important factors, but to serve the purpose of an examination of what makes a respondent give a productivity factor a higher importance score. Initially meant as a control question to examine to what extent the participants read the questions properly, we also added the productivity factor "Having a good lunch restaurant nearby". As we will describe later, this question turned out to serve another purpose, and did not work well as a control questions. The questionnaire is enclosed as Appendix A, which also include introductory text, the actual question formulations and more on the scales used.
The survey	The survey was distributed as an on-line link to a questionnaire developed using Qualtrics (www. Qualtrics.com). The median time spent on completing the survey was 14 minutes, and all spent more than five minutes. The survey had three separate parts (Parts A, B and C), where we: A. Asked the respondents to give an importance score, for high team productivity, for 14 productivity factors. B. Asked the respondents to assess their previous teams' performance for each of the productivity factors. C. Asked the respondents to assess how often each of the factors had caused productivity problems previously. When completing one part of the questionnaire and starting on a new, they were sent to a new questionnaire page, and could not see their previous responses. To avoid systematic sequence effects of the responses, we randomized the sequence of the productivity factors for each part of the questionnaire and for each participant.
The analysis	The analysis connecting the respondents prior experience and the perceived importance of a productivity factors is based on comparisons of mean values for ordinally scaled responses, such as the scale 1="very low importance" … 5="very high importance". While mean values of ordinal (Likert) scales may be debatable, we think that it is a reasonable choice in this context, see for example (Brown, 2011) for support of interval-scale analyses when using Likert scales. Where we have reasons to believe that there is a linear relationship between the scores on two scales, we include correlational analyses (Spearman rank correlation coefficient). When appropriate, we add analyses of statistical significance, where we claim statistical significance when $p<0.05$.
Excluded responses	As described earlier, we included a check question about the importance of having a good lunch restaurant nearby. The intention was to exclude those who gave a high importance score here. Several of the participants gave, however, this factor a score of

	"moderate" or higher. We asked many of them, after finalizing the questionnaire, about why they thought a good lunch restaurant was important. All had good answers, arguing that having a good lunch restaurant nearby was indeed important for productivity in their workplace. When examining their remaining responses, we found no indications of low quality, and we did not remove these responses. We found no reason to exclude any of the responses from the survey participants.
Validity and limitation of the study	The perhaps most critical part of survey-based studies of this type is to enable responses with sufficiently high quality, i.e., avoiding that the respondents are not reading and thinking sufficiently carefully before they give their answers. We believe the quality of the responses in this survey is good, perhaps as a consequence that answering the questionnaire was contracted, paid work for the respondents and because they were to receive an evaluation score from us as clients important for their future work. In addition, the strict criterion of only selecting experienced software professionals, with extensive management background and very good score from previous clients, may have added to the quality. We make no attempt to generalize the results regarding the importance of the productivity factors to other contexts (quite the opposite, as we argue that this is very challenging). What is more likely to be possible to generalize from our study are the results on the connections between previous experience and the perceived importance of a productivity factor. As will be seen in the analysis section, many of connections we claim to find are not very strong (although statistically significant) and the study design do not enable causal claims. While we find patters there are reasons to believe show causal connections, we cannot exclude that the connections are just correlational, and that there are other, perhaps more important, causal connections not identified by us.

Table 3. Characteristics of the respondents

Countries	Argentina (1), Armenia (2), Belarus (1), Brazil (1), Bulgaria (3), Canada (1), Colombia (1), Egypt (4), Estonia (1), France (1), Georgia (1), India (9), Macedonia (2), Moldova (1), Netherlands (1), Pakistan (11), Philippines (5), Romania (3), Serbia (1), South Africa (1), Taiwan (1), Turkey (1), UK (2), Ukraine (20), US (2), and Venezuela (2).
Median years of experience as software professional	8 years
Median number of software development *projects* as a developer/programmer	6 projects
Median number of software development *teams* as a developer/programmer	8 teams
Median number of software development projects and teams in *management role* (project leader, team leader etc.)	10 projects and/or teams
Highest education level ("Other" includes both incomplete responses and other degrees).	Master's degree: 36 participants Bachelor's degree: 38 participants College: 5 participants
Experienced productivity in previous teams and projects (as perceived by themselves) in mean percentage per productivity category	Very high productivity: 22% High productivity: 29% Medium productivity: 31% Low productivity: 13% Very low productivity: 5%

As can be derived from the above descriptions of the participants, the majority of them were from typical outsourcing, lower-cost countries. In addition, they had extensive experience both as developers and managers, were well-educated, and perceived that most of their previous teams and projects had had high or very high productivity. All of them worked internationally, offering team or project management services. An examination of the participants' previous employers, as presented on their personal page at UpWork.com and in their cv-s, shows that nearly all of them currently worked in small or medium-large offshoring providers, or had worked in such software companies before offering services through UpWork.com.

3. Results

This section first reports results on the perceived importance and previous experience regarding the productivity factors (Section 3.1), and then reports on the connections between the importance and the previous experience regarding the productivity factors (Section 3.2)

3.1 Descriptive results

Tables 4-6 display the distributions of responses for Part A (perceived importance of the productivity factors), Part B (previous perceived performance regarding the productivity factors) and Part C (previous perceived productivity problems caused by low performance on the productivity factors) of the survey.

Table 4: Perceived importance of productivity factors for achieving high software development productivity (three most important in bold)

Factor	Very low (1)	Low (2)	Mod. (3)	High (4)	Very high (5)	Mean	Rank
Development skill	0%	0%	16%	52%	32%	4.15	8
Management skill	0%	5%	27%	39%	29%	3.92	12
Domain knowledge	0%	8%	33%	46%	14%	3.66	13
Autonomy	0%	6%	43%	33%	18%	3.62	14
Psychological safety	0%	0%	13%	48%	39%	4.27	4
Trust	**0%**	**1%**	**4%**	**38%**	**57%**	**4.51**	**2**
Job satisfaction	0%	0%	15%	49%	35%	4.20	6
Processes and tools	0%	0%	19%	46%	35%	4.16	7
Innovate and learn	**0%**	**0%**	**8%**	**54%**	**38%**	**4.30**	**3**
Focus and prioritize	0%	1%	18%	47%	34%	4.14	9
Motivation and enthusiasm	0%	3%	9%	51%	38%	4.24	5
Commun. and collab.	**0%**	**0%**	**3%**	**33%**	**65%**	**4.62**	**1**
Composition of team	0%	5%	20%	38%	37%	4.06	10
Relations/emotional intel.	0%	4%	19%	49%	28%	4.01	11

The perhaps most striking result in Table 4, is that all productivity factors are, on average, quite similar in mean perceived importance and that all are perceived to be at least moderately important. The top three factors were good communication and collaboration, trust, and innovate and learn. All these factors are frequently found to be perceived as important in other surveys (see for example the analyses of reviews of surveys of productivity factors in the (Oliveira, Conte, Cristo, & Valentim, 2018)), i.e., our results may not deviate much from those of other surveys including some of these productivity factors.

As argued earlier, the interpretation of the above results is not trivial. As an illustration, the factor with the lowest importance was found to be domain knowledge. In contexts where the domain knowledge is nearly absent and the other productivity factors are at a satisfactory level, this factor may sometimes, we argue, have the strongest influence on productivity and be the most important one to improve to increase productivity.

Perhaps even more illustrative for the problems of interpreting the results are the responses to the control question about the importance of having a *good nearby lunch restaurant*. Although the mean value was as low as 2.05 ("Low importance"), as many as 23 of the respondents gave this factor a "moderate" or higher importance (the majority of them located in Pakistan, India, or Egypt). When asking them for an explanation, they typically gave good rationales for the importance of a good nearby lunch restaurant, such as "Saves time to have it nearby" and "Good food is important for job satisfaction and productivity". We have no reason to doubt that these respondents perceived that this factor was important for productivity, sometimes even more important than a few of the other factors. The interpretation challenges are related to what this means. A good nearby lunch restaurant is hardly an important productivity factor in most contexts, as indicated by the responses from the majority of the respondents. One of the respondents even perceived a good lunch restaurant to be more important than development skills. This judgment sounds strange but it is possible to defend. That project manager may, for example, have experienced that project members have had low productivity due to leaving the office, for lunch, for a long time every day.

Table 5: Frequency of experiencing good performance on productivity factors in previous projects/teams

Factor	**Nearly all (1)**	**Most (2)**	**About half (3)**	**Some (4)**	**Few or none (5)**	**Mean**	**Rank**
Development skill	11%	41%	29%	14%	5%	2.61	4
Management skill	5%	41%	28%	20%	6%	2.82	11
Domain knowledge	10%	25%	37%	24%	4%	2.86	12
Autonomy	6%	23%	39%	20%	11%	3.08	14
Psychological safety	**24%**	**27%**	**25%**	**18%**	**6%**	**2.56**	**2**
Trust	15%	34%	25%	18%	8%	2.68	8
Job satisfaction	16%	32%	29%	18%	5%	2.63	6
Processes and tools	14%	38%	24%	20%	4%	2.62	5
Innovate and learn	13%	39%	23%	20%	5%	2.66	7
Focus and prioritize	10%	34%	34%	19%	3%	2.70	10
Motivation and enthusiasm	11%	35%	30%	19%	4%	2.68	8
Commun. and collab.	**15%**	**41%**	**23%**	**14%**	**8%**	**2.58**	**3**
Composition of team	**16%**	**42%**	**27%**	**14%**	**1%**	**2.42**	**1**
Relations/emot. intel.	8%	25%	34%	28%	5%	2.97	13

As can be derived from Table 5, the three productivity factors that the respondents perceived as having the, on average, best performance score (lowest mean value) were those related to the composition of the team, psychological safety, and communication and collaboration. The three productivity factors with the, on average, worst (highest) performance were autonomy, relations and emotional intelligence, and domain knowledge.

Table 6: Frequency of experiencing that poor performance on a factor caused low productivity in previous teams and/or projects

Factor	Very often (1)	Often (2)	Several times (3)	A few times (4)	Never (5)	Mean	Rank
Development skill	18%	23%	29%	23%	8%	2.80	4
Management skill	14%	25%	24%	27%	10%	2.94	8
Domain knowledge	8%	25%	23%	38%	6%	3.10	12
Autonomy	8%	16%	39%	28%	9%	3.14	13
Psychological safety	8%	20%	30%	28%	14%	3.20	14
Trust	14%	24%	28%	25%	9%	2.91	7
Job satisfaction	**15%**	**30%**	**28%**	**19%**	**8%**	**2.79**	**3**
Processes and tools	13%	24%	28%	25%	10%	2.96	9
Innovate and learn	9%	24%	28%	29%	10%	3.08	11
Focus and prioritize	**13%**	**34%**	**22%**	**25%**	**6%**	**2.78**	**2**
Motivation and enthusiasm	18%	20%	28%	28%	6%	2.85	5
Commun. and collab.	**35%**	**32%**	**16%**	**16%**	**0%**	**2.14**	**1**
Composition of team	11%	33%	23%	25%	8%	2.85	5
Relations/emot. intel.	14%	19%	34%	23%	10%	2.96	9

Table 6 shows that the respondents have experienced poor performance on the productivity factors causing low productivity relatively often. The three productivity factors that most often caused low productivity, were poor communication and collaboration, poor ability to focus and prioritize, and low job satisfaction. As can be derived from the table, all productivity factors had more than 50% of the responses in the categories "several times", "often", or "very often".

3.2 Connections

This section analyses the connection between the previous experience regarding productivity factors and the perceived importance of these productivity factors.

Table 7 summarizes the connections examined, how we analyze them, and the results of the analyses. The details of the analyses are displayed in Tables 8 and 9 and discussed below these tables.

Table 7. Summary of the analyses

Tested connection	Consequence for analysis	Results of analysis
1. A *larger variation* in how well previous projects and teams have performed regarding that productivity factor is connected with higher perceived importance.	When experiencing that "about the half" of previous projects and teams had good performance on a productivity factor, this suggests the largest perceived variation on that factor. This should then be connected with higher mean importance of that factor.	*No support* for the interpretation that the respondents give higher importance to factors where they previously have experienced much variance in performance.
2. A *good performance* in previous projects and teams regarding a productivity factor is	When experiencing that "nearly all" or "most" of previous projects and teams had good performance on a productivity factor, this suggests the best perceived	*Support* for the interpretation that the respondents give higher importance to factors where they previously have

connected with higher perceived importance.	performance on that factor. This should then be connected with higher mean importance of that factor.	experienced very good performance.
3. A *poor performance* in previous projects and teams regarding a productivity factor is connected with higher importance.	When experiencing that only "some" or "few" of previous projects and teams had good performance on a productivity factor, this suggests the worst perceived performance on that factor. This should then be connected with higher mean importance of that factor.	*Weak support* for the interpretation that the respondents give higher importance to factors where they previously have experienced bad performance.
4. A *higher frequency* of observing that a *low performance on a productivity factor has caused low productivity* is connected with higher importance.	The more frequently low performance on a productivity has been perceived to cause productivity problems, the higher the importance of that factor will be. This analysis is similar to the one in 3., but analyses a more direct connection between poor performance and productivity *problems*.	*Support* for the interpretation that the respondents give higher importance to factors they frequently have experienced have caused productivity problems. (This suggests an important difference between performing poorly on a factor and experiencing that a factor has caused productivity problems.)

Table 8: Mean importance of a factor, for categories of frequency of good performance in previous teams (highest value for each factor in bold)

Factor	Nearly all (1)	Most (2)	About half (3)	Some (4)	Few or none (5)
Development skill	4.00	4.06	4.26	4.18	**4.50**
Management skill	**4.50**	3.94	3.82	3.94	3.80
Domain knowledge	**4.50**	3.45	3.55	3.58	4.33
Autonomy	**4.00**	3.72	3.61	3.44	3.56
Psychological safety	4.37	4.33	4.05	4.29	**4.40**
Trust	**4.75**	4.37	4.65	4.43	4.33
Job satisfaction	4.23	**4.28**	4.22	4.00	4.25
Processes and tools	**4.73**	4.13	3.95	4.06	4.33
Innovate and learn	**4.80**	4.19	4.28	4.38	3.75
Focus and prioritize	**4.88**	4.15	3.89	4.20	4.00
Motivation and enthusiasm	**4.56**	4.21	4.21	4.20	4.00
Commun. and collab.	4.92	4.59	4.44	4.45	**5.00**
Composition of team	**4.46**	4.15	3.67	4.09	4.00
Relations/emot. intel.	**4.83**	3.90	4.11	3.77	4.00
Overall mean value	**4.54**	4.11	4.05	4.07	4.16

An examination of the above mean importance values suggests that the main pattern is that the highest importance is typically put on factors where the projects and teams have previously scored well, i.e., when nearly all or most previous teams and projects have had a good performance on the productivity factor. It may also be the case, but mainly for three of the factors, that higher importance is put on factors with very low previous performance. For none of the factors, it is the case that those with the most variance (as indicated by reporting that "about half of the teams and projects have had a good performance") are connected with the highest importance. This gives support to the connections that productivity factors are given high importance when previous experience has been very good, but no support to a connection between more variance in experience and higher perceived importance of a productivity factor. A connection between poor previous performance on a productivity factor and the high perceived importance of that factor cannot be excluded for some factors, e.g., development skill. Notice that we have not included a correlational analysis here, as opposed to Table 9, because the analyzed connection is not likely to be linear.

Table 9: Mean importance of a productivity factor, for categories of frequency of experience that poor performance has caused low productivity (highest values for each factor in bold, correlations with * indicate $p<0.05$ and with ** $p<0.01$)

Factor	**Very often (1)**	**Often (2)**	**Several times (3)**	**A few times (4)**	**Never (5)**	**Corr. (r)**
Development skill	**4.79**	4.22	3.91	4.06	3.67	-0.42**
Management skill	**4.36**	4.00	3.63	3.76	4.25	-0.13
Domain knowledge	**4.83**	3.90	3.39	3.53	3.00	-0.39**
Autonomy	**5.00**	3.54	3.55	3.36	3.71	-0.24*
Psychological safety	**4.83**	4.38	4.17	4.14	4.27	-0.17
Trust	**4.82**	4.37	4.55	4.35	4.71	-0.04
Job satisfaction	**4.50**	4.17	4.14	4.13	4.17	-0.13
Processes and tools	**4.90**	4.16	4.05	4.05	3.88	-0.32**
Innovate and learn	4.14	**4.58**	4.36	4.09	4.25	-0.20
Focus and prioritize	4.70	4.11	3.88	3.95	**4.80**	-0.14
Motivation and enthusiasm	**4.57**	4.19	4.14	4.18	4.20	-0.13
Commun. and collab.	**4.79**	4.64	4.38	4.46	-	-0.29**
Composition of team	**4.67**	4.04	4.17	3.65	4.33	-0.18
Relations/emot. intel.	**4.64**	3.93	4.00	3.89	3.63	-0.25**
Overall mean value	**4.68**	4.16	4.02	3.97	4.07	-0.22*

The results in Table 9 show a clear pattern. For nearly all productivity factors, the high importance of a factor is connected with the experience of that factor having caused low productivity "very often." The correlation column suggests that the connection between the frequency of previous experience of a factor and perceived importance of that factor is linear for many of the factors, i.e., the more frequently a respondent has experienced that a productivity factor has caused low productivity, the higher the importance put on that factor. This is especially the case for the productivity factors development skill, domain knowledge, processes and tools, communication and collaboration, and relations and emotional intelligence. All productivity factors have a negative correlation between previous problems and perceived importance.

4. Discussion and conclusion

It should not be surprising that the current lack of clarity in how to interpret software development productivity, partly vaguely defined productivity factors, together with the lack of commonly agreed upon criteria on how to score the importance of productivity factors, lead to problematic interpretation of survey-based results on the importance of productivity factors. This was, amongst others, demonstrated by the responses on a factor we expected everyone taking the survey seriously would give a low importance score, i.e., the importance of a good lunch restaurant nearby. Several of the participants perceived this productivity factor to have a "moderate" or "high" importance and gave rational arguments for this. This is consistent with a strong context dependency on the importance of productivity factors, and the challenges of aggregating responses across a variety of contexts. Without understanding the work context of survey participants, it will be hard to interpret the results properly and make meaningful use of them. In addition, we have no access to the judgment processes behind the judgment or the criteria used for assessing one factor as more important than another, and it may be the case that the respondents themselves have no explicit criteria and just provide judgments based on what "feels right". We know from studies on unconscious judgmental processes (expert judgment) that people may use simple heuristics (Gigerenzer, 2008; Tversky & Kahneman, 1973), such as *availability* (if, for example, the first association with a productivity factor is an event where the team lost a deadline because of too long lunch breaks or article about the importance of psychological safety the strength of the message in this association may affect the importance given to the factor), *recency* (the last event experienced with strong influence on team productivity may be deemed more important), and *representativeness* (the most typical experience regarding a productivity factor is what is believed to represent its importance). The observation that software professionals are willing to answer poorly defined questions on the importance of productivity factors, including those in our study (where several respondents gave very positive feedback on the importance and the meaningfulness of the study), is perhaps not surprising, but not very confirming for the quality and interpretability of such studies.

If challenging to interpret what a high or higher importance of a productivity factor means, what can we then learn from the results of surveys on such factors? The results in this paper suggest that such results may tell us something about the previous experience of those responding. Respondents who have experienced that poor performance on a productivity factor has caused low productivity, are likely to give a high importance score on that factor. Another connection with perceived higher importance on a productivity factor, supported by our findings, is that prior performance on that factor has been good, i.e., that all or nearly all previous teams and projects have scored well on that factor. These two processes potentially guiding the decision on importance of a productivity factor are quite different, and it may be hard to know which will be the strongest and when they are used. There may also be other sources leading to the higher perceived importance of a productivity factor. It is easy to think of contexts where almost any reasonable factor may contribute to higher or lower productivity, and qualify as a productivity factor. The number of such factors may consequently be as high as desired, given a sufficiently large variety of contexts.

Our recommendation based on the above reflections and our empirical results is that we should avoid conducting surveys on the importance or influence of productivity factors unless we come up with better ideas of how to pose the questions in more concrete, well-defined ways and include the context necessary to be able to give a proper interpretation of the results. A possible use of the results of such surveys may be to get some insight into the previous experience with the performance of these factors and how frequently they have caused productivity problems. If, however, that is the purpose of the survey, it would probably be a better idea to ask directly about their experience regarding the productivity factors and their connection to productivity problems.

References

Blackburn, J. D., Scudder, G. D., & Van Wassenhove, L. N. (1996). Improving speed and productivity of software development: a global survey of software developers. *IEEE Transactions on Software Engineering, 22*(12), 875-885.

Brown, J. D. (2011). Likert items and scales of measurement. *Statistics, 15*(1), 10-14.

Chattopadhyay, S., Nelson, N., Au, A., Morales, N., Sanchez, C., Pandita, R., & Sarma, A. (2022). Cognitive biases in software development. *Communications of the ACM, 65*(4), 115-122.

de Barros Sampaio, S. C., Barros, E. A., de Aquino, G. S., e Silva, M. J. C., & de Lemos Meira, S. R. (2010). *A review of productivity factors and strategies on software development.* Paper presented at the 2010 fifth international conference on software engineering advances.

Gigerenzer, G. (2008). Why heuristics work. *Perspectives on psychological science, 3*(1), 20-29.

Jørgensen, M. (2013). Myths and over-simplifications in software engineering. *Lecture Notes on Software Engineering, 1*(1), 7.

Jørgensen, M., & Papatheocharous, E. (2015). *Believing is seeing: Confirmation bias studies in software engineering.* Paper presented at the 2015 41st Euromicro Conference on Software Engineering and Advanced Applications.

Machuca-Villegas, L., Gasca-Hurtado, G. P., Puente, S. M., & Tamayo, L. M. R. (2022). Perceptions of the human and social factors that influence the productivity of software development teams in Colombia: A statistical analysis. *Journal of systems and software, 192*, 111408.

Machuca-Villegas, L., Hurtado, G. G., Puente, S. M., & Tamayo, L. M. R. (2021). An Instrument for Measuring Perception about Social and Human Factors that Influence Software Development Productivity. *J. Univers. Comput. Sci., 27*(2), 111-134.

Oliveira, E., Conte, T., Cristo, M., & Valentim, N. (2018). Influence factors in software productivity—a tertiary literature review. *International Journal of Software Engineering and Knowledge Engineering, 28*(11n12), 1795-1810.

Paiva, E., Barbosa, D., Lima Jr, R., & Albuquerque, A. (2010). Factors that influence the productivity of software developers in a developer view. In *Innovations in computing sciences and software engineering* (pp. 99-104): Springer.

Tversky, A., & Kahneman, D. (1973). Availability: A heuristic for judging frequency and probability. *Cognitive psychology, 5*(2), 207-232.

Wagner, S., & Ruhe, M. (2018). A systematic review of productivity factors in software development. *arXiv preprint arXiv:1801.06475.*

Appendix A: The survey questions

A) Factors connected with software development team productivity

Below is a list of factors potentially connected with the productivity of software development teams (productivity = developed software of value to the users/work-effort spent). Evaluate **how important you believe each of these factors are to achieve high software development team (inclusive project teams) productivity.**

	Very low/no importance to achieve high team productivity (1)	Low importance (2)	Moderate importance (3)	High importance (4)	Very high importance to achieve high team productivity (5)
High software development competence/skill of the team members	○	○	○	○	○
High competence/skill in team management	○	○	○	○	○
Good domain and business experience of the team members	○	○	○	○	○
High team autonomy (freedom to choose when and/or how to develop the software)	○	○	○	○	○
High psychological safety ("The belief that one will not be punished or humiliated for speaking up with ideas, questions, concerns, or mistakes, and that the team is safe for interpersonal risk-taking")	○	○	○	○	○
High trust between the team members (high trust in that all are doing the right things and with the right intentions)	○	○	○	○	○
High job satisfaction and well-being of the team members	○	○	○	○	○
Good use of efficient software development processes and tools (e.g. good use of agile software development practices)	○	○	○	○	○
Strong ability of team members to learn from and/or innovate based on feedback/experience	○	○	○	○	○
Strong ability of team members' to focus and prioritise	○	○	○	○	○
Strong job motivation and enthusiasm of team members	○	○	○	○	○
Good communication and collaboration within the team, with management, and with clients	○	○	○	○	○
Good composition of the team (good mix of roles, skills and personalities within the team)	○	○	○	○	○
Good interpersonal relationship and emotional intelligence	○	○	○	○	○
Good lunch restaurant nearby	○	○	○	○	○

B) Your experience of frequency of teams with good performance on each of the productivity factors

Below are the same productivity factors you evaluated earlier. This time, think back on the teams (including project teams) you have experience from and assess how well they scored on each of the productivity factors.

For each of the productivity factors evaluate whether you think "nearly all", "most", "about half", "some (but less than half)" or "few or none" of the teams you have experience from were "good" (or better than good) on each of the productivity factors.

You should consider a team to have been "good" regarding a productivity factor if the team's performance on this factor did not cause any productivity problems, but instead was a factor contributing to at least medium high productivity.

	Nearly all teams were good on this productivity factor (1)	Most teams were good (2)	About half of the teams were good (3)	Some of the teams were good (4)	Few or none of the teams were good on this productivity factor(5)
Software development competence/skill of the team members	○	○	○	○	○
Competence/skill in team management	○	○	○	○	○
Domain and business experience of the team members	○	○	○	○	○
Team autonomy (freedom to choose when and/or how to develop the software)	○	○	○	○	○
Psychological safety ("The belief that one will not be punished or humiliated for speaking up with ideas, questions, concerns, or mistakes, and that the team is safe for interpersonal risk taking")	○	○	○	○	○
Trust between the team members (trust in that all are doing the right things and with the right intentions)	○	○	○	○	○
Job satisfaction and well-being of the team members	○	○	○	○	○
Use of efficient software development processes and tools (e.g. good use of agile software development practices)	○	○	○	○	○
Team member's ability to learn from and/or innovate based on feedback/experience	○	○	○	○	○
Team members' ability to focus and prioritize	○	○	○	○	○
Team members' job motivation and enthusiasm	○	○	○	○	○
Communication and collaboration within the team, with management, and with clients	○	○	○	○	○
Composition of the team (the mix of roles, skills and personalities within the team)	○	○	○	○	○
Interpersonal relationship and emotional intelligence	○	○	○	○	○

C) Your experience on how often low performance on a productivity factor has been an important cause of low productivity of the team and/or the project

Similarly to the previous question, we ask you to use your experience from teams you have been part of or observed and evaluate them for each of the factors.

This time we would like you to assess **how often you have experienced that poor performance on a factor has STRONGLY REDUCED the productivity of the team/project (has been an important cause of LOW PRODUCTIVITY).**

	Very often experienced that this factor has caused low productivity (1)	Often (2)	Several times (3)	A few times (4)	Never experienced that this factor has caused low productivity (5)
Low software development competence/skill of the team members strongly reduced the team productivity	○	○	○	○	○
Low competence/skill in team management strongly reduced the team productivity	○	○	○	○	○
Poor domain and business experience of the team members strongly reduced the team productivity	○	○	○	○	○
Low team autonomy (freedom to choose when and/or how to develop the software) strongly reduced the team productivity	○	○	○	○	○
Poor psychological safety ("The belief that one will not be punished or humiliated for speaking up with ideas, questions, concerns, or mistakes, and that the team is safe for interpersonal risk taking") strongly reduced the team productivity	○	○	○	○	○
Low trust between the team members (trust in that all are doing the right things and with the right intentions) strongly reduced the team productivity	○	○	○	○	○
Low job satisfaction and well-being of the team members strongly reduced the team productivity	○	○	○	○	○
Poor use of software development processes and/or tools (e.g. good use of agile software development practices)	○	○	○	○	○
Team member's poor ability to learn from and/or innovate based on feedback/experience strongly reduced the team productivity	○	○	○	○	○
Team members' poor ability to focus and prioritise strongly reduced the team productivity	○	○	○	○	○
Team members' low job motivation and enthusiasm strongly reduced the team productivity	○	○	○	○	○
Poor communication and collaboration within the team, with management, and with clients strongly reduced the team productivity	○	○	○	○	○
Poor composition of the team (poor mix of roles, skills and personalities within the team) strongly reduced the team productivity	○	○	○	○	○
Poor interpersonal relationship and emotional intelligence strongly reduced the team productivity	○	○	○	○	○

Exploring Terminological Consistency of Project Management Glossaries

María Fernanda Papa, Pablo Becker, Luis Olsina

GIDIS_Web, Facultad de Ingeniería, UNLPam, General Pico, LP, Argentina

{pmfer, beckerp, olsinal}@ing.unlpam.edu.ar

Abstract. *The present paper deals with an exploratory study on the terminological consistency of four selected project management glossaries. To systematically carry out the study, eight activities were established. Regarding the information consistency sub-characteristic, this work includes a comparison and analysis of both the syntactic and semantic consistency of the terms in the glossaries. To do this, nine terminological categories were conceived for the project area, in which, for each glossary, a given term is included in a category, considering the semantics intended in the definition of the term by the authors. This categorization of terms allows us to comparatively analyze syntactic and semantic similarities, and in turn consistencies and inconsistencies. As a final goal, this study will help us examine our previously developed project ontology and recommend adoptions and adaptations.*

1. Introduction

To support the understanding and learning of frequently used concepts for the project management discipline, there are several initiatives that have developed project management glossaries. A glossary, regardless of whether it is for project management or not, includes entries, that is, terms that designate concepts and their definitions –and occasionally synonyms, acronyms, references, and additional notes- often taking into account recognized sources in a given area.

Therefore, glossaries serve as an authoritative reference to establish a common conceptual foundation for terms and definitions, not only in understanding and learning but also in communicating with different stakeholders.

Thus, an entire profession and discipline have been focused on improving software engineering approaches, processes, methods, and tools, so any professional in the field of software engineering will have come across and used many glossaries, whether in their formal training or their daily work. In particular, most professionals in the field of project management are familiar to some degree with glossaries such as PMBOK which stands for Project Management Body of Knowledge (PMBOK, 2021), APM which stands for Association for Project Management (APM, 2021), IAPM which stands for International Association of Project Managers (IAPM, 2021), and PRINCE2 which stands for PRojects IN Controlled Environments (PRINCE2, 2017), to mention just a few existing project management glossaries, but which were the ones selected for the present study.

Terminologies can be conceived and developed from lesser to greater structural richness, such as glossaries, taxonomies, and ontologies. In Rivera et al. (2016), the authors built the first version of a project ontology, which adapted some terms from PMBOK. Later, in 2019, a five-tired ontological architecture was developed by Olsina (2021) where the cited project ontology was located at the core level. However, a current review of its core concepts and relationships will be beneficial by considering terms from a selected set of up-to-date project management glossaries.

For this, we carry out an exploratory study in order to analyze the most frequent terms in the abovementioned glossaries, which in turn present the highest levels of syntactic and semantic consistency. The main goal of this study is to help us examine the previously developed project ontology concepts and recommend adoptions and adaptations of some terms from project management glossaries. It is important to remark that the comparative analysis to recommend the adoption or adaptation of terms in the new version of the project ontology will be limited to generic terms that can be placed at the core level rather than at the domain level.

Additionally, this comparative analysis will allow us to gauge the level of syntactic and semantic harmonization existing in these terminologies. Since glossaries serve as a common conceptual basis for different stakeholders, a given discipline or field –like project management- will become more mature if terminological consistency and harmonization are promoted and achieved.

To systematically conduct this research, eight activities or steps were established. To compare and analyze the information consistency sub-characteristic, this work includes both the syntactic and semantic consistency of the terms in the glossaries. To perform this, nine terminological categories were conceived for the project area, in which, for each glossary, a given term is included in a category, considering the semantics intended in the definition of the term by the glossary authors. This categorization of terms allows us to comparatively analyze syntactic and semantic similarities, and in turn consistencies and inconsistencies.

The remaining sections of this paper are organized as follows. Section 2 establishes the eight activities carried out for this exploratory study on terminological consistency, in addition to developing and illustrating each activity in detail, dedicating a subsection to each one. Section 3 highlights related work. Finally, Section 4 outlines our conclusions and future work.

2. Process and Development of the Exploratory Study on Syntactic and Semantic Consistency in Terms of Project Management Glossaries

To carry out this exploratory study on the comparative analysis of the consistency of both syntactic and semantic information for project management glossaries, we have established the following activities or steps:

- **A1**. Define the evaluation goal and scope of the comparative analysis.
- **A2**. Select project management glossaries to be compared.
- **A3**. Design terminological categories for the project management area to evaluate syntactic and semantic consistency.
- **A4**. Put glossary terms into categories taking into account the semantics intended by glossary authors in their definitions and count them.

- **A5**. Calculate the frequency of terminological occurrence (syntactic similarity) considering the primary terms or their synonyms.
- **A6**. Calculate the categorical coincidence (semantic similarity) considering the syntactic similarity of the terms.
- **A7**. Analyze syntactic and semantic consistency.
- **A8**. Recommend adoptions and adaptations.

It is worth noting that while this process instance deals with our current study applied to project management glossaries, this activity sequence can be used and adapted for any syntactic and semantic comparative analysis of terms in glossaries of other domains. Thus, in previous studies applied to software testing glossaries by Tebes et al. (2022) and Olsina et al. (2022), although the above process was not explicitly listed, we can affirm that the only slightly adapted activity was A8, in which improvement actions were recommended instead of adoptions and adaptations as in the present work.

The following eight subsections discuss and illustrate the procedures and results of the activities listed above.

2.1. Defining the Goal and Scope of the Exploratory Study

Activity A1 aims to define the objective of the evaluation, the motivation, and the scope of this study within the area of project management terminologies.

The statement of the evaluation goal of this exploratory study can be briefly formulated as "Compare and analyze the syntactic and semantic consistency of terms in the latest versions of project management glossaries used for training and certification worldwide". Hence, the purpose of the evaluation goal is to 'compare'; the purpose of the information need goal is to 'analyze' –by performing a comparative analysis of categorized terms with the ultimate end of adopting/adapting them in a previously developed ontology; the main particular entity is 'project management glossary'; the evaluation focus is 'consistency' –by considering the suitability of both syntactic and semantic information; and the context is 'the latest versions of official or de facto international glossaries used for training and certification worldwide'.

The motivation of this study lies in the further updating of a previously developed project ontology (Rivera et al., 2016), which should be located at the core level in the context of a five-tired ontological architecture. For this, we conduct this study in order to analyze mainly the most frequent terms in the selected glossaries, which in turn evidence the highest levels of syntactic and semantic consistency. The scope for the comparative analysis to recommend the adoption or adaptation of terms in the new version of the project ontology will be limited to generic terms that can be placed at the core level rather than terms that are more domain-specific such as "Agile project management", "Agile method", "Sprint", or "Scrum", among others.

Note that Table 1 defines a reduced set of sub-characteristics and attributes of Information Quality, which was also used in a previous study by Olsina et al. (2022). In particular, it defines the Consistency sub-characteristic and its two attributes that will be used in subsections 2.5 through 2.7 to design metrics, get values, and analyze results.

Table 1. Extract of sub-characteristics and attributes of Information Quality

Characteristic/*Attribute*	Definition
Information Quality	The degree to which a product or system delivers accurate and suitable information which meets stated and implied needs when used under specified conditions.
1 Information Accuracy	The degree to which a product or system delivers information that is correct, credible, and current.
2 Information Suitability	The degree to which a product or system delivers the information with the right coverage, added value, and **consistency**, considering the specified user tasks and intended goals.
2.1 **Consistency**	The degree to which the information is coherent both semantically and syntactically against informational things, parts, categories, or human expressions previously shown or stated and agreed upon.
2.1.1 Syntactic consistency	*The degree to which the information has the necessary and sufficient keywords to coherently convey the message in a given natural language in front of something previously stated and agreed upon.*
2.1.2 Semantic consistency	*The degree to which the information coherently conveys and harmonizes meaning with something previously stated and agreed upon.*

2.2. Selecting Project Management Glossaries

As pointed out in the Introduction Section, the four project management glossaries analyzed are PMBOK, APM, IAPM, and PRINCE2. Table 2 shows in the first row the edition/year of each glossary. These four project management glossaries were chosen among eight shortlisted candidates applying the following selection criteria, namely: i) It must be written in English; ii) Must be used for training and certification purposes; iii) Must be updated between January 2017 and January 2022; and, iv) The latest version/edition can be accessed publicly or through our academic institution. The reader can find summary information and criteria met by the eight glossaries in Appendix I at https://bit.ly/CIbSE_Appendices. Note that the excluded glossaries are mainly due to criterion iii). A brief description and figures of the four included glossaries follow.

The PMBOK is a go-to document for effective project management in any industry. This resource results from work overseen by the Project Management Institute, which also offers certifications. It includes the standard for Project Management, which is the foundation upon which the vast body of knowledge builds, and the guide serves to capture and summarize that knowledge. The glossary generally does not include domain-specific terms. The current version is the 7th edition, which was released in July 2021 and includes a glossary with 350 primary terms and 3 synonyms (see Table 2).

The APM glossary was created by the Association for Project Management and was last updated in 2021. It is a collection of popular project management terms sourced from the 5th, 6th, and 7th editions of the APM Body of Knowledge and other APM publications. APM says its glossary is the common reference for project professionals in their daily work, for students studying APM qualifications, and for training providers looking to create study materials. Table 2 shows the term numbers that are overwhelmingly larger than the other three.

The IAPM Glossary is currently an online English-language resource for agile and project management terms created by the International Association of Project Managers. This organization is a global certification authority for project managers. The glossary has 333 primary terms and 41 synonyms.

Table 2. Number of terms for the four project management glossaries

Metric name	PMBOK	APM	IAPM	PRINCE2
Glossary edition/year	7th Ed./2021	2021	2021	6th Ed./2017
Total Number of Primary Terms per Glossary	350	753	333	197
Number of Synonyms per Glossary	3	51	41	3

PRINCE2 is a glossary, which is also a process-based method for effective project management, as well as a project manager certification program. The PRINCE2 certification is recognized worldwide. It has 197 primary terms and 3 synonyms.

2.3. Designing Terminological Categories for Project Management Glossaries

Concerning activity A3, nine terminological categories were designed, in which, for each glossary, a certain term is included only in one category in activity A4, considering the semantics intended by the authors of a given glossary. Designing categories followed by placing glossary terms in them will allow us to calculate syntactic and semantic similarities and then analyze consistency and give recommendations for adoption.

Table 3 exhibits the nine terminological categories we have conceived for project management glossaries. The terms that we are going to include in categories 1 (C1) to 8 (C8) are those terms that are primarily related to the area of project management. Instead, C9 is intended to incorporate terms belonging chiefly to other areas, although they may also be used in projects, such as the term "Contract".

The rationale for the design of these categories takes into account those developed in the exploratory studies for the software testing glossaries mentioned above. A similar approach is considered in the present research. For example, we share the same conceptual patterns for C2, C3, C5, C6, and C7 categories. However, the former C3 (Test Goal-, Requirements-, Entity-related Terms) is now divided into two categories, i.e., in C1 and C8, as shown in Table 3. What is new, is the category C4. It is worth mentioning that the project management area has a greater number of generic terms than the software testing domain, as we will discuss later.

Table 3. Names of the nine terminological categories for terms in project management glossaries

Category ID	Terminological Category name
C1	Goal-, Objective-, Purpose-, Intention-related Terms
C2	Strategy-, Approach-, Framework-, Principle-, Policies-related Terms
C3	Work Process-, Activity-, Step-related Terms
C4	Situation-, Event-, Condition-, Action-related Terms
C5	Method-, Technique-, Procedure-, Decision Criterion-, Rule-related Terms
C6	Work Product-, Artifact-, Result-, Representation-related Terms
C7	Agent-, Role-, Tool-, Responsibility-, Skill-, Capability-related Terms
C8	Organizational Entity-, Asset-related Terms
C9	Miscellaneous Terms

Category 1 is called "Goal-, Objective-, Purpose-, Intention-related Terms", which is devoted to covering terms with the semantics of goal, objective, and purpose. Olsina et al. (2021) define the term "Goal" as "*an intention-related assertion, that is, the statement of the aim to be achieved by the organization which considers the propositional content of a goal's purpose in a given situation and time frame*".

Category 2 is labeled "Strategy-, Approach-, Framework-, Principle-, Policies-related Terms". In the project ontology built by Rivera et al. (2016), the term "Strategy" is defined as "*Principles, patterns, and particular domain concepts and framework that can be specified by a set of tailored processes, in addition to a set of appropriated methods and tools, as core resources, for helping to achieve the project's goal purpose.*" According to this definition, a strategy or approach simultaneously encompasses at least the concepts of process or activity -what to do- and method or technique -how to do it- when established and used in a given project. As a consequence, the concept of strategy or approach has a broader meaning than the concept of work process or technique alone. In addition, it should be noted that the terms principles and framework appear explicitly in the definition above. Moreover, a strategy may include knowledge and skills as well.

Category 3 is named "Work Process-, Activity-, Step-related Terms", which is intended to include terms with the semantics of work process or activity. The concepts of the work process, activity, or task in projects generally encompass only the meaning of 'what to do' rather than 'how to do' an activity or step. So, the terms with the semantics of method or technique pertain to C5. Also, note that these terms are defined in a process ontology at the core level in an updated work by Becker et al. (2022).

Category 4 is called "Situation-, Event-, Condition-, Action-related Terms". Olsina et al. (2021) define the term "Situation" as "*an assertion that explicitly states and specifies the combination of circumstances, episodes and relationships/events embracing particular entities and their surroundings [...], which is of interest and relevant to be represented by a human agent/organization with an established goal.*" Furthermore, a particular event is seen as an action-related assertion that explicitly states and specifies the occurrence of an entity action.

Category 5 (labeled "Method-, Technique-, Procedure-, Decision Criterion-, Rule-related Terms" in Table 3) is dedicated to including method/technique terms, which have the semantics of 'how to do' an activity or task specification. The explicit semantic distinction between glossary terms that represent 'what to do' (work process) and 'how to do' has a clear benefit for understanding and consistency (Henderson-Sellers et al., 2014). Note that to perform a given activity specification more than one method or technique may be available to be selected.

Category 6 is labeled "Work Product-, Artifact-, Result-, Representation-related Terms", which is devoted to covering terms with the semantics of artifacts (e.g. reports, specifications, and representations such as models or graphs) or results (values, outcomes) that are produced or consumed by project processes, activities, or tasks.

Category 7 (labeled "Agent-, Role-, Tool-, Responsibility-, Skill-, Capability-related Terms") is expected to encompass terms with the semantics of automated or human agents. The term tool represents an instrument that facilitates the automation and execution of procedures and rules of methods and techniques, whereas the term role embraces skills that a project agent must possess to perform activities or tasks.

Lastly, Category 8 (labeled "Organizational Entity-, Asset-related Terms") is expected to encompass terms with the semantics of organizational entities such as the term "Project", among others. An asset is an entity with added value for an organization.

After designing the above categories, we classified each glossary term into its suitable category, as shown below.

2.4. Placing Glossary Terms into Terminological Categories and Counting them

The inclusion of terms in categories for the four glossaries was initially carried out independently by the authors of the present work. Subsequently, the three authors met face-to-face many times to check the consistency. As a result, many issues were raised and categorization discrepancies in the placement of terms according to their given semantics in the definitions were agreed upon and resolved. Note that the volume of primary terms is 1,633. Therefore, the work demanded a lot of effort. The entire period, from the search and selection of the glossaries to the categorization and verification of the terms, was from February to October 2022.

To better understand A4, let us illustrate this step using the term "Project", which is found in all four glossaries. Each glossary entry also has its definition as exhibited in Table 4. In order to categorize a glossary term, we only look at its definition. So the question is, to which category does a term pertain, considering its intended semantics and the conceptual category with previously agreed semantics? Remembering the meaning of each of the nine categories (subsection 2.3), and reading the definition of "Project" in each glossary, it accordingly belongs to C8. The reader may observe a close match in the meaning of "Project" in all four glossaries, although definitions are not identical. This is not the case for many other common terms.

In the first version of the project ontology built by Rivera et al. (2016), we adapted the term "Project" mainly from PMBOK. It was defined as "*an entity representing a temporary and goal-oriented endeavor with definite start and finish dates, which considers a managed set of interrelated activities, tasks, and resources aimed at producing and modifying unique work products (i.e., artifacts, services or results) for satisfying a given requester need*". In subsection 2.8 we will recommend adoptions/adaptations of terms for the new version of this ontology to be updated.

Table 4. Definitions of the "Project" term in each glossary

Term	Term definition	Glossary
Project	A **temporary endeavor** undertaken to create a unique product, service, or result.	PMBOK
Project	A **unique, transient endeavour** undertaken to bring about change and to achieve planned objectives.	APM
Project	**Undertaking** that is characterised by an overall uniqueness of conditions, such as objectives, time, financial, human resource-related and other constraints, difference from other projects and project-specific organisation structures.	IAPM
Project	A **temporary organization** that is created for the purpose of delivering one or more business products according to an agreed business case.	PRINCE2

Once all the primary terms –with corresponding synonyms, if any- were placed in categories, the produced tables were documented in Appendices. The reader can find the PMBOK glossary terms categorized in Appendix III of the document at https://bit.ly/CIbSE_Appendices. The glossary terms of APM, IAPM, and PRINCE2 are classified and documented in Appendixes IV, V, and VI, respectively.

Another result of A4 is the count of terms by category and glossary as shown in Table 5. Appendix VII also documents the sum of terms by category for all four glossaries together, as well as the percentages. The total sum of primary terms is 1,633, which is obtained by adding each value in the first row of Table 5. This calculation procedure was applied accordingly in each row to obtain the sums by category.

Table 5. Numbers of all categorized terms by glossary

Metric name	PMBOK	APM	IAPM	PRINCE2
Total Number of Primary Terms per Glossary	350	753	333	197
Number of Primary Terms per Glossary in C1	1	4	9	1
Number of Primary Terms per Glossary in C2	27	52	15	10
Number of Primary Terms per Glossary in C3	26	125	43	12
Number of Primary Terms per Glossary in C4	30	86	38	41
Number of Primary Terms per Glossary in C5	40	28	16	6
Number of Primary Terms per Glossary in C6	147	206	95	73
Number of Primary Terms per Glossary in C7	15	51	38	22
Number of Primary Terms per Glossary in C8	7	26	13	10
Number of Primary Terms per Glossary in C9	57	175	66	22

Thus, calculating percentages and excluding C9 (with 19.60%), the highest is observed for C6 (work product) with 31.90%, then for C3 (work process) with 12.61% followed by C4 (situation/event/action) with 11.94%. Besides, C2 (strategy/framework) represents 6.37%, while C5 (method/technique) is 5.51% of all main terms. The lowest percentage is for C1 (goal/intention) with 0.92% which is what could be expected.

2.5. Calculating Syntactic Similarity of Terms

A5, listed at the beginning of Section 2, deals with the computation of the syntactic similarity of terms. The frequency of terminological occurrence considering the primary terms or some of their synonyms (if needed and available) is obtained following a procedure of matching terms between glossaries. Let's see it observationally with the example of Table 4. As a result of looking at the term name or label, we can state that the term "Project" syntactically matches and thus has full syntactic similarity. Or, we can say that it has an occurrence frequency of 4, simultaneously considering the four glossaries as the target entity to be analyzed. Note that this term does not have synonyms in any glossary, which, if available, are not necessary to be included in the calculation procedure. Once the results of the syntactic frequency were obtained for each glossary term through the tool procedure described in Olsina et al. (2022), we calculated the numbers and percentages shown in Table 6.

Table 6. Metrics and their values for syntactic frequencies (syntactic similarity) of the terms from all four glossaries together

Metric name/acronym/formula	Value
Total sum of primary Terms (TpT)	1,633
Number of Terms with Frequency 4 (#TFq4)	16
Percentage of Terms with Full Syntactic Similarity [%TFSyS = ((#TFq4 * 4) / TpT) * 100]	3.92%
Number of Terms with Frequency 3 (#TFq3)	46
Percentage of Terms with high-Partial Syntactic Similarity [%ThiPSyS = ((#TFq3 * 3) /TpT) * 100]	8.45%
Number of Terms with Frequency 2 (#TFq2)	164
Percentage of Terms with low-Partial Syntactic Similarity [%TloPSyS = ((#TFq2 * 2) / TpT) * 100]	20.09%
Number of Terms with Frequency 1 (#TFq1)	1,103
Percentage of Terms without Syntactic Similarity [%TwSyS = (#TFq1 / TpT) * 100]	67.54%

As represented in Table 6, we designed four indirect metrics (percentages) with their related direct metrics. Percentage metrics calculate the proportion of terms with full syntactic similarity, high-partial syntactic similarity, low-partial syntactic similarity, and without syntactic similarity.

The frequency results were taken from the data processed by the tool, so the values of the base and derived measures are recorded in Table 6. The first direct metric for frequency is the "Number of Terms with Frequency 4", which resulted in 16. Then, we calculated the "Percentage of Terms with Full Syntactic Similarity", which is 3.92%. The reader can see the other obtained values for frequencies 3, 2, and 1. Note that frequency 1 implies that a term is either absent from the other three glossaries, or has a slightly different primary term label, with no matching synonyms. Also, note that we have pre-processed some terms such as "Program" and "Programme" for syntactic uniformity. Thanks to this, "Program" has a frequency of 4 instead of 3, since "Programme" is the label used in the APM glossary.

Finally, if we look at the yielded percentages, we can say that the project management glossaries assessed have a low proportion of common terms with full syntactic similarity (16 common terms representing 3.92%) and even with a frequency of 3 (46 common terms representing 8.45%). Considering that since the 1950s, organizations began to systematically apply project management approaches, processes, techniques, and tools to engineering projects, we expected a greater full syntactic match in the glossary terms.

2.6. Calculating Semantic Similarity of Terms

Activity A6 deals with metrics and calculations of categorical semantic similarity based on the frequency of syntactic similarity of glossary terms and their semantic correspondences with designed terminological categories.

Let's apply this activity with the term "Project" shown in Table 4 and exemplified in subsection 2.5, where it turned out to have full syntactic similarity as it has a frequency of occurrence of 4. Also, the definition of "Project" in all four glossaries has a semantic reference to *transient/temporary organization*, *endeavor*, or *undertaking*. For this reason, they belong to the conceptual category C8 called "Organizational Entity-, Asset-related Terms". The reader may notice that the "Project" entry in each glossary has a variation in its definition. However, they are similar considering the categorical keywords, which is why they fall into the same semantic category. Ultimately, we can state that these entries are syntactically and semantically similar and therefore syntactically and semantically consistent concerning the information suitability sub-characteristic defined in Table 1.

Taking into account both the syntactic and semantic aspects of this exploratory study, we have designed a set of direct and indirect metrics whose names and values are shown in Table 7. Note that the formulas for indirect metrics are formulated in Appendix IX at https://bit.ly/CIbSE_Appendices.

On the one hand, regarding the categorical semantic similarities of the 16 terms with a syntactic frequency of 4 (Table 6), only 12 terms have full semantic similarity (#TFSSFq4 = 12). This means that per each common entry, the 4 syntactically equal terms in the 4 glossaries have the same intended semantics as well.

Table 7. Metrics and their values for syntactic frequencies and categorical semantic similarities/discrepancies of the terms from all four glossaries together

Metric name/acronym/formula	Value
Number of Terms with Full Semantic Similarity for Frequency 4 (#TFSSFq4)	12
Number of Terms with high-Partial Semantic Similarity for Frequency 4 (#ThPSSFq4)	3
Number of Terms with low-Partial Semantic Similarity for Frequency 4 (#TlPSSFq4)	1
Number of Terms without Semantic Similarity for Frequency 4 (#TwSSFq4)	0
Number of Terms with Full Semantic Similarity for Frequency 3 (#TFSSFq3)	28
Number of Terms with Partial Semantic Similarity for Frequency 3 (#TPSSFq3)	16
Number of Terms without Semantic Similarity for Frequency 3 (#TwSSFq3)	2
Number of Terms with Full Semantic Similarity for Frequency 2 (#TFSSFq2)	124
Number of Terms without Semantic Similarity for Frequency 2 (#TwSSFq2)	40
Percentage of total Terms with Full Syntactic and Semantic Similarity (%TFS&SS)	2.94%
Percentage of total Terms with high-Partial Semantic Similarity (%ThiPSS)	5.70%
Percentage of total Terms with low-Partial Semantic Similarity (%TloPSS)	17.27%
Percentage of total Terms without any Semantic Similarity (%TwSS)	74.10%

Thus, the Percentage of total Terms with Full Syntactic and Semantic Similarity (%TFS&SS) gives 2.94% from $(\frac{12*4}{1633} * 100)$.

On the other hand, 3 common terms have a high-partial semantic similarity (#ThPSSFq4 = 3), i.e., they have a semantic similarity of only 3 primary terms out of 4. In addition, the Number of Terms with Full Semantic Similarity for Frequency 3 (#TFSSFq3) gives 28. Therefore, the Percentage of total Terms with high-Partial Semantic Similarity (%ThiPSS) gives 5.70% from $(\frac{3*3 + 28*3}{1633} * 100)$.

It is worth noting that for the frequency of 4, there is 1 common term with low-partial semantic similarity, that is, a semantic similarity of only 2 primary terms out of 4. While no term for this frequency has 4 different semantics (#TwSSFq4 = 0).

Table 8. Names of the terms with frequency 4 including the semantic categorization by glossary. Note that a green-colored row indicates full semantic similarity, a yellow-colored row indicates high-partial semantic similarity, an orange-colored row indicates low-partial semantic similarity, and a red one indicates no semantic similarity

Term name or label	PMBOK	APM	IAPM	PRINCE2
portfolio	C8	C8	C8	C9
program	C8	C8	C8	C8
project	C8	C8	C8	C8
project life cycle	C4	C2	C6	C6
project management	C2	C2	C2	C3
project management team	C7	C7	C7	C7
project management office	C8	C8	C8	C8
project manager	C7	C7	C7	C7
quality	C9	C9	C9	C9
report	C9	C6	C6	C6
risk	C4	C4	C4	C4
sponsor	C7	C7	C7	C7
sprint	C4	C4	C4	C4
stakeholder	C7	C7	C7	C7
user story	C9	C9	C9	C9
work package	C6	C6	C6	C6

Finally, Table 8 shows the 16 labels (names) of the project management glossary terms with a syntactic frequency of 4 and their semantic category per glossary, from which the values of the direct metrics in Table 7 were obtained. In addition, Table 8 exhibits a different color for term rows with full, high-partial, low-partial, and no semantic similarity. The reader can see the remainder tables for frequencies 3, 2, and 1 in Appendix X at https://bit.ly/CIbSE_Appendices.

2.7. Analyzing Syntactic and Semantic Consistency

A7 is mainly concerned with the comparative analysis of the syntactic and semantic consistencies of categorized terms. Based on the results of A5 and A6 activities that recorded syntactic and semantic similarities of terms, the detection of consistency issues can be analyzed not only for the four glossaries as a whole but also for the terms within each glossary. Also, many other quality aspects of glossaries could be analyzed.

Firstly, if we look at the glossary term "Project" as a single term designating the intended concept, or "Project" as the word of other compound terms designating related concepts, Table 8 shows 6 common terms (with a frequency of 4) containing the label "Project". If we browse this for a frequency of 3 (see Appendix X of the linked document), there are 3 common terms, while there are 10 common terms for a frequency of 2. However, 91 terms include the label "Project" with a frequency of 1, which imply no syntactic similarity. These figures are a bit surprising taking into account that all the glossaries are for the project management area.

Secondly, if we observe the green-shaded rows for the terms in Table 8, we find 12 syntactically and semantically consistent common terms. That is to say, each one of them shares not only the same label but also falls under the same conceptual category. Therefore, as illustrated in the previous subsection, the common term "Project" is consistent considering the four glossaries. Or, in other words, there is to a large extent a terminological harmonization. But the same is not the case with the common term "Project management", which has a categorical semantic similarity of 3. Table 9 shows its definition in the four glossaries as well as the categories. In Prince 2 this term has process/activity semantics (C3), whereas in the other glossaries it falls into C2. However, in Table 10 we see the term "Project management process" as another related concept existing only in APM and IAPM. So if the Prince 2 term "Project management" had the final word 'process' it would be consistent with that in APM and IAPM.

Table 9. Definitions of the "Project management" term in the four glossaries

Term	Term definition	Gloss.	Cat
Project management	The application of knowledge, skills, tools, and techniques to project activities to meet the project requirements.	PMBOK	C2
Project management	The application of processes, methods, knowledge, skills and experience to achieve specific objectives for change.	APM	C2
Project management	Project management involves *the application of methods and management tools (administration task), *techniques and concepts of leadership (leadership task) and *integration of the competences ... [*continues*]	IAPM	C2
Project management	The planning, delegating, monitoring and control of all aspects of the project, and the motivation of those involved, to achieve the project objectives within the expected performance targets for time, cost, quality, scope, benefits and risk.	PRINCE2	C3

Table 10. The term "Project management process" is available only in two glossaries

Term	Term definition	Gloss.	Cat
Project management processes	The generic processes that need to apply to each phase of the project life cycle. These may be described as a starting or initiating process, a defining and planning process, a monitoring and controlling process and a learning or closing process.	APM	C3
Project management process	All processes to be performed by the project management team within the scope of a project, including project preparation, project start-up, project implementation (= management of technical planning and implementation) and project close-out.	IAPM	C3

Moreover, the PMBOK term "Project management process group" has a syntactic frequency of 1 with the semantics of process (C3). So if this term had had "Project management process/es" as a synonym or without the word 'group' then it would also have been in Table 10, consistently.

Finally, if we observe the row shaded in orange in Table 8, the inconsistency corresponds to the shared term "Project life cycle" since it has three different semantics.

2.8. Recommending Adoptions and Adaptations

A8 focuses on recommendations for the adoption or adaptation of glossary terms to the new version of the project ontology to be updated, which is located at the core level, as indicated in subsection 2.1. Note that a core ontology should contain generic concepts rather than domain-specific concepts. Thus, if "Project management process" is a generic term, then the term "Agile project management process" is a specialization of it, hence a domain-specific term for a top domain-specific ontology for agile projects. An example of a recently updated core ontology is ProcessCO (Becker et al., 2022).

On the one hand, looking at Table 8, there are terms such as "Sprint" and "User Story" that are rather domain-specific. So they will not be part of the updated project core ontology. Likewise, another term such as "Quality" represents a cross-cutting concept that can be applied to different entities and not only to projects. For this reason, "Quality" was placed in the miscellaneous category (C9). On the other hand, the first eight terms of Table 8 must be considered in the updated project ontology, among others with less frequency of occurrence such as the term "Project management process".

Table 11 shows only four terms, i.e., their labels and definitions of the project ontology developed in 2016. We can make some recommendations in light of the present study.

Table 11. A subset of terms from the project ontology by Rivera et al. (2016)

Term	Term definition	Cat
Project	An entity representing a temporary and goal-oriented endeavor with definite start and finish dates, which considers a managed set of interrelated activities, tasks, and resources aimed at producing and modifying unique work products (i.e., artifacts, services or results) for satisfying a given requester need.	C8
Project life cycle	The series of phases that a Project passes through from its initiation to its closure.	C4
Project management	It is the set of managerial processes and activities intended to achieve the goal operationalized by a project.	C3
Project management plan	The document that describes how the project will be executed, monitored, and controlled.	C6

Regarding the term "Project", the definition made in 2016 can be maintained, since it covers the key concepts given in the four glossaries (see Table 4). We foresee adding the word 'organizational' to the beginning of its definition as "*An organizational entity representing a temporary…*" to explicitly include this C8 keyword.

The term "Project life cycle" was adopted in the first version of the ontology from PMBOK (2013). But the current edition (PMBOK, 2021) rephrases it as "*The series of phases that a project passes through from its start to its completion*", which we will adopt in the new version.

Considering the discussion carried out in the previous subsection for the term "Project management", and taking into account that this term has process/activity semantics (C3) in Table 11, we propose to change the former label to "Project management process" in the new version of the project ontology. Also, we can consider leaving its definition as it is or adapting it a bit. Lastly, for the term "Project management plan" we reused the definition given by PMBOK (2013). The current edition of PMBOK (2021) has the same definition, but only "… *and closed*" was appended to the end of the sentence in Table 11.

In summary, many recommendations can be considered for adoptions and adaptations to the project ontology to be updated, but we are limited in the present analysis for reasons of space. Anyway, we hope that the main aspects of this work have been conveyed.

3. Related Work

To the best of our knowledge, no directly related work in the literature considers a comparative analysis of syntactic and semantic consistency for a set of project management glossaries.

Somewhat related work is Wideman's (2012) glossary on project management, which is comparative and hyperlinked. It contains over 6,400 entries covering over 4,400 primary terms derived from over 200 sources. This glossary was built considering the syntactic similarity of terms. For example, its glossary version 5.5 lists thirty-four definitions of the term "Project". So, the author highlights the preferred definition of it. However, categorical semantic similarity and consistency issues are not taken into account. Note that the glossary version 6.1 was released in July 2017 but is not publicly accessible. Also, it is not used for training and certification purposes.

To search related work in digital libraries, we primarily used Scopus with a variety of keywords and operators, even including glossaries outside the project management area. The result was about 10 articles, which we thoroughly analyzed. Outside the project management area, we found some work related to the software testing domain. Among them, the oldest research was carried out by Arnicane et al. (2016). The authors analyzed only inconsistencies in one software testing glossary, without conducting a comparative analysis between terms of different glossaries.

More recently, Tebes et al. (2022) carried out a comparison and analysis of syntactic and semantic similarities and discrepancies between terms of three software testing glossaries for two terminological categories, i.e., for the categories of process/activity and method/technique. Olsina et al. (2022) widened this exploratory study by considering the label 'testing' as a single word or included at the end of a compound label for eight terminological categories. The present work is similar to the approach followed in the two papers cited, but now its steps are explicitly specified. In addition, we deal with another area (project management), so we have redesigned some categories. Moreover, the goal of this exploratory study differs from previous ones.

4. Final Remarks

This paper has shown the results of analyzing the syntactic and semantic similarities and consistencies between terms of four selected project management glossaries documented in PMBOK (2021), APM (2021), IAPM (2021), and PRINCE2 (2017). We have supported this comparative analysis by using a set of metrics in addition to a set of conceptual categories which helped us to semantically categorize all glossaries' terms.

We have established in Section 2 the list of activities that systematically guided us in the execution, discussion, and documentation of the present study. As an end goal, this exploratory study will help us to examine in a more disciplined way our previously developed project ontology and recommend adoptions and adaptations from glossaries, as described in subsection 2.8. Additionally, the comparative analysis has permitted us to assess the level of syntactic and semantic consistency and harmonization existing in the selected glossaries.

In a nutshell, what has become evident from this early research on project management glossaries is that are many opportunities to improve these terminologies to achieve greater consistency, harmonization, and standardization in the field.

As for a threat to the validity of this exploratory study, particularly for a task from activity A4 (Put glossary terms into categories taking into account the semantics intended by glossary authors in their definitions), we cannot guarantee the absence of miscategorizations in the process of placing the terms in the proper category. Although category names or labels have a set of well-defined keywords (see Table 3) that, after reading a given term definition, guide the process of identifying the term semantics by a human agent, term definitions are often not well structured. For example, in some cases, the term starts with a note and then comes with some kind of definition. Or, rarely the definitions of terms are structured by using the hypernym-hyponym relationship.

Faced with this situation, in future work, we will explore the sub-characteristics and attributes of information quality that can be considered for the evaluation and comparison of glossaries, such as syntactic correctness, semantic correctness, and non-redundant coverage, among other aspects of quality.

Ultimately, in the short term, we will update the project core ontology mentioned above.

Acknowledgments. This line of research is supported partially by the Engineering School at UNLPam, Argentina, in the project coded 09/F079.

References

Arnicane, V., Arnicans, G., & Borzovs, J. (2016). Building of Concept System to Improve Systematic Collection of Terminology. *Frontiers in Artificial Intelligence and Applications*, vol. 291, pp. 313–326. https://doi.org/10.3233/978-1-61499-714-6-313.

APM, (2021). Association for Project Management, APM Glossary, Available at: https://www.apm.org.uk/resources/glossary/. Accessed by November 15, 2022.

Becker, P., Papa, M.F., Tebes, G., Olsina L. (2022). Discussing the Applicability of a Process Core Ontology and Aspects of its Internal Quality, Software Quality Journal, Springer, 30:(4), pp. 1003–1038. DOI: 10.1007/s11219-022-09592-3.

Henderson-Sellers, B., Gonzalez-Perez, C., McBride, T., Low, G. (2014). An ontology for ISO software engineering standards: 1) Creating the infrastructure. Computer Standards & Interfaces, 36(3), pp. 563–576. https://doi.org/10.1016/j.csi.2013.11.001.

IAPM. (2021). International Association of Project Managers, Project Managers' Guide and Agile Project Managers' Guide, Available at: https://www.iapm-cert.net/documents/glossary-en/a.html. Accessed by November 16, 2022.

Olsina, L., Lew, P., Tebes, G. (2022). Analyzing Quality Issues from Software Testing Glossaries Used in Academia and Industry. In: Vallecillo, A., Visser, J., Pérez-Castillo, R. (eds) Quality of Information and Communications Technology. QUATIC 2022. Communications in Computer and Information Science, Springer, vol. 1621, pp. 140–155, https://doi.org/10.1007/978-3-031-14179-9_10.

Olsina, L. (2021). Applicability of a Foundational Ontology to Semantically Enrich the Core and Domain Ontologies. In: 13th International Joint Conference on Knowledge Discovery, Knowledge Engineering and Knowledge Management, vol. 2: KEOD (Knowledge Engineering and Ontology Development), Portugal, pp. 111–119.

PMBOK. (2021). PMBOK® Guide, A Guide to the Project Management Body of Knowledge. 7th Edition. Available at: https://www.pmi.org/pmbok-guide-standards/foundational/pmbok?sc_camp=D750AAC10C2F4378CE6D51F8D987F49D. Accessed by November 15, 2022.

PMBOK. (2013). A Guide to the Project Management Body of Knowledge. 5th Edition.

PRINCE2. (2017). PRINCE2®, 6th Edition Glossaries of Terms, Available at: https://www.axelos.com/resource-hub/glossary/prince2-6th-edition-glossaries-of-terms. Accessed by November 16, 2022.

Tebes, G., Lew, P., Olsina, L. (2022). Syntactic and Semantic Similarities and Discrepancies between Terms of Glossaries for Software Testing. XXV Conferencia Iberoamericana en Software Engineering (CIbSE'22), Córdoba, Argentina, pp. 278-291. Proceedings published by SBC_OpenLib (https://sol.sbc.org.br/index.php/cibse) and Curran Associates 2022, ISBN: 9781713855583.

Rivera, B., Becker, P., Papa, M.F., Olsina, L. (2016). A Holistic Quality Evaluation, Selection, and Improvement Approach driven by Multilevel Goals and Strategies. In *CLEI Electronic Journal*, 19:(3), Paper 3, pp. 1–28, ISSN 0717-5000.

Wideman, M. (2012). Wideman's Project Management Glossary v5.5. Available at: http://www.maxwideman.com/pmglossary/intro.htm. Accessed by November 15, 2022.

Supporting software evolution actions with process mining

Daniel Calegari[1], **Andrea Delgado**[1]

[1]Instituto de Computación, Facultad de Ingeniería, Universidad de la República, Montevideo, Uruguay

{dcalegar,adelgado}@fing.edu.uy

Abstract. *There are several forces driving software evolution. One is the business process (BP) misalignment, i.e., when the behavior of the information systems supporting the BPs, or its users, is not aligned with the intended behavior of the BPs identified during the requirement engineering phase. Process Mining (PM) is an essential strategy for BP alignment evaluation. Nevertheless, PM initiatives do not usually focus on connecting BP alignment misfits with concrete software requirements for software evolution. This paper provides initial insights into how PM can support software evolution actions by considering research questions posed during a PM initiative. We exemplify this idea by analyzing administrative procedures within an Electronic Document Management System, providing action guides for its evolution obtained from the PM initiative.*

1. Introduction

Business Processes (BPs) are at the center of organizations' daily operation, supported by a combination of traditional Information Systems (IS) and Process-Aware Information Systems (PAIS) [Dumas et al. 2005]. Many different internal and environmental forces require the software to be corrected, adapted, and improved, guiding its evolution [Sommerville 2016]. One is BP misalignment, i.e., when the actual behavior of the information systems supporting the BPs, or its users, is not aligned with the intended behavior of the BPs identified during the requirement engineering phase.

BPs life-cycle [Weske 2019] is closely linked with the software engineering life-cycle since there must be an evaluation phase measuring business alignment [Aversano et al. 2012, Rabelo et al. 2019] pushing process improvement and the corresponding software evolution. Alignment between the BPs and the supporting software systems requires comparing the actual behavior of an information system or its users with the intended behavior of the BPs identified during the requirements phase [van der Aalst 2005]. BPs could be not entirely aligned, e.g., their execution does not comply with performance requirements, there were environmental changes (e.g., policies and laws) that are not considered, or there is evidence of unexpected behaviors caused by a flexible execution of the BP or an incorrect interpretation of the process during their implementation. Depending on the source of the misalignment, the BPs need to be redesigned, and/or the supporting system needs to evolve.

Process Mining (PM) ([van der Aalst 2016]) is an essential strategy for BPs alignment evaluation. It allows for analyzing the records (logs) of events associated with the execution of processes in information systems. There are several techniques to discover corresponding business process models (process discovery) from the recorded events and verify the correspondence of the enacted BPs concerning the defined one (conformance checking). It also allows obtaining measures such as the duration of the processes, bottlenecks, or the underuse of resources, among others.

There are also methodologies, e.g., [Eck, van et al. 2015, Delgado et al. 2021], to guide the execution of PM initiatives (projects), defining activities, roles, and artifacts. They usually start with a planning stage for setting up the initiative with the definition of research questions that guide the mining and analysis activities. These methodologies also identify an evaluation stage that relates analysis findings to improvement opportunities. Although many possible use cases exist for PM [Milani et al. 2022], they focus on identifying BP alignment misfits. They do not focus on connecting problems that arise during the execution of the PM methodology with concrete requirements of the software systems supporting the BPs that must be addressed during software evolution. Moreover, since these research questions are separate from the requirement engineering stage, some business requirements for evaluation are only sometimes considered during software construction. Even if there is a perfect fit in BPs alignment, how data is recorded may obstruct or prevent answering the research questions. For example, the supporting systems register the activities performed but not the responsible users; thus, the process can be (mostly) enacted as expected. However, it is necessary to include data about who performs the activities to perform resource analysis.

This paper explores how PM can support software evolution actions such that improvements from these actions complement BP alignment needs. We define a general schema that connects research questions posed during a PM initiative with software evolution actions. We explore the feasibility of the schema by performing a PM initiative to an Electronic Document Management System (EDMS) [ISO 2016] providing such action guides for software evolution. In particular, we perform an in-depth analysis of open-access information on administrative procedures from our university. As a complementary objective of this initiative, we identify challenges for applying PM in EDMS.

The rest of the paper is structured as follows. In Section 2, we analyze some related work. In Section 3, we present the approach we followed. In Section 4, we present the PM initiative, and in Section 5, we discuss the initiative concerning the general approach and identify some challenges in applying PM for EDMS. Finally, in Section 6, we provide conclusions and an outline of future work.

2. Related Work

PM has many applications to software engineering [Keith and Vega 2017]. Most of them are focused on what is called Software Process Intelligence (SPI), which is the application of mining and analysis to software processes. The information needed for applying PM comes from software repositories such as version control systems, bug trackers, and mail archives. Using this information, the data can be extracted, combined [Poncin et al. 2011], and integrated with the perceptions of stakeholders [Vavpotic et al. 2022] to determine deviations and take corrective actions or provide improvement recommendations for the whole process. Generally, it is possible to study how to use PM to monitor the development process to demonstrate adherence to methodologies, rules, regulations, guidelines, or best practices [Bala and Mendling 2018]. Moreover, it is possible to apply the same idea to concrete software engineering disciplines, e.g., testing [Hernandez-Resendiz et al. 2023] and maintenance [Gupta et al. 2017].

The alignment between business requirements and software systems is also an active research line [Aversano et al. 2012, Rabelo et al. 2019]. In [Aversano et al. 2016], the authors present a general approach for monitoring and managing the alignment level. It comprises a modeling stage for BPs and software systems, an evaluation phase for measuring the alignment level between them, and a final step for identifying and executing the evolution actions. This approach is based on the existence of the previous modeling of the software systems and a mapping between software and business entities, which can be restrictive. In [van der Aalst 2005], PM is used for measuring business alignment based on predefined process models and discovered models that are compared using delta and conformance analysis, similar to the works about PM application to software engineering described before.

Works applying PM techniques to EDMS focus on extracting information from the system's database rather than identifying challenges. In [Berti et al. 2021], the authors propose an approach to guide and ease the extraction of event logs from SAP ERP, which, in a broader sense, can be seen as an EDMS. In [Osman and Ghiran 2019], the authors exemplify the application of PM as part of Industry 4.0 by analyzing an event log describing a document management process. In [Repta et al. 2018], the authors analyze processes related to e-government systems, focusing on the discovery and extraction of document flows. Finally, in [Markowski and Przybylek 2016], the authors present an example of the application of PM to analyze the loss of documents in a document flow.

3. Connecting a PM initiative with software evolution actions

Any PM initiative tends to analyze the actual execution of BPs within traditional IS or PAIS, supporting them for the organization's daily operation. We claim that from these initiatives, it is possible to discover BP alignment misfits and determine concrete actions for software evolution. This section presents the general idea of linking a PM initiative to identifying software evolution actions and a proposal to guide such identification.

3.1. PM initiatives for software evolution

Although there are many PM methodologies to guide a PM initiative, we take PRICED [Delgado et al. 2021] as a reference since we have applied it in several PM efforts before and in the EDMS example we present here. It provides guidance and support for organizational data science projects, i.e., from a traditional process mining project to a more complex project requiring integrating process data, and organizational data [Calegari et al. 2021]. From a very abstract perspective, as depicted in Figure 1, the PRICED methodology defines four phases. The **Enactment** phase involves the actual execution of processes within the supporting software systems. The **Data** phase involves determining the research questions that will lead the mining effort and extracting, integrating, and loading data to build event logs which are the primary source of information to analyze. An event log consists of cases (executions) of a process. For each case, there is a partially ordered collection of events that describe such execution, each with possibly many attributes describing the event and its environment (e.g., resources involved, timestamps, etc.) The **Mining/Analysis** phase focuses on executing the analysis and providing many outputs, such as process and analytic models, which are evaluated to provide findings for the organization. Finally, the **Improvement** phase corresponds to the organization's improvement efforts after the analysis.

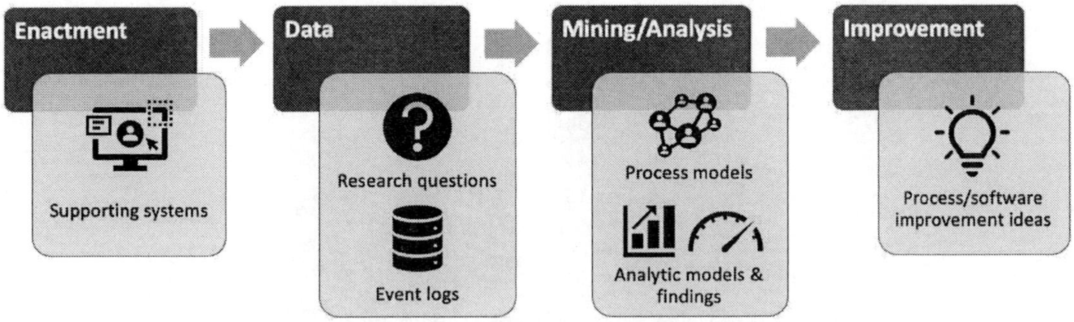

Figure 1. An overview of the PRICED methodology

Within the Improvement phase, there are two different kinds of improvement ideas to consider. On the one hand, process improvement ideas come from identifying BP alignment misfits, e.g., some activities can be improved by assigning more resources, or the process can be uniformly performed by avoiding undesirable paths. On the other hand, software evolution actions can be taken indirectly from process improvement ideas, i.e., the software system needs to evolve to better align with the business processes it supports.

In this paper, as a second kind of software improvement idea, we connect problems that arise during the execution of the PM methodology with concrete software requirements that must be addressed during the evolution of the supporting systems. A PM initiative could be used to ensure that the software provides the organization with the answers it needs for evaluating its operations.

3.2. Identifying software evolution actions

Based on the motivation presented above, we defined an approach to connect PM initiatives with software evolution actions as another result of the PM effort. As depicted in Figure 2, we consider three dimensions: the purposes guiding a PM initiative, the perspectives addressed by the research questions, and the existing challenges and guidelines for building an event log.

The **Purpose dimension** was taken from [Milani et al. 2022], in which PM use cases are classified, as well as the business questions they might address. The authors define the following categories, each with specific questions to be addressed: *Transparency* focuses on discovering process perspectives: process models, resource interactions, decision rules, etc.; *Efficiency* focuses on performance analysis; *Quality* focuses on process variants and deviation analysis; *Compliance* focuses on conformance checking and compliance monitoring; and *Agility* focuses on predictive monitoring, concept drift, etc.

The **Perspective dimension** was taken from [van der Aalst 2016], in which the following perspectives are defined: *Control-flow* focuses on finding a good characterization of all possible paths within a process; *Organizational* focuses on the resources enacting the process and their relations; *Case* focuses on the data that characterizes process instances, i.e., organizational data related to each event; and *Time* focuses on analyzing the timing and frequency of events, e.g., on discovering bottlenecks.

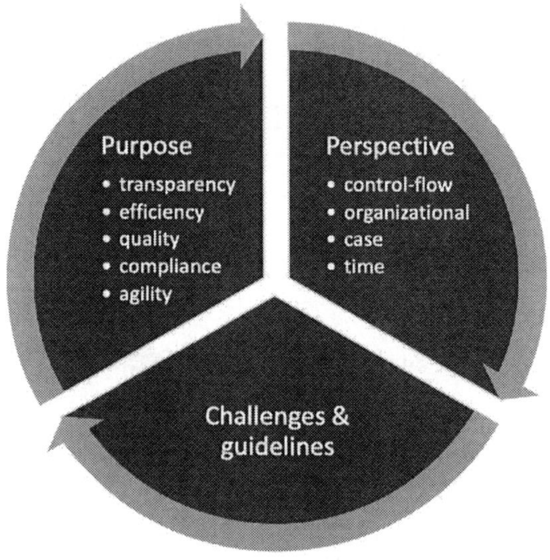

Figure 2. Dimensions considered within a PM initiative

There are also **Challenges & Guidelines** that apply to an event log [van der Aalst 2016]. Essential aspects to consider are: *events* need to be grouped and (partially) ordered per case. They also need to be all at the same level of granularity; Every event needs at least two *attributes*: a name and a timestamp that partially orders them within a case. There can be other attributes of interest, e.g., the resource causing the event or any other type of data (costs, risk, age, etc.); *attribute values* must have clear semantics and be structured, precise, and stable within a log.

The three dimensions depicted in Figure 2 could be overlapped sometimes (e.g., the efficiency purpose is related to the time perspective) and are non-exhaustive. Nevertheless, they provide an initial approach to identifying software improvement (evolution) actions from a PM initiative. Figure 3 depicts our proposed general schema. Once the initiative's **purpose** is defined, many research **questions** must be addressed, and each question involves a particular **perspective** related to a set of guidelines. During the PM initiative, some **challenges** could arise related to the perspective involved, thus inducing some guidelines to consider. These guidelines can be mapped to specific software evolution **actions** by looking at the former software requirements and how they were addressed within the software system. Sometimes different challenges can be connected to the same guideline, and different guidelines could be related to the same improvement action.

For example, a transparency initiative could be focused on the organizational perspective. In such a case, as described in [Milani et al. 2022], specific research questions can be addressed, e.g., what are the relationships among the resources involved in a process? This research question leads to specific log requirements (guidelines), e.g., events must have an attribute describing the resource involved with the event, which also needs to be appropriately connected with the organizational structure. During the PM initiative, we can find some events that need more information about the people performing them or the role people have within the organization. It identifies how the organizational structure is managed and which software requirements involve associating these events with concrete people/roles allowed to perform certain activities in the BP.

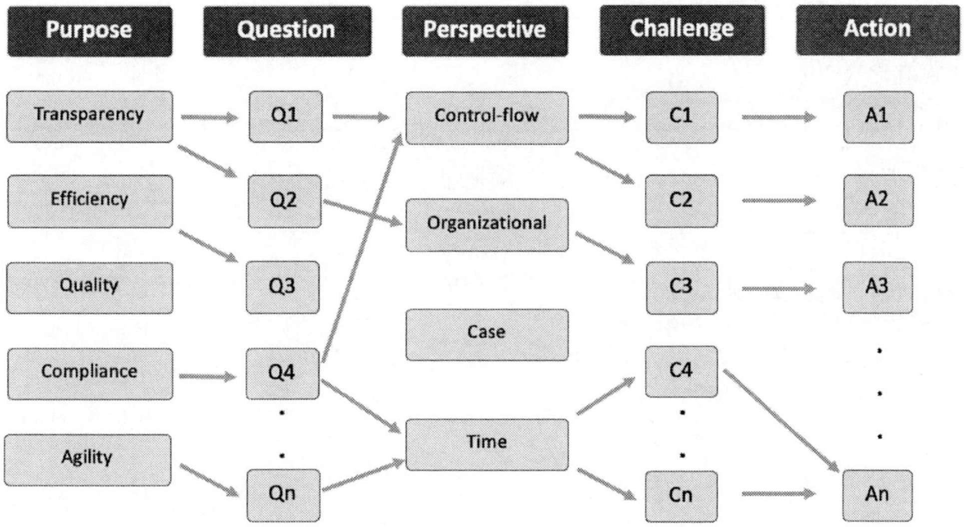

Figure 3. Schema for identifying improvement actions from a PM initiative

4. PM initiative example: EXPE+

To assess the general schema depicted in Figure 3, we performed an exploratory PM initiative following the PRICED methodology for analyzing the EXPE+[1] system. In what follows, we present the system and the main results of the Data and the Mining/Analysis phases of the PRICED methodology application.

4.1. EXPE+

The EXPE+ system is an Electronic Document Management System (EDMS) used at Universidad de la República, Uruguay's main public university. EXPE+ manages the electronic creation, storage, and control of documents, supporting the organization's processes. It is used to carry out every administrative procedure helping to organize and exchange data in a distributed environment with more than six thousand administrative people and a hundred administrative areas within their twenty decentralized schools.

EXPE+ defines how records need to be expressed to trace an administrative procedure and what information can be accessed as public. Every administrative procedure has a physical document attached to new information at each step. The system registers primary data used to carry out the administrative procedure, e.g., the step that has to be done, the person and organizational section that performs it, and when it is done. The procedures follow flexible but optional guidelines, i.e., a predefined process may need to be carried out as intended. It could generate deviations in the processes and the impossibility of objectively analyzing their execution.

An open-access web application enables tracking of the stage of the process in which an administrative procedure is. The application shows the cover of an administrative procedure, e.g., the one depicted in Figure 4, which provides the primary information about it, e.g., the procedure ID, the kind of procedure, and a summary of it, and the data of each step that has been enacted, as well as the active step.

[1]EXPE+. `http://www.expe.edu.uy/`

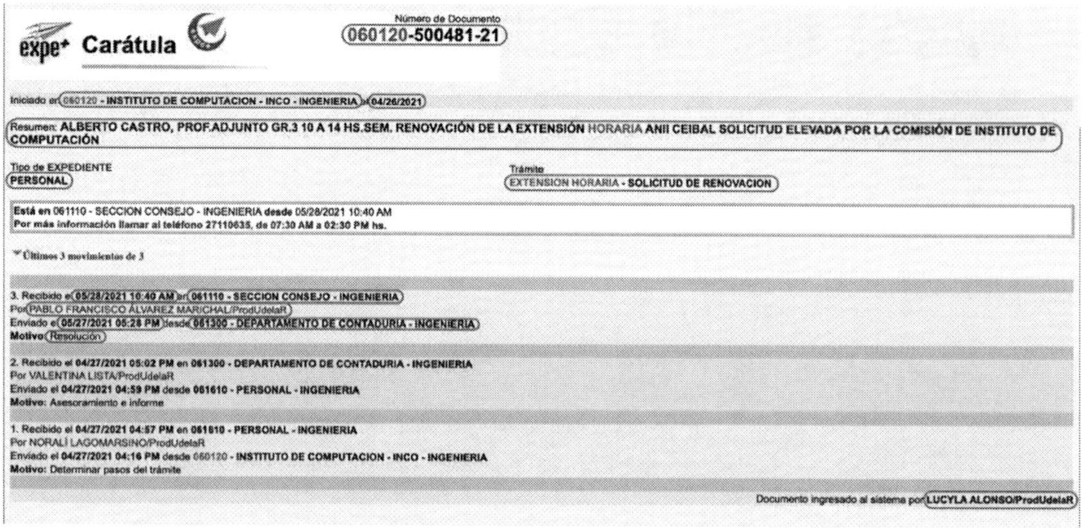

Figure 4. EXPE+: exampling cover of an administrative procedure

4.2. Data phase

We selected well-known processes for us: the "Extension of working hours" and "Reduction of working hours" for teachers within the Computer Science Institute (InCo). The processes are commonly used to extend/reduce working hours, in the first case mainly to participate in research projects or to teach extra courses. The university has a theoretical high-level base procedure specified in the text for those processes. These routes should be followed within the EXPE+ system, and one of the critical interests of the analysis is to be able to contrast the actual process execution with the defined procedures.

- Procedure: *"Extension of working hours"*
  - *Step 1:* Organizational unit request with the consent of the interested party
  - *Step 2:* Human Resources: position report
  - *Step 3:* Accounting: availability report
  - *Step 4:* Faculty Council: resolution
  - *Step 5:* Human Resources: Registration, notification, and archiving
  - *Step 6:* Secretary: Archive
- Procedure: *"Reduction of working hours"*
  - *Step 1:* Interested party request with the endorsement of the requesting organizational unit
  - *Step 2:* Human Resources: position report and preventive reserve
  - *Step 3:* Accounting: preventive confirmation
  - *Step 4:* Faculty Council: resolution
  - *Step 5:* Human Resources: Registration, notification, and archiving
  - *Step 6:* Secretary: Archive

We carry out a process mining initiative answering basic questions of any initiative [van der Aalst 2015], which is focused on detecting and analyzing deviations regarding the control-flow and throughput time. These basic questions are:

(RQ1) *Are the processes executing as expected regarding the defined base procedures?*
(RQ2) *Which is the average/minimum/maximum throughput time of the processes?*

The website of the EXPE+ system was identified as the primary data source since the data published there is the public one corresponding to the steps (activities) carried out within the procedures, and it is directly connected to its database. The supporting database provides no additional information for the study. We used web scraping to extract the data from the pages and store it in a database for further manipulation. In this way, we could evaluate the web application and perform the PM initiative without adding the risk of delays in access to information. We recovered processes from 2000 to 2021, totaling 2072 cases containing 12513 events. We automatically generated the event log as a CSV sheet which can be used directly as input in PM tools such as Disco[2].

Mapping events as activities was indirect since the EXPE+ names for the activities are unrelated to the specific process. They are generic for all processes in the system and refer to the movement's objective from one organizational unit to the next, i.e., what the receiving organizational unit should do. For example, when the aim is to resolve, the activity following the transition will be named "Resolution", or when the objective is to analyze and report regarding the procedure's content, the activity's name following the transition will be "Advice and report". Names are selected from a predefined list of options.Using only the activity names to identify the events leads to erroneous loops. Although the names are repeated, they are not the same activity as the origin, and the target organizational unit is different; hence the correct path in the process should not be a loop but moving forward. After analyzing different combinations for the identification of activities, we identified the name activity + target organizational unit (i.e., the one executing the activity) as the one that leads to the expected paths.

We analyzed the event log concerning quality characteristics and improved it accordingly. Each attribute was scanned to check whether it did not present a null value. In particular, we found 22 cases with null values in the sending date, which were solved using the same date as the reception date for the next movement. Regarding the names of the activities, although they are currently available in a list to choose from, some previous records had the names in uppercase, lowercase, or misspelled. To solve this, all the names were standardized to use uppercases. We also checked the timestamps of the registered dates, which in the EXPE+ extend up to minutes. It is not the best granularity to allow exact calculation of waiting and processing times. Still, in this context, it should be sufficient.

4.3. Mining/Analysis phase

We analyzed and filtered the data in the log to get a consistent one to apply the PM tasks. Table 1 presents descriptive statistics regarding the raw and filtered data.

The "Extension of working hours" log contains 1766 cases and 10785 events from 10/10/2000 to 19/11/2021, with a median duration of 90.8 days and a mean of 142.1 days (20.3 weeks) and 140 activities. As expected, most cases have 5-6 events (1112 representing 63% of the cases), with a maximum of 19 events and a minimum of 2 events per case. After filtering incomplete cases (i.e., ongoing and canceled), we get 817 cases (46%) and 4380 (40%) of the events, with a median duration of 88.1 days and a mean of 106.4 days (15.2 weeks).

[2]Fluxicon Disco. https://fluxicon.com/disco/

Table 1. Descriptive statistics of the raw and filtered event logs

Name	#traces raw	#traces filtered	#events raw	#events filtered	#steps raw	#steps filtered
Extension of working hours	1766	817	10785	4380	140	21
Reduction of working hours	201	94	1238	510	111	22

The "Reduction of working hours" process event log contains 201 cases with 1238 events, from 02/03/2001 to 15/11/2021, with a median duration of 84.8 days and a mean duration of 142.1 days (20.3 weeks), and activities. Also, as expected, most cases have 5-6 events (118 cases representing 59% of the cases), with a maximum of 13 events and a minimum of 2 events per case. After filtering incomplete cases (i.e., ongoing and canceled), we get 94 cases (46%) and 510 events (41%), with a median duration of 83.9 days and a mean of 90.9 days.

Figure 5 depicts the general paths of the filtered event logs. It can be seen that the two start activities selected correspond to the organizational units InCo (Instituto de Computación-InCo-Ingeniería) and Human Resources (HR, Personal). In both processes, the ones initiated in HR correspond to expiration notices of an already previous Extension granted. These are sent to the InCo to inform if the renewal should be processed. The ones passed through the organizational unit Secretary of the Faculty Council was renewed.

To answer the first question of interest, whether the processes are executing as expected when comparing the process models' general paths with the procedures defined, it can be easily seen that the real execution of the processes added several activities to the ones planned. Mainly, there are several variants in which cases go through no needed activities and are returned to where they were before to continue within the correct paths. It is caused by participant mistakes since there is a free route option in which an underlying process model does not predefine the activities. Although the most frequent path is similar to the one defined for the procedure, it only represents around 7% of the cases.

We detected five organizational units enacting the process not described in the procedure defined. It probably happens since the ones named in the procedure are the high-level ones, i.e., Accounting, but not the sub-units that are part of them, e.g., Salaries, or the Secretary of the Faculty Council, when only the Faculty Council is named.

To answer the second question regarding the throughput time of the processes (using the filtered log), both processes take several months, but their duration is around the expected times. The Extension process has a median duration of 88.1 days and a mean of 106.4 days (15.2 weeks) with a maximum of 3 years and 265 days and a minimum of 9 days 23 hours. The Reduction process has a median duration of 83.9 days and a mean of 90.9 days, with a maximum of 252 days and a minimum of 19 days and 7 hours.

Reviewing the maximum durations for the unfiltered log, we found that in most cases with long duration, the final archiving activity was missing and added several years later, particularly in 2017, probably due to reviews of the system data. The cases with minimum duration were ongoing cases that we filtered out when adding the endpoint filter to keep only complete cases. Both observations also hold for the Reduction process.

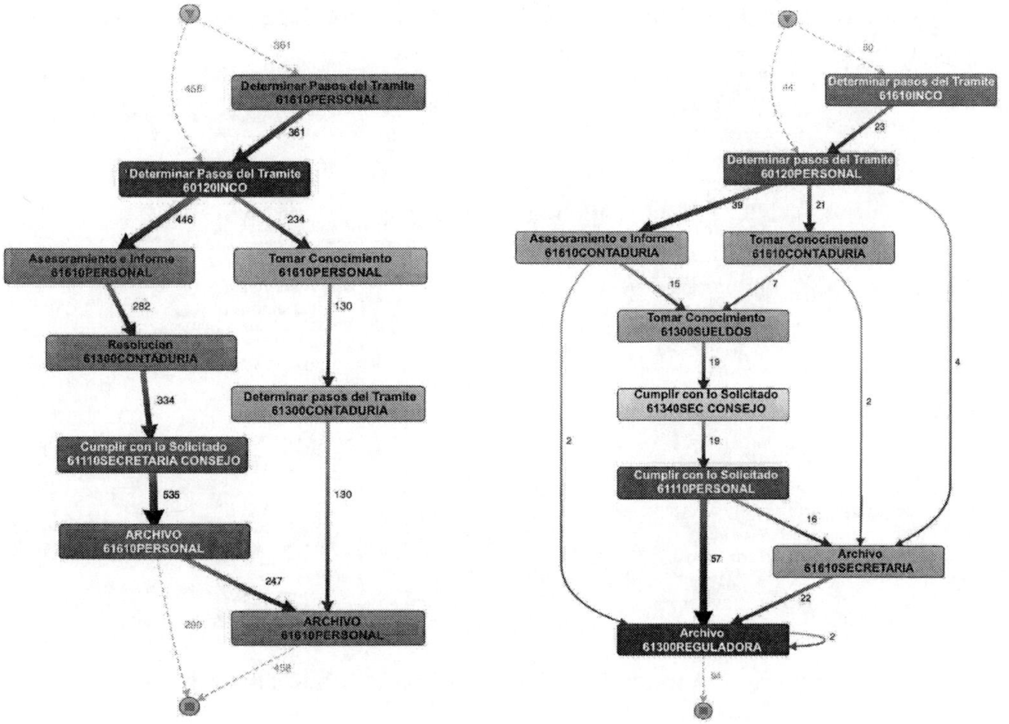

(a) Extension of working hours

(b) Reduction of working hours

Figure 5. Process models general paths from the filtered event logs

5. Discussion & Challenges

Using the PM initiative, we can now discuss how PM can help support software evolution as well as identify challenges for applying PM in EDMS.

5.1. PM for software evolution

Figure 6 summarizes the application of the schema described in Section 3. The initiative had transparency, quality, compliance, and efficiency purposes. From the two main research questions, some other specific ones arise, according to [Milani et al. 2022], involving the control-flow, organizational, and time perspectives, e.g.,

The alternatives can be accumulative. For example, action (A1) involves three accumulative possibilities. As a minimum requirement, activity names must be refined (A1.a). Moreover, the list of predefined activity names in EXPE+ could be extended. A filtering option could be implemented to provide only the list of activities directly associated with the corresponding process (A1.b). The specific activity names for each process can be identified from the theoretical description of the process or the business people involved in each unit. A third and more advanced alternative, while keeping the free routing capabilities of the EDMS, is to incorporate functionality to suggest the following activity to be performed (A1.c), considering the prescribed process or even a software component for predictive analysis that can also be based on PM strategies. Moreover, the alternatives can be opposite or considered exclusive. For example, action (A2) involves

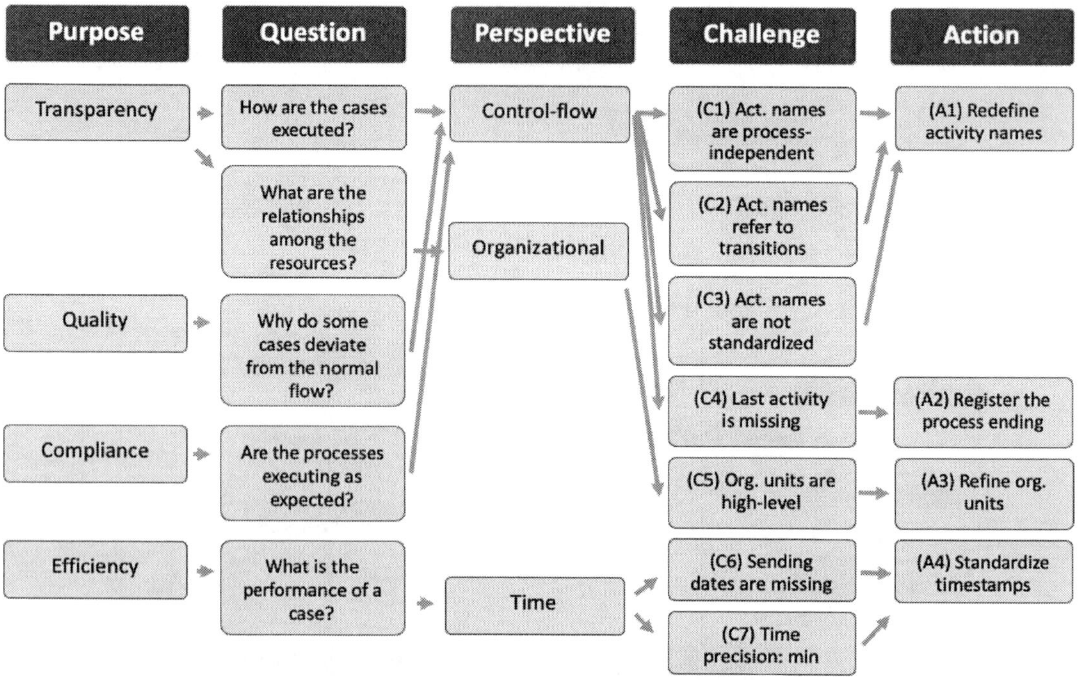

Figure 6. Application of the schema to the PM initiative

two potentially exclusive possibilities. The first (A2.a) consists of locating the concrete requirement that ends the process and changing their implementation for registering the last activity. The second one (A2.b) involves keeping the implementation as is and adding an automatic mechanism to identify "suspended" cases and mark them as ended.

Actions could also imply changing the architecture, e.g., adding new or third-party software components, such as an LDAP (A3.a) or a logging mechanism (A4.b). They could also be considered recommendations and not mandatory requirements. For example, action (A4) implies refining the precision of timestamps which is optional since the way timestamps are registered is sufficient for analyzing the selected procedures.

From the organization's perspective, the EXPE+ software system complies with their former requirements, e.g., it allows managing administrative processes, provides customization capabilities for adding new users and roles, etc. We are not evaluating the functional alignment level between the BP and the supporting software systems. On the contrary, we are adding new requirements about how to register data (e.g., activity names), technologies to incorporate (e.g., LDAP), and additional functionalities (e.g., listing potential routing destinations). The potential actions to perform could vary depending on the software system supporting the business process. Moreover, no BP reengineering is needed from a business perspective. Nevertheless, we can identify ideas that lead to updating or refining the processes and their available information, e.g., the procedures could be updated to reflect the paths and participants in more detail.

The initiative was carried out with missing or incorrect data, as usual when working with traditional systems. We assumed that building the log is performed considering the best practices, so if something obstructs the initiative, it can be linked to some software weaknesses. In this sense, we can detect software improvement ideas.

Table 2. Challenges identified within the PM initiative EXPE+

Id	Challenge	Description
(C1)	Activity names are process-independent	Names are generic for all processes in the system.
(C2)	Activity names refer to transitions	Names refer to the objective of the transition from one unit to the next.
(C3)	Activity names are not standardized	Although they are available in a list to choose from, some records had the names in uppercase, lowercase, or misspelled.
(C4)	Last activity is missing	The end archiving activity was missing and added several years later.
(C5)	Organizational units are high-level	Organizational units referred are the high-level ones, but not the sub-units that are part of them.
(C6)	Sending dates are missing	There are null values in the sending date.
(C7)	Time precision: minutes	Timestamps extend up to minutes

Table 3. Software evolution actions identified within the PM initiative EXPE+

Id	Action	Description
(A1)	Redefine activity names (C1, C2, C3)	(a) Rename activities in a standardized process-specific way; (b) extend the list of predefined activity names and filter them w.r.t. each process; (c) suggest the following activity to be performed.
(A2)	Register the process ending (C4)	(a) Locate the requirement ending the process and registering the activity there; (b) periodically check and finish "suspended" cases that are waiting to be completed.
(A3)	Refine organizational units (C5)	(a) Include sub-units, and relate them to people, e.g., use an LDAP to store the organization information; (b) list only appropriate sub-units to be selected as the routing destination of an activity.
(A4)	Standardize timestamps (C6, C7)	(a) Change the precision of timestamps to include seconds; (b) log timestamps mandatory for every system's action.

5.2. Challenges for PM in EDMS

EDMS are generally integrated by several software modules, including a workflow for routing administrative procedures and a web interface that allows publishing public information about the administrative procedure to ease inquiries from interested parties. Workflow technologies have advanced in the last decades to complete BPMS solutions. , including introducing the BPMN 2.0 standard for enacting BPs. However, these systems mostly use limited capacities for process enactment and allow working with free routes, even defining ad-hoc paths within the process based on specifying the movement and the target organizational unit. It leads to several problems in the control-flow, such as errors when routing procedures to an organizational unit that is not the correct one, or selecting the wrong type of movement, adding unnecessary complexity and duration to the process. It could be helpful to use a predefined most frequent path as the preferred one for execution, leaving the free routing option for exceptional cases.

We can discuss the experience from the perspective of [Burattin 2015] about the most common problems regarding the applicability of PM in real-world environments. Although our findings cannot be generalized to other EDMS, it could be helpful to consider them as potential scenarios in similar initiatives.

- **P-01 Incompleteness of information**. There were several issues regarding the representation of elements on the website. The system is from 2000, and there were no easy ways to identify the elements within the web pages. Also, the back-end system for handling the procedures changed in 2020. Additionally, some cases had extra events not listed on the main page, for which other links had to be followed and parsed to get all the events for the cases.
- **P-02 Exploiting as much information as possible**. The EXPE+ database contains only a little more information than the one accessed through the website. For example, there is no information about each step's start and end timestamps, only the timestamp of when the procedure is sent to another administrative unit. Moreover, there are no attached documents with concrete information on the administrative procedure, approvals, etc., since they are stored on paper. However, this information could be digitally stored using standardized formats, not just PDFs. Explaining this information in a broader context could be possible, e.g., integrating process and organizational data using the PRICED methodology.
- **P-03 Difficulties in using tools and algorithms**. It could be interesting to validate the comprehension of the results within the same organization and analyze the possibility that non-expert users perform some process mining analysis.
- **P-04 Results interpretation**. Following the line above, we should validate it. The processes carried out in EXPE+ are linear, and there is a training of the experts in carrying out the processes (as part of their test competitions), so the interpretation of the models would not be a challenge.
- **P-05 Computational power and storage capacity required**. The scrapping process and the storage of logs were fine in EXPE+. The processes are usually short, and less information is stored. However, as we see in e-gov environments, the logs are larger and more complicated in larger organizations.

6. Conclusions

This paper explored how PM can support software evolution by connecting the research questions posed during a PM initiative with software evolution actions. We also essayed the general schema through the analysis of administrative procedures registered within the EXPE+ system of our University. We need further assessment for validating and identifying limitations of the general schema since we just performed a promising but initial experience. To improve the schema, we need to strengthen the connection between the challenges and the evolution actions, e.g., by expressing the actions in the form of concrete software requirements and using them for performing feasibility and cost analysis. We can also apply the idea to software testing, in which artificially created data could address an idealized PM initiative.

As a complementary objective of the PM initiative, we also identified challenges for applying PM in EDMS. We discussed some findings, such as the problems gathering information from basic (and old) web technologies and the free routing that allows defining where the procedure should go next. Applying PM techniques to EDMS is crucial in checking the operation of the administrative procedures with the predefined or desired one. Since the EXPE+ is being partially replaced by a new solution looking for complete digitalization of the administrative procedures, our analysis provides valuable input for implementing the new system to enable the analysis of processes and improve the University's operations. As ongoing work, we are currently validating the results with business experts to determine the contribution the inputs can generate.

7. Acknowledgements

We want to thank the undergraduate students who worked on the practical application: Ignacio Jorge and Nicolás Menna.

References

Aversano, L., Grasso, C., and Tortorella, M. (2012). A literature review of business/it alignment strategies. *Procedia Technology*, 5:462–474. 4th Conf. of ENTERprise Information Systems, aligning technology, organizations and people (CENTERIS).

Aversano, L., Grasso, C., and Tortorella, M. (2016). Managing the alignment between business processes and software systems. *Information and Software Technology*, 72:171–188.

Bala, S. and Mendling, J. (2018). Monitoring the software development process with process mining. In *Business Modeling and Software Design*, pages 432–442. Springer.

Berti, A., Park, G., Rafiei, M., and van der Aalst, W. M. P. (2021). An event data extraction approach from SAP ERP for process mining. In *Process Mining Workshops - ICPM 2021 Intl. Workshops, Revised Selected Papers*, volume 433 of *LNBIP*, pages 255–267. Springer.

Burattin, A. (2015). Obstacles to applying process mining in practice. In *Process Mining Techniques in Business Environments: Theoretical Aspects, Algorithms, Techniques and Open Challenges in Process Mining*, pages 59–63. Springer.

Calegari, D., Delgado, A., Artus, A., and Borges, A. (2021). Integration of business process and organizational data for evidence-based business intelligence. *CLEI Electron. J.*, 24(2).

Delgado, A., Calegari, D., Marotta, A., González, L., and Tansini, L. (2021). A methodology for organizational data science towards evidence-based process improvement. In *Software Technologies - 16th Intl. Conf., ICSOFT*, volume 1622 of *Communications in Computer and Information Science*, pages 41–66. Springer.

Dumas, M., van der Aalst, W. M., and ter Hofstede, A. H. (2005). *Process-Aware Information Systems: Bridging People and Software through Process Technology*. John Wiley & Sons, Inc.

Eck, van, M., Lu, X., Leemans, S., and Aalst, van der, W. (2015). PM2 : a process mining project methodology. In *Advanced Inf. Systems Engineering: 27th Intl. Conf., CAiSE 2015*, LNCS, pages 297–313. Springer.

Gupta, M., Serebrenik, A., and Jalote, P. (2017). Improving software maintenance using process mining and predictive analytics. In *IEEE Intl. Conf. on Software Maintenance and Evolution (ICSME)*, pages 681–686.

Hernandez-Resendiz, J. D., Ramirez-Alcocer, U. M., and Tello-Leal, E. (2023). *An Approach Based on Process Mining Techniques to Support Software Development*, pages 25–49. Springer.

ISO (2016). ISO 15489-1:2016 information and documentation — records management. Technical report, ISO/TC 46/SC 11.

Keith, B. and Vega, V. (2017). Process mining applications in software engineering. In *Trends and Applications in Software Engineering*, pages 47–56. Springer.

Markowski, P. and Przybylek, M. R. (2016). Process mining methodology in industrial environment: Document flow analysis. In *Proc. of the 2016 Federated Conf. on Computer Science and Information Systems (FedCSIS)*, volume 8, pages 1175–1178. IEEE.

Milani, F., Lashkevich, K., Maggi, F. M., and Francescomarino, C. D. (2022). Process mining: A guide for practitioners. In *Research Challenges in Information Science - 16th Intl. Conf., RCIS, Proc.*, volume 446 of *LNBIP*, pages 265–282. Springer.

Osman, C. and Ghiran, A. (2019). When industry 4.0 meets process mining. In *Knowledge-Based and Intelligent Information & Engineering Systems: Proc. of the 23rd Intl. Conf. KES-2019*, volume 159 of *Procedia Computer Science*, pages 2130–2136. Elsevier.

Poncin, W., Serebrenik, A., and Brand, M. v. d. (2011). Process mining software repositories. In *15th European Conf. on Software Maintenance and Reengineering*, pages 5–14.

Rabelo, L. C., Habba, M., Fredj, M., and Benabdellah Chaouni, S. (2019). Alignment between business requirement, business process, and software system: A systematic literature review. *Journal of Engineering*, 2019:6918105.

Repta, D., Moisescu, M. A., Nae, A. C., Sacala, I. S., and Dumitrache, I. (2018). Towards document flow discovery in e-government systems. In *2018 Intl. Symp. on Electronics and Telecomms. (ISETC)*, pages 1–4.

Sommerville, I. (2016). *Software engineering, 10th Edition*. International computer science series. Pearson.

van der Aalst, W. M. P. (2005). Business alignment: using process mining as a tool for delta analysis and conformance testing. *Requirements Engineering*, 10(3):198–211.

van der Aalst, W. M. P. (2015). *Extracting Event Data from Databases to Unleash Process Mining*, pages 105–128. Springer.

van der Aalst, W. M. P. (2016). *Process Mining - Data Science in Action, 2nd Ed.* Springer.

Vavpotic, D., Bala, S., Mendling, J., and Hovelja, T. (2022). Software process evaluation from user perceptions and log data. *J. Softw. Evol. Process.*, 34(4).

Weske, M. (2019). *Business Process Management - Concepts, Languages, Architectures, 3rd Ed.* Springer.

Patterns in Microservices-based Development: A Grey Literature Review

Fabio Gomes Rocha[1], **Michel S. Soares**[1], **Guillermo Rodriguez**[2]

[1]Universidade Federal de Sergipe
Sergipe, Brazil

[2]ISISTAN (UNICEN-CONICET) Research Institute
Tandil, Buenos Aires, Argentina

fabio.gomes@souunit.com.br, michel@dcomp.ufs.br

guillermo.rodriguez@isistan.unicen.edu.ar

Abstract. *Microservices emerged due to the massive adoption of cloud computing and the need to integrate legacy systems. However, there still needs to be a greater understanding of adopting a microservice-based architectural style. Besides, there is a need for guidelines to operationalize those microservices. We conducted a grey literature review to identify commonly used architectural patterns and how they are implemented following design patterns. We present two key contributions. Firstly, we identified four architectural patterns and 23 design patterns. Secondly, we identified a catalog of tools for implementing the main patterns adopted when using the microservices style. The Proxy and the SAGA patterns are the most used in communicating and linking data for services. Additionally, tools such as Kubernetes, Docker, and Amazon WS are the most used for implementing microservices and deploying them into containers.*

1. Introduction

Software Architecture deals with the properties a system has, incorporating the elements and their relationships, design and evolution [ISO 2011]. In this sense, designing the architecture of the software is a complex activity, requiring analysis beyond the modular structure of the software, and it is necessary to consider the required technology and the dependencies between technology and modules [Sievi-Korte et al. 2019]. Thus, to design a high-level system, it is necessary to make decisions related to the various quality requirements. However, without this harming the system as a whole [Yang et al. 2016], [Ribeiro et al. 2018]. In this sense, microservices emerge, a software architecture pattern that emerges from systems based on service-oriented architecture (SOA), with characteristics arising from the adoption of the cloud in a distributed and independent way [Balalaie et al. 2015].

Microservices emerged as a result of the massive adoption of cloud computing and the need to integrate legacy systems [Balalaie et al. 2015]. Thus, the adoption of microservices architecture results in flexibility related to scalability and availability. However, according to Christoforou et al. [Christoforou et al. 2017], such a model brings with it new complexities, requiring analysis for adoption. In this sense, the authors point out the redistribution, as a high operational cost point, in addition to the difficulty of maintaining the various resources and addresses [Balalaie et al. 2015], [Christoforou et al. 2017]. In addition to the problems pointed out, there is a need for new patterns for how these services' communications will be performed and how they will be implemented and operationalized. Thus, this article seeks to characterize the standards adopted by the industry through a systematic review of grey literature. We selected 125 articles between the years 2014 to 2021, divided into six bases. We identified four architectural patterns and 23 design patterns. In addition, we identified ten tools with five or more occurrences. We developed a catalogue of the main patterns adopted when using the microservices style based on the data. The rest of the paper is divided as follows: in section II, we present the background of the research, followed by the related work in section III. Section IV offers the grey literature methodology adopted in the study. Section V presents the results, answering the research questions, discussions about the results in section VI, and finally, the paper's conclusions.

2. Background

Using Microservices [Balalaie et al. 2016] as a solution for distributed software architecture has grown rapidly in the business environment in recent years [Balalaie et al. 2016]. Companies such as Netflix, eBay and Uber have adopted Microservices for the architecture of their systems to replace the monolithic architecture design. However, the lack of consensus in defining what a microservice is and what methodology to adopt when migrating from traditional services to this new paradigm has created several challenges for IT teams. Microservices require differentiated forms of infrastructure, here called agile infrastructure. Agile infrastructure consists of three layers: Technical, Project and Operations. Technical relates to hardware and software used in the environment. Project is about the process that introduces the changes into the environment. Operations is the process of keeping the environment working [Debois 2008]. Within this paradigm arise new technologies such as containerization environments, automation of deliveries, among others.

The microservices architecture paradigm can be considered an approach for developing a single application as a set of small services, each working in an isolated process and communicating through mechanisms [Kitchenham and Charters 2007]. Along this line, microservices have their growth linked to the platform of container [Pahl et al. 2020]. Containerization is a technology for virtualizing applications in a light way that resulted in a significant absorption in the management of cloud applications. How to orchestrate the construction and deployment of containers individually and in clusters has become a central problem [Pahl et al. 2017].

3. Related work

Systematic mapping studies and systematic literature reviews are used to find and assess relevant data for a research issue or topic. However, for this type of secondary research, only academic materials, often known as white literature, are used. We claim that grey literature is crucial for supplying useful insights to researchers from the industrial community. In this Section, we present the grey reviews already conducted on this field.

Based on an online survey (with three questions answered by 25 interviewed practitioners), Ghofrani and Lübke gave a preliminary analysis of state-of-practice on microservices. Ghofrani and Lübke (2018)'s findings provide a high-level summary of industry-oriented microservices' difficulties without going into the specifics of their actual pains and rewards. Instead, the research attempts to provide a more in-depth examination of the technical/operational challenges and benefits of microservices as identified by industrial researchers and practitioners who work with microservices [Ghofrani and Lübke 2018].

Based on interviews with developers who have worked with microservice-based systems, Taibi and Lenarduzzi identified 11 microservice-specific bad practices. Some of the problems that we discover in our study, whose goal is distinct from Taibi and Lenarduzzi, reflect such faulty behaviors. Rather than conducting interviews to uncover problematic practices, the goal is to carefully analyze the grey literature on the topic to elicit microservices' primary technical/operational challenges and gains [Taibi et al. 2018].

The authors of [Taibi et al. 2020] wanted to help practitioners understand the various patterns by classifying them and reporting potential benefits and concerns. They used a multivocal literature review process, sifting through peer-reviewed and grey literature and categorizing patterns (standard solutions to common problems) as well as benefits and drawbacks. They found 32 patterns in 24 works, organizing them as orchestration, aggregation, event management, availability, communication, and authorization.

In [Soldani et al. 2018], the authors chose 51 industrial studies and analyzed them to distill the hardships and rewards of designing, implementing, and managing microservices due to their review. It also revealed that the industry's grasp of the benefits and drawbacks of microservices is reasonably advanced, implying that academia has a lot to learn from the industry on the subject. Valdivia et al. sought to expand knowledge on the design of microservices-based systems by presenting a multivocal systematic literature evaluation for microservices-related patterns, linking them together with quality attributes and metrics identified in academia and industrial research [Valdivia et al. 2020].

In summary, our research differs in that it examines architectural patterns to characterize them in terms of microservices from the perspective of professionals, development businesses, or independent researchers who have worked on the subject in the context of real projects.

4. Methodology

Grey literature refers to informal literature commonly published in blogs and web sites. Normally, grey literature is collected by using regular search engines, such as Google. Moreover, grey literature comprises of unpublished studies or doctoral theses, conference sessions, book chapters, government and agency reports, as well as blog entries, white papers and video presentations [Calderón et al. 2018]. Garousi, Felderer, and Mäntylä [Garousi et al. 2019] emphasize that software development professionals produce relevant and scaled Grey Literature, usually disregarded by academic research and that it is essential to read this literature in order to gather practical knowledge. This section presents how this review was conducted.

4.1. Research Question

The research objective is defined using part of the model GQM (Goal-Question-Metric) [Mashiko and Basili 1997, Van Solingen et al. 2002]: **Analyze** architectural patterns; **with the purpose of** characterising, **with respect** to microservices; **from the point of view** of professionals, development companies or independent researchers who have experience on the subject **in the context of** real projects. For this study, four research questions are established, as depicted in Table 1.

Table 1. Research Questions

Research Question	Description
RQ1	What is the profile of the publications on standards related to Microservices Architecture? This research question intends to find out (i) the number of publications on Microservices Architecture per year, (ii) the distribution by subjects of the papers, and (iii) the distribution of papers on scientific bases.
RQ2	What types of results were obtained, and what types of validation were adopted in the article? The intention is to identify, using Shaw [Shaw 2003] as a basis, and explain the articles' contributions to the knowledge of Software Engineering.
RQ3	What are the software architecture patterns/styles adopted on microservices projects? The intention is to identify which architectural patterns are adopted for the development of microservices.
RQ4	Which methods are adopted and used for operationalizing the architecture of microservices? The aim is to identify the methods and technologies used for the continuous delivery and operation of microservices.

4.2. Search sources

According to Garousi, Felderer, and Mäntylä [Garousi et al. 2019], the search sources of *grey literature* are generally classified into three levels:

- **Level 1**: Self-level of decision control and credibility - books, magazines, reports from government and reputable organisations in the field.
- **Level 2**: Medium level of decision control and credibility - annual reports, new articles, presentations, videos, and *sites* such as *StackOverflow*.
- **Level 3**: Low level of decision control and credibility - *blogs*, *tweets*, pages from social networks.

We formulated the string *"(architecture OR design) AND (microservice OR "micro-service" OR microservices OR "micro-services") AND (pattern OR style)*" to identify and select search sources as listed below, regarding only Level 2 sources:

- Website of Martin Fowler[1] (level 2). Selected by the author's credibility, who was one of the disseminators of the concept of microservices.

[1] https://martinfowler.com/

- DZone[2] website articles (level 2): created in 1997, the site has diverse content in the form of articles to discuss software development, considered one of the largest communities on the subject, and the submission of works performed by professionals and quality reviewed by the DZone team.
- Medium.com[3] Articles (level 2): appeared in 2012, and described as a blogging platform, or as described, a platform of things that matter, maintained by the company Obvious. Medium.com has diverse content, being highly accessed, mainly because it has a recommendation system.
- NewRelic[4] Blog (level 2) created in 2008 brings articles about what is new on software development, usually linked to services offered by the company.
- OpenSource[5] (level 2) is a portal maintained by RedHat created in 2010 with articles on various topics, with more than two million readers in 2020.
- InfoQ[6] (level 2) is a portal that focuses on helping progressive software development teams with diverse materials such as articles, interviews, and books, and content in several languages including English, Japanese, Chinese, Portuguese and French.

4.3. Criteria for Selecting Publications and Stopping the Search

For the selection of items in the search sources, Garousi, Felderer, and Mäntylä [Garousi et al. 2019] suggest that criteria for inclusion and exclusion of these items have to be applied, safeguarding the systematisation of choice. Thus, we defined the criteria presented in Table 2.

Table 2. Selection Criteria

ID	Inclusion Criteria
IC01	The article proposes guidelines or patterns according to developers' general experience
ID	**Exclusion Criteria**
EC01	Duplicated material
EC02	Material presenting only a brief summary
EC03	Material is not written in English
EC04	Material that does not deal with microservices standards

4.4. Process of Work Selection and Data Extraction

The material selection process was systematized in three stages:

1. execution of the search;
2. first filter; and
3. second filter. Then, the search was performed in the sources that were selected.

[2]https://dzone.com
[3]https://medium.com/
[4]https://blog.newrelic.com/
[5]https://opensource.com/
[6]https://www.infoq.com/

In the first filter, the titles and abstracts of the works found were read. For the videos, the title and descriptions were read, and the inclusion and exclusion criteria were applied. In the second filter, the studies were read in total, and the videos included in the first filter were watched in full. Again, the inclusion and exclusion criteria were applied. Thus, the items whose content did not meet the selection criteria were excluded, justifying the decision.

The execution of the search took place in May 2021, and there was no restriction on the time interval of publication. After execution of the search and application of the first filter, 156 items were returned. Next, following the application of the second filter, 125 items were selected, originating from six sources, as described in Table 3. The papers are distributed between years 2014 and 2021, as depicted in Figure 1. Furthermore, the trend of articles is appreciated in Figure 2.

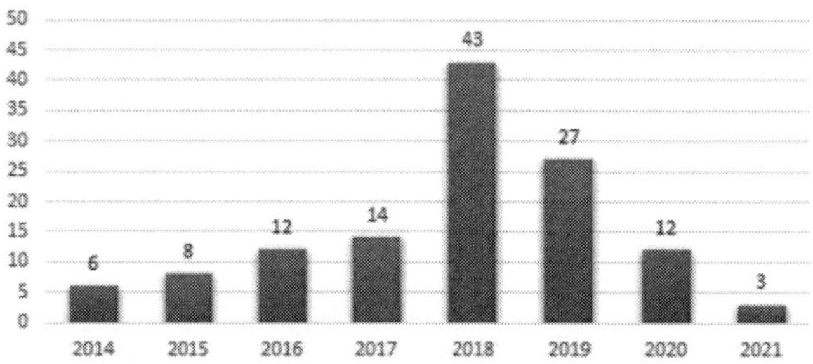

Figure 1. Distribution of works per year

Following the completion of selection of the second filter, the extraction of data was performed. The study was conducted by eight researchers (P1 to P8). The search strategy was developed as follows: Researcher P1 and P2 did a test search, identifying the number of papers and preparing a spreadsheet with the total volume of one hundred and fifty-six papers. Then, it was distributed to researchers P1 to P5 to read and identify the papers that would be part of the study. Then it was rotated; that is, P1 validated the results of P2, P2 of P3 and so on. Finally, P6 made a general validation. For data extraction, the papers were divided among researchers P1 to P5, and the extraction is validated by P6. Finally, researchers P7 and P8 performed the validation together, and all researchers performed the analysis of results.

Table 3. Distribution of works per year

Source	**Total of works**	**Selected**	**Disclosures**
Medium	18	15	3
Martin Fowler	9	9	0
DZone	44	44	0
New Relic	3	1	2
Open Source	32	10	22
InfoQ	50	46	4
Total	156	125	31

Data extraction is one of the main phases of conducting a literature review, including a grey literature review. It is from the data collected that one can answer the research questions. Thus, for this purpose, a detailed reading of each collected item was conducted to identify, categorise and analyze the following items to answer the research questions.

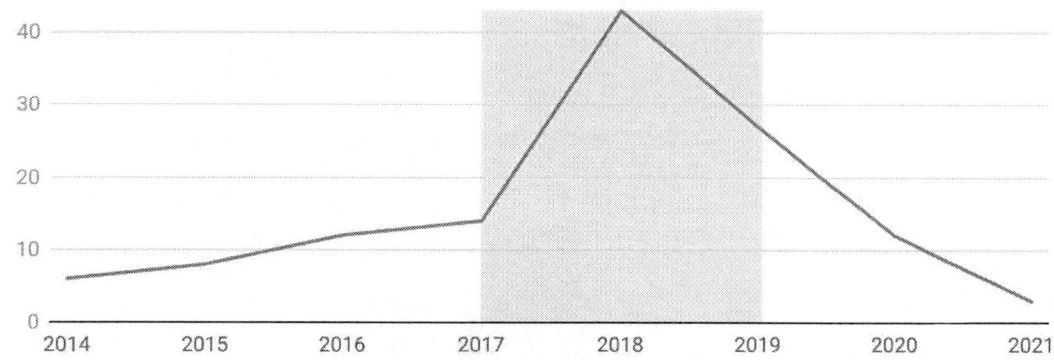

Figure 2. Distribution of works per year

5. Results

In response to **RQ1**, we have a total of 125 selected papers. The year 2018 was the peak of published papers, as depicted in Figure 2. One point to be monitored in the coming years is that in 2020 there was a drop. However, given that it was a year with drastic changes due to the COVID-19 pandemic, it will be necessary to monitor in the coming years if the theme stabilises, if it will still expand or if it is decreasing.

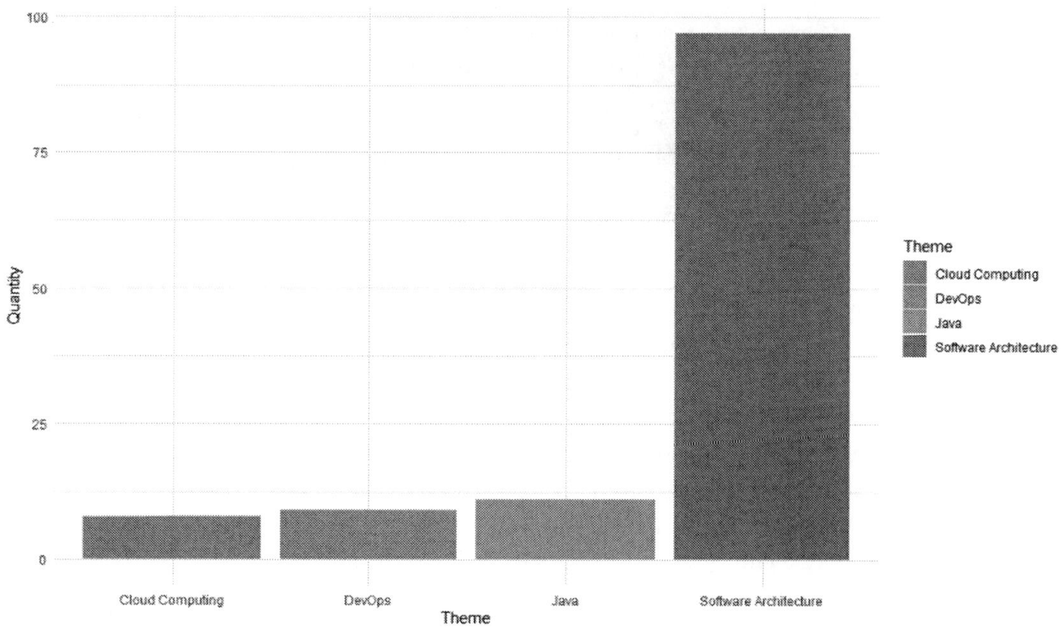

Figure 3. Distribution of works per Theme

Regarding the distribution concerning the work themes, four areas were identified: Architecture, DevOps, Cloud and Java, highlighting the theme of software architecture with 78% of the works, as depicted in Figure 3. About the scientific bases, out of the six bases, all had selected papers, highlighting the bases InfoQ and DZone (Figure 4).

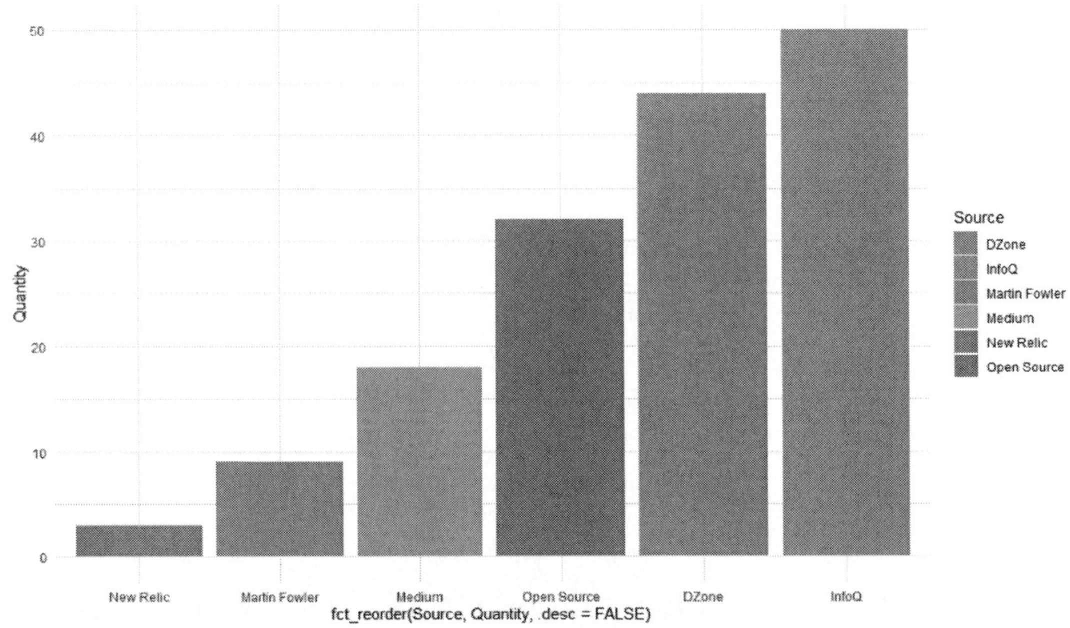

Figure 4. Distribution of works per Source

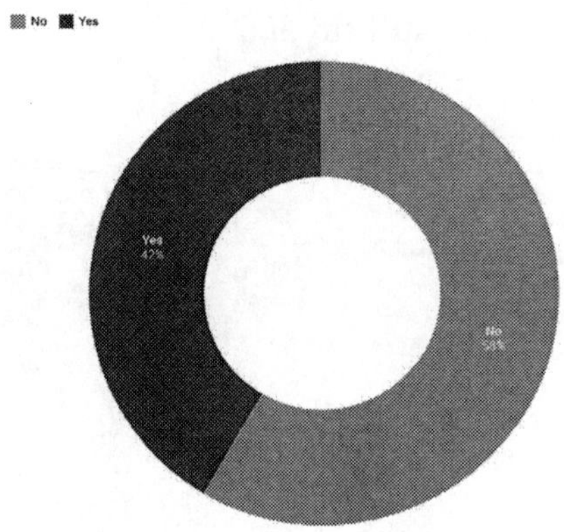

Figure 5. Type of work result

Regarding **RQ2**, first, we sought to understand if the papers published as grey literature had results. At this point, 41.6% had results. That is, they were not only theoretical papers, as depicted in Figure 5. Also, based on [Shaw 2002], of the papers that present any result, the results are validated, being that the same result can be validated in more than one way. The type of validation that stood out the most was the example, followed by statement - Figure 6.

In response to **RQ3**, an article may contain more than one pattern or style of architecture. The highlight is for the Pattern style with 40 works. However, 49 do not

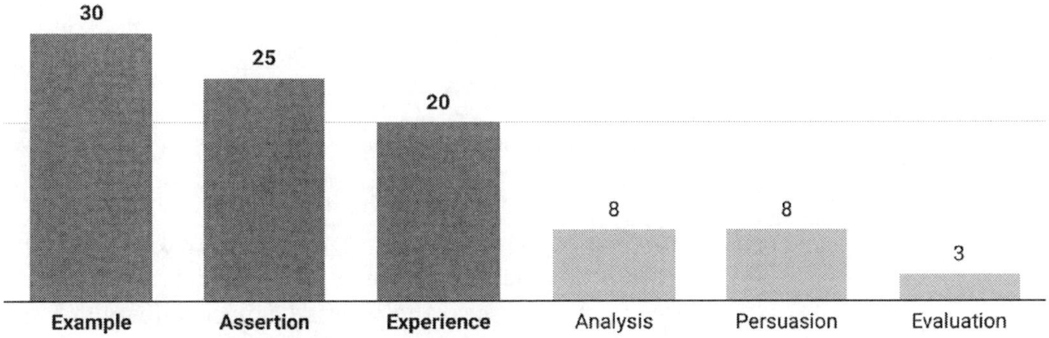

Figure 6. Type of validation

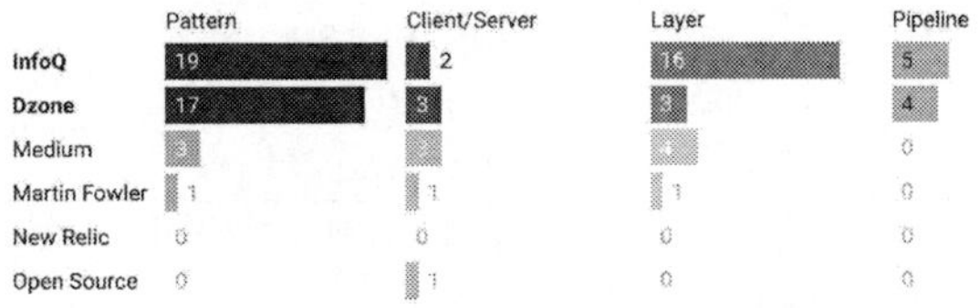

Figure 7. Distribution of Pattern per Source

present styles or patterns of architecture - Figure 7. As for the design patterns employed in microservices works, 23 patterns were identified - Figure 8 - but we can highlight the Proxy pattern with ten works.

InfoQ, Dzone and Medium are the bases that aggregate the most in Design Patterns - Figure 9. As a result, we obtained a set of patterns adopted in microservices architecture and presented them in Table 4 and Table 5.

In response to **RQ4**, of the one hundred and twenty-five papers selected for this article, nine deal with DevOps as a way to operationalize microservices. In addition, another eight deal with this operationalization in the cloud. It was also identified that three methodologies appear only once in the works: BDD, Pragmatic Microservices and Twelve-Factor app. The latter focuses on the delivery of software as services.

To support the operationalization, we identified one hundred and fifty tools. However, we described in Figure 10 those that were mentioned in at least two works. One highlight is Kubernetes with twenty-two occurrences, Docker and AWS with fourteen and Spring with 12. At this point, we can notice that the two items with the most significant highlights are related to the application infrastructure.

6. Discussion

The bibliography that deals with microservices bring some patterns starting in 2014, and since then added new works, highlighting the year 2018 with 48 new works. In total, we obtained 125 works dealing with DevOps, Architecture, Cloud and the Java programming language.

Another critical point is that, despite being grey literature, 42% of the papers presented some results. That is, it was not only an explanation article. In addition, from

Table 4. Patterns Catalogue.

Pattern	Description
Proxy	A proxy is a Structural design pattern intended to provide a substitute or placeholder for another object. Thus, the proxy controls access to the original object, allowing one to execute something before or after the request arrives at the original object. It has been adopted to control access to external microservices in this context.
SAGA	Thus, the proxy controls access to the original object, allowing one to execute something before or after the request arrives at the original object.
Low Coupling	It has been adopted to control access to external microservices in this context.
Strangler	The Strangler pattern focuses on application migration and consists of two types of services, where one implements already existed as monolithic, without new features. Subsequently, a second service implements new resources, thus generating value for the business by adopting the microservice without stopping the existing service.
Bulkhead	The Bulkhead pattern aims at fault tolerance, so the elements must be isolated in containers so that, if one fails, the others keep working.
Sidecar	Sidecar Pattern works together with the main container, with the actual application in a symbiotic way, acting as a single component, used as a reverse proxy, monitoring service, and observability and ambassador.
API Gateway	The API Gateway pattern creates a single entry point for all clients handling the requests.
Aggregator	Microservices should be independent, autonomous, and small. The Aggregator Pattern focuses on receiving customer requests xecutes requests to several microservices and combines the results to answer the initial request.
Gateway Routing	The Routing Gateway acts as a request router, i.e., a single point for clients to make their requests, and this route to the microservices.
Chained Microservice	The Chained Microservice Pattern produces a single, consolidated response to a request, even if it depends on several microservices.

Table 5. Patterns Catalogue (II).

Pattern	Description
Branch	The Branch Pattern is a set of other Aggregator and Chain design patterns that allows the simultaneous processing of several requests and generation of responses from two or more microservices
Client-Side Up Composition	The Client-Side Up Composition allows the independent development of user interface components responsible for a region of the page/screen for a specific service. In this way, it is possible to generate independence in developing screens and working with the composition of user interface components.
Service Discovery	The API Gateway consulted the Service Discovery pattern, which is responsible for discovering the available services. It usually works with the Service Registry pattern, which is responsible for registering the available services.
Circuit Breaker	The Circuit Breaker Pattern avoids cascading catastrophes when a service generates an error. The idea is that the call is packaged with a Circuit Breaker function that monitors failure. Once it reaches a certain threshold, the function stops, and new calls start to return errors without the protected call being performed, thus avoiding a problem.
Blu-Green Deployment	The Blu-Green Deployment pattern is a model for application deployment. The goal is to gradually transfer user traffic from an existing version to a new version; when both are running in the production environment, the old version is blue, while the new one is green. Thus, traffic is transferred from blue to green, and when completed, it can be removed from production or kept for reversion.
High Cohesion	High Cohesion is a Grasp Pattern and is usually linked to low coupling, aiming to keep objects focused, manageable and understandable. The term cohesion is used, in this context, to indicate the degree to which a microservice or class has single and well-focused responsibility.
State	The State is a GOF behavioral pattern that allows an object to change behavior when its internal state changes.
Singleton	Singleton is a creative GoF pattern that aims to ensure that a class has only one instance while providing a global access point.

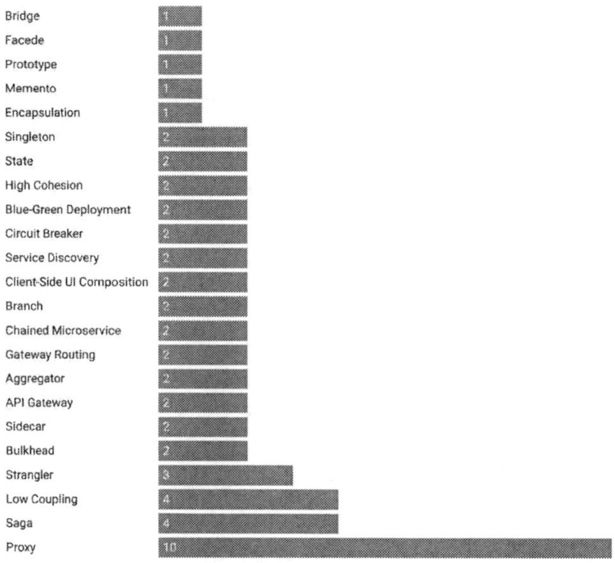

Figure 8. Distribution of Pattern

Figure 9. Distribution of Design Pattern per Source

these articles, we obtained some validations about the result, especially the validation by example, assertion and experience. In terms of patterns or styles of architecture, the highlight is the pattern of layers, and InfoQ and Dzone have more works that present these patterns. When it comes to Design Patterns, we obtained 23 patterns with at least one reference. Based on this, we prepared a table with the patterns refer.

6.1. Threats to Validity

According to Zhou, Xin et al. zhou2016map, we should address several aspects regarding the validity of a systematic review, the main ones being constructed, internal, external and conclusion validity.

6.1.1. Construct Validity

The results may not address the research questions related to the topic. To mitigate this threat, a pilot was conducted to validate the protocol and search chain to minimise this threat. All selection was conducted by one researcher and validated by another researcher, making it as broad as possible. Thus, the researchers searched independently, checking whether the results were related to the research questions and exchanging their results for validation.

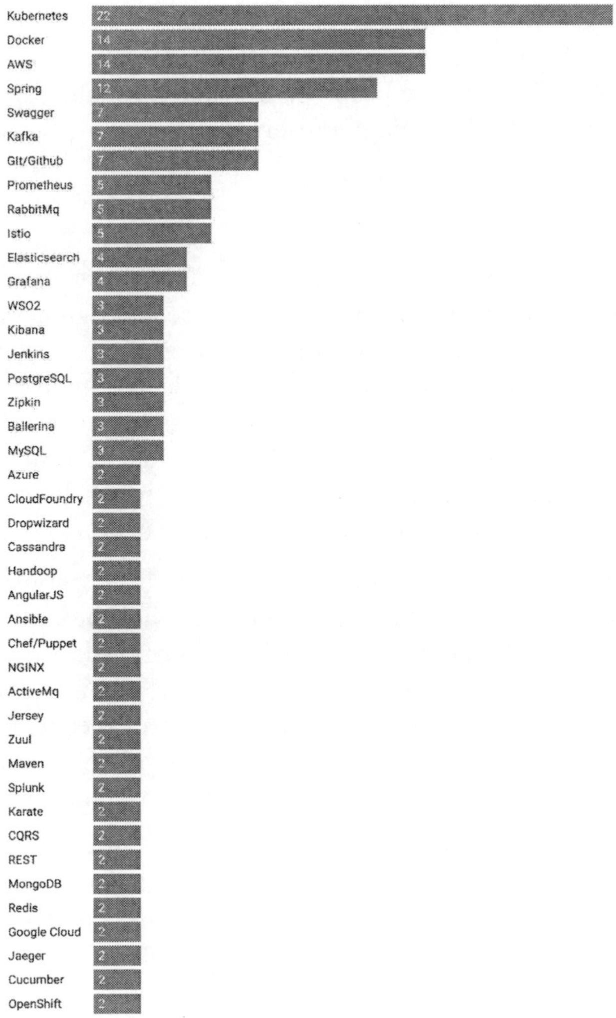

Figure 10. Tools for operationalizing microservices

6.1.2. Internal Validity

Threats to validity include those related to the protocol and the process of selecting papers. Thus, for both tasks, a double validation was performed. After the protocol was defined, a series of searches were tested before the search string was defined. In case of doubts about whether a paper should be selected, all researchers discussed the paper's suitability to the topic. The same occurred with the selection.

6.1.3. External Validity

This information cannot be generalised because no significant number of papers address architecture patterns applied to microservices. Thus, it was possible to identify other papers suitable for the context of patterns and/or microservices, but no references were made to them. The search chain was designed to reach as many documents as possible to mitigate this threat, allowing the work to become a catalogue of patterns. However, it is well known that the software industry uses microservices in essential projects and that all this knowledge may not be published as papers. Therefore, although the grey literature brings a vast body of knowledge about microservices, many practices are not published.

7. Conclusions

It is noted that, beyond the academy, microservices have been receiving attention from professionals, with the main focus being: independence and lightness. This study sought to understand how the gaps left by the academy have been treated, in terms of standards for microservices, by the industry. We observed that the selected studies started publishing in 2014, with an apse in 2018 and a considerable reduction of works on the subject between 2020 and 2021. This can be attributed to the problems arising from COVID19; however, we would need more data and time for such a statement. It is, at this point, only an empirical finding, requiring a follow-up in the coming years on the subject.

Several mappings and systematic reviews have been published in this field, as presented in the related papers; however, unlike the studies presented, this paper sought to characterize architectural patterns and relationships of results and methods, but from an industry perspective, through grey literature. Thus, for this study, we followed a systematic and rigorous protocol, based on Garousi [Garousi et al. 2019], obtaining 125 studies and sought, based on these, to produce a view of the state of the practice on patterns/architecture styles adopted in practice with microservices.

As a result, it was possible to present a catalog of patterns currently adopted by professionals who develop using microservices architecture, highlighting the Proxy pattern, part of GOF, and the SAGA pattern used in the communication and linking of data for services. Consequently, we identified the main tools that allow the operationalization of microservices, highlighting Kubernetes, followed by Docker and AWS, demonstrating that the operationalization in containers with cloud load distribution has focused on the works presented.

In future work, we plan to extend our work as a multivocal literature review, considering formal literature. Furthermore, as part of our ongoing research, we want to apply a survey to gather data on the technologies used by practitioners to develop microservices from scratch or by migrating a legacy system. We want to learn more about the most popular tools, how people use them, and how they are integrated. With this knowledge, we may describe an implementation technique that supports academic or professional projects that call for a quick, secure, and dependable agile infrastructure.

References

Balalaie, A., Heydarnoori, A., and Jamshidi, P. (2015). Migrating to cloud-native architectures using microservices: an experience report. In *European Conference on Service-Oriented and Cloud Computing*, pages 201–215. Springer.

Balalaie, A., Heydarnoori, A., and Jamshidi, P. (2016). Migrating to Cloud-Native Architectures Using Microservices: An Experience Report. In *Communications in Computer and Information Science*, pages 201–215. Springer International Publishing.

Calderón, A., Ruiz, M., and O'Connor, R. V. (2018). A multivocal literature review on serious games for software process standards education. *Computer Standards & Interfaces*, 57:36–48.

Christoforou, A., Garriga, M., Andreou, A. S., and Baresi, L. (2017). Supporting the Decision of Migrating to Microservices Through Multi-Layer Fuzzy Cognitive Maps. In *Service-Oriented Computing*, pages 471–480. Springer International Publishing.

Debois, P. (2008). Agile infrastructure and operations: how infra-gile are you? In *Agile 2008 Conference*, pages 202–207. IEEE.

Garousi, V., Felderer, M., and Mäntylä, M. V. (2019). Guidelines for including grey literature and conducting multivocal literature reviews in software engineering. *Information and Software Technology*, 106:101–121.

Ghofrani, J. and Lübke, D. (2018). Challenges of microservices architecture: A survey on the state of the practice. *ZEUS*, 2018:1–8.

ISO (2011). ISO/IEC/IEEE 42010:2011 Systems and Software Engineering — Architecture Description.

Kitchenham, B. and Charters, S. (2007). Guidelines for performing systematic literature reviews in software engineering.

Mashiko, Y. and Basili, V. R. (1997). Using the gqm paradigm to investigate influential factors for software process improvement. *Journal of Systems and Software*, 36(1):17–32.

Pahl, C., Brogi, A., Soldani, J., and Jamshidi, P. (2017). Cloud container technologies: a state-of-the-art review. *IEEE Transactions on Cloud Computing*, 7(3):677–692.

Pahl, C., Jamshidi, P., and Zimmermann, O. (2020). Microservices and containers. *Software Engineering 2020.*

Ribeiro, F. G. C., Rettberg, A., Pereira, C. E., Steinmetz, C., and Soares, M. S. (2018). An Approach to Formalization of Architectural Viewpoints Design in Real-Time and Embedded Domain. In *21st IEEE International Symposium on Real-Time Distributed Computing, ISORC 2018, Singapore, Singapore, May 29-31, 2018*, pages 59–66. IEEE Computer Society.

Shaw, M. (2002). What makes good research in software engineering? *International Journal on Software Tools for Technology Transfer*, 4(1):1–7.

Shaw, M. (2003). Writing good software engineering research papers. In *25th International Conference on Software Engineering, 2003. Proceedings.*, pages 726–736. IEEE.

Sievi-Korte, O., Richardson, I., and Beecham, S. (2019). Software Architecture Design in Global Software Development: An Empirical Study. *Journal of Systems and Software*, 158:110400.

Soldani, J., Tamburri, D. A., and Van Den Heuvel, W.-J. (2018). The pains and gains of microservices: A systematic grey literature review. *Journal of Systems and Software*, 146:215–232.

Taibi, D., El Ioini, N., Pahl, C., and Niederkofler, J. R. S. (2020). Patterns for serverless functions (function-as-a-service): A multivocal literature review.

Taibi, D., Lenarduzzi, V., and Pahl, C. (2018). Architectural patterns for microservices: A systematic mapping study. In *CLOSER*, pages 221–232.

Valdivia, J. A., Lora-González, A., Limón, X., Cortes-Verdin, K., and Ocharán-Hernández, J. O. (2020). Patterns related to microservice architecture: a multivocal literature review. *Programming and Computer Software*, 46(8):594–608.

Van Solingen, R., Basili, V., Caldiera, G., and Rombach, H. D. (2002). Goal question metric (gqm) approach. *Encyclopedia of software engineering*.

Yang, C., Liang, P., and Avgeriou, P. (2016). A Systematic Mapping Study on the Combination of Software Architecture and Agile Development. *Journal of Systems and Software*, 111:157–184.

Can Multi-Agent Consensus Improve Quality Tradeoffs in Software Architecture Optimization?

J. Andres Diaz-Pace[1], **Santiago A. Vidal**[1], **Antonela Tommasel**[1], **Sebastian Frank**[2], **Andre van Hoorn**[2]

[1]ISISTAN Research Institute – UNCPBA University & CONICET
Tandil – Buenos Aires – Argentina

[2]University of Hamburg – Hamburg – Germany

{andres.diazpace, santiago.vidal, antonela.tommasel}@isistan.unicen.edu.ar
{sebastian.frank, andre.van.hoorn}@uni-hamburg.de

Abstract. *When designing a software architecture to fulfill quality-attribute requirements, architects normally explore and assess alternative solutions leading to different quality-attribute tradeoffs. In this context, we developed the* `SQuAT` *framework to support automated multi-objective optimization in large design spaces.* `SQuAT` *provides a modular, multi-agent architecture in which each agent represents and optimizes a particular quality attribute. However, this search strategy has problems identifying tradeoffs that satisfy all the parties (or architects' concerns), particularly when searching for many candidate solutions and evaluating them becomes computationally costly. This is actually a general challenge for architecture optimization tools. To deal with it,* `SQuAT` *features an agent negotiation protocol that seeks consensus based on the utility of solutions as judged by each agent. In this paper, we present a parameterized heuristic that enhances the integration between search and negotiation in* `SQuAT`*, and also report on an empirical evaluation with two case studies. The results show initial evidence that using negotiation is more effective than doing a pure search to identify solutions having a balanced utility across agents, and thus, offer alternative quality-attribute tradeoffs to the architect.*

1. Introduction

The software architecture of a system is a blueprint that captures the main design decisions for satisfying the functional requirements and quality attributes (e.g., performance, modifiability, reliability, among others) posed by the system stakeholders [Bass et al. 2021]. Designing a software architecture in such a way it meets its quality-attribute requirements can be a complex process, as architects often need to consider alternative solutions satisfying the same requirements, and furthermore, these solutions lead to tradeoffs. A tradeoff means that a given architecture (or any of its design decisions) has a positive impact on a given quality attribute at the cost of negatively affecting another one — e.g., separating functions into modules favors modifiability but might have a performance impact.

Given an initial architecture, the number of possible solutions for improving it (with respect to predefined quality-attribute requirements) can be too big to be assessed by a human, even for medium-sized problems. For this reason, automated optimization approaches for the architecture domain have been developed [Aleti et al. 2013]. The optimization process is normally cast to a heuristic search driven by multiple objectives and constraints, in which an initial architecture undergoes different transformations (or refactorings). As output, this search is expected to produce a number of architecture candidates with different tradeoffs, according to the architect's criteria as the decision maker. An instance of such optimization approaches is the `SQuAT` framework [Rago et al. 2017], which relies on a multi-agent architecture organized into separate modules (agents) called *dbots*. `SQuAT` takes a *model-based approach* and uses the Palladio Component Model (PCM) [Becker et al. 2009] for representing software architectures. Departing from an initial PCM architecture, each *dbot* performs a local search, evaluating and optimizing candidates with respect to a single quality attribute. Afterward, the *dbots* rely on a negotiation protocol to identify candidates that globally satisfy all the qualities. To do so, the *dbots* try to reach "agreements" (or consensus) [Rekha and Muccini 2018] based on the utility of the solutions explored by each agent.

The `SQuAT` framework has evolved over the years, and encouraging experiments with case studies involving modifiability and performance have been reported. However, applying the approach in larger, more real architectural settings brings several challenges. A first problem refers to the *computational cost* of the optimization. For example, analyzing a PCM architecture with a performance analytical solver [Koziolek and Reussner 2008] to determine whether an objective is met can take a considerable amount of time (from seconds to minutes), and this effort increases as more objectives and architectural candidates are evaluated during the search. This is the case when multiple architectural transformations are explored, increasing the depth of the search. Therefore, pruning must be considered to avoid a combinatorial explosion of candidates while still being able to return a set of "interesting" solutions to the architect. A second problem is about the utility of solutions regarding their quality-attribute tradeoffs. In practice, architects might not be interested in optimal solutions (in the sense of maximizing or minimizing objectives or reaching the Pareto front) but in *satisfying solutions*, i.e., solutions being good enough for the objectives (or other architects' preferences) tackled by the *dbots*. Within `SQuAT`, this means searching for candidates having *balanced* tradeoffs, that is, architectures providing more or less the same utility to all the agents. We should note that these challenges are not unique to `SQuAT` and apply to any architecture optimization tool [Di Pompeo and Tucci 2023].

A (pure) search strategy cannot always produce balanced solutions unless a significant portion of the design space is explored. However, as mentioned above, increasing the computational resources (for the search) is not always feasible. This is where the negotiation strategy comes into play. We argue that a judicious combination of search and negotiation can help steer the search toward solutions with balanced tradeoffs without a large exploration of the design space. This idea was proposed in previous work [Monteserin et al. 2017], but the combined strategy has neither been fully developed nor empirically evaluated yet. Here, we formalize and enhance the strategy as a heuristic that depends on several parameters. We also analyze its behavior by simulating search traces in two PCM design spaces: *ST+* and *CoCoME*. Although preliminary, the results show that the *dbots* using negotiation are able to find many solutions with balanced tradeoffs while keeping the number of examined solutions bounded, which is an advantage over pure search. An adequate strategy parameterization and the complexity of the optimization space are also drivers to consider. Beyond SQuAT, we believe that the techniques and insights from this work contribute to improving the usage and adaptation of optimization techniques in the software architecture domain.

The rest of the paper is organized as follows. Section 2 provides the basic concepts of architecture optimization using *ST+* as a motivating example and briefly introduces SQuAT. It also covers related work. Section 3 presents the search heuristic integrated with negotiation and its main parameters, which is the central part of this work. Section 4 reports on the evaluation of the combined strategy for the *ST+* and *CoCoME* case studies. Finally, Section 5 gives the conclusions and outlines future work.

2. Background

To contextualize the SQuAT concepts, we describe a quality-driven optimization problem for software architectures and how it can be tackled using search techniques and architectural transformations. We also introduce a simplified version of the *ST+* system [Koziolek 2013, Rago et al. 2017] to illustrate the concepts.

2.1. Motivating Example

Extended Simple Tactics (*ST+*) [Rago et al. 2017] is a trip management system, adapted from [Koziolek 2013], in which users can search and book trips with different payment options and request reimbursements for cancellations. The system architecture is specified in PCM, as shown in Figure 1. In PCM, the architecture consists of several models, each representing an architectural view: *i)* the component types and interfaces (repository), *ii)* the system assembly, and *iii)* the deployment of this assembly to the infrastructure (e.g., servers interconnected via network links). *ST+* also includes a behavioral specification for the component implementations in the repository and a usage model with an open workload for the system-provided services. For brevity, these two models are not shown.

In the repository (top level), ST+ has several components and interfaces available. BUSINESSTRIPMGMT is the system entry point for the users. BOOKINGSYSTEM is invoked for handling a booking. PAYMENTSYSTEM is called to process payments or reimbursements. QUICKBOOKING is an alternative to BOOKINGSYSTEM. ST+ saves trip (and reimbursement) information to TRIPDB, which can be replaced by the alternative components FASTREADTRIPDB or FASTWRITETRIPDB, for instance, based on performance considerations. The database can export information about trips and payments as a PDF file using EXPORTER. In addition, since logos must be added to a PDF file, ALTERNATIVEEXPORTER stores them in a compressed version. For the initial architecture (middle level), a subset of the above components is instantiated and assembled: BUSINESSTRIPMGMT, BOOKINGSYSTEM, PAYMENT SYSTEM, EXPORTER, and TRIPDB. The deployment infrastructure (bottom level) comprises three servers (SERVER1, SERVER2, and SERVER3) and a DB CLUSTER with two nodes connected via a LAN. The allocation of components to servers is depicted with black arrows.

In the example, we assume that *ST+* must fulfill stakeholders' performance and modifiability requirements. These requirements are captured by *scenarios* [Bass et al. 2021], which specify objectives in quantitative measures (e.g., change effort for modifiability or response time for performance) that architectures must meet. Let us consider two scenarios (i.e., optimization objectives) for *ST+* as follows:

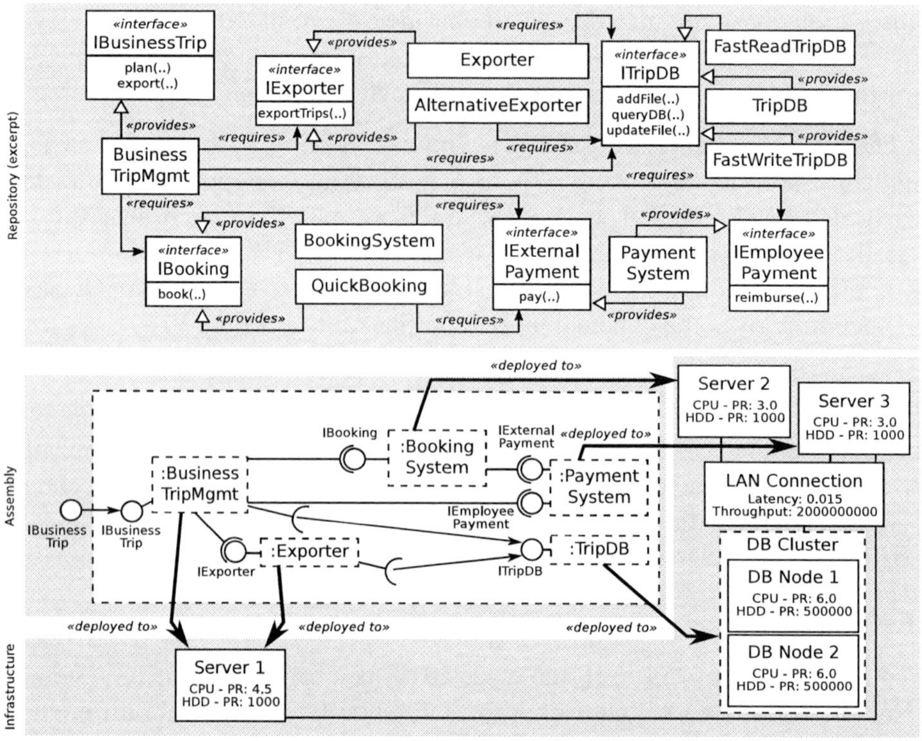

Figure 1. PCM models for the *ST+* system (initial architecture) [Rago et al. 2017].

• **M1** (modifiability) refers to adding a new payment option and specifies that the number of affected components should be less than 5, with a total complexity of 120.

• **P1** (performance) is about the system workload and requires the response time to stay below 30 ms.

In the scenarios, their quality-attribute measures are treated as satisfaction thresholds; that is, any architecture whose performance and modifiability scores are below 120 and 30, respectively, are considered *satisfying* solutions for the problem. We refer to the space of quality-attribute measures as the *quality-attribute space*. To determine the quality-attribute scores of PCM architectures, we rely on existing analysis models, such as (layered) queueing networks for performance [Koziolek and Reussner 2008] and change impact analysis for modifiability [Stammel and Reussner 2009]. In this way, we can assess how far the *ST+* initial architecture (A_0) is from satisfying the thresholds in the quality space. Let us assume that quantitative analyses are run on A_0, and it turns out that A_0 satisfies $M1$ but does not satisfy $P1$, as shown in Figure 3. Thus, the architect would like to explore candidate solutions for improving both scenarios, as denoted by the blue area in the figure, which we refer to as the *satisfaction area*.

2.2. Architectural Transformations and Search Tree

One way of generating candidate architectures is through design transformations, also known as *tactics* [Bass et al. 2021]. In this paper, we are interested in transformations targeting modifiability and performance objectives. To improve modifiability, architects have several options at their disposal. For instance, the transformations can: i) divide a component dealing with multiple responsibilities into two or more sub-components, ii) reduce the coupling between two components by placing an intermediary or wrapper

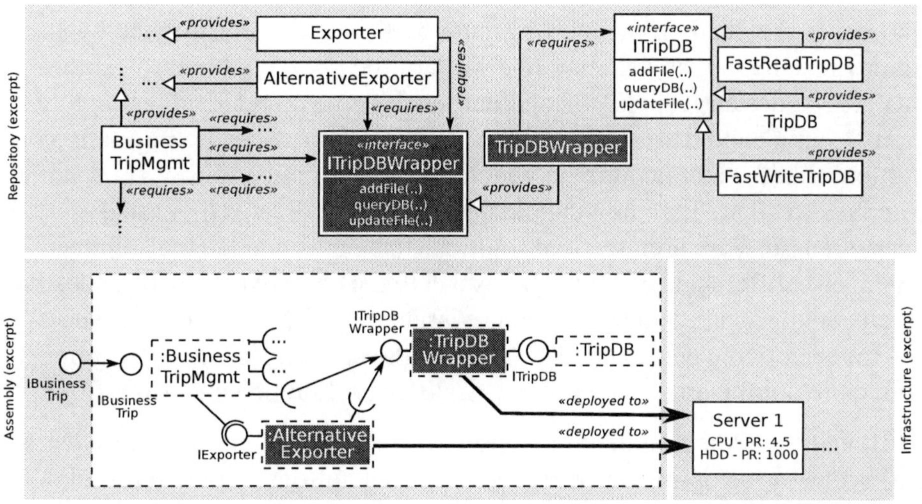

Figure 2. Modifiability and performance tactics applied to *ST+* [Rago et al. 2017].

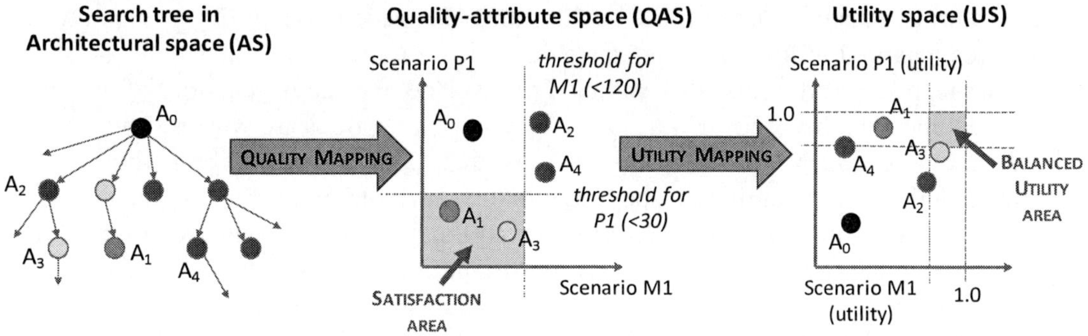

Figure 3. Relation between search tree (left-side), quality-attribute space (center) and the utility space (right side). The green circles refer to architectures that satisfy all the quality-attribute scenarios, while the red circles correspond to architectures that do not satisfy any of the scenarios. The yellow circles indicate that the architectures satisfy some of the scenarios.

component, or iii) remove responsibilities from non-cohesive components, among other tactics. An example of the wrapper tactic applied on *ST+* is shown in Figure 2 (top). A wrapper component and an interface (ITRIPDBWRAPPER and TRIPDBWRAPPER) are created to avoid rippling effects after changing ITRIPDB operations. This tactic might cause a performance drop since another component is deployed to the servers, and the component communications with the DB are indirect through the wrapper. The candidate architecture resulting from the wrapper tactic is denoted as A_1 in Figure 3.

From a performance perspective, possible tactics for the architect are: i) select a particular component alternative, ii) allocate components to different servers, or iii) introduce performance-specific components such as a cache or a load balancer, among other transformations. Figure 2 (bottom) shows the replacement of the EXPORTER component by the more efficient ALTERNATIVEEXPORTER component, which ensures that the additional load (as required by *P1*) can be handled. Applying this performance tactic impacts modifiability, e.g., due to additional maintenance efforts. The candidate architecture resulting from the replacement tactic is denoted by A_2 in Figure 3.

The successive application of tactics (from the initial architecture) gives place to a search tree, as sketched on the left of Figure 3. This tree is constructed by an optimization engine (actually, by the collaborative work of the *dbots*) in order to explore candidate solutions. The nodes correspond to candidates, while the directed edges capture the transformations from a candidate to its children in the search. A tactic normally comes with preconditions that the architecture on which it is applied must fulfill. Thus, not all tactics can be applied to all architectural candidates. Those candidates that satisfy any or all the objectives (scenarios) are architectural solutions to be presented to the architect. These solutions will have different tradeoffs with respect to the objectives. In principle, the tree can grow in breadth or depth, and become quite large, even for small design spaces. Controlling how the search tree gets expanded is one of the challenges when designing heuristics for architecture optimization [Quesada et al. 2018, Di Pompeo and Tucci 2023].

Although getting candidate solutions that fall in the satisfaction area (center of Figure 3) is one of the optimization drivers, not all solutions might be useful to the architect. To this end, we introduce the notion of *utility* to capture architects' preferences and also avoid situations of "over-optimization", given the computational costs of the search. Thus, a utility function converts the quality-attribute space into a *utility space*, in which 1 indicates maximal utility and 0 indicates no utility. Figure 3 illustrates how A_0, A_1, and A_2 get mapped to different utility values. For instance, we can have a utility function (for both $M1$ and $P1$) that tends to 1 as the quality-attribute values are within a short distance of the scenario thresholds and decreases towards 0 otherwise. Along this line, the candidate solutions are quantified in both the quality-attribute and utility spaces. Assuming that all scenarios must be (mostly) satisfied, an ideal solution should get a utility in the right-upper quadrant of the utility space. Furthermore, such a solution should have a *balanced* utility across all scenarios, meaning that it is useful to all parties. This utility space region is regarded as the *balanced utility area*, as marked in Figure 3. Because of the discrete nature of the (feasible) architectural transformations, finding these candidates is not straightforward. Not all satisfying candidates will necessarily have a balanced utility. In practice, the search process might eventually find candidates with a balanced utility, but a challenge is how to increase the chances of finding them.

2.3. Quality-driven Architecture Optimization

We consider a multi-objective architecture optimization along the lines of the PAD (Predictable Architecture Design) model [Bachmann et al. 2005, Pace and Campo 2008]. We assume an *architectural space* for a family of systems that encompasses all possible solutions in terms of a (finite) set of *design decisions*. More formally, let $AS = \{A_0, A_1, A_2, ..., A_n\}$ be a space in which each A_i corresponds to a (valid) architecture resulting from predefined design decisions $A_i = \{d_{1i}, d_{2i}, ..., d_{mi}\}$. In this work, we restrict the possible decisions to *architectural tactics* [Bass et al. 2021]. A tactic is a transformation that affects parts of an architectural structure (e.g., PCM components and interfaces) to improve a particular quality attribute. Thus, the architectures in AS are linked to one another through the application of tactics. AS can be visualized as a directed graph in which each node represents an architecture, while an edge between two nodes A_i and A_j captures a tactic from the former to the latter. A tactic T_ij changes the architectural structure of A_i to become that of the target A_j.

An architecture A_i can be assessed with respect to multiple quality attributes (objectives) through quantitative measures (or scores). Let $QAS =< O_1, O_2, ..., O_m >$ be a *quality-attribute space* in which each objective O_k represents a quality-attribute metric (e.g., response time, change complexity, etc.) associated with some candidate in AS. Hence, the evaluation function $f : AS \rightarrow QAS$ maps architectures to multi-valued vectors in $\Re^m$. Furthermore, let $IS =< I_1, I_2, ..., I_p >$ be a *utility space* in which I_k represents a utility metric in the range $[0..1]$ for some multi-valued vector in QAS. Consequently, we have a utility function $u : QAS \rightarrow IS$ that maps quality-attribute values to utilities. Note that $u = f(AS)$. In Figure 3, the quality-attribute values and utilities for the architecture examples are 2-dimensional vectors in QAS and IS, respectively. In the general case, all these spaces can be n-dimensional.

2.4. Related Work

Two approaches related to our work are *EASIER* [Arcelli et al. 2018] and *GATSE* [Procter and Wrage 2019], which implement a multi-objective search strategy using evolutionary algorithms. The rationale of this technique differs from that of the *dbots*, in the sense that a collection of multiple candidates (population) is evolved through several iterations (generations). Furthermore, the architecture solutions are encoded as chromosomes and transformed by means of genetic operators. On the one hand, *EASIER* relies on architectural specifications written in *AEmilia*, which enables performance and reliability analyses. They also consider the number of architectural changes from one candidate to another as an additional objective to be minimized. On the other hand, *GATSE* provides a visual explorer for *AADL* (Architecture Analysis and Design Language) specifications that displays quality-attribute analyses of selected architectural configurations, enabling the architect to focus on regions of the quality space and progressively narrow down the search, also referred to as "design by shopping". Like in PCM, the usage of model-based analysis techniques for quality attributes is a shared characteristic of the specifications used by *GATSE* and *EASIER*, respectively.

Unlike the previous approaches, our work focuses on quality-attribute tradeoffs and tries to manage them (in the sense of reaching a consensus among parties), instead of seeing tradeoffs from the traditional view of a Pareto frontier. The usage of negotiation is a novel aspect, which has the potential of exploring different tradeoffs than an evolutionary search. Furthermore, the improvements for `SQuAT` discussed in this paper can reduce the computational costs of the optimization of architectural models, which is currently a challenge for *GATSE* and *EASIER*, among other optimization approaches.

3. Integrating Search and Negotiation

In general, an automated heuristic is needed to drive the exploration of the design space and generate alternative solutions according to the architecture optimization formulation. `SQuAT` provides a multi-agent modeling approach and a modular architecture for PAD, which supports various search strategies. The main aspects of the framework for achieving this goal are explained next — the reader is referred to our previous work [Rago et al. 2017] for more details. This work focuses on mechanisms to address the two challenges discussed in previous sections. Specifically, we expect to obtain architecture candidates at the intersection between the satisfying and balanced utility areas while reducing the computational overhead of the (pure) search.

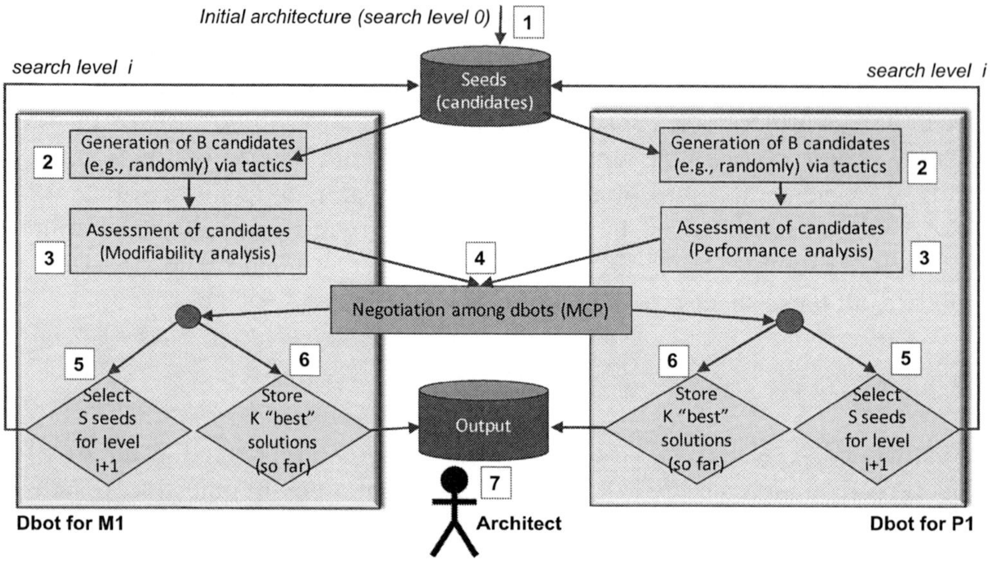

Figure 4. Distributed search process (individual *dbots*) and negotiation phase.

3.1. *SQuAT* Overview

The `SQuAT`[1] framework is structured around the notion of *dbots*—agents encapsulating the required knowledge to analyze and improve a particular quality attribute [Rago et al. 2017]. This knowledge involves: *i)* an automated analyzer (or solver) that takes an architectural description (e.g., PCM) and computes a quality metric, and *ii)* a set of tactics implemented as architectural transformations. Unlike other architecture optimization tools, the rationale behind SQuAT is that each *dbot* performs a single-objective optimization with little knowledge about the objectives being pursued by other *dbots*. From a modeling perspective, a *dbot* is intended to capture the interests of a particular stakeholder regarding the architecture. These interests are expressed by means of quality-attribute scenarios [Bass et al. 2021] and utility functions.

The search strategy followed by the *dbots* is summarized in Figure 4. For simplicity, we assume two agents optimizing scenarios $M1$ and $P2$, respectively, although it can be generalized to n agents. Each agent accesses a storage, called `Seeds`, with the candidates to be explored and potentially improved in its next round of search (or tree level). There is another storage, called `Output`, in which all agents persist their best candidates so far. These are the candidates presented to the architect once the process ends. A round of search consists of seven steps, namely:

[1] An initial architecture specified in PCM (and provided by the architect) is configured as the first seed (candidate) to trigger the *dbots* activity. In intermediate rounds of search, the *Seeds* storage is updated with candidates from the *dbots*, as denoted by the feedback loops in the figure.

[2] Each *dbot* takes the first architecture from the *Seeds* storage (using some priority criterion) and generates several children candidates by applying predefined tactics to different parts of the architecture. The *dbot* $M1$ will only use modifiability tactics, while the *dbot* $P1$ will only use performance ones. Within a *dbot*, this step entails a local, single-objective search. The *dbots* also check that the resulting configuration of the candidates is valid; otherwise, the child is discarded.

[1] *SQuAT* is an acronym for *S*earch Techniques for Managing *Qu*ality-*A*ttribute *T*radeoffs in Software Design Optimizations. It started in 2016 as part of an international collaboration project.

3 The *dbot* runs a quality-attribute analyzer to get quantitative values for both the seed architecture and its children. Analogously to the previous step, the *dbot* $M1$ will rely on a modifiability analyzer (e.g., [Stammel and Reussner 2009]) and the *dbot* $P1$ will rely on a performance analyzer (e.g., [Koziolek and Reussner 2008]). Executing these analyzers usually involves a computational overhead. After the analysis, each *dbot* ranks its candidates according to quality-attribute (or utility) criteria.

4 The *dbots* engage in a negotiation protocol based on the available candidates, their scenario thresholds, and utility function. This step simulates a human negotiation about (the utility of) the candidates, in which some agents might be willing to accept inferior candidates (in their rankings) to reach an agreement with the other agents.

5 Each *dbot* gets a new ranking for its candidates, which might include candidates agreed during the negotiation. At this point, a set of candidates must be selected as seeds for the next round of search. These candidates are chosen using the same criteria from step 3. The process is repeated from step 2.

6 In parallel, each *dbot* gets a new ranking for its candidates. At this point, a set of "interesting" candidates must be sent to the `Output` storage as intermediate solutions of the current round. These candidates are expected to have quality-attribute tradeoffs and (ideally) balanced utility.

7 Once the maximum number of tree levels is reached, the process is finished, and all the stored solutions are presented to the architect.

3.2. The Negotiation Protocol

In step 4, the *dbots* use the Monotonic Concession Protocol (MCP) for negotiation [Endriss 2006]. We give here an intuition of how MCP works since full coverage is out of scope — the MCP instantiation for `SQuAT` can be found at [Monteserin et al. 2017]. Essentially, MCP supports agent coordination allowing the *dbots* to exchange and retain candidates (either as seeds or outputs) that could be otherwise disregarded. The goal is to keep solutions with better (or more useful) tradeoffs than those obtained through the agents' local search.

In MCP, the *dbots* are assumed to be cooperative and abide by rules about: *i)* the agreement criterion; *ii)* if no agreement is achieved, which *dbot* makes the next concession; and *iii)* how much a *dbot* should concede. Initially, each *dbot* makes an initial proposal with its first (best) candidate for the current search level. All proposals are interchanged to check if an agreement on any of them can be reached. The agreement is defined in terms of the proposal utility for the *dbots*. As mentioned previously, a utility function $u_i(A_j)$ that assigns non-negative values to the proposals is assumed. There is an agreement if one *dbot* proposes a candidate A_x that is at least as good (regarding utility) for any other *dbot* as their own current proposals [Endriss 2006]. If so, A_x is chosen, and the negotiation ends successfully. If not, a conflict exists, and some *dbot* should make a concession. A concession means that a *dbot* seeks an alternative proposal in its list of candidates. If no *dbot* can concede, the process finishes with conflict, which means that nothing is obtained from the negotiation. The selection of the *dbot* that must concede is determined by the Zeuthen rule [Endriss 2006], which evaluates each dbot's willingness to risk conflict and prefers a conflict-free proposal being close to Nash equilibrium. As for the concession itself, a *dbot* makes a new proposal that is worse for itself (usually, the next candidate in its ranking).

For example, coming back to Figure 3, let us assume that in level 2 the *dbots* $M1$ and $P1$ enter a negotiation with A_1 and A_3 as proposals from $M1$ and A_4 from $P1$. A_1 seems like a good candidate in terms of quality, but let us suppose that its utility is not good for $P1$, and the *dbot* proposes A_4 instead. Although this proposal is closer to the quality thresholds, let us suppose it conflicts with the expected utility by $M1$. At this point, $M1$ makes a concession and picks A_3

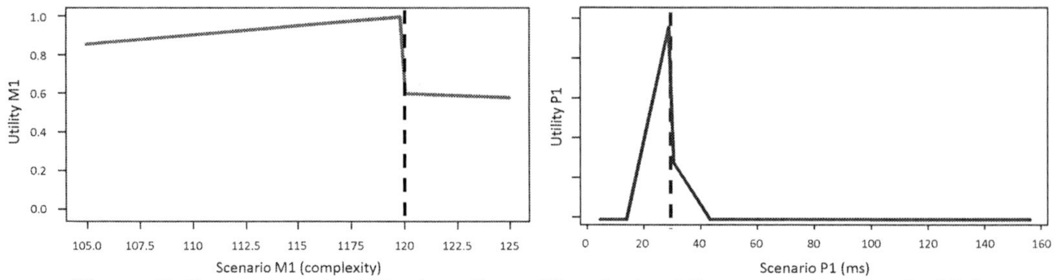

Figure 5. Examples of utility functions (the dashed lines are the thresholds).

from its ranking. Upon this candidate, which has a higher complexity but a slightly lower utility for $M1$, $P1$ and $M1$ reach a utility consensus, and the negotiation succeeds.

For the negotiation strategy to work, utility functions need to be configured in the *dbots*. We defined a utility function (for all *dbots*) that takes into account the desired scenario threshold and the actual scenario value for the candidate under analysis. This is a variant of the Boulware function [Fatima et al. 2004], which gives the maximum value to candidates whose quality value is equal to the threshold, as exemplified in Figure 5, and penalizes values otherwise (with different slopes). Other parameterizations of the function or alternative utility functions are possible.

3.3. Proposed Strategy

To deal with projects of different complexity, we designed the search process of Figure 4 as a parameterized heuristic. The parameters can be seen as knobs to control the expansion of the search tree, the tactics being considered at each level, and the criteria to rank certain candidates while discarding others. The heuristic is shown by Algorithm 1 and the parameters are below.

- *Branching factor (`B`):* It gives the maximum number of children a *dbot* is allowed to create for a given seed, with a predetermined set of available tactics (step 3). Candidate generation via tactics is performed randomly until the B limit is reached (line 8 in the algorithm). Large B values can promote candidate diversity at the cost of increasing the number of candidates being evaluated.

- *Ranking criteria:* It is the *dbot*'s rule to sort candidates (at a given level). The default criterion, which takes a quality-attribute perspective, is to rank first those candidates with the smallest quality value (assuming objective minimization). An alternative criterion is to look at the utility of the quality values, ranking candidates with the highest utility first.

- *Seeding factor (`S`):* It determines how many children candidates, once generated and assessed, a *dbot* can pass on as seeds for the next level (step 5). Some of these candidates might come from the negotiation phase. *S* controls the tree growth in subsequent levels of search (line 12 in algorithm). Each *dbot* retains the top-*S* candidates and deletes the rest, using the `filteringCriterion`. It can be configured either as quality- based or utility-based criterion.

- *Retaining factor (`R`):* It limits the number of candidates a *dbot* can return at a given level of search. The union of all the candidates (by all the *dbots*) is presented to the architect at the end of the process (step 6). This parameter might be useful to filter the *dbots*' output and reduce information overload on the architect. The `outputCriterion` is employed to filter the solutions (line 13 in algorithm), which can also be quality-based or utility-based.

- *Tree depth (`maxLevel`):* It bounds the search tree to a maximum number of levels.

Determining the right parameters for the heuristic is not straightforward, because it depends on project-specific characteristics (e.g., a family of architectures and scenarios).

Algorithm 1 Heuristic search for architecture candidates.

Inputs: A_0 : initial architecture
$dbots$: available *dbots* (one per scenario)
B : branching factor
S : seeding factor
$maxLevel$: maximum depth to be explored in the tree
R : retaining factor
Outputs: $outputs$: list of architectures to be shown to the architect
$level \leftarrow 0$
$currentSeeds \leftarrow \{A_0\}$
$outputs \leftarrow \emptyset$
while $level < maxLevel$ **do**
  $candidates \leftarrow \emptyset$
  foreach $dbot \in dbots$ **do**
    foreach $s \in currentSeeds$ **do**
      $candidates \leftarrow generateCandidates(B, S, dbot)$ {Expand each seed via valid tactics}
    end for
  end for
  {Add additional architectures coming from negotiation}
  $candidates \leftarrow candidates \cup doNegotiation(dbots, candidates)$
  {Rank and filter architectures}
  $currentSeeds \leftarrow filterCandidates(S, candidates, filteringCriterion)$
  {Filter resulting architectures to present as output}
  $outputs \leftarrow outputs \cup selectOutputs(R, candidates, outputCriterion)$
end while
return $outputs$

4. Evaluation

To empirically assess the behavior of the combined strategy (and its parameters), we performed a series of experiments with two case studies [Frank 2019]: *ST+* and *CoCoME*, which involve small-to-medium size design spaces. The research questions were the following:

- **RQ1.** How does the *dbots* negotiation affect the number of solutions with satisfying and balanced utility characteristics?
- **RQ2.** What is the role of the branching and seeding factors in reducing the search space?

For each case study, we sampled a large number of candidates (without considering branching or seeding restrictions) up to a fixed search level. For this sampling process, we configured `SQuAT` with *dbots* assigned to performance and modifiability scenarios with their quality thresholds. We set a threshold of ≈ 0.8 for balanced utility. As a result, each dataset comprises a predetermined set of solutions with different characteristics (e.g., satisfying, balanced utility, negotiated, and non-satisfying ones). The two datasets[2], structured as search trees, are shown in Figure 6. The *ST+* tree is balanced, while the *CoCoME* tree has a more irregular structure.

On the (full) tree computed from each dataset, we ran a grid search with alternative configurations and classified the solutions explored by the heuristic according to their characteristics. We were mainly interested in parameters `B` and `S`, but also considered the quality-based and utility-based `filteringCriterion`. For every parameter configuration, we simulated 30 search traces over the tree in order to account for the randomness of the process. An average pruning rate was computed based on the candidates being visited (by the search) in the traces. The pruning

[2]For the sake of reproducibility, the datasets with all the information used in the study are accessible at `http://bit.ly/3RfpOY5`.

(a) ST+ (3 levels)　　(b) CoCoME (5 levels)

Figure 6. Graphical representations of the search trees for the two case studies.

(*P*) is the ratio of nodes assessed by the *dbots* with respect to the total nodes in the tree (i.e., the dataset). *P* is an indicator of the computational effort required by the search, recalling that the highest costs come from executing the quality-attribute analyzers on each architecture candidate.

Case study 1 (ST+). The *Extended Simple Tactics* system[3] was partially introduced in Section 2 [Koziolek 2013, Rago et al. 2017]. The PCM specification comprises 9 component types. For optimizing the initial architecture, we set two scenarios for performance and two for modifiability. The search tree contained 554 candidates, including: 154 satisfying solutions (28%), 75 negotiated ones (13.5%) , and 76 solutions with balanced utility (14%). The number of candidates in the sampled space increased significantly with each level, exhibiting a fair distribution of architectures with different characteristics.

We ran search simulations with `B` and `S` in the range $[2-50]$, based on the maximum number of children per node. The `P` values obtained for these configurations are shown in Figure 7a. The darker parts of the heatmap correspond to a more aggressive tree pruning (i.e., high `P` values), which means a faster execution time for the search. As expected, increasing `B` or `S` makes the heuristic explore more candidates, and `P` decreases accordingly. Both `B` and `S` have approximately the same influence on `P`, which can be attributed to the balanced tree structure of *ST+*.

The violin plots in Figure 8a show the kinds of solutions generated by the heuristic when considering pure search or adding negotiation (for all the $P \times B$ configurations). When the *dbots* engaged in negotiation, we observed a higher number of satisfying (*Satisfying-QA*) solutions ($\approx 10\%$) as well as a higher number of solutions ($\approx 20\%$) with a balanced utility (*Balanced-QA*). The improvements were smaller ($\approx 3\%$ and $\approx 10\%$) when using the utility-based criterion (*Satisfying-U* and *Balanced-U*, respectively). We performed a paired samples test (with $\alpha = 0.05$) that confirmed the statistical significance of these differences. We argue that the negotiation is able to find candidates that are not necessarily satisfying but close enough to the thresholds, which cannot be easily detected when the *dbots* try to minimize their quality values. Alternatively, when using the utility-based criterion, the *dbots* seek to maximize utility values; thus, increasing the chances of getting candidates with balanced utility along the way. When checking for differences between pure search and negotiation for low pruning rates, the positive effects of negotiation were attenuated, and both strategies retrieved the same number of solutions.

[3]The *ST+* system specification is publicly available at: `http://bit.ly/3JGFWjV`

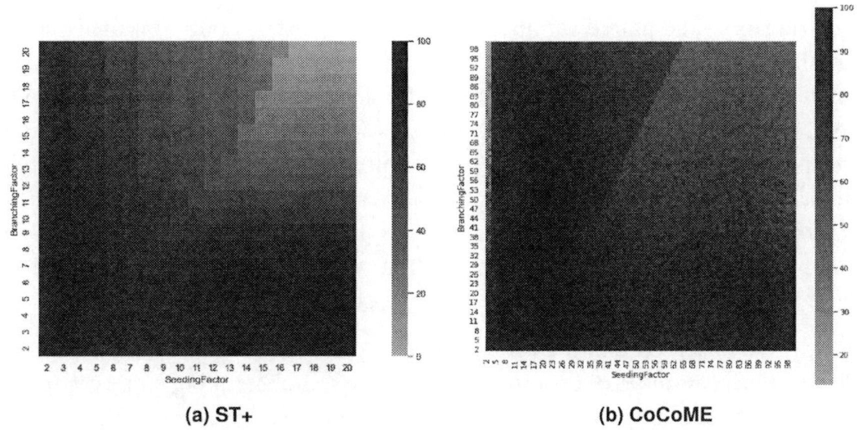

Figure 7. Tree pruning (P) for different branching (*B*) and seeding (S) factors.

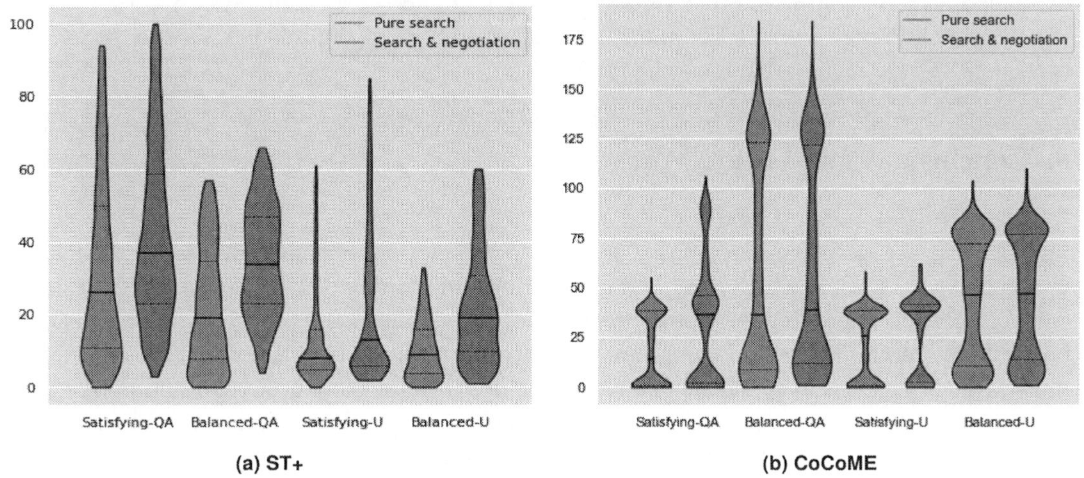

Figure 8. Distribution of the number of solutions with and without negotiation.

Case study 2 (CoCoME). The *Common Community Modeling Example* [Herold et al. 2007] is a benchmark for model-based approaches. It specifies the trading system of a supermarket with many requirements and components. *CoCoME* is a much larger and more realistic model than *ST+*, with a PCM specification[4] having 55 component types. For optimizing the initial architecture, we set twice as many *dbots* as for *ST+*, with four performance scenarios and four modifiability scenarios. The search tree contained 1238 candidates, including: 282 satisfying solutions (23%) , 175 negotiated ones (14%), and 241 solutions with balanced utility (19%) . Unlike the *ST+* design space, the *CoCoME* space had a "wicked" structure with an uneven distribution of the different kinds of solutions. This happened because not all the transformations tried by the *dbots* led to valid architectures, which is a common situation in complex models.

For *CoCoME*, we ran search simulations with B and S in the range $[2-100]$. The P values obtained for these configurations are shown in Figure 7b. The heatmap reveals a similar pattern as for *ST+*, although with higher pruning rates due to the size and shape of the *CoCoME* tree. Figure 8a shows the kinds of solutions obtained with pure search or adding negotiation. There is a small difference in favor of the negotiation for the number of satisfying solutions ($\approx 8\%$) and almost no difference with respect to the balanced solutions, either using a quality-based or a

[4]The *CoCoME* system specification is publicly available at `http://bit.ly/3JGFWjV`

utility-based criterion. The paired samples tests (with $\alpha = 0.05$) only revealed statistical differences for combinations of `P` and `S` in specific ranges, although no clear patterns were identified. For instance, negotiation showed higher numbers for satisfying solutions with `S` in $[65 - 100]$ (irrespective of `B`) and for balanced solutions with `B` in $[2 - 10]$ (irrespective of `S`). When comparing this trend to the more uniform trend in *ST+*, we think the design space complexity is a causal factor since many satisfying candidates were located in the leaves (level 5) of particular sub-trees. Thus, the *dbots* had trouble finding the right paths to those candidates, even if a few intermediate nodes (for those paths) were obtained via negotiation. Certainly, more experiments and other case studies should be analyzed in order to make stronger claims.

Overall, we observed that the proposed heuristic can reduce the computational overhead due to exploring a large number of candidates during the search, making some compromises in the quality of the output. The usage of negotiation seems to improve the tradeoffs of the solutions in terms of meeting the scenario thresholds or having a balanced utility. However, this potential benefit depends on the structure of the search tree, as evidenced by the case studies. An insight from the experiments is that the desired values of branching and seeding should be properly chosen, ideally in a mid-range with respect to the (estimated) number of children per node in the tree.

5. Conclusions and Future Work

In this work, we have presented and assessed a parameterized search heuristic for architecture optimization in `SQuAT`, which combines negotiation and pruning mechanisms in order to strike a balance between improving the quality tradeoffs of the solutions and reducing the computational costs of the search. The core assumption of our work is that stakeholders aim for balanced solutions, which translates to candidates on which the *dbots* can reach a utility consensus. An initial assessment with two case studies has shown that negotiation can be effective, particularly when limiting the exploration parameters. Beyond `SQuAT`, we believe that the mechanisms and insights discussed in the paper can be helpful to other architecture optimization approaches, as they often face similar challenges with respect to the effectiveness of the search process.

As discussed in the evaluation, the characteristics of the design space being explored (including the target scenarios) can affect the effectiveness of the proposed heuristic. Unfortunately, such characteristics are difficult to estimate in advance, that is, when configuring the *dbots*. Nonetheless, it should be possible to adapt the search parameters of `SQuAT` dynamically, as new information (about the space) becomes available [Hoos 2012]. To overcome performance and scalability issues, we plan to investigate the usage of surrogates [Jiang et al. 2020] and parallel-distributed mechanisms, given the multi-agent foundations of `SQuAT`. This would allow us to apply the approach to larger, more complex architectural models. Along this line, we expect to run `SQuAT` on some case studies used by related approaches, like *GATSE* and *EASIER*, and compare the performance of our heuristic with that of evolutionary algorithms.

Another interesting mechanism to direct the search or improve its effectiveness is to include human feedback (e.g., regarding architectural preferences) as part of the optimization process. Some studies with evolutionary algorithms have been reported [Quesada et al. 2018]. In `SQuAT`, currently the architect's preferences (e.g., the utility function, the negotiation policies) have to be entered before the optimization takes place. In future work, we will explore mechanisms to make the *dbots* search process more interactive with the architect, and provide some explanations of the decisions being made in the search, so that the architect can understand and have more confidence in the results of the optimization process.

References

Aleti, A., Buhnova, B., Grunske, L., Koziolek, A., and Meedeniya, I. (2013). Software architecture optimization methods: A systematic literature review. *IEEE Trans. on Soft. Eng.*, 39(5):658–683.

Arcelli, D., Cortellessa, V., D'Emidio, M., and Di Pompeo, D. (2018). Easier: An evolutionary approach for multi-objective software architecture refactoring. In *2018 IEEE International Conference on Software Architecture (ICSA)*, pages 105–10509.

Bachmann, F., Bass, L., Klein, M., and Shelton, C. (2005). Designing software architectures to achieve quality attribute requirements. *IEE Proceedings - Software*, 152:153–165(12).

Bass, L., Clements, P., and Kazman, R. (2021). *Software Architecture in Practice*. Addison-Wesley Professional, 4th edition.

Becker, S., Koziolek, H., and Reussner, R. (2009). The palladio component model for model-driven performance prediction. *Journal of Systems and Software*, 82(1).

Di Pompeo, D. and Tucci, M. (2023). Quality attributes optimization of software architecture: Research challenges and directions.

Endriss, U. (2006). Monotonic concession protocols for multilateral negotiation. In *5th International Joint Conference on Autonomous Agents and Multiagent Systems*, pages 392–399. ACM.

Fatima, S., Wooldridge, M., and Jennings, N. (2004). An agenda-based framework for multi-issue negotiation. *Artificial Intelligence*, 152(1):1–45.

Frank, S. (2019). Techniques for visualization and interaction in software architecture optimization. Master's thesis, University of Stuttgart.

Herold, S., Klus, H., Welsch, Y., Deiters, C., Rausch, A., Reussner, R. H., Krogmann, K., Koziolek, H., Mirandola, R., Hummel, B., Meisinger, M., and Pfaller, C. (2007). Cocome - the common component modeling example. In *The Common Component Modeling Example: Comparing Software Component Models [result from the Dagstuhl research seminar for CoCoME, August 1-3, 2007]*, volume 5153 of *Lecture Notes in Computer Science*, pages 16–53. Springer.

Hoos, H. H. (2012). *Automated Algorithm Configuration and Parameter Tuning*, pages 37–71. Springer Berlin Heidelberg, Berlin, Heidelberg.

Jiang, P., Zhou, Q., and Shao, X. (2020). *Surrogate Model-Based Engineering Design and Optimization.*

Koziolek, A. (2013). *Automated Improvement of Software Architecture Models for Performance and Other Quality Attributes*. PhD thesis, KIT.

Koziolek, H. and Reussner, R. H. (2008). A model transformation from the palladio component model to layered queueing networks. In Kounev, S., Gorton, I., and Sachs, K., editors, *Proceedings of the SPEC International Performance Evaluation Workshop (SIPEW 2008)*, volume 5119 of *Lecture Notes in Computer Science*, pages 58–78. Springer.

Monteserin, A., Díaz Pace, J. A., Gatti, I., and Schiaffino, S. N. (2017). Agent negotiation techniques for improving quality-attribute architectural tradeoffs. In *Proc. PAAMS '17*, pages 183–195.

Pace, J. A. D. and Campo, M. R. (2008). Exploring alternative software architecture designs: A planning perspective. *IEEE Intell. Syst.*, 23(5):66–77.

Procter, S. and Wrage, L. (2019). Guided architecture trade space exploration: Fusing model based engineering amp; design by shopping. In *2019 ACM/IEEE 22nd Int. Conf. on Model Driven Engineering. Languages and Systems (MODELS)*, pages 117–127.

Quesada, A. R., Romero, J. R., and Ventura, S. (2018). Interactive multi-objective evolutionary optimization of software architectures. *Inf. Sci.*, 463-464:92–109.

Rago, A., Vidal, S. A., Diaz-Pace, J. A., Frank, S., and van Hoorn, A. (2017). Distributed quality-attribute optimization of software architectures. In *Proceedings of the 11th Brazilian Symposium on Software Components, Architectures and Reuse, Fortaleza, CE, Brazil, September 18 - 19, 2017*, pages 7:1–7:10.

Rekha, V. S. and Muccini, H. (2018). Group decision-making in software architecture: A study on industrial practices. *Information and Software Technology*, 101:51 – 63.

Stammel, J. and Reussner, R. (2009). Kamp: Karlsruhe architectural maintainability prediction. In Engels, G., Reussner, R., Momm, C., and Sauer, S., editors, *1st. Workshop des GI-Arbeitskreises Langlebige Softwaresysteme (L2S2): "Design for Future - Langlebige Softwaresysteme"*, pages 87–98.

Exploratory Analysis of the Structural Evolution of public REST APIs

Nicolás Robles[1], Nicolás Potes[1], Kelly Garcés[1], Javier Luis Canovas Izquierdo[2], Jordi Cabot[2]

[1]Department of Systems and Computing Engineering
Universidad de los Andes, Colombia

[2]IN3 - UOC; ICREA, Spain

{nr.robles, n.potes, kj.garces971}@uniandes.edu.co

jcanovasi@uoc.edu, jcabot@icrea.cat

Abstract. *The software industry is in continuous evolution, forcing developers to quickly adapt to new requirements to catch up with the latest trends. A clear example is the huge demand for web-based APIs to connect all kinds of services among them. Like any other piece of software, a Web API is continuously changing, and with each change, all client applications must evolve. This adaptation process is critical and essential for software developers. In this paper, we present an exploratory evaluation of the most common changes occurring during the evolution of REST APIs. We define a taxonomy of structural API changes, which we classify according to their impact on client-side software; and propose a repository mining process to identify these changes in real Web APIs. We apply this process to a large set of Azure APIs from* APIsGuru, *a well-known Open Source API repository. Based on the analyzed dataset from* APIsGuru, *we found that breaking changes tend to decrease when a new version of an API from this dataset is released. Other useful findings and insights are discussed throughout the article.*

1. Introduction

The digital transformation has created a world where services and data are accessed through the Internet; and therefore service providers make their data available through Application Programming Interfaces (APIs). APIs can be classified as *libraries* or *remote APIs* considering the place where they are hosted. The former runs in the same environment as the client software, whereas the latter is hosted in a different environment and reached by the client application using remote access protocols. When the protocol is HTTP, the APIs are called Web APIs. This work targets the evolution of REST Web APIs which are the most common type of Web API used today [Halili and Ramadani 2018]. It is worth mentioning that REST (REpresentational State Transfer) is an architectural style that guides the design and development of Web APIs.

Like any other piece of software, service providers need to evolve their APIs, which frequently implies the introduction of changes in the released API versions. As a result, developers need to adapt (co-evolve) their software to support the new API version, which requires full knowledge of API changes and their impact. [Li et al. 2013] note that updating Web API clients is a more critical task than updating library clients because the former generally can not keep using the old API version (as it may not be available anymore).

Change detection between REST API versions is generally addressed by manual reviewing the API documentation and perusing the API controllers used on a client application to find the occurrences of evolving methods [Koçi et al. 2019, Wang et al. 2014]. However, these approaches are time-consuming and dependent on the API's implementation. This situation has motivated us to mine a public REST API repository to expand the body of knowledge about Web API evolution. By knowing better how the API evolution happens in practice, developers could be adequately prepared for it, both in terms of determining what types of changes they should be prepared for and in terms of how impactful those changes risk to be for the client applications consuming the APIs.

We mined a large set of APIs by Azure available at APISGURU[1], a well-known API repository, to better understand the most common changes occurring in the evolution of REST APIs. Each change was classified either as a *breaking* or *non-breaking* change. A breaking (BR) change means there is an impact on the API client applications that damages their functionality. In turn, a non-breaking (NON-BR) change preserves the compatibility with previous API versions, and thus, the client code will keep running [Dig and Johnson 2006]. Understanding the frequency and type of changes is therefore key to prioritize and plan any API evolution process. The importance of this problem appeared often in our discussions with practitioners working in the development and maintenance of APIs.

Besides this characterization of API changes, this paper also contributes: (i) a taxonomy of possible REST API changes classified by their impact on client software; (ii) a tool to identify API changes and (iii) a mining process to (semi) automate the extraction and analysis of APIs in an API repository. We use OPENAPI, a standard to describe REST APIs in a language-agnostic way, to analyze and compare REST APIs. Thus, our approach does not require any access to API source code and therefore is independent of the programming language the API is implemented with. Note that there are ways to generate the OpenAPI specification out of API implementation if needed [Cao et al. 2017].

The article is organized as follows. Sections 2, 3 and 4 present the research questions, method and results, respectively. Sections 5 and 6 present the validation and the threats to validity. Section 7 reports the related work, while Section 8 ends the paper and presents the future work.

2. Research Questions

This section states the three research questions to guide our understanding of REST APIs evolution:

RQ1 How frequent are breaking changes in API evolution?
RQ2 What are the most frequent types of changes introduced in API evolution?
RQ3 Is it possible to get insights on the stability of an API by reviewing its evolution process?

These questions can be responded at two different levels of granularity: *repository level* and *API level*. *Repository level* refers to when the analysis is based on all the APIs of

[1] https://apis.guru/

the dataset (general), on the other hand, *API level* refers to when the analysis is based on certain APIs (particular). We answer RQ1 and RQ2 at repository level to provide overall information on the evolution of the analyzed APIs. Researchers could take advantage of the findings to develop techniques and tools to ease the adaptation of client programs to frequent changes. On the other hand, R3 will be addressed at API level to compare the stability of APIs and get insights about its quality (i.e., the fewer changes, the more stable the API, meaning the less potential impact on client software).

We reached these questions and the granularity level based on our own experience and the opinion of a group of senior software developers with whom we had informal meetings during this research.

3. Research method

The research method we developed to answer our research questions covers the following steps: (1) definition of a taxonomy of API changes, (2) development of a tool to mine changes in evolving APIs, (3) execution of the mining process. The subsequent sections describe each step in detail.

3.1. Taxonomy of API changes

To build our taxonomy of API changes, we followed a process composed of three phases: (1) kick-start the taxonomy by analyzing existing proposals; (2) manual review of existing Web APIs to identify new change types; and (3) taxonomy consolidation.

Our taxonomy is inspired by the proposal made by [Li et al. 2013], which we extended with the following types of changes: i) add path; ii) change parameter lower bound; iii) relocate parameter; and iv) change default parameter value. We identified these new categories after manual reviewing twenty OPENAPI specifications available on the APISGURU repository. To ensure high representativity, each reviewed API satisfies three criteria: it has at least two versions, it includes at least ten endpoints, and it has had commits recently. We removed the XML Tag type change because we focus on REST APIs which do not use XML [Halili and Ramadani 2018]. Table 1 lists the APIs changes of the taxonomy (see first column). We use the severity column to distinguish between breaking (BR) and non-breaking (NON-BR) changes.

We compared our taxonomy with the ones proposed by [Li et al. 2013], [Wang et al. 2014], [Sohan et al. 2015]. Table 1 shows the results of such comparison (see last four columns). For each API change, the row indicates whether they are included or not in each proposal. As can be seen, our taxonomy covers most of the changes proposed by the aforementioned authors and includes additional ones. It is worth noting that our taxonomy does not cover API changes related to authentication and authorization, as those changes are not identifiable using static analysis and also because the OPENAPI v2.0 lacks elements to represent with accuracy the different types of API authorization.

3.2. API Changes Detection Tool

In this section we present the elements of the tool developed to detect API changes, called API Detection Tool (ADT). We first describe the *Diff Changes Metamodel*, that serves to represent our changes taxonomy and is instantiated by the tool; and then present the ADT tool architecture.We use the Model-Driven Engineering (MDE) approach to create and

Change Name	Severity	Ours	[Li et al. 2013]	[Wang et al. 2014]	[Sohan et al. 2015]
Change parameter Type	Br	Y	Y	Y	N
Rename parameter	Non-Br	Y	Y	Y	Y
Increase number of parameters	Br	Y	N	Y	Y
Decrease number of parameters	Br	Y	Y	Y	Y
Change return type	Br	Y	Y	Y	Y
Delete path	Br	Y	Y	Y	Y
Change parameter schema type	Br	Y	Y	Y	N
Unsupported request method	Br	Y	Y	N	N
Change default parameter value	Non-Br	Y	N	N	N
Change parameter upper bound	Non-Br	Y	Y	Y	N
Change parameter lower bound	Non-Br	Y	N	Y	N
Change return type schema	Br	Y	Y	Y	N
Relocate parameter	Br	Y	N	N	N
Change consumed type	Br	Y	Y	N	N
Remove restricted access	Non-Br	Y	N	N	Y
Add restricted access	Non-Br	Y	Y	N	Y
Change produced type	Br	Y	Y	Y	N
Rename method	Br	Y	Y	Y	Y
Combine methods	Br	Y	Y	N	N
Split method	Br	Y	Y	N	N
Add path	Non-Br	Y	N	Y	Y
Change auth model	Br	N	N	Y	Y
Change required parameter type	Br	Y	N	Y	N
Add status code	Non-Br	Y	N	N	N
Remove status code	Br	Y	N	N	N

Table 1. Taxonomies comparison.

develop the tool. MDE is a Software development approach which focuses on models, as opposed to source code. Models are built representing different views on a Software system. The main goal is to raise the level of abstraction, and to develop and evolve complex Software systems by manipulating models.

3.2.1. Diff Changes Metamodel

We have designed a metamodel to represent the API changes based on our taxonomy and the metamodel proposed by [Polák and Holubová 2015]. The root concept of our metamodel is *Diff*, which is composed of a set of changes. A change can be *Simple* or *Complex*. A simple change refers to an individual element of a given API undergoing a unique change, either a *Deletion*, an *Addition*, or a *Modification*. Depending on the type of change, a simple change may have references to API elements presented in the former and latter compared versions. A *Complex* change is a set of simple changes that affect multiple API elements. Finally, we represent the changes shown in Table 1 as specializations of the concepts *Simple* and *Complex*.

3.2.2. ADT Architecture

ADT aims to identify changes introduced in a given REST API by comparing two of their versions. The discovery process is performed by a transformation chain which takes as input two OPENAPI models corresponding to different versions of the same API. These models conform to the already existing *OpenAPI metamodel* [SOM RESEARCH LAB 2018] and are later processed by a comparator that executes EMFCOMPARE and gets a *comparison model*. This comparison model has generic differences (i.e., ADD, DELETE, CHANGE and MOVE), which are processed and transformed to obtain a model conforming to the *Diff changes metamodel* presented before.

3.3. Mining process

We performed a mining process by applying ADT to a large set of OPENAPI definitions by Azure from APISGURU. We selected those APIs having multiple versions and whose definitions conform to OPENAPI v2.0. In the following, we report the main challenges found during the mining process.

OPENAPI models representing OPENAPI definitions were ordered in pairs including the consecutive versions of the API. For example, if an API has three versions, the resulting pairs would be (v1, v2) and (v2, v3). Then, we called ADT for each pair of versions to be compared. We processed the versions in the aforementioned order to ensure the comparisons follow the API evolution path so that the results show the state of the API on each evolutionary step. Finally, we studied the results and generated a set of charts to address our research questions.

4. Results

We have designed a set of visualizations that aims at answering the research questions stated in Section 2 from two different perspectives: i) repository level (overall evolution of analyzed APIs); ii) API level (evolution of selected APIs). Section 5 presents the findings of a survey on the usefulness of the contributed visualizations. Our process mined 225 different APIs, including 1568 different versions, in other words, 784 pairs of versions. Each API reviewed had, on average, 6.97 versions and also on average, 1.72 breaking changes per comparison in each pair of versions. In the following, we take advantage of the visualizations provided to answer the research questions for this dataset. For the sake of space we present the results of RQ1 and RQ2 at repository level, but the same graphics can be generated for a particular API specified by the user. In the section associated to RQ3 we present results at repository and API level because the charts are different at each granularity.

4.1. RQ1: How frequent are breaking changes in API evolution?

An API is considered affected when there is at least one change (breaking or non-breaking). Based on this, the number of affected APIs with respect to the total is: 157 out of 225 studied. That is, 69.78% were affected APIs.

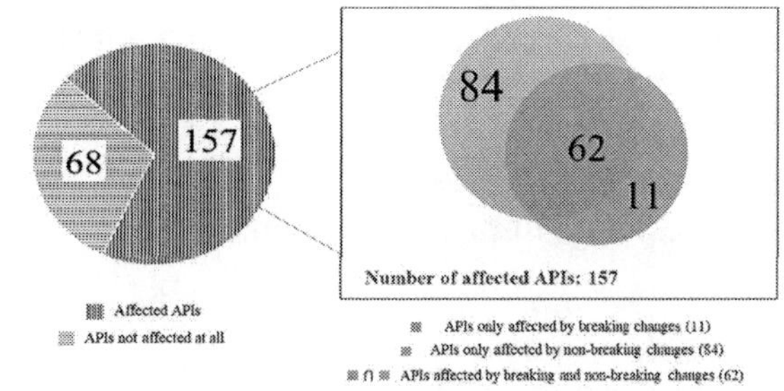

Figure 1. Distribution of APIs by type of change

Figure 1 shows the distribution of APIs by type of change. 11 APIs were affected only by breaking changes, 84 APIs were affected only by non-breaking changes, of these two sets, the intersection was 62 APIs, i.e., APIs affected by both breaking and non-breaking changes. Finally, 68 APIs of the dataset were not affected by any change.

Additionally, we decided to analyze the percentage of pairs of versions that include a breaking change. Based on this, we found that of the 784 pairs of versions analyzed, 102 pairs of versions include at least one breaking change. That is, **13.01%** of the pairs of versions have a breaking change in the studied dataset.

Finally, we performed an analysis by API looking at the percentage of endpoints[2] that changed versus those that did not. In general, for all the APIs in the dataset under study, the following distribution was found:

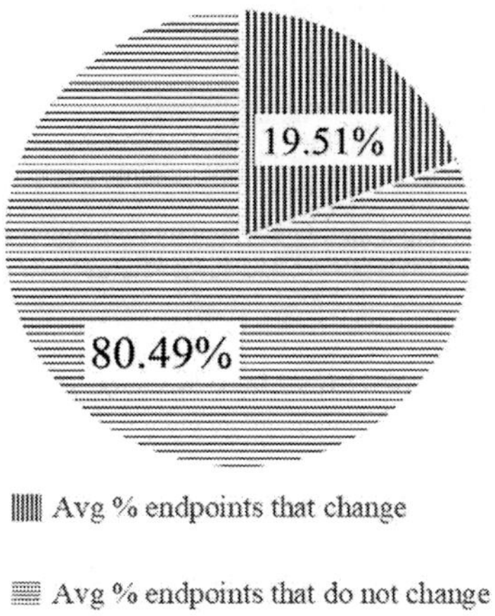

Figure 2. Average % of endpoints that change vs. those that do not)

As can be seen in figure 2, most endpoints of the APIs under study do not tend to change.

[2]An endpoint is a point at which an API connects with a client program

4.2. RQ2: What are the most frequent types of changes introduced in API evolution?

We obtained the following distribution from the dataset of the most popular breaking and non-breaking changes, represented in the figures 3 and 4:

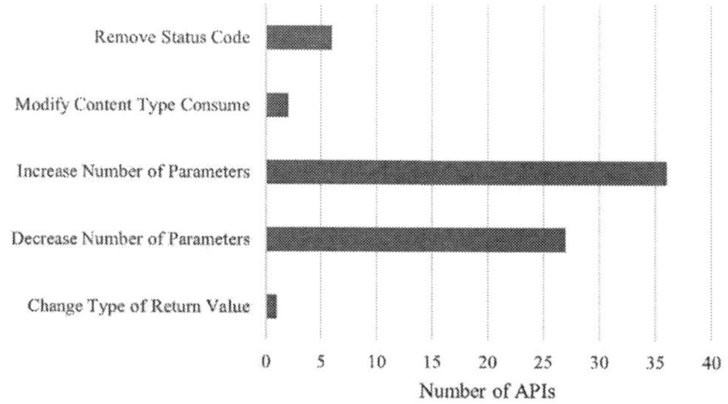

Figure 3. Most popular breaking changes per API

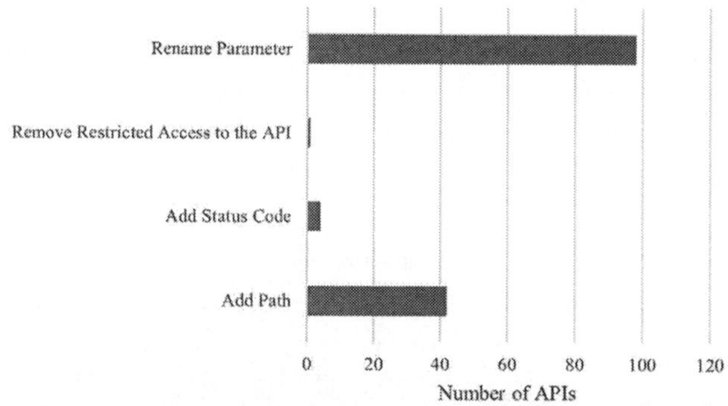

Figure 4. Most popular non-breaking changes per API

- **Breaking change most repeated:** *Increase Number of Parameters* with 658 occurrences

- **Non-breaking change most repeated:** *Rename Parameter* with 1473 occurrences

As can be seen, both changes are very common and are therefore the most frequently repeated. On one hand, the *Increase Number of Parameters* change occurs when the definition of a method is changed by adding more parameters. On the other hand, the *Rename Parameter* change occurs when the name of a parameter is changed.

4.3. RQ3: Is it possible to get insights on the stability of an API by reviewing its evolution process?

To address this research question, we decided to conduct analyses at both repository and API levels.

4.3.1. Repository level

Firstly, to visualize the trend regarding the average age of APIs, measured in the number of versions, figure 5 shows the number of pairs of versions on the x-axis (1-21) and the number of APIs that have n pairs of versions on the y-axis . For example, there are 133 APIs that have two pairs of versions, i.e., 4 versions in the dataset.

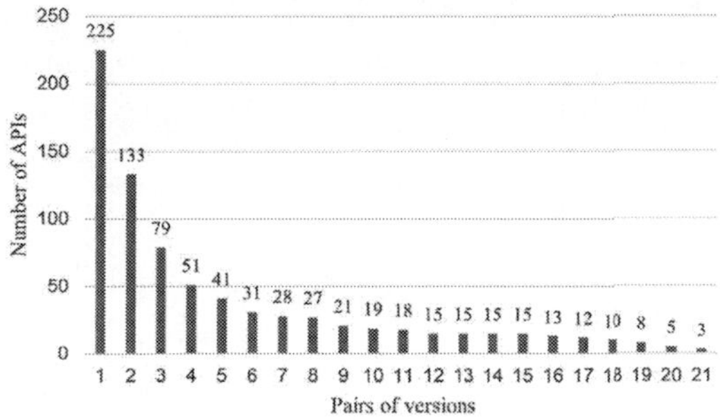

Figure 5. Number of APIs per pair of versions

Based on Figure 5, we can see that the vast majority of APIs have 1 to 4 version pairs in this dataset. Therefore, their average age is around this range.

Secondly, we conducted an analysis of the 225 APIs to find out what was the average disappearance time of breaking changes, measured in versions. To determine that breaking changes are disappearing (decreasing) in APIs, we compared the number of breaking changes found in a given pair of version with that of its immediately previous pair. Based on this, we found that only APIs that have two pairs of versions decrease the breaking changes without increasing them again. Therefore, the average disappearance time for this dataset is **two pairs of versions** (4 versions) To clarify, table 2 exemplifies the above with two concrete APIs: *apimcaches* and *apimdeployment*.

API	PV1	PV2	PV3
apimcaches	10	5	7
apimdeployment	5	2	0

Table 2. Descending breaking changes in APIs' pairs of versions

As shown in table 2, *apimcaches* has 10 breaking changes in its first pair of versions, in its next pair of versions it decreases to 5 breaking changes but finally in its third pair of versions it increases again its breaking changes (7), therefore, this API is not considered to completely decrease its breaking changes since in some pair of versions it increased again its number of breaking changes or it never decreased them. On the other hand, *apimdeployment* decreases its breaking changes without increasing them again, therefore, this API is considered to have totally decreased its breaking changes.

In addition, we performed an analysis of the evolution of breaking changes for each number of API pairs of versions in the dataset. To this end, we obtained the pairs of versions of each API in the dataset and found that there are APIs that have only one pair of versions up to APIs that have 21 pairs of versions. In addition, we calculated the number of breaking changes for each pair of version. Then, we summed the breaking changes observed in the first pairs of version (i.e., version 1 and 2) of all APIs. We did the same for the second pairs (i.e., version 2 and 3), third pairs and so on. It is worth noting that the number of pairs of versions is variable among the studied APIs. From these aggregated values, we created a Scatter graph that shows the behavior of the breaking changes (y-axis) through the different pairs of versions (x-axis).

Figure 6 shows the pairs of versions on the X-axis and the number of breaking changes per pair of versions on the Y-axis.

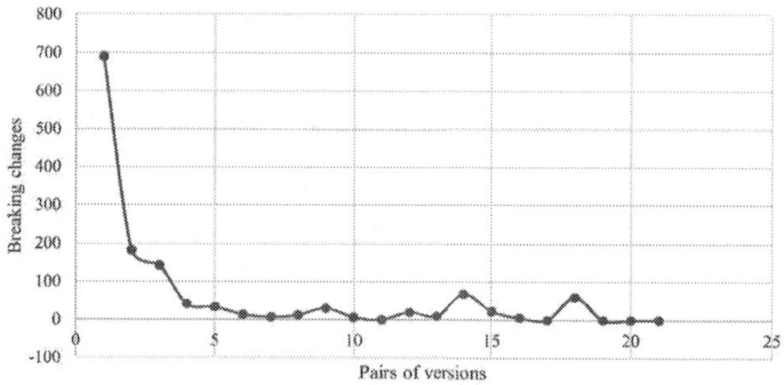

Figure 6. Scatter of pairs of versions and breaking changes

The scatter line shows a decreasing trend in most of the pairs of versions, this indicates that last versions have less BR changes than older ones. An assumption to explain this behaviour is the effort from the developers of this particular dataset to decrease the number of breaking changes over time by fixing the problems that affect the applications that consume the API, in order to guarantee the evolutionary improvement in each of the versions released. When performing the same analyses on other datasets outliers may be present since the decrease of breaking changes in new API versions depends on the API developers.

4.3.2. API level

Below is a chart that allows you to see the comparison between two specific APIs (azure.com:apimanagement-apimapis-network versus azure.com:apimanagement-apimsubscriptions-blue), where both have two pairs of equal versions: *2018-06-01-preview-2019-01-01-01* and *2019-01-01-01-2019-12-01-01-preview*. Figure 7 shows the behavior of decreasing breaking changes in the first API (apimapis) and an increase of breaking changes in the second one (apimsubscriptions):

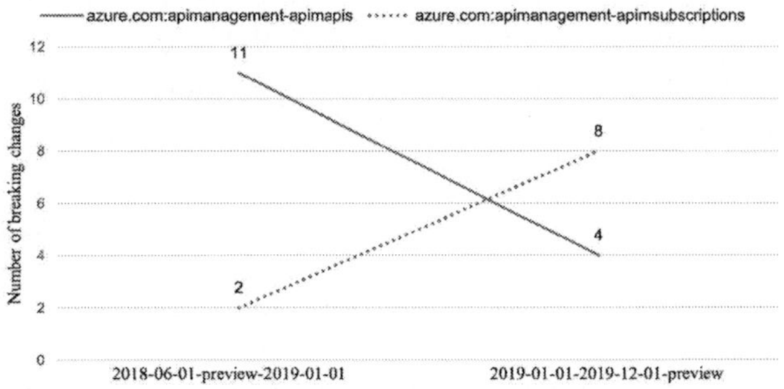

Figure 7. Comparison of breaking changes between two APIs.

Based on the three previous analyses, it is possible to obtain insights about the stability of an API. The first analysis helps one review the average number of endpoints changing in an API. The second analysis showed that for this dataset the breaking changes tend to decrease when a new version of an API is released. Finally, the last analysis shed light on the increase/decrease of the number of breaking changes in the different API version pairs.

5. Usefulness of the results

To validate whether the analysis presented so far was perceived as useful by practitioners, we prepared a survey to see how the previous charts could be insightful for a number of use case scenarios around API evolutions.

The survey was responded by ten practitioners (eight men and two women), all of them software engineers in the private sector and with 3-5 years working on the development and maintenance of APIs.

For each chart, we asked the participants two questions: i) what kind of decisions/processes would the charts help to make/perform; and ii) usefulness of the charts.

With respect to the first group of questions, we gave the participants four possible charts usage options and prompted them to suggest new usage ideas. The initial usages were: (U1) define work priorities to adjust the client software to the changes introduced in the API's latest version; (U2) define concrete actions to reduce the impact of changes found in client applications; (U3) identify the need to refactor the API to improve its maintainability; (U4) if the compared APIs satisfy the same functionality, the comparison could motivate to choose one API over the other because the first one changes less. The participants agreed with some of the usages listed before but also proposed the following two usages: (U5) identify the volatility/stability of an API over time; (U6) get an initial idea about the effort to adapt client applications in response to API changes. The more breaking changes, the greater the effort to move client software to the new version of the API. Table 3 shows for each chart the aforementioned usage scenarios selected by the participants. On this table, an X on a row means that the particular chart is useful in that usage scenario.

Regarding the second question, the participants evaluated the usefulness of each chart by using a likert scale, with levels of agreement/disagreement being the dimension used. All the participants strongly agreed that the classification of changes in breaking and non-breaking changes (i.e., charts 3 and 4 in Table 3) are of great value for them. Participants perceived the usefulness/easiness of charts 6 and 7 in a lower amount compared to that of the other charts: 50% of the participants agreed, 30% remained neutral and the rest disagreed on the usability.

Chart	U1	U2	U3	U4	U5	U6
(1) Total changes per severity	X	X				X
(2) Br / Non-Br distribution	X	X	X			
(3) Single API stability	X	X	X			
(4) Br changes proportion	X		X	X	X	

Table 3. Chart Usage According to Practitioners

6. Threats to validity

Our work is subjected to both (1) internal validity (i.e., related to the inferences we made); and (2) external validity (i.e., generalization of our findings). Regarding the internal validity, it is worth mentioning that at the time we obtained the information from *APIsGuru*, the only APIs that had several version-pairs and that were specified in the OpenAPI version (i.e., v2.0), requested by the ADT tool, were those provided by Azure. This is a thread of validity but it was necessary at the time in order to obtain a set of APIs to analyze. Additionally, note that the APIsGuru was selected because they provide publicly available APIs actively supported by developers. Also, the repository is continuously updated, and the API definitions are reviewed to ensure its correctness. The proposed taxonomy covers API changes presented by both other authors and us but additional changes may have been missed. As for the external validity, our study is based on a subset of OpenAPI APIs and therefore our results should not be generalized to any other kinds of APIs.

7. Related work

The topic of API evolution has been largely studied in the literature [Dig and Johnson 2006, Wu et al. 2016, Xavier et al. 2017, Sawant et al. 2019, D.Rivières 2019, Henkel and Diwan 2005, Hora et al. 2014, Nguyen et al. 2010, Zhong et al. 2009, Wu et al. 2014, Bartolomei et al. 2010, Lamothe et al. 2021]. Some of the earlier works focused on the evolution of software libraries and have served as inspiration for the taxonomy definition. More recent ones target specifically web-based APIs. We have identified two categories of works in this context: (i) those focusing on understanding the API evolution process by classifying API changes; and (ii) those that study API usages on client software by mining repositories. Our work falls in the intersection of these categories in the sense that it focuses on API evolution itself (excluding client applications) but the research method includes mining techniques. In what follows we compare our approach with the closely related literature.

Web API evolution. Regarding the works studying the API evolution process, [Li et al. 2013] establish Web API evolution patterns and how different those are from the ones found on regular APIs. [Romano and Pinzger 2012] report the differences found between pairs of API versions represented in the Web Services Description Language (WSDL). The authors transform the representations into models and compare them using EMFCompare [Eclipse Fundation 2019]. [Koçi et al. 2019] present a classification that shows which REST API elements are prone to change. This classification takes into account paths, parameters, requests, and changes in authority level. [Wang et al. 2014] study online discussions about REST API changes by analyzing the StackOverflow questions. They identify 21 types of changes and claims that 7 of them are new compared with existing studies. [Polák and Holubová 2015] represent the initial version of a given API in a model called ReM. Whenever a new change requirement appears, the change is specified in the ReM model and generates a new version of said model, so that the users can trace the API evolution in time. The authors also provide model transformations that generate API source code, in a specified programming language, from a ReM model version.

In particular, our approach differs from existing related works in three key aspects. Firstly, we specialize in REST APIs, the most popular ones at the moment. The proposals of [Koçi et al. 2019] and [Wang et al. 2014] are the only ones that target this kind of APIs. Nevertheless, their change detection approach is entirely manual and based on the revision of documentation and API controllers used on client software, thus making their process technology specific. In contrast, our change identification process is automated and compares APIs using OPENAPI documents, which allow us to process APIs written in any programming language while focusing on structural changes. Second, we use a more extensive taxonomy of changes to detect and classify the API evolution. Third, our approach compares the APIs using a model-based representation of each API version. This allows us to further process the changes detected and add metadata to them. In our review, we found [Romano and Pinzger 2012] to be the only one that uses model-based comparisons to detect changes. However, they do not perform any additional processing on the comparison model returned by EMFCOMPARE. In contrast, we have added a step to the comparison process that enriches the EMFCOMPARE results with complex changes that go beyond the classical simple changes (i.e., delete, add, modify).

API usages in client software. [Wang et al. 2019] propose a mining engine called *Crmac* which recommends APIs based on regularity of use taking into account code from both open-source projects and local projects. [Sawant and Bacchelli 2015] analyze the use of certain APIs consumed by projects in GitHub. This approach differentiates from others in that it establishes the connection between the API class and the invocation in the client application. This allows developers to understand the use of an API with greater precision. [Lamothe 2020] establishes practical and scalable guidelines/tools regarding the evolution of APIs based on what is found mining public code repositories. The insights are delivered to both stakeholders: API developers and consumers. [Huppe et al. 2017] identify patterns of API usages, by utilizing genetic programming, to inform non-trivial patterns that allow developers who consume these APIs to understand their usage more efficiently. [Bae et al. 2014] detect possible misuses of Web APIs on client applications written in Javascript. [Yasmin et al. 2020] identify depreciated elements in different versions of REST APIs. The authors mined 1368 APIs from APIsGuru and determined that there are many problems related to the deprecation of REST APIs.

[Koçi et al. 2021b, Koçi et al. 2021a][Koçi et al. 2020] propose to inform providers about API usage patterns and usability by regarding the interaction of consumers with APIs reported in logs. Finally, [Di Lauro et al. 2021] study evolution by mining open-source API versions specified in the OpenAPI standard. Their analyzes focuses on the following three aspects: overall number of changes, API age, and API growth.

Like most aforementioned approaches, we mine public API datasets. However, we focus on the API versions themselves by plotting the mining results in graphics, at aggregated (repository) and isolated level (API). Our approach differentiates from others in that it classifies changes in a taxonomy that has categories (either breaking or non breaking) and subcategories (e.g., rename parameter, delete path, etc.). This information may help developers and consumers to understand API evolution and make decision to improve maintainability as shown in the validation. The analyses of API usages in client applications is out of the paper scope.

8. Conclusion and future work

We mined a set of APIs from APISGURU to better understand the common changes when evolving APIs. We concluded that the category of breaking changes has more types of changes, thus showing that the adaptation of client applications to API evolution is a critical step in any migration/evolution process and should be planned as such. Further validation with practitioners showed that the results and proposed charts are useful to assist them in their API adaptation process, mainly to help to prioritize the required adaptation work. In addition, we concluded for the API Evolution Analysis section that most of the APIs in the dataset were affected by some change and that most of them were non-breaking changes. We also observed that the most repeated breaking change was *Increase Number of Parameters* with 658 occurrences and the most repeated non-breaking change was *Rename Parameter* with 1473 occurrences. Lastly, we verified that the APIs of the dataset under study follow the behavior of decreasing the number of breaking changes in each new version that is released. This is a good indicator for the dataset, most API releases tended to decrease their breaking changes, which is an ideal behavior and benefits those who consume these APIs. However, this behavior is not always the case, therefore, good practices should be followed when releasing new versions of an API.

Regarding the further work, we would like to develop new methods and tools to recommend/apply client software adaptations to the frequent API changes found in this analysis. Another possible step would be to prioritize the adaptations based on breaking changes severity. We are interested in supporting other API definition formats (e.g., OPENAPI v3.0). Also, we would like to explore the change detection beyond static analysis of the APIs definition. For example, as depicted in our taxonomy section, a change in the authentication model may only be detectable at runtime by perusing the API HTTP responses.

References

Bae, S., Cho, H., Lim, I., and Ryu, S. (2014). Safewapi: Web api misuse detector for web applications. *Proceedings of the ACM SIGSOFT Symposium on the Foundations of Software Engineering*, 16-21-November-2014:507–517.

Bartolomei, T. T., Czarnecki, K., and Lämmel, R. (2010). Swing to SWT and back: Patterns for API migration by wrapping. In *26th IEEE International Conference on*

Software Maintenance (ICSM 2010), September 12-18, 2010, Timisoara, Romania, pages 1–10.

Cao, H., Falleri, J.-R., and Blanc, X. (2017). Automated generation of rest api specification from plain html documentation. In *Service-Oriented Computing*, pages 453–461, Cham. Springer International Publishing.

Di Lauro, F., Serbout, S., and Pautasso, C. (2021). Towards large-scale empirical assessment of web apis evolution. In Brambilla, M., Chbeir, R., Frasincar, F., and Manolescu, I., editors, *Web Engineering*, pages 124–138, Cham. Springer International Publishing.

Dig, D. and Johnson, R. (2006). How do apis evolve? a story of refactoring. *J. Softw. Maint. Evol.*, 18.

D.Rivières (2019). Evolvingjava-basedapis2.

Eclipse Fundation (2019). Emf compare.

Halili, F. and Ramadani, E. (2018). Web services: A comparison of soap and rest services. *Modern Applied Science*, 12.

Henkel, J. and Diwan, A. (2005). Catchup! capturing and replaying refactorings to support api evolution. *Int. Conf. on Software Engineering*, 27:274 – 283.

Hora, A., Etien, A., Anquetil, N., Ducasse, S., and Valente, M. (2014). Apievolutionminer: Keeping api evolution under control. *Int. Conf. on Software Maintenance, Reengineering, and Reverse Engineering.*

Huppe, S., Saied, M. A., and Sahraoui, H. (2017). Mining complex temporal api usage patterns: An evolutionary approach. In *2017 IEEE/ACM 39th International Conference on Software Engineering Companion (ICSE-C)*, pages 274–276.

Koçi, R., Franch, X., Jovanovic, P., and Abelló, A. (2021a). Improving web api usage logging. In Cherfi, S., Perini, A., and Nurcan, S., editors, *Research Challenges in Information Science*, pages 623–629, Cham. Springer International Publishing.

Koçi, R., Franch, X., Jovanovic, P., and Abelló, A. (2021b). Patternlens: Inferring evolutive patterns from web api usage logs. In Nurcan, S. and Korthaus, A., editors, *Intelligent Information Systems*, pages 146–153, Cham. Springer International Publishing.

Koçi, R., Franch, X., Jovanovic, P., and Abelló, A. (2019). Classification of changes in api evolution. In *2019 IEEE 23rd International Enterprise Distributed Object Computing Conference (EDOC)*, pages 243–249.

Koçi, R., Franch, X., Jovanovic, P., and Abelló, A. (2020). A data-driven approach to measure the usability of web apis. In *2020 46th Euromicro Conference on Software Engineering and Advanced Applications (SEAA)*, pages 64–71.

Lamothe, M. (2020). Bridging the divide between api users and api developers by mining public code repositories. In *2020 IEEE/ACM 42nd International Conference on Software Engineering: Companion Proceedings (ICSE-Companion)*, pages 178–181.

Lamothe, M., Guéhéneuc, Y.-G., and Shang, W. (2021). A systematic review of api evolution literature. *ACM Comput. Surv.*, 54(8).

Li, J., Xiong, Y., Liu, X., and Zhang, L. (2013). How does web service api evolution affect clients? *Int. Conf. on Web Services.*

Nguyen, H., Nguyen, T. T., Jr., G. W., Nguyen, A., Kim, M., and Nguyen, T. (2010). A graph-based approach to api usage adaptation. *ACM SIGPLAN Notices - OOPSLA '10*, 45:302–321.

Polák, M. and Holubová, I. (2015). Rest api management and evolution using mda. *Int. Conf. Proceeding Series*, 13:102–109.

Romano, D. and Pinzger, M. (2012). Analyzing the evolution of web services using fine-grained changes. In *2012 IEEE 19th International Conference on Web Services*, pages 392–399.

Sawant, A., Robbes, R., and Bacchelli, A. (2019). To react, or not to react: Patterns of reaction to api deprecation. *Empiric Software Engineering*, 24:3824–3870.

Sawant, A. A. and Bacchelli, A. (2015). A dataset for api usage. In *2015 IEEE/ACM 12th Working Conference on Mining Software Repositories*, pages 506–509.

Sohan, S., Anslow, C., and Maurer, F. (2015). A case study of web api evolution. *IEEE World Congress on Services*.

SOM RESEARCH LAB (2018). Apicomposer.

Wang, C., Yang, Y., Liu, H., and Kang, L. (2019). Statistical api completion based on code relevance mining. In *2019 IEEE Workshop on Mining and Analyzing Interaction Histories (MAINT)*, pages 7–13.

Wang, S., Keivanloo, I., and Zou, Y. (2014). How do developers react to restful api evolution? *Int. Conf. in Service-Oriented Computing*, 8831:245–259.

Wu, W., Adams, B., Guéhéneuc, Y., and Antoniol, G. (2014). Acua: Api change and usage auditor. In *Int. Conf. on Source Code Analysis and Manipulation*, pages 89–94.

Wu, W., Khomh, F., Adams, B., Guéhéneuc, Y., and Antoniol, G. (2016). An exploratory study of api changes and usages based on apache and eclipse ecosystems. *Emp. Softw. Eng.*, 21:2366–2412.

Xavier, L., Brito, A., Hora, A., and Valente, M. T. (2017). Historical and impact analysis of api breaking changes: A large-scale study. *Int. Conf. on Software Analysis, Evolution and Reengineering*, pages 138–147.

Yasmin, J., Tian, Y., and Yang, J. (2020). A first look at the deprecation of restful apis: An empirical study. In *2020 IEEE INTERNATIONAL CONFERENCE ON SOFTWARE MAINTENANCE AND EVOLUTION (ICSME 2020)*, Proceedings-IEEE International Conference on Software Maintenance, pages 151–161. IEEE; IEEE Comp Soc. 36th IEEE International Conference on Software Maintenance and Evolution (ICSME), ELECTR NETWORK, SEP 27-OCT 03, 2020.

Zhong, H., Xie, T., Zhang, L., Pei, J., and Mei, H. (2009). Mapo: Mining and recommending api usage patterns. *Europ. Conf. on Object-Oriented Programming*, 5653:318–343.

Cross-language Clone Detection for Mobile Apps

Stephannie Jimenez[1], **Gordana Rakic**[2], **Silvia Takahashi**[1], **Nicolás Cardozo**[1]

[1]Systems and Computing Engineering Department - Universidad de los Andes, Colombia

[2]Faculty of Sciences - University of Novi Sad, Serbia

{s.jimenez16,stakahas,n.cardozo}@uniandes.edu.co, gordana.rakic@dmi.uns.ac.rs

Abstract. *Clone detection provides insight about replicated fragments in a code base. With the rise of multi-language code bases, new techniques addressing cross-language code clone detection enable the analysis of polyglot systems. Such techniques have not yet been applied to the mobile apps' domain, which are naturally polyglot. Native mobile app developers must synchronize their code base in at least two different programming languages. App synchronization is a difficult and time-consuming maintenance task, as features can rapidly diverge between platforms, and feature identification must be performed manually. Our goal is to provide an analysis framework to reduce the impact of app synchronization. A first step in this direction consists on a structural algorithm for cross-language clone detection exploiting the idea behind enriched concrete syntax trees. Such trees are used as a common intermediate representation built from programming languages' grammars, to detect similarities between app code bases. Our technique finds code similarities with* 79% *precision for controlled tests where Type 1-3 clones are manually injected for the analysis of both single- and cross-language cases for Kotlin and Dart. We evaluate our tool on a corpus of 52 mobile apps identifying code similarities with a precision of* 65% *to* 84% *for the full application logic.*

1. Introduction

In software systems it is usual to find repeated code fragments, also known as code clones. Large modern software systems' code base has 20% to 50% clones [Ain et al. 2019]. Normally, clones are innocuous, but add complexity to a code base and induce higher maintenance costs. For instance, the time to add a feature or fix a bug increases as the code requiring changes may be replicated across multiple modules, requiring the propagation of the changes to all clone locations. Moreover, assuring that the applied changes are consistent across clones remains a challenge [Mondal et al. 2020].

Clones refer to similar but not necessarily identical code fragments. Clones are classified into four hierarchical types: *Type 1* or *exact clones*, refer to identical code fragments not including code comments, layout, or whitespaces. *Type 2* or *renamed clones*, refer to code fragments that have a similar structure or equivalent syntax without including identifiers, types, or literals. *Type 3* or *near miss clones*, refer to fragments that have been altered further, such as adding or removing statements and changes in whitespaces, identifiers, layout, comments, and types. *Type 4* or *semantic clones*, refer to code fragments that are functionally similar, but implemented as syntactic variants [Ain et al. 2019]. Figure 1 exemplifies the differences among clone types in a multi-language setting for Kotlin[1] and

[1] https://kotlinlang.org

Dart[2] Line 1 shows a Type 1 clone for an assignment of variable `i`. Line 3 shows a Type 2 clone for an assignment where the variable names differ. Line 5 shows a Type 3 clone as the increment operation changes its form. Lines 7-9 show a Type 4 clone where the syntax changes completely but both code fragments increase the value of a variable by 9.

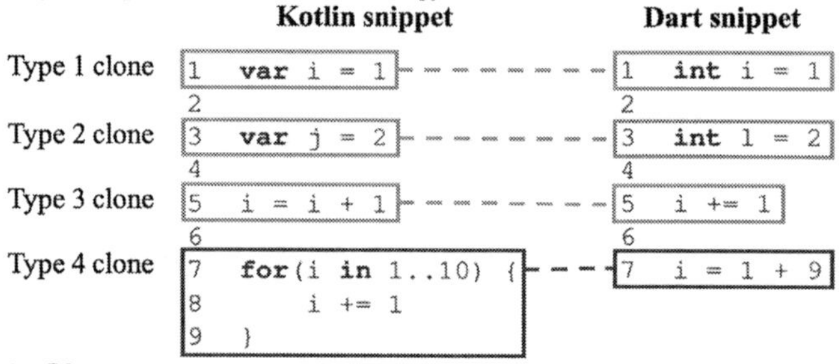

Figure 1. Clone type examples between Kotlin and Dart code bases.

In addition to the four clone types, clones may also be grouped in two families, *structural clones* and *function clones*. Structural clones refer to code fragments that follow the syntactic structure of a given language with a syntactic boundary. Function clones are limited to the procedure or function granularity level [Ain et al. 2019].

Clone detection techniques can be advantageous in code plagiarism, intellectual property protection, or code quality analysis [Ain et al. 2019]. Another example of the usefulness of clone detection tools is that of bug fixing. As mentioned previously, fixing a bug on a cloned functionality is costly. Identifying all similar code snippets to a bug will reduce the technical debt for the development team, as they can incorporate the fix in all existing clones, or refactor the code to reuse a single instance of the clone.

In mobile app development, it is common to find separate code bases using different programming languages to target mobile platforms natively (*i.e.,* iOS and Android), while keeping the functionality between platforms as close as possible. However, app features across platforms often differ due to the separate development teams targeting each platform, and the available platform APIs. We highlight three challenges with maintaining separate code bases for different platforms. First, developers need to ensure that the features across the platforms are equivalent. Second, bug fixes knowledge needs to be transferred across platforms. Third, the maintenance costs of two development teams for each platform is high. To address these challenges, cross-platform code generation frameworks are becoming increasingly popular. However, such approaches may result in a limited use of specific native APIs that may not translate easily across platforms [Patkar et al. 2020].

As a counterpart to multi-platform code generation, the use of a tool to help development teams synchronize feature evolution across mobile platforms is desired. Furthermore, we argue that a cross-language analysis tool that keeps track of equivalent code fragments constitutes a first step to achieve this goal. However, currently no such tool exists. This paper presents the first algorithm and tool for cross-language clone detection for mobile apps, called OUT OF STEP. The main contributions of OUT OF STEP are:

- A generalized model for Enriched Concrete Syntax Trees (eCSTs) (Section 2.1).
- A new clone detection algorithm and metric based on structural clone detection using eCSTs to abstract commonalities across languages (Sections 2.2-2.4).
- A corpus for the evaluation of cross-language clone detection including basic examples, 30 sorting algorithms exemplars, and 52 medium and large mobile apps (Section 3).

[2] `https://dart.dev`

2. OUT OF STEP

This section describes our proposed approach for cross-language clone detection. OUT OF STEP follows a structured approach for clone detection based on the comparison of eCSTs generated from the grammars of modern mobile programming languages as Kotlin and Dart.[3] First, we present the generalized definition of eCSTs. Second, we describe the underlying algorithm and metric to compare eCST structures used to determine clones.

2.1. Enriched Concrete Syntax Trees

To compare of code bases written in different languages we first build an intermediate representation based on the languages' grammars. For our representation, we extend eCSTs by introducing new node types, which allow us to capture the general abstractions of the languages used for mobile app development. Concretely, we use the ANTLR4 [Parr 2013] parse generator to generate the eCSTs focusing on the standard grammar definitions of Kotlin, and Dart. This is applicable to other languages, as Swift, Java, or C++.

2.1.1. eCST Definition

Given that the generated syntax trees may result in highly divergent tree structures, we define a tree structure that is able to capture more information of the input source code. Our solution extends the original proposal of eCST [Rakić and Budimac 2013], with *universal*, *advance*, and *stop* nodes, to uniformly shape trees, structure grammar elements as a group, and ease sub-tree structure comparisons.

Originally, eCSTs are extracted from the generated Abstract Syntax Tree (AST) by the parser. eCSTs introduce universal nodes to shape trees for a Concrete Syntax Tree (CST) or Parse Tree (PT) [Budimac et al. 2012, Vislavski et al. 2018]. In our case, eCSTs are generated directly from PTs and contain a subset of the original universal nodes, as well as a set of mobile app specific nodes (introduced as domain specific universal nodes [Rakić and Budimac 2013]).

Every syntactic rule defined in the languages' grammar is translated to one node. Each node type of the eCST is designed to be as generic as possible, with the objective that rules from different languages generate the same universal node types. Yet, we are required to faithfully represent all expressions defined in a program.

The eCST structure extends the original AST structure by holding more information at nodes, in pursuit of standardizing programming languages to a critical set of features (*e.g.,* grammar concepts). In order to achieve the required behavior, we extend the standard ANTLR4 parsers and lexers for each of the languages. Using this approach, we are no longer required to build programs' ASTs to then translate them to the eCST. Rather, we build the eCSTs directly from the PT generated for each language.

Additionally, eCST nodes keep a keyword token stored as plain text, and a mapping to the line and column of the original source code file in which the keyword appears. With this information, we are able to map the final clones to the original source code file from the tree representation. Moreover, having the actual keyword text helps us recognize

[3]available at: `https://github.com/FLAGlab/CloneDetection/`

the appropriate category of the clones (*i.e.,* Type 1, 2 or 3). As an example, if a node is of type `comparison_operator`, the keyword text information in the node token should be one of the <, <=, >, or >= operators.

Figure 2 shows the tree structure including the new node information. Node types are shown to their right, and the token is shown inside each node. Tokens' line and column are omitted from the figure for clarity. Universal nodes ease tree comparison and analysis by making their structures more similar. Flat structures, as Dart's, now contain information on eCST nodes that will help us map clones (*e.g.,* `assignment_operator`).

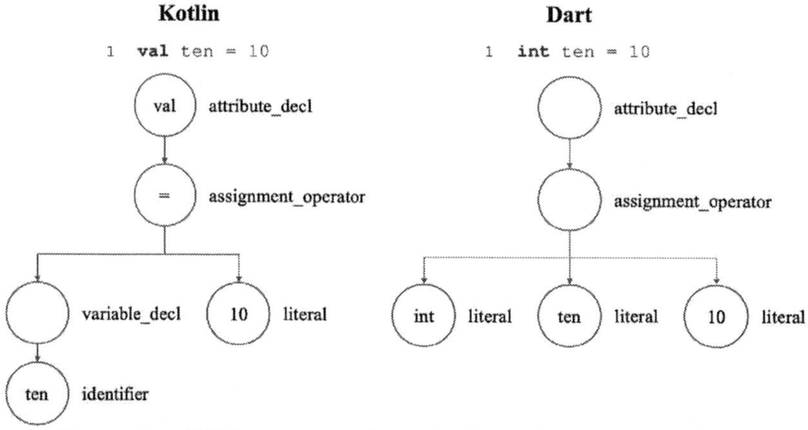

Figure 2. eCST examples for a Kotlin (left) and Dart (right)

In our extension of the eCST, we introduce *advance nodes*. The purpose of these nodes is to group structures of the grammar that should be together. For example, to group the body of the `for loop`, increasing the trees's hierarchy, as in Figure 3. Advance node `body`, in the loop Dart example, helps us create a parent structure, making the grammar more hierarchical than it originally is. The grammar elements represented with advance nodes include `type`, `body`, and `expression`. Advance nodes are used as information sources, but they are not taken into account in the actual clone detection. A full list of the nodes introduced for eCSTs is available in the project's documentation.

Given that clone types exclude comments, layout, and white spaces, these elements are excluded in the generation of eCSTs. The parser focuses on grammar rules to generate the eCST from the associated code, as in Figure 3.

```
main(int num) {
    int sum = 0;
    for (i in i..num){
        // Count numbers
        // sum = sum + 1;
        sum += 1;
    }
}
```

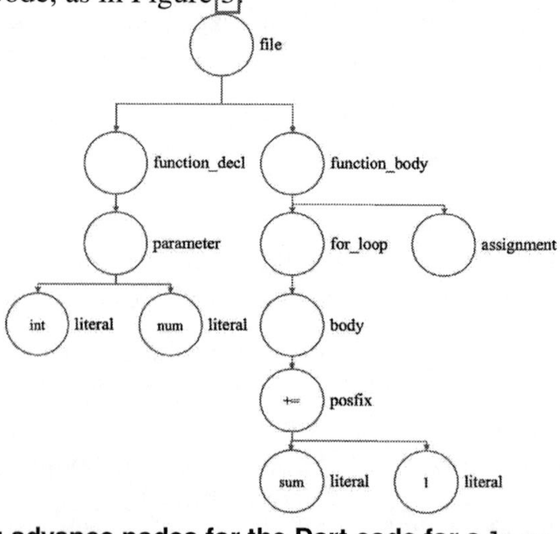

Figure 3. Increased hierarchy using advance nodes for the Dart code for a `loop`

2.1.2. eCST Comparison

Multiple tree comparison algorithms exist in the literature (*cf.* Section 4), the approach taken in OUT OF STEP is to find similar subtree structures between eCST pairs. Under this approach, a pair of similar trees may not be completely identical in their node types, but the types may be closely related. This resemblance is defined via a new mapping, where one type of node can map to multiple other nodes. For example, the similar nodes for the type `parameter_list` will include `value_parameter_list` and itself. All relationships between nodes are established in pursuit of finding Type 3 clones. The complete list of nodes' similarity mapping is also available in the repository's documentation.

Additionally, we define *stop nodes*. These nodes are of special importance in the tree comparison process, as they break down the complete eCST into smaller subtrees to ease comparison. The universal node types that are represented as *stop nodes* are: *function declaration*, *function body*, *class declaration*, and *class body*. As these structures are normally present in scripts, the detector can use them to identify clones, independent and unbiased of their position in the eCST's hierarchy.

The motivation of stop nodes' fragmentation is centered in the idea that clones can be disperse throughout the files. This means that is not necessary for the first function of the first file to map to a clone in the first function on the second file. In this way, having separated substructures of the eCST enables us to compare them among each other and find clones that could map to different locations across source code files.

2.2. Code Clones Detection

The generality of the eCST intermediate representation enables us to map code written in any programming language to this structure. That is, any two eCST trees use the same set of universal nodes making them comparable and agnostic to the specific programming language they abstract.

Using the fragmentation technique introduced with *stop nodes*, multiple subtrees become comparable. For every pair of trees their nodes are visited to see if they are clones of each other, based on the similarity mapping. Once two nodes' types are deemed equivalent, we compare their tokens for (simple) equality. In the case where the type of the nodes is equivalent and the token is exactly the same, we mark them as Type 1 clones. If the type of the nodes is equivalent but the tokens are not equal, we mark them as Type 2 clones. If the nodes are only similar, then they are Type 3 clones.

2.3. Filter Final Code Clones

As we are able to differentiate among clone types, we posit a similarity metric for code fragments based on the number of clones detected. This metric is the weighted sum of the total number of clones found for each type, where their importance follows the restriction that clone types are weighted as Type 1 > Type 2 > Type 3, as shown in Equation (1).

$$m = 3 * T_1 + 2 * T_2 + T_3 \qquad (1)$$

This metric is defined for filtering the possible clones detected in the comparison of all the possible pair-wise combinations of the subtrees. In this way, we are able to define the closest pair among all the possibilities. Our metric shows the most identical clones, and gives precedence to exact clones over others clone types.

For complex and hierarchical structures, a merging mechanism is used where we define if the root node of a tree is similar to some other node by counting the number of clones that are within its children nodes. In this way, we are able to recognize not only the clones that are in the tree leafs, but also clones in intermediate nodes.

Figure 4 exemplifies how clone type weight broadcasting helps us determine when a subtree is more similar to another. In this example, the leaf nodes broadcast their type weights up to the `func_decl` nodes. This way, the corresponding function clone pairs are based on leaf nodes' precedence by their broadcasting rather than by their parent nodes.

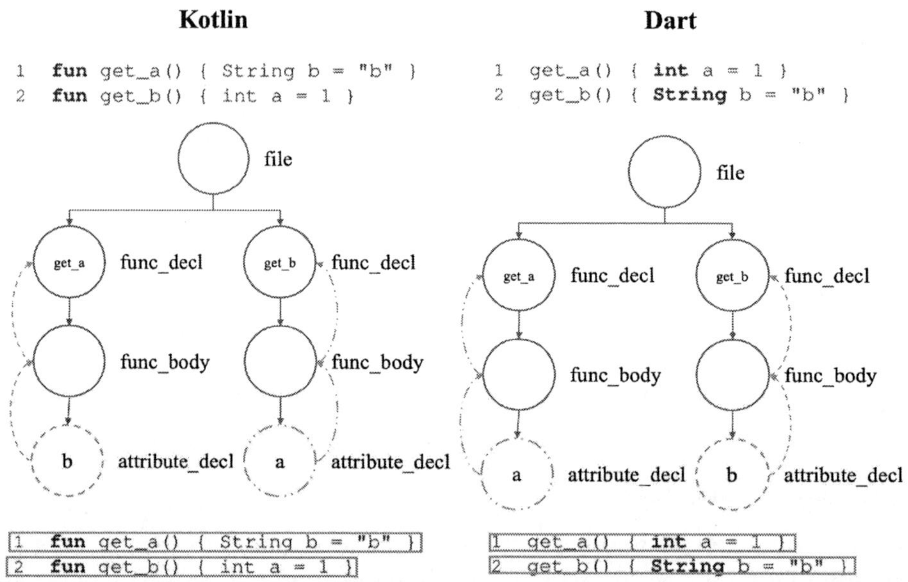

Figure 4. Broadcast method determining the similarity of sub-tree structures

The algorithm returns a list of all detected clones. Each clone is defined as a pair of tokens with a mapping to the original files, the actual string, line and column number, eCST node type, and clone type. All analysis information is reported back to users.

2.4. Out of Step Implementation

The implementation of our proposed approach (*i.e.,* tool and algorithm) exhibits different improvements when compared to other clone detection tools. In this section we describe the details of Out of Step in comparison with other tools.

A key feature of Out of Step, not present in any other tool, is the support for complete programming projects. Normally, existing tools receive as input two specific source files to compare, which might be limiting for large code bases, where users may want to detect clones across full programming projects (*e.g.,* to check feature compatibility, or plagiarism verification). Out of Step can take multiple files as input, as well as whole projects. This enhancement is presented considering the exploration of mobile apps, where developers may need to compare the complete application source code. To attain this need, given a complete project as input, Out of Step performs an exhaustive pair-wise comparison of all the possible source code files, finding all possible clones in the application, which comes with a high complexity ($O(n^3)$) of the comparison algorithm.

Additionally, the Out of Step analysis parametrizes the amount of clones to analyze in the algorithm –that is, to view all detected clones, or to use clone filtering.

This can be useful when the motivation of using OUT OF STEP is to detect repeated code fragments rather than just the most identical fragments in the code base.

Finally, we isolate grammars, with their parsers and lexers, so that adding a new programming languages is completely modular, requiring new folder with the grammar definition to include it in the tool The grammar definition must follow the ANTLR4 specification, as it is the dependency we use to automatically generate langauges' lexer and parser, otherwise a custom lexer and parser must be provided. To complete the integration of new languages, we require a manual mapping between the language's grammar rules and the universal nodes. Not all the grammar rules need to generate a node in the eCST; this depends on the desired granularity of generated trees.

3. OUT OF STEP Evaluation

We evaluate OUT OF STEP in two phases. First we validate clone detection correctness by means of the basic language features for Kotlin, and Dart. Second, we validate the effectiveness of OUT OF STEP to analyze complete mobile app projects. We close this section with a discussion about our results[4]

3.1. Clone Detection in Structural Elements

To evaluate our clone detection algorithm we first focus in analyzing the basic abstractions across Kotlin and Dart. The goal of this evaluation is to correctly identify clones using general universal nodes in the base case examples of the languages. Due to space constraints, here we show only the case for loops and classes in Kotlin, and Dart. We introduce Type 1 and Type 2 clones to our examples, to verify their correct detection.

3.1.1. Loop nodes

Managing loops is an interesting case for universal nodes. Loop abstractions are defined using different keywords in Kotlin, Dart, and Swift (*e.g.*, `for`, `while`). In OUT OF STEP we process loop abstractions as semantically equivalent, and define them as Type 3 clones. To evaluate this, we manually inject Type 1 and Type 3 clones in our tests.

Snippet 1. Kotlin for loop - version A

```
var sum = 0;
for (i in 1..100)
   sum = sum + i
```

Snippet 2. Kotlin while loop - version B

```
var sum = 0
var i = 1
while (i <= 100) {
   sum = sum + i
   i = i + 1
}
```

Snippet 3. Dart for loop - version A

```
int sum = 0;
for (int i = 1; i <= 100; i++)
   sum = sum + i;
```

Snippet 4. Dart while loop - version B

```
int sum = 0;
int i = 1;
while ( i <= 100) {
   sum = sum + i;
   i = i + 1;
}
```

[4]The full evaluation is available as an online appendix https://flaglab.github.io/CloneDetection/ All evaluation data is available at: https://doi.org/10.5281/zenodo.5228822

The analysis for Kotlin (Snippets 1 and 2), and Dart (Snippets 3 and 4) in the same language results in two Type 3 clones. These match the **for** and **while** statements and the i variable declaration. The clone for the postfix statement i++ and the variable assignment i = i + 1 is not correctly detected as a Type 3 clone due to their node representations in the eCST, an assignment_operator unary node, and a binary node respectively. Nonetheless, we identify the complete **for** and **while** blocks as clones of each other, as the algorithm broadcasts clones inside the body of blocks. Additionally, OUT OF STEP identifies the declarations and assignment of variables as Type 1 clones in Line 1 of both snippets, and Line 3 of version A with Line 4 of version B.

The cross-language comparison between code versions A and B is also successful in detecting the corresponding clones. This is because the node information and the eCST structure are the same for the two code snippets. Every node is matched to its corresponding node on the other eCST, even though the programming languages differ. When comparing any A vs any B versions, we find that there are Type 3 clones for the **for** and **while** statements, and the definition of variable i. Additionally, we can find the Type 1 clones for the declaration and assignment of the sum variable, as before.

In the loop analysis, OUT OF STEP finds a couple of Type 2 false positives, due to the two assignments that are present in versions B of the code. In this case, the detection algorithm points to the body of the **for** and **while** statements to be clones. This happens because the intermediate type node for both of them is the same. The exact same behavior takes place with the assignment before the loop statement in both cases.

3.2. Clone Detection in Classes and Functions

Given that our proposed algorithm detects Type 1, 2, and 3 clones in simple code snippets, we turn our attention to evaluate its performance with more complex code structures that involve nested eCSTs with a large variety of universal nodes.

3.2.1. Classes

To identify clones in classes and objects, we implement a program that creates and instantiates a class in the main function. Type 1 clones are inserted in this example for versions A (Snippets 5 and 7), and B (Snippets 6 and 8) for the two languages.

Snippet 5. Kotlin class definition - version A

```
fun main(args: Array<String>){
  Person A = Person("A")
  Person B = Person("B")
}
class Person(val name : String){
  fun present() = "Yes"
  fun greet(other: String) = other
}
```

Snippet 6. Kotlin class definition - version B

```
class Person(val name: String){
  fun present(){
    return "Yes"
  }
  fun greet(other: String){
    return other
  }
}
fun main(args: Array<String>){
  Person A = Person("A")
  Person B = Person("B")
}
```

Snippet 7. Dart class definition - version A

```
main(){
  Person A = Person("A");
  Person B = Person("B");
}
class Person{
  Person(String name){
    this.name = name;
  }
  String present(){
    return "Yes";
  }
  void greet(String other){
    return other;
  }
}
```

Snippet 8. Dart class definition - version B

```
class NestingPerson { class Person{
    Person(String name){
      this.name = name;
    }
    String present(){
        return "Yes";
    }
    void greet(String other){
        return other;
    }
} }
main(){
    Person A = Person("A");
    Person B = Person("B");
}
```

The version of the class definitions are similar to their counterparts in the other language. We use two different syntax forms for Kotlin to show that we support the latest major version of the language. Additionally, we swap the order of the class and main declarations in the file and scope the `Person` class differently in Dart. This, to test our algorithm is agnostic to the elements' definition order and scope. OUT OF STEP is able to find exact clones in different file locations, scopes, or eCST hierachy.

The analysis of the two versions for a single language yields a complete match of Type 1 clones throughout the document. This is true even for Kotlin, where we use different syntactic elements to define the same class. When comparing Kotlin versions A and B, we also identify a clone in the definition of the function `greet` and `main`. This is because of the similarity in their definition and structure making them a false positive.

In the cross language analysis, when versions B are compared OUT OF STEP performs better than with versions A. This is due to the compressed syntax of Kotlin, which changes slightly the structure of the eCST. Notwithstanding, in general, our algorithm can detect the exact same classes and the `main` function.

This experiment reinforces the case where the code is exactly the same but it differs in definition order and scope. This means our algorithm detects clones using the eCST structure even if the root nodes of the clones are at different tree levels.

3.3. Clone Detection in Mobile Apps

We further evaluate the clone detection for complete mobile apps. To do this, we built a corpus of 52 functionally equivalent apps implemented in Kotlin (26) and Dart (26), spanning different application domains. The apps are extracted from two sources: 40 apps come from of a mobile app development course taught at Unandes between 2018 and 2021. For the course each app must be developed for Android and iOS, normally using two development teams of 2-3 students per language/platform. The remaining 12 apps are extracted from GitHub. We make sure these repositories are maintained by the same development team or are under the same organization, to assure feature equivalence.

We verify that all apps compile and run using the standard IDEs for each language, *i.e.,* Android Studio for Kotlin, and the Flutter framework for Dart. The selected apps for

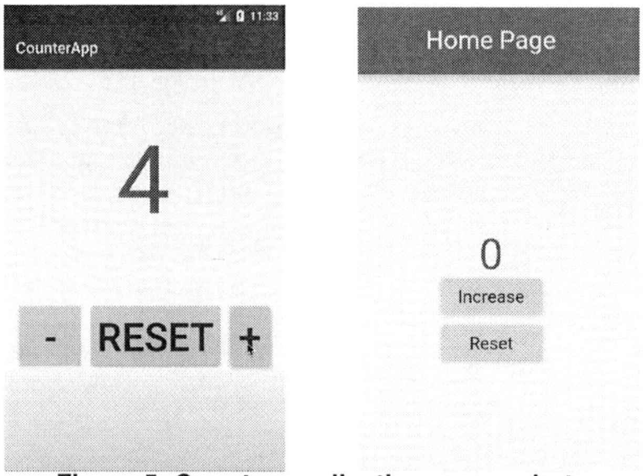

Figure 5. Counter application screenshots

our evaluation vary in application domain (covering 9 domains), and size of the code bases. Since the previous evaluation scenarios used small codebases, we are interested in medium to large apps for this evaluation (with an average of 3100 LOC per application) spanning over several files (an average of 41 files per app). We only take into account the main logic of the project, not including any presentation, configuration, or GUI files.

The analysis between mobile apps is exemplified by a counter application developed by the authors (bold in Table 1). The app counts the number of times a button on the screen is pressed. A screenshot for the Kotlin and Dart versions is shown in Figure 5.

The differences between the apps are immediate. First, the Kotlin version has one extra feature than its Dart counterpart, as users can reduce the counter. However, we expect for the clone detector to be able to find similar features that exist between the two code bases. This follows from the algorithm's clone detection through a pairwise comparison of all files and the functions therein. The result of such exhaustive comparison results in the detection of a large amount of clones.

Snippet 9. Counter app main function in Kotlin

```
class MainActivity:AppCompatActivity(){
   var count = 0
   override fun onCreate(savedInstanceState:Bundle?){
      super.onCreate(savedInstanceState)
      setContentView(R.layout.activity_main)
      textView.text = count.toString()
   }
}
```

Snippet 10. Counter app main function in Dart

```
class MyApp extends StatelessWidget{
  @override Widget build(BuildContext context){
    return MaterialApp(title: 'Flutter Demo',
      theme: ThemeData(primarySwatch: Colors.blue),
      home: MyHomePage(title: 'Home Page'),
    );}
}
```

Our algorithm is capable to find one correct Type 3 clone across the whole code base (that in Snippets 9 and 10). However the algorithms finds common nodes across the two implementations resulting in many small clones identified for variables and single lines of code. This causes over 60 false positives upon the manual inspection of the code. The high rate of false positives is due, in part, to the frameworks used to implement each of the mobile apps. The implementation frameworks have their own independent APIs, which change the functions used to achieve a particular task in the different programming languages. This has an important impact in the way in which we build the eCST. For example, Snippet 11 shows the signature for the functions used to retrieve an app's splash screen. These functions are semantically equivalent. However, their syntactic difference implies a difference in the the eCST's location and shape. A similar analysis from the manual inspection of OUT OF STEP's results on the other evaluated apps confirms the behavior of our tool, obtaining a precision of 0.65 to 0.84 for mobile app clone detection.

Snippet 11. Kotlin's and Dart's API usage

```
public final SplashScreen getSplashScreen() //Kotlin code
public SplashScreen provideSplashScreen() //Dart code
```

Table 1 shows the clones found by OUT OF STEP in the evaluation of mobile apps. Given the size of the apps, we do not disaggregate Type 2 and Type 3 clones or identify false positives, as these tasks are manual.

Table 1. Cross-language clone detection results for the mobile apps corpus

App Type	Avg. LOC		# of Files		Total	Type 1	Type 2 & 3
	Dart	Kotlin	Dart	Kotlin			
Shopping	1220	3180	6	51	192395	66566	125829
Health	5463	4776	46	48	733716	167673	566043
Health	2956	2236	29	21	110573	27768	82805
Games	2499	3408	20	40	260244	65166	195121
Productivity	4220	3321	85	47	584825	161981	422844
Shopping	3449	1913	74	29	240201	57909	182386
Library	3909	2432	30	32	219373	51978	167395
Shopping	3468	2951	39	84	327299	90354	236945
Shopping	8139	3771	72	84	803354	210749	592605
Health	3660	1836	28	40	106931	27068	79863
Health	4215	1087	39	23	136150	34199	101951
Bookings	4953	3433	44	50	463125	112528	350597
Services	3927	2700	27	31	178192	38384	139808
Lifestyle	3123	1547	21	26	92305	27354	64951
Productivity	2429	1652	21	26	140574	31716	108858
Bookings	1045	1982	25	67	83825	26741	57084
Discounts	2380	1781	37	27	120956	30090	90866
Pets	5754	2615	41	51	250769	70000	180769
Pets	3039	1724	23	26	96517	24828	71689
Bookings	5490	2538	58	81	564947	150226	415011
Productivity	136	104	1	1	149	23	126
Productivity	144	104	1	1	149	23	126
Productivity	**57**	**23**	**1**	**1**	**90**	**25**	**65**
Information	367	2383	6	47	60215	25139	35076
Lifestyle	510	1831	14	59	55591	18471	37120
SmartHome	759	3248	9	33	111810	28052	83758

3.4. Discussion

Running OUT OF STEP on different types of projects across languages for mobile platforms shows the effective clone identification even when dealing with complex project structures and large code bases. Section 3.1 verifies that the basic structures of the two languages are correctly identified as clones. Moreover, from the results in Section 3.2, our algorithm obtains a precision between $[0.65, 0.84]$ for large code bases, demonstrating the correct identification of code clones across languages uniformly in the two data sets.

In the case of mobile apps, we observe that OUT OF STEP finds clones covering complete code bases, as direct consequence of the exhaustive behavior of our algorithm. However, we identify two limitations in the clone detection for mobile apps. First, eCST nodes sometimes lack information to be able to determine whether a code structure can be marked as Type 2 or Type 3 clone. This can reduce the precision of our algorithm, as well as increase required manual verifications. Second, for mobile apps, OUT OF STEP works strictly with the standard definition of the programming languages. As a consequence we do not take into account additional UI or configuration files (*e.g.,* `.xml` files) that developers may use to define the apps' layout. Therefore, we do not detect clones of GUI elements because they are not programmatically defined in the code base. GUI clone identification can give way to further feature divergence analysis across applications.

To enhance the clone detection for mobile platforms, we can extend the languages' grammars to incorporate specific aspects of the UI and native frameworks used in the development. For instance, in the case of Dart, the programming language grammar can be extended to have new eCST nodes defined by the Flutter framework. Taking into account all the new syntax, we can have nodes for threads, GUI elements, and mobile events. This means that our comparison algorithm for the eCST will have more information available, and therefore raise the precision of our algorithm.

4. Related Work

This section discusses existing strategies for clone detection in both the single-language and multi-language settings. We compare these strategies with our work.

Existing clone detection tools focus on a single programming language, and are not directly applicable to our case. There is a vast diversity in the target language to analyze; with prominence in C/C++, Java, JavaScript, and Python tools [Roy et al. 2009]. Existing tools aim for language independence so that clone detection is independent from tools' language, still, detection is possible for fragments of a single language [Cheng et al. 2017]. We note the approaches for single language clone detection are not easily transferable to the multi-language case, and therefore the algorithms and metrics are not comparable with OUT OF STEP.

C2D2 is one of the first approaches to detect clones across the .NET language family [Kraft et al. 2008]. Very similarly to our approach, C2D2 applies a hybrid method on tokens and ASTs for clone detection. However, contrary to our approach where any language may be supported, C2D2 may support only .Net languages which is a restriction caused by the intermediate representation chosen. A similar analysis of .NET languages uses a representation based on the Common Intermediate Language (CIL) [Al-Omari et al. 2012]. CIL is a stack-based machine-independent object-oriented assembly language focused on .Net languages. Again, this tool differs from OUT OF STEP as it applies the Longest Common Sub-sequence (LCS) algorithm for detection, which can be restrictive in the detection of Type 2 and 3 clones.

LICCA [Vislavski et al. 2018] uses the original version of eCSTs to detect clones across different language types (*e.g.,* Java, Scheme). The eCST structure used in LICCA is the base for OUT OF STEP. As a consequence, this is the approach closest to our proposal. However, in OUT OF STEP we extend the generation of eCSTs to start directly from the PT and not use the AST. Moreover, we extend the definition of nodes in eCSTs (universal, advance, and stop nodes) to enable finer-grained analysis of tree sub-structures. Finally, while LICCA applies the LCS algorithm, our detection algorithm relies on tree mappings and broadcasting to map different node types, giving us more flexibility and possibilities to compare trees from across languages.

CLCSD [Zhang et al. 2020] is a hybrid framework for cross-language clone detection based on flowcharts as a means to abstract language constructs. Flowcharts in CLCSD have a tree-like structure similar to our eCSTs, standardizing different program structures. However, the standardization of flowcharts restricts the analysis for the base language grammar (Java and Python), not extensible to multiple different languages as OUT OF STEP. The closest approach to OUT OF STEP uses unified PTs generated from a language grammar linearized and pre-processed at the function level, comparing the linearized sequences [Nichols et al. 2019]. However, this approach differs from OUT OF STEP in the detection algorithm.

In addition, one of the main problems with existing clone detection tools is their lack of support [Walker et al. 2020]. We identified 20 clone detection tools from the literature, summarized in Table 2 with their maintainability state. Out of all the tools, 9 where downloadable, and only 3 of them could be installed and gave an output to a test file. Furthermore, most of the tools are available do not support the latest versions of the target programming languages. This means that to analyze code exploiting new features, the tools will return unexpected results.

Table 2. Existing clone detection tools

#	Name	Multi-language	Type	Runs
1	NICAD [Cordy and Roy 2011]	No	Textual	No
2	CCFinderX [Kamiya et al. 2002]	No	Lexical	No
3	Simian [Harris 2018]	No	Textual	No
4	Duploc [Gordon and Bannier 2021]	No	Textual	Yes
5	SourcererCC [Sajnani et al. 2016]	No	Lexical	No
6	iClones [Göde and Koschke 2009]	No	Lexical	No
7	PMD/CPD [pmd 2021]	No	Lexical	Yes
8	Deckard [Lingxiao et al. 2018]	No	Tree-based	No
9	Licca [Vislavski et al. 2018]	**Yes**	Hybrid	**Yes**

5. Conclusion and Future Work

Cross-language clone detection can enhance coed quality analysis, bug detection and feature divergence for polyglot software systems. Currently there are a small set of working tools for cross-language clone detection, mainly focused on classic languages (*e.g.,* Java, C++, Python). We identify a need for new algorithms and tools capable of performing such task on modern languages. In this work, we propose an approach, with its accompanying functional tool, for the detection of Type 1, 2, and 3 clones across mobile programming languages. Our approach to cross-language clone detection, OUT OF STEP, uses a mixture of the abstract representation of programs based on their programming language grammars, and the textual code. For this purpose, we posit an extension to eCSTs that uses universal node types, where tree nodes carry token information. This helps us to explore the code and find the best corresponding clone matches.

The evaluation results confirm the main contribution of OUT OF STEP as an effective tool to detect clones across languages: (1) detecting clones for programming languages' main features with precision of over 79%, and (2) detecting clones with a precision of 65% to 84% for large mobile app code bases. Additionally, we posit a new corpus for cross-language clone detection, as no comprehensive data set exist to date, which is unfavorable for algorithm comparison. The corpus is used to contrast the divergence in application examples and target programming languages and application domains not covered by existing tools. Our corpus, evaluates basic language features, known domain algorithms, and equivalent mobile apps to maintain a common standard across languages.

OUT OF STEP is a first effective approach and tool for cross-language clone detection for mobile apps. While our results are promising, we identify further improvements for our approach. In the analysis of mobile apps, it is necessary to extend the eCST to include characteristics specific to mobile GUIs and frameworks. This will enable us to identify clones for GUI elements, threads, and mobile events. Another approach to consider is to investigate the comparison of the code not from the source, but once it is compiled to an intermediate or native representation, removing the layer of mobile frameworks. The main idea behind these improvements is to standardize eCSTs so that analyses do not diverge across languages, and therefore increase the precision of our algorithm. Additionally, we can introduce new tree transformations for fragments in which we can manipulate and reorder statements as to reduce the number of comparisons improving the complexity of the algorithm. Finally, we will extend the coverage of OUT OF STEP to include Swift (currently under development) to cover all languages for mobile platforms.

References

(2021). PMD: An extensible cross-language static code analyzer.

Ain, Q. U., Butt, W. H., Anwar, M. W., Azam, F., and Maqbool, B. (2019). A Systematic Review on Code Clone Detection. *IEEE Access*, 7:86121–86144.

Al-Omari, F., Keivanloo, I., Roy, C. K., and Rilling, J. (2012). Detecting clones across microsoft. net programming languages. In *2012 19th Working Conference on Reverse Engineering*, pages 405–414. IEEE.

Budimac, Z., Rakić, G., and Savić, M. (2012). Ssqsa architecture. In *Balkan Conference in Informatics*, BCI'12, page 287–290, New York, NY, USA. ACM.

Cheng, X., Peng, Z., Jiang, L., Zhong, H., Yu, H., and Zhao, J. (2017). Clcminer: detecting cross-language clones without intermediates. *IEICE TRANSACTIONS on Information and Systems*, 100(2):273–284.

Cordy, J. R. and Roy, C. K. (2011). The NiCad Clone Detector. In *IEEE International Conference on Program Comprehension*, pages 219–220.

Göde, N. and Koschke, R. (2009). Incremental Clone Detection. In *European Conference on Software Maintenance and Reengineering*, SMR'09, pages 219–228.

Gordon, S. and Bannier, B. (2021). xsgordon/duplo-fork: C/C++/Java Duplicate Source Code Block Finder.

Harris, S. (2018). Simian - Similarity Analyser — Duplicate Code Detection for the Enterprise — Overview.

Kamiya, T., Kusumoto, S., and Inoue, K. (2002). CCFinder: A multilinguistic token-based code clone detection system for large scale source code. *IEEE Transactions on Software Engineering*, 28(7):654–670.

Kraft, N. A., Bonds, B. W., and Smith, R. K. (2008). Cross-language clone detection. In *SEKE*, pages 54–59.

Lingxiao, J., Ghassan, M., Zhendong, S., and Stephane, G. (2018). skyhover/Deckard: Code clone detection; clone-related bug detection; sematic clone analysis.

Mondal, M., Roy, C. K., and Schneider, K. A. (2020). A survey on clone refactoring and tracking. *Journal of Systems and Software*, 159(110429):27.

Nichols, L., Emre, M., and Hardekopf, B. (2019). Structural and nominal cross-language clone detection. In Hähnle, R. and van der Aalst, W., editors, *Fundamental Approaches to Software Engineering*, FASE'19, pages 247–263. Springer International Publishing.

Parr, T. (2013). *The Definitive ANTLR 4 Reference*, volume 1. 1 edition.

Patkar, N., Ghafari, M., Nierstrasz, O., and Hotomski, S. (2020). Caveats in eliciting mobile app requirements. In *Proceedings of the Evaluation and Assessment in Software Engineering*, EASE'20, pages 180–189, New York, NY, USA. ACM.

Rakić, G. and Budimac, Z. (2013). Introducing enriched concrete syntax trees. In *Proceedings of the International Multiconference on Information Society*, pages 211–214.

Roy, C. K., Cordy, J. R., and Koschke, R. (2009). Comparison and evaluation of code clone detection techniques and tools: A qualitative approach. *Science of Computer Programming*, 74(7):470–495.

Sajnani, H., Saini, V., Svajlenko, J., Roy, C. K., and Lopes, C. V. (2016). SourcererCC: Scaling code clone detection to big-code. In *International Conference on Software Engineering*, pages 1157–1168. IEEE Computer Society.

Vislavski, T., Rakić, G., Cardozo, N., and Budimac, Z. (2018). Licca: A tool for cross-language clone detection. In *International Conference on Software Analysis, Evolution and Reengineering*, SANER'18, pages 512–516. IEEE.

Walker, A., Cerny, T., and Song, E. (2020). Open-source tools and benchmarks for code-clone detection. *ACM SIGAPP Applied Computing Review*, 19(4):28–39.

Zhang, F., Li, L., Liu, C., and Zeng, Q. (2020). Flow Chart Generation-Based Source Code Similarity Detection Using Process Mining. *Scientific Programming*, 2020.

Using Software Architecture Descriptions to Detect Architectural Smells at Design Time

Everton Cavalcante, Thais Batista

Federal University of Rio Grande do Norte
Natal, Brazil

everton.cavalcante@ufrn.br, thaisbatista@gmail.com

Abstract. *Architectural smells are decisions made at the software architecture level, whether intentional or not, that may negatively impact the quality of a software system. In the literature, architectural smells are identified mainly by relying on the source code or other implementation artifacts. However, architectural smells could be detected at design time, even before employing implementation efforts and preventing them from being reflected at the system implementation. This research investigates how software architecture descriptions realized through architecture description languages (ADLs) can be used to identify architectural smells at design time. This work focuses on how architectural smells manifest and can be detected in SysADL, an ADL that allows describing both structure and behavior of software architectures using standardized diagrams from the OMG's SysML language.*

1. Introduction

Software architectures are acknowledged as essential assets for the success of software systems, contributing to satisfying both functionalities and quality requirements and incorporating principles and decisions guiding their design and evolution [Bass et al. 2022]. Such architectures can be visualized at a high level in the form of components representing the functional elements of the system, connectors that promote communication between those components, and their behavior.

Even though a software system can work with a poor architecture resulting from inadequate or incorrect decisions, future problems will arise in its operation, maintenance, and evolution. One of these problems, which has been of growing interest in the Software Architecture field, refers to the so-called *architectural smells*. An architectural smell is an architectural-level decision, whether intentional or not, that may negatively impact a software system's quality, despite not representing an error that prevents the system from working [Garcia et al. 2009a]. A typical example of architectural smell is cyclic dependencies among software architecture components, which strongly impact the system's maintainability and harm its quality.

Architectural smells are identified mainly in the advanced stages of the software development life cycle. A recent literature review aimed to identify the existing techniques and tools for detecting architectural smells and their limitations concluded that most of these techniques and tools primarily analyze artifacts such as the source code [Mumtaz et al. 2021]. However, detecting architectural smells from a recovered architecture is undoubtedly problematic because the system is already implemented. This means that some effort has already been employed to implement the system, and additional effort will be required to fix existing architectural smells.

Although many works in the literature use the source code to identify the occurrence of architectural smells, there is evidence that not every architectural smell can be detected from it, and the existence of a problem in the code does not necessarily imply an architectural smell [Macia et al. 2012, Arcelli Fontana et al. 2019]. The available tools to detect architectural smells cannot be used at design time when the system implementation does not exist yet [Azadi et al. 2019, Mumtaz et al. 2021]. Moreover, almost all existing techniques and tools focus only on detecting architectural smells related to dependencies, and many others still need to be covered.

Detecting architectural smells at design time can prevent this problem from being reflected at the system implementation, hampering later development stages and negatively affecting software quality attributes [Stafford and Wolf 2001, Chondamrongkul et al. 2020]. *Architecture descriptions* can play a crucial role at this point as they constitute a first representation of the software system under development. However, the literature on using architectural descriptions to detect architectural smells is relatively scarce. The existing works (see Section 3) have limitations concerning the set of identified architectural smells and the considered architectural viewpoints.

This ongoing research investigates how software architecture descriptions realized through architecture description languages (ADLs) can be used to identify architectural smells at design time when these architectures are being conceived. This work focuses on how architectural smells manifest and can be detected in SysADL [Oquendo et al. 2016]. SysADL is an ADL complying with the ISO/IEC/IEEE 42010 International Standard for architectural descriptions and allows describing both structure and behavior of software architectures using standardized diagrams and elements from the OMG's SysML language. The ultimate result will be implementing a mechanism into the SysADL tool to automatically detect architectural smells from architecture descriptions and assist software architects in mitigating them at design time.

The remainder of this paper is organized as follows. Section 2 briefly introduces some architectural smells. Section 3 discusses related work. Section 4 describes the identification of architectural smells from the perspective of software architecture descriptions in the SysADL architectural language. Section 5 brings final remarks and directions for ongoing and future work.

2. Architectural Smells: A Bird's Eye View

Architectural smells mainly stem from the poor use of software architecture elements such as components, connectors, interfaces, etc., including how they handle the different system concerns and interact with each other. Despite the relevance of addressing architectural smells and the negative consequences on the quality of software systems, the literature still needs a uniform understanding of their characteristics and root causes. Garcia et al. [Garcia et al. 2009a, Garcia et al. 2009b] were the pioneers in defining the first catalog of architectural smells. This collection was revisited and expanded throughout the years [Azadi et al. 2019, Mumtaz et al. 2021].

[Le et al. 2017] present a framework to understand and classify architectural smells. They proposed five different classes of architectural smells and described only the ones that could be detected through architectural recovery. Table 1 lists those categories along with well-known architectural smell instances. It is worth mentioning that

Table 1. Architectural smell categories and some instances.

Categories	Causes	Architectural smell instances
Concern-based smells	Inappropriate or inadequate separation of concerns	*Concern Overload, Scattered Parasitic Functionality, Functionality Overload*
Dependency-based smells	Inappropriate interconnections and interactions among system elements	*Dependency Cycle, Link Overload*
Interface-based smells	Deficiency in defining component's interfaces	*Ambiguous Interface, Unused Interface, Ununsed Component, Sloppy Delegation, Lego Syndrome*
Coupling-based smells	Couplings among components	*Duplicate Function, Co-change Coupling*
Connector-based smells	Inappropriate definition or use of connectors	*Extraneous Adjacent Connector, Connector Envy*

the literature presents a high diversity of names and definitions, even though referring to the same architectural smell [Azadi et al. 2019, Mumtaz et al. 2021].

3. Related Work

The Stafford and Wolf's work is one of the first studies related to the software architecture analysis from architecture descriptions to specifically detect dependencies among architectural elements, which is the most common architectural smell [Stafford and Wolf 2001]. These authors argue that ADLs allow reflecting on software system properties at a high abstraction level, e.g., identifying if a given component affects or is affected by another, thus meaning that there is some dependency between these components.

[Sanchez et al. 2015] proposed an approach to verify the nonexistence of architectural smells from architecture descriptions in Archery, a formal ADL proposed by them. In their approach, the structure of software architectures is represented in Archery. An extension called Archery-Constraints allows formally specifying the nonexistence of architectural smells as constraints to be formally verified.

[Chondamrongkul et al. 2020] proposed and implemented an approach to detect architectural smells at design time from formalized software architecture descriptions. The structural viewpoint is represented through ontologies in the OWL language, and the behavioral viewpoint is represented through specifications in Wright#, a formal ADL. Relationships and rules in the ontology codify possible occurrences of architectural smells in the architecture's structure. Next, formal verification is used to detect architectural smells related to behavioral concerns.

In general, the works related to detecting architectural smells through architecture descriptions are limited to analyzing a small set of smells. They do not also consider standardized notations such as UML, SysML, and its derivations, which are preferred for use by practitioners in industry [Malavolta et al. 2013, Ozkaya 2018]. In the Sanchez et al.'s work, the used ADL does not offer an appropriate distinction between architectural elements (components and connectors) as typically expected for an ADL, besides focusing only on the structural viewpoint and not providing mechanisms for the automatic detection of architectural smells. The Chondamrongkul et al.'s approach considers both structural and behavioral viewpoints in the identification of the occurrence of architectural smells. However, it uses different notations to describe architecture's structure and behavior, and the verification relies on computationally-limited model-checking.

4. Identifying Architectural Smells in SysADL Architecture Descriptions

SysADL [Oquendo et al. 2016] is an architectural language designed to support multiple-view modeling, cross-view checking, and execution of software architectures. It relies on the diagrammatic notation from the SysML Systems Modeling standard and is aligned with the ISO/IEC/IEEE 42010 International Standard. SysADL encompasses three viewpoints for software architectures, namely *structural*, *behavioral*, and *executable*. The structural viewpoint concerns the structure of the software architecture, specifying its elements (components, ports, connectors) and how they are interconnected. The behavioral viewpoint is related to the behavior of the architecture and its elements through activities, actions, constraints, and protocols. The executable viewpoint copes with implementing the behavioral viewpoint and allows for simulating the architecture behavior at runtime.

The structural viewpoint of SysADL primarily relies on two diagrams, namely (i) the structural *Block Definition Diagram* (BDD) for defining components, connectors, configurations, ports, and types, and (ii) the *Internal Block Definition Diagram* (IBD) to detail a configuration by instantiating the elements defined in the BDD. In the behavioral viewpoint, SysADL uses a *behavioral BDD* for defining actions, activities, and constraints. An *Activity Diagram* (AD) defines an activity in terms of actions. A *Parametric Diagram* allows relating constraints to activities and actions. At last, the executable viewpoint of SysADL allows for the early detection of architectural problems, thus saving valuable time and human resources for the final deliverable implementation.

Almost all categories of architectural smells (see Section 2) can be identified in SysADL architecture descriptions as SysADL comes with typical ADL structural constructs and allows describing the behavior of architectural elements. Architectural recovery techniques used to identify architectural smells fail to address connector-based smells, i.e., those caused by inappropriate definition or use of connectors. Consequently, these techniques cannot differentiate between components and connectors reliably [Le et al. 2017]. However, connector-based smells can be identified in SysADL architecture descriptions since connectors are first-class architectural elements in the language, explicitly distinct from components.

In general, the identification of architectural smells using architecture descriptions consists in first characterizing how a given architectural smell manifests through the constructs of the ADL used to describe the software architecture. This characterization leads to the specification of rules stating the occurrence of an architectural smell in an architecture description. If some automation is envisioned, then a mechanism can be implemented to concretize the previously specified rules and point out if the architecture description matches any of these rules, thereby indicating the occurrence of architectural smells. Once an architectural smell is detected in the architecture description, software architects can be assisted on how to mitigate the smell.

This section describes how architectural smells can show up in software architecture descriptions in SysADL by using an adapted version of the Automated Guided Vehicle (AGV) system [Araújo et al. 2021, Gomaa 2011] as an illustrative example. In the AGV system, a real-time system controls a vehicle to start/stop moving along a track and relies on an arrival sensor to detect when it has arrived at a station. The AGV system interacts with two other existing systems by (i) receiving commands from a Supervisory System and sending vehicle acknowledgments and (ii) sending the vehicle status to an external Display System.

For the sake of space, this section presents only some instances of the architectural smells listed in Table 1[1]. This paper focuses on the steps related to characterizing architectural smells in software architecture descriptions using SysADL as architectural language. The detection tool support and mitigation is an ongoing work.

***Dependency Cycle* (DC).** DC is a dependency-based smell that occurs when two or more components depend on each other in a circular chain [Azadi et al. 2019], causing high coupling among components. A DC can be identified in the structural viewpoint of SysADL through the IBD. In an IBD, a DC appears when two connectors link the components in opposite directions, from an output port to an input port and vice-versa. Figure 1 depicts part of an IBD describing the AGV system as a composite component. There is a DC between instances of the *RobotArm* and *VehicleControl* components as they are linked through instances of the *CommandArm* and *NotificationArm* connectors in a bidirectional flow between their input/output ports.

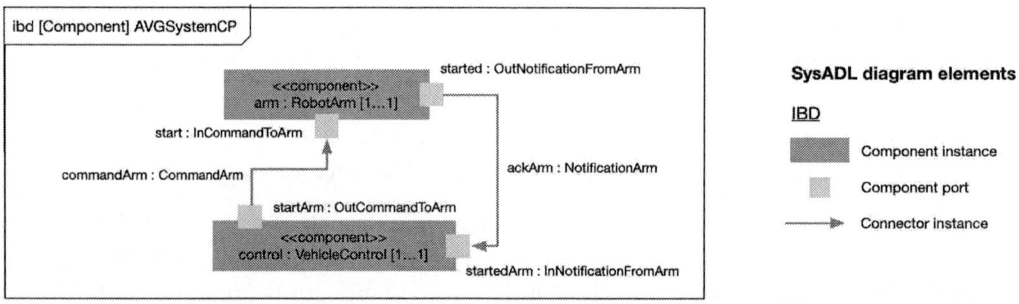

Figure 1. Part of a SysADL Internal Block Diagram with occurrences of *Dependency Cycle* and *Extraneous Adjacent Connector* in the AGV system.

***Extraneous Adjacent Connector* (EAC).** EAC is a connector-based architectural smell that occurs when two or more different connector types are used to link the same pair of components, even though it may be acceptable in certain cases [Garcia et al. 2009b]. An EAC can be identified in the structural viewpoint of SysADL through the IBD when instances of different connector types link the involved components. Figure 1 also presents a manifestation of EAC as the instances of the *RobotArm* and *VehicleControl* components are linked through instances of two different connectors, namely *NotificationArm* and *CommandArm*.

[1]The figures presented in this paper are excerpts of a complete architecture description of the AGV system in SysADL available at https://doi.org/10.5281/zenodo.6546959.

***Ambiguous Interface* (AI).** AI is an interface architectural smell that refers to a single general interface provided by a component that accepts requests and dispatches them internally. An AI can be identified in the structural viewpoint of SysADL through the IBD when a composite component has a proxy input port linked via a binding connector to multiple input ports of different internal components. In SysADL, ports of composite components are always proxy ports, so they need to be delegated to the ports of internal components [Oquendo et al. 2016]. Figure 2 depicts another part of an IBD describing the AGV system as a composite component. The AGV system interacts with the Supervisory System by receiving start/stop moving and loading/unloading commands. These commands are received via *commands*, a single input proxy port of the AGV system linked to two input ports of the *VehicleControl* component through binding connectors. The commands received via the proxy input port are dispatched to those internal input ports according to their nature. If the command is about start/stop moving the AGV, then the delegation is to the *move* input port. If the command is about loading/unloading onto and off the AGV, then the delegation is to the *load* input port.

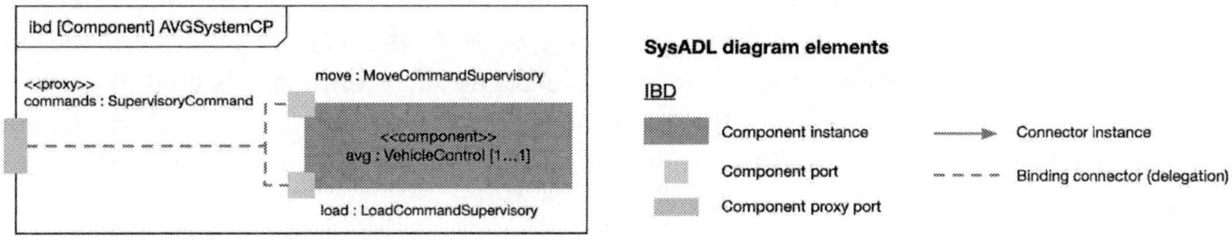

Figure 2. Part of a SysADL Internal Block Diagram with an occurrence of *Ambiguous Interface* in the AGV system.

***Functionality Overload* (FO).** FO is a concern-based smell that indicates that a component accumulates excessive functionalities and control, being an inappropriate form of modularity and violating the principle of separation of concerns. An FO can be identified in the behavioral viewpoint of SysADL through the behavioral BDD. A highly complex BDD with many actions composing an activity may indicate FO. Nevertheless, defining a certain threshold is required to judge a fair number of actions for describing the behavior of an architectural element. It is worth highlighting that existing tools that detect FO relying on architectural recovery adopt thresholds for this purpose [Azadi et al. 2019]. Figure 3 depicts a BDD specifying of the *MoveAC* activity performed by the *VehicleControl* component of the AGV System. This activity is defined as a composition of four actions, namely *ProcessCommandAN*, *SendDestinationAN*, *SendCommandAN*, and *SendStartMotorAN*. Suppose that a customizable threshold establishing the maximum number of actions to compose an activity is set to $ac_{max} = 3$. In this case, the *MoveAC* activity would be considered as possibly suffering from FO as its number of composing actions exceeds the established threshold ac_{max}.

5. Final Remarks

This paper aimed to present ongoing work on investigating how software architecture descriptions realized through ADLs can be used to identify architectural smells at design time before the system implementation. The main thrust behind these ideas is to avoid employing efforts to implement an architecture that may already manifest an architectural smell. This represents a different research direction from what has been done in the state

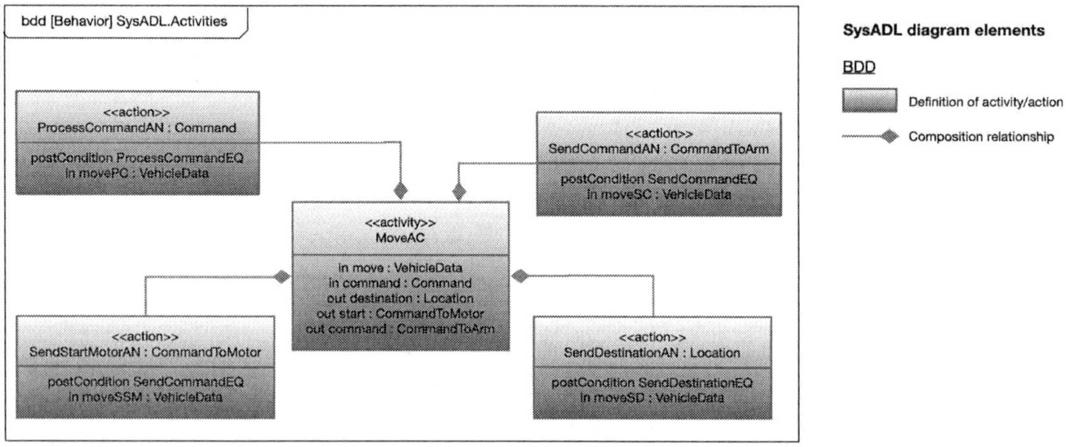

Figure 3. Part of a SysADL Block Definition Diagram with an occurrence of *Functionality Overload* in the AGV system.

of the art since almost all techniques currently used to detect architectural smells rely on architectural recovery or metrics from the source code of the system's implementation. The literature reports that the existing tools to detect architectural smells cannot be used at design time when the system implementation does not even exist. Architectural smells should be detected and eradicated before implementing the system since doing this at later stages through refactoring is costly.

This paper also showed how some architectural smells could be identified in SysADL architectural language. Ongoing work focuses on continuing the specification of rules that state the occurrence of architectural smells in SysADL diagrams. The following stages will be devoted to implementing a mechanism to automatically identify architectural smells in SysADL architecture descriptions. This mechanism will ultimately be integrated into the SysADL Studio tool [Leite et al. 2018], enabling software architects to analyze the occurrence of architectural smells when designing their software architectures. As SysADL complies with the ISO/IEC/IEEE 42010 International Standard and offers well-known, consolidated abstractions to describe software architectures, the same principles presented in this work for identifying architectural smells can be applied with other ADLs relying on the typical architectural abstractions.

References

Araújo, C., Batista, T., Cavalcante, E., and Oquendo, F. (2021). Generating formal software architecture descriptions from semi-formal SysML-based models: A model-driven approach. In Gervasi, O. et al., editors, *Computational Science and Its Applications – ICCSA 2021*, Lecture Notes in Computer Science, vol. 12951, pages 394–410. Springer Nature Switzerland AG, Switzerland.

Arcelli Fontana, F., Lenarduzzi, V., Roveda, R., and Taibi, D. (2019). Are architectural smells independent from code smells? An empirical study. *Journal of Systems and Software*, 154:139–156.

Azadi, U., Arcelli Fontana, F., and Taibi, D. (2019). Architectural smells detected by tools: A catalogue proposal. In *Proceedings of the 2019 IEEE/ACM International Conference on Technical Debt*, pages 88–97, USA. IEEE.

Bass, L., Clements, P., and Kazman, R. (2022). *Software Architecture in practice*. Addison-Wesley/Pearson Education, Inc., USA, 4th edition.

Chondamrongkul, N., Sun, J., Warren, I., and Lee, S. U.-J. (2020). Semantic-based architecture smell analysis. In *Proceedings of the 8th International Conference on Formal Methods in Software Engineering*, pages 109–118, USA. ACM.

Garcia, J., Popescu, D., Edwards, G., and Medvidovic, N. (2009a). Identifying architectural bad smells. In *Proceedings of the 13th European Conference on Software Maintenance and Reengineering*, pages 255–258, USA. IEEE.

Garcia, J., Popescu, D., Edwards, G., and Medvidovic, N. (2009b). Toward a catalogue of architectural bad smells. In Mirandola, R., Gorton, I., and Hofmeister, C., editors, *Architectures for Adaptive Software Systems*, Lecture Notes in Computer Science, vol. 5581, pages 146–162. Springer-Verlag Berlin Heidelberg, Germany.

Gomaa, H. (2011). *Software modeling and design: UML, use cases, patterns, and software architectures*. Cambridge University Press, USA.

Le, D., Link, D., Shahbazian, A., Zhao, Y., Mattmann, C., and Medvidovic, N. (2017). Toward a classification framework for software architectural smells. Technical report, Center for Systems and Software Engineering, University of Southern California, USA.

Leite, J., Batista, T., Oquendo, F., Silva, E., Santos, L., and Cortez, V. (2018). Designing and executing software architecture models using SysADL Studio. In *2018 IEEE International Conference on Software Architecture Companion*, pages 81–84, USA. IEEE.

Macia, I., Arcoverde, R., Garcia, A., Chavez, C., and von Staa, A. (2012). On the relevance of code anomalies for identifying architecture degradation symptoms. In *Proceedings of the 16th European Conference on Software Maintenance and Reengineering*, pages 277–286, USA. IEEE.

Malavolta, I., Lago, P., Muccini, H., Pelliccione, P., and Tang, A. (2013). What industry needs from architectural languages: A survey. *IEEE Transactions on Software Engineering*, 39(6):869–891.

Mumtaz, H., Singh, P., and Blincoe, K. (2021). A systematic mapping study on architectural smells detection. *Journal of Systems and Software*, 173.

Oquendo, F., Leite, J., and Batista, T. (2016). *Software Architecture in Action: Designing and executing architectural models with SysADL grounded on the OMG SysML Standard*. Springer International Publishing, Swizerland.

Ozkaya, M. (2018). The analysis of architectural languages for the needs of practitioners. *Software: Practice and Experience*, 48(5):985–1018.

Sanchez, A., Barbosa, L. S., and Madeira, A. (2015). Modelling and verifying smell-free architectures with the Archery language. In Canal, C. and Idani, A., editors, *Software Engineering and Formal Methods*, Lecture Notes in Computer Science, vol. 8938, pages 147–163. Springer International Publishing, Switzerland.

Stafford, J. A. and Wolf, A. L. (2001). Architecture-level dependence analysis for software systems. *International Journal of Software Engineering and Knowledge Engineering*, 11(4):431–451.

Software Engineering Education in the DevOps Era: Experiences and Recommendations

Nicolás Paez[1,2], **Carlos Fontela**[2]

[1]Departamento de Ciencia y Tecnología - Universidad Nacional de Tres de Febrero
Saenz Peña, Argentina

[2]Facultad de Ingeniería - Universidad de Buenos Aires
Buenos Aires, Argentina

nicopaez@computer.org, cfontela@fi.uba.ar

Abstract. *DevOps has reached the mainstream, in part, because it proposed a way to solve the last mile of the software delivery process. It brought to the industry concrete solutions to some concerns that software engineering and academia have traditionally ignored. The popularity and success of DevOps got the attention of the academia and some universities have started to include DevOps related content in their programs. After doing our own experience, we found out that introducing DevOps is not as simple as adding a new course. In fact, it requires a major redesign of the Software Engineering curriculum. In this article we share some key ideas and recommendations to include DevOps in Software Engineering programs.*

1. Introduction

The Software Engineering discipline has traditionally ignored what we call the "last mile" of the delivery process. This "last mile" includes how to get the software solution into the production environment and, once in the production environment, how to operate the software solution. There is no mention to these delivery and operational concerns in the Guide to the Software Engineering Body of Knowledge (SWEBoK) [Bourque and Fairley 2014]. The same happens with classical Software Engineering textbooks. That was acceptable in the past. After all, going into production was a very special situation that happened once in a while. But at a certain point, the business requirements began to change more frequently, forcing deliveries to become more frequently. As a result, the "last mile" of the process became more important. These business needs, along with the lack of formal knowledge and guidance, lead to the raise of the DevOps movement. DevOps brought concrete solutions to industry problems and it did not take long for it to go mainstream. DevOps grew in the industry and it gradually got the attention of the academia because it proved to be effective to solve industry problems. In the context of this article we will use the term "DevOps" as a generic way to refer to all those concerns in the last mile of the delivery process which includes the ones related to the delivery itself and also to operations. All these DevOps topics are gradually being incorporated in the Software Engineering discipline. In fact, the version four of the Guide to the Software Engineering Body of Knowledge (which is still in beta) [IEEE Computer Society 2022], contains a new knowledge area called "Software Engineering Operations". At the same time, these topics are also getting interest from academic and scientific environments.

In our role of practitioners, we believe that these DevOps topics must be part of the Software Engineering body of knowledge. As a consequence, Software Engineering education needs to include these topics in their programs too. The challenge here, in our opinion, is that including those topics is not as simple as adding a new course. DevOps topics should be considered at the program level to be enable them to be to distributed in different courses.

In this article we aim to share some recommendations based on experiences in order to include DevOps concerns in Software Engineering education.

2. About DevOps

The term DevOps was coined back in 2009. There are several definitions of what DevOps is. Some of them are related to specific products or technologies. But one that is generally enough and is still compatible with most definitions is the one by Len Bass: *DevOps is a set of practices intended to reduce the time between committing a change to a system and the change being placed into normal production while ensuring high quality.* [Bass et al. 2015]. Even when Bass' view of DevOps may sound exclusively focused on delivery, it also encompasses operational concerns because they are needed in order to get fast changes in production without compromising the stability of the system.

Approximately at the same time that DevOps started to get popular, there was another movement that got important visibility too: Site Reliability Engineering (SRE). This term was coined by Google long time ago but after the publication of the book "Site Reliability Engineering: How Google Runs Production Systems" [Beyer et al. 2016] it was widely spread in the industry. SRE incorporates Software Engineering practices to infrastructure and IT operation management. Some people consider SRE something different from DevOps or even an alternative, but Google proposes SRE as an specific implementation of DevOps [Fong-Jones and Vargo 2018].

3. Related work

Scientific publications about DevOps grow up every year. Some institutions have started to include DevOps in their programs. In some cases specific DevOps courses have been created [Demchenko et al. 2019, Hobeck et al. 2021, Jennings and Gannod 2019]. In some other cases DevOps topics have been added to existing Software Engineering courses [Hills 2020, Paez and de la Fuente 2022]. Hobeck et al. [Hobeck et al. 2021] delivered a DevOps course in two universities using a inverted classroom strategy. Alves and Rocha [Alves and Rocha 2021] designed a project-oriented DevOps course and conducted an empirical study to evaluate it. Their results evidence that first-hand experience paves the way for the comprehension of DevOps. Demchenko et al. [Demchenko et al. 2019] proposed a "DevOps Software Engineering Body of Knowledge" and described their implementation in a course at the University of Amsterdam. Chatley and Procaccini [Chatley and Procaccini 2020] describe how they introduced students to DevOps practices early in their degree program, and then wove their use through many different projects.

In the research field, Schilling [Schilling 2022] discusses the justification for including DevOps within a Software Engineering program and the associated challenges it places upon an instructor to teach. Fernandes et al. have studied DevOps challenges and recommendations for teaching DevOps. They initially performed a literature review, and after that, they performed an interview study with 14 DevOps educators from different universities [Fernandes et al. 2022]. They identified 83 challenges and over 180 recommendations.

Our approach to teach DevOps topics, which is described in the rest of this article, is different from the mentioned works because: 1) we are doing a proposal at the program level and 2) at the same time we are giving concrete recommendations regarding the teaching strategy.

4. Our Current Program

What we describe in this section is related to the four-and-half year degree in System Analysis [1] offered by the Engineering School of the University of Buenos Aires. This degree had a major update in 2014 that, among other things, introduced several changes in the Software Engineering area. The body of knowledge that covers from business needs to the delivery, operation and support of the solution is organized in four core courses:

- Software Engineering Fundamentals 1 (95.20): this course is focused on the first part of the delivery process, which includes concerns like product discovery, requirements, domain modeling, but also covering some architecture, development and deployment concerns. In fact, as part of the course, the students have to develop a web application and deploy it to the cloud. More details about this course in Software Engineering and the program in general have been described by Villagra et al. [Villagra et al. 2020].
- Software Engineering Fundamentals 2 (95.21): this course is more focused on the second part of the delivery process which implies more technical concerns like design, configuration management, deployment strategies and several topics that are usually associated with DevOps. This course is described in detail in a recent publication by Paez and de la Fuente [Paez and de la Fuente 2022].
- Software Development Management (95.24): this course is guided by the project management knowledge areas as defined by the PMBOK (scope, time, costs, risks, quality, etc.), but applied to software development and with more than one approach. Therefore, students are confronted with management from both traditional and agile perspectives, following iterative-incremental and continuous flow life cycles, both in project and product mode. Special attention is given to team and people issues, including soft skills, such as communication, meetings, collaboration, collective learning, and working environment. More details about this course have been described by Fontela and Santos [Fontela and Santos 2022].
- Software Operations Management (95.59): this course is focused on design, operation and management of informatic services. This is far beyond the traditional Software Engineering scope, although is closely related to operational concerns which is under the scope of DevOps.

A matter worth mentioning is that the two courses on Software Engineering Fundamentals cover all the disciplines of the software delivery process but with different focus and level of detail. Figure 1 shows how these courses maps on to the software delivery stream.

[1] The name of the degree in Spanish is *Licenciatura en Análisis de Sistemas* and it could be considered a Master Degree in Software Engineering

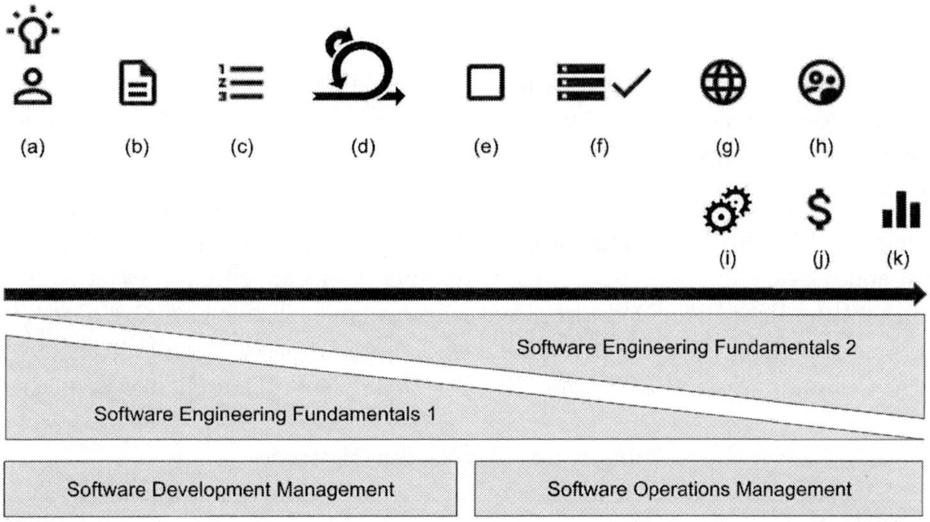

Figure 1. Software Delivery Stream and Software Engineering core Courses
It starts with a user need(a), that leads us to create a project vision (b), we create a product backlog (c) and start working in an iterative and incremental way (d). At the end of each iteration we have a product increment (e), we verify it (f) and pass it through different environments in its way to production (g). There, it finally meets the end user (h) and the software finally provides value (j). We operate it to ensure its availability (i) and get run-time metrics (k) to understand user behavior and it all starts over again

In addition to these four core courses, there are others that focus on specific aspects of Software Engineering, like Software Quality, Software Architecture and Object-oriented Programming and Design.

We know program updates tend to take too much time while knowledge, practices and tools in this area are in constant evolution. At the same time, professors in the software engineering area in our university, are usually practitioners. Therefore, professors try to keep their courses up-to-date moving faster than the program updates.

5. Recommendations

Recently, the School of Engineering decided to renew the programs of all degrees that it had been offering. In this context, we, as professors in the Software Engineering area, developed a set of recommendations to cover the Software Engineering body of knowledge in the new program of the System Analysis degree. Our recommendations are based on: a) the experiences we made in the Software Engineering courses during the last 10 semesters [Villagra et al. 2020, Paez and de la Fuente 2022, Fontela and Santos 2022] , 2) some recommendations made by other professors and researchers [Fernandes et al. 2022, Hobeck et al. 2021, Hills 2020] and 3) the guidance provided by the Guide to the SWEBoK version 4 [IEEE Computer Society 2022].

In the following subsections we describe each of our recommendations. They are listed in a sequential way but they are interrelated. Even when we are already applying some of these recommendations in our courses, we intend to make them an explicit part of the orientation of the upcoming program. It is worth mentioning that even when some of our recommendations are in some way generic and can be applied to many different topics, we consider them to be especially important when trying to teach DevOps.

5.1. DevOps Concerns

DevOps comprises a wide field of knowledge integrating organizational and technical aspects. It is too much content to be covered in one course. So our recommendation is to introduce DevOps topics in gradual way along several courses.

In our current program we are already covering some DevOps topics but not all what we would like to. Our idea for the new program is to add some topics to existing courses, and we plan to create new courses to cover some specific topics as well. In table 1 we present the list of DevOps topics we want to cover in our program along with our strategy to cover them. This list of topics was elaborated based mainly on the SWEBoK-V4[IEEE Computer Society 2022] and the DevOpsSEBoK [Demchenko et al. 2019].

Table 1. DevOps Topics Coverage

Topic	Course
DevOps mindset and Culture	C
Organisational impact of DevOps and Team structure	C
Continuous Integration and Delivery	C
Infrastructure as Code and Configuration Management	C, N
Cloud Computing Architectures, Service and Deployment models	C, N
Virtualization, Containerization and Container Orchestration	A, N
Networking	C, A
Monitoring, Telemetry and Observability	A, N
Resilience and Chaos Engineering	N
Operations, Service Levels, Outage and PostMortem Analysis	A
Security, Auditing and Compliance	A

C: already covered in existing courses; A: to be added to existing courses; N: new course

Some of the topics on the list are not new and have been in the Software Engineering body of knowledge for years. But for some reason, they might have been ignored and now, with the DevOps movement, they got more relevance.

5.2. Iterative and Incremental Delivery

Just as software is delivered in a iterative and incremental way, we believe that we should follow the same strategy to deliver knowledge. This implies that some topics should be studied in more than one course but, of course, with different level of detail, and possibly from different perspectives. This idea applies to traditional Software Engineering topics as well as DevOps topics.

At the same time, those practices learned in one course should be applied in all subsequent courses. This may sound obvious and it happens with some topics, but it does not always happen with Software Engineering ones. For example, a situation that we have detected in our institution is that students learn unit testing in a certain course, but they do not write unit tests in subsequent courses unless teachers explicitly ask them to do it.

We are applying this strategy in the Software Engineering core courses but now we are proposing this as an explicit guideline at the program level.

5.3. Transversal contents

There are some topics that are typically treated in Software Engineering courses but that we consider it could be much better to see them early in academic formation and along several courses. This idea applies to classical Software Engineering topics, like unit testing, but also to some DevOps related topics like Build Automation and Continuous Integration. This idea complements our iterative and incremental delivery approach. Let us consider the Continuous Integration (CI) practice. Early in the program the students could have a first contact with this practice by using a pre-configured CI pipeline. Later, in another course, the students could go deeper with the CI practice and design and configure themselves their CI pipeline.

We currently apply this strategy with several topics in our program. In particular, some Software Engineering topics like architecture and quality, are initially presented in the Software Engineering Fundamentals courses, and later the students take specific courses on those topics.

5.4. Hands-on Approach

Teaching effectively underlying lasting concepts, principles and practices of Software Engineering requires to put them into practice. At the same time, new generations of students want to understand what problems we need to solve before facing the theory that supports the solutions. Therefore, we think a hands-on approach is a good fit for this context. A hands-on approach allows the students to better understand the relation between tools, technologies and its underlying concepts, principles and practices.

When it comes to DevOps, tools and technologies may represent a major challenge for educators trying to deliver a hands-on approach because they are in constant evolution at a fast rate. This challenge compromises three dimensions: knowledge, guidance and support.

- **Knowledge**: in order to teach a topic educators must dedicate recurrent time and effort to stay up to date with tools and technologies.
- **Guidance**: educators must provide guidance and resources for students to learn and practice. This may require generating exercises, videos, guides, etc.
- **Support**: it is common, when dealing with tools and technologies for the first time, to face blocking issues, so educators must give support to the students to help them unblock.

This situation leads us, as educators, to reconsider how to plan our classes and here is where the flipped classroom may be an interesting option.

5.5. Flipped classroom

A flipped classroom approach proposes a reversal of the traditional class flow: the students "carry out" the lecture at home (for example, watching a video or reading an article) and then the "in-class" time is used for interactive activities. There is extensive bibliography regarding the usage of this technique to teach Software Engineering. Given the challenges brought by the hands-on approach, taking a flipped classroom approach sounds like a good match: deliver content in video to be watched at home and then use the class time to perform hands-on activities. These videos can be used to deliver different kinds of content like lectures, tools demonstrations and tools configuration/installation instructions.

Our Software Engineering Fundamentals courses have applied this strategy since their first edition in 2015 and several other courses have been adopting it recently, forced in part by COVID-19 pandemic.

5.6. Cloud Labs and virtual classes

In some institutions, the set of DevOps tools and technologies may represent a challenge for the laboratories. Frequent laboratory updates may be required. This may be partially mitigated by the use of cloud services, in fact some of the DevOps tools and technologies are cloud-based. Most of the cloud vendors have some kind of academic subscriptions that provide access to their services for free or at a very low cost. This may imply some initial bureaucracy for the institution to access to the cloud subscription while reducing the cost of laboratories.

At the same time, COVID-19 forced education to switch to virtual classes, at least for a while. In our own case, virtual classes result to be very convenient for some courses. In those cases where students have to work on development projects using a stack composed of several tools, the virtual classes allow the students to work on their own computers while the professors can give them remote-online support during the class time.

From a institution point of view, virtual classes require the institution to provide some service/subscription to allow professors to delivery online classes. At the same time, there may be some regulations limiting the virtual classes, but in our own experience, the combination of online and onsite classes allowed to have the best of both worlds.

6. Conclusions

DevOps came to stay and be part of the Software Engineering body of knowledge. It brings organizational and technical concerns, and teaching them face Software Engineering educators with major challenges. At the same time, DevOps is a wide topic and each institution may decide how deeply to cover it, depending on the program's profile.

In this article we shared how we started to include DevOps topics in some courses of our current program and some ideas we want to be implemented in the upcoming program. We also shared a set of recommendations to consider when including DevOps topics in Software Engineering education. While some recommendations may be applied to Software Engineering in general, we consider that using a flipped classroom strategy combined with a hands-on approach and virtual classes to be the best approach to teach the DevOps topics. A possible combination that proved to be effective in our case is: a) Deliver lectures in video, b) Use the class time to perform hands-on activities, c) Combine onsite and online classes, d) Use cloud-based services, e) Use online classes to give remote support to students working on their own computers and f) Provide tool guidance in video.

The surveys run at the end of each course have revealed that students are very pleased with the way we deliver the software engineering courses and the topics covered, in part because they see that are aligned with what they see in the daily work (most of our students are already working in the industry when they take the Software Engineering courses.)

References

Alves, I. and Rocha, C. (2021). Qualifying software engineers undergraduates in devops - challenges of introducing technical and non-technical concepts in a project-oriented course. In *2021 IEEE/ACM 43rd International Conference on Software Engineering: Software Engineering Education and Training (ICSE-SEET)*, pages 144–153.

Bass, L., Weber, I., and Zhu, L. (2015). *DevOps: A Software Architect's Perspective*. Addison-Wesley Professional, 1st edition.

Beyer, B., Jones, C., Petoff, J., and Murphy, N. (2016). *Site Reliability Engineering: How Google Runs Production Systems*. O'Reilly Media, Incorporated.

Bourque, P. and Fairley, R. E. (2014). *Guide to the Software Engineering Body of Knowledge, Version 3.0*. IEEE Computer Society.

Chatley, R. and Procaccini, I. (2020). Threading devops practices through a university software engineering programme. In *2020 IEEE 32nd Conference on Software Engineering Education and Training (CSEE&T)*, pages 1–5.

Demchenko, Y., Zhao, Z., Surbiryala, J., Koulouzis, S., Shi, Z., Liao, X., and Gordiyenko, J. (2019). Teaching devops and cloud based software engineering in university curricula. In *2019 15th International Conference on eScience (eScience)*, pages 548–552.

Fernandes, M., Ferino, S., Fernandes, A., Kulesza, U., Aranha, E., and Treude, C. (2022). Devops education: An interview study of challenges and recommendations.

Fong-Jones, L. and Vargo, S. (2018). What's the difference between devops and sre? (class sre implements devops).

Fontela, C. and Santos, G. D. (2022). Learning communication skills in software development management courses: an active learning experience. In *2022 IEEE Biennial Congress of Argentina (ARGENCON)*, pages 1–8.

Hills, M. (2020). Introducing devops techniques in a software construction class. In *2020 IEEE 32nd Conference on Software Engineering Education and Training (CSEE&T)*.

Hobeck, R., Weber, I., Bass, L., and Yasar, H. (2021). Teaching devops: A tale of two universities. In *Proceedings of the 2021 ACM SIGPLAN International Symposium on SPLASH-E*, SPLASH-E 2021, page 26–31, New York, NY, USA. ACM.

IEEE Computer Society (2022). Software engineering body of knowledge v4 public review.

Jennings, R. A. K. and Gannod, G. (2019). Devops - preparing students for professional practice. In *2019 IEEE Frontiers in Education Conference (FIE)*, pages 1–5.

Paez, N. and de la Fuente, H. (2022). Software engineering education meets devops: an experience report. In *2022 IEEE Biennial Congress of Argentina (ARGENCON)*.

Schilling, W. W. (2022). Wip: Integrating modern development practices into a software engineering curriculum.

Villagra, S., Benedetti, G. D., Bruno, T., Fernández, L., and Outeda, N. (2020). Teaching software engineering: an active learning experience. In *2020 IEEE Congreso Bienal de Argentina (ARGENCON)*, pages 1–6.

Mi Superpoder es la Programación: Una herramienta para la enseñanza de la programación en niños y jóvenes

Erika J. Gutiérrez Beltrán, Juan C. Martínez Arias

Facultad de ingeniería y ciencias – Pontificia Universidad Javeriana
Calle 18 #118-250 – Cali – Valle del Cauca – Colombia

{ejgutierrb, juancmartinez}@javerianacali.edu.co

Abstract. *"Mi Superpoder es la Programación" is an educational web tool developed with modern technology and Severless-based techniques to teach children and youth the basics of programming with an educational focus on logic, sequences, flowcharts, and advanced object-oriented programming concepts. "Mi Superpoder es la Programación" evolved to its current form after seeing the impacts of a social program of the same name founded in 2017 which impacted more than 100 children in Colombia. While many tools are available to teach children and youth, none of them focus on strengthening other computing skills beyond just coding. In this work, we will review "Mi Superpoder es la Programación" as a methodology and tool for teaching programming, compare it with other currently available programming tools, and validate its value, impact, and interest in use with children and youth.*

Resumen. *"Mi Superpoder es la Programación" es una herramienta web para enseñar programación a niños y jóvenes enfocada en lógica, secuencias, diagramas de flujo, y conceptos avanzados de programación orientada a objetos. La herramienta se desarrolló utilizando tecnologías y técnicas modernas basadas en Serverless. La aplicación web surgió del proyecto social del mismo nombre, que comenzó en 2017 y ha impactado a más de 100 niños de Colombia. Aunque se utilizaron varias herramientas para enseñar a los niños y jóvenes, ninguna de ellas se enfoca en fortalecer otros componentes de la computación más allá de la codificación. En este trabajo se presenta la plataforma web para enseñar programación, una comparación con otras herramientas, y la validación de la solución en niños y jóvenes, para conocer el impacto e interés en su uso.*

1. Introducción

Durante los últimos años, la enseñanza de la programación para niños y jóvenes ha tomado relevancia, por lo que gran parte de las escuelas, colegios y universidades de Colombia están transformando sus planes de estudio, con el fin de involucrar la computación y la tecnología, ya que se reconoce el gran impacto de los dispositivos electrónicos y el internet en diversas actividades de la cotidianidad. A raíz de toda esta revolución se ha generado en la industria una gran demanda en campos y roles asociados a la tecnología e investigación y desarrollo (I+D) [Dane 2018], incrementando el interés por capacitar a los más pequeños en temas relacionados.

Con el fin de promover el acceso a los conocimientos relacionados a la programación desde cortas edades, diversas entidades públicas y privadas se han enfocado en enseñar programación a través de cursos extracurriculares. Estos cursos pueden ser gratuitos o de pago. Sin embargo, en Colombia se identifica que la gran mayoría de los niños de sectores vulnerables, principalmente aquellos de escasos recursos o con problemas socioeconómicos, son desertores de estos cursos, ya que en sus hogares no cuentan con las herramientas necesarias para desempeñar los ejercicios de práctica.

El aprendizaje de la programación está en auge, puesto que se ha demostrado que aporta al desarrollo de habilidades lógicas y creativas para la resolución de problemas, y contribuye al fortalecimiento de otras áreas del conocimiento, como por ejemplo las matemáticas. Algunas investigaciones como el caso de "Analizar por qué se debe enseñar la lógica de programación a niños y jóvenes en los hogares de la ciudad de Medellín" [Patiño et al 2016], describe a partir de las necesidades y situaciones culturales de los niños y jóvenes de Medellín, las ventajas de la programación y como cada herramienta existente tiene un objetivo particular en la enseñanza, por lo que se debe recurrir a más de una herramienta para enriquecer el proceso de aprendizaje.

La mayoría de herramientas para la enseñanza de la programación a niños y jóvenes utiliza los videojuegos, para facilitar la creación de estrategias de gamificación, ya que se ha identificado que a través de estas estrategias, se incrementa el compromiso por parte de los estudiantes, además del interés y mejor disposición en la participación de actividades de clase. Esto se pone en evidencia en el trabajo "Evaluación del uso de un Juego Serio no virtual en Programación" [Pisabarro et al 2018]

Debido a las ventajas que se adquieren por medio del aprendizaje de la programación, en el año 2017 se crea el proyecto social llamado ***Mi Superpoder es la Programación***, el cual tiene como objetivo llegar a las poblaciones más vulnerables de Colombia, para transformar el entorno de niños y jóvenes por medio del uso de la tecnología, principalmente el aprendizaje de la programación [MSP 2017].

En los inicios del proyecto social, se utilizaron herramientas gratuitas como Scratch [MIT 2007] y Pilas Bloques [Program.AR 2016], para enseñar conceptos de programación como ciclos, variables, funciones e iteradores. Sin embargo, al no contar con módulos avanzados para continuar con el proceso de aprendizaje, fue necesario hacer uso de otras herramientas como CodeMonkey [Schor 2014], donde es necesario realizar el pago de una licencia anual.

Estos talleres se realizaron inicialmente en la ciudad de Cali, en los puntos Vive Digital, ya que son espacios diseñados por el gobierno para la capacitación y el entretenimiento [MinTic 2014]. Al ser lugares públicos, los niños y jóvenes sin acceso a internet y sin computadores en sus hogares, podían acceder a los talleres, para así vincularse a la transformación digital que les permitirá no ser solo consumidores potenciales de tecnología, sino que además puedan generar contenidos útiles para compartir.

En el año 2020, con la pandemia de COVID-19, los talleres pasaron a ser dictados de manera virtual. Muchos de los niños y jóvenes desertaron de los talleres debido a múltiples dificultades asociadas a mala conexión de internet, puesto que principalmente utilizaban plan de datos para conectarse desde sus dispositivos celulares. Adicionalmente, las herramientas web usadas para la enseñanza no se adaptaban correctamente a los dispositivos, lo que generaba gran frustración y bloqueos en el proceso de aprendizaje.

Teniendo en cuenta las problemáticas identificadas, como la adaptabilidad de las herramientas a los dispositivos de los niños, la falta de recursos para su capacitación, el uso de múltiples herramientas que agregan complejidad al proceso de enseñanza de la programación, y los costos asociados, se decide crear una herramienta web con el mismo nombre del proyecto social: ***Mi Superpoder es la Programación***.

Esta herramienta incluye todo lo necesario para la capacitación y aprendizaje de conceptos de programación, partiendo de conceptos básicos como las partes de un computador, hasta diagramas de flujo, secuencias, patrones y pseudocódigo, conocimientos necesarios antes del paso de la construcción de código, y del cual carecen las herramientas utilizadas.

En el presente trabajo se describe la herramienta web para la enseñanza de la programación en niños y jóvenes, descripción de las tecnologías utilizadas, arquitectura, resultados de las pruebas de la herramienta y comparación con otras herramientas existentes.

2. Antecedentes

Mi Superpoder es la Programación como proyecto social, ha logrado impactar a más de 100 niños y jóvenes de diferentes ciudades de Colombia. Desde el año 2017 se han analizado herramientas, libros y trabajos relacionados, que han permitido llevar a cabo mejoras en la metodología de enseñanza para transmitir conocimientos no solo en programación, sino también en conceptos asociados al desarrollo de la lógica computacional e informática.

En el pasado se requería el uso de distintas herramientas, debido a la carencia de módulos que permitieran enseñar sobre las bases de la programación a través de secuencias, patrones, diagramas de flujo y pseudocódigo. Para lograr transmitir estos conocimientos, se diseñaron algunos ejercicios a partir de los libros de Linda Liukas, Hello Ruby: Adventures in Coding [Liukas 2015] y Hello Ruby: Journey Inside the Computer [Liukas 2017].

Para llegar a los niños y jóvenes de sectores vulnerables de Colombia, se ha recurrido y obtenido apoyo de diferentes entidades, comunidades de voluntariado, colegios y universidades, lo que ha permitido dar visibilidad al proyecto. Este a su vez ha sido presentado en eventos como Campus Party, realizado en la ciudad de Bogotá en el año 2019 y TecnoFest, evento de la alcaldía de la ciudad de Cali en los años 2018 y 2019, bajo el concepto de que cualquiera puede aprender sobre programación.

La posibilidad de impartir talleres en sectores vulnerables ha permitido identificar las necesidades de los niños y jóvenes para aprender sobre temas relacionados a la tecnología e informática. Se está en búsqueda constante por mejorar la metodología de enseñanza, para proporcionar recursos de valor que aporten a su desarrollo.

El impacto del COVID-19 sobre la educación y las técnicas de enseñanza de la programación, las cuales se impartían principalmente de manera presencial, tuvieron que ser trasladadas de manera virtual, revolucionando por completo a las herramientas web para el aprendizaje. Algunas herramientas como SATReLO [Martínez et al

2018][Martínez et al 2019], demuestran el potencial de la web y los videojuegos para transmitir conocimientos y educar, en este caso en las terapias del lenguaje en niños con discapacidad auditiva [Álvarez et al 2021]. Esto amplió el panorama y aportó a la construcción de la metodología y plataforma de enseñanza de la programación, bajo un paradigma similar, utilizando videojuegos con diferentes niveles de dificultad y adaptación a los recursos disponibles en los hogares de los niños.

3. Trabajos relacionados

En la actualidad, existen sistemas que han sido creados con el propósito de enseñar a los niños y jóvenes todo lo relacionado con los lenguajes de programación, los cuales se enfocan principalmente en la codificación y la comprensión de la sintaxis.

Estas herramientas fueron evaluadas durante la realización de los talleres de *Mi Superpoder es la Programación*, con el fin de identificar: 1) si el ambiente de ejecución era adaptable a dispositivos móviles; 2) cuenta con el idioma nativo del usuario, en este caso el español; 3) permite incrementar el nivel y agregar complejidad a los ejercicios; y 4) variedad en contenidos para aprender desde conceptos básicos hasta avanzados.

Previo a la definición, implementación y creación de la nueva herramienta se realizó una evaluación y análisis previo de las herramientas más conocidas y utilizadas durante los talleres. Gracias a ello, fue posible identificar las principales problemáticas y enfocarse en ofrecer elementos innovadores que no se encuentran en las herramientas existentes, con el fin de mejorar los recursos de aprendizaje para los niños y jóvenes.

Para comprender las necesidades de la herramienta construida, se analizaron las plataformas utilizadas y se destacan componentes claves e importantes de los trabajos de investigación relacionados. Se resalta el impacto de la pandemia vivida en el año 2020, la cual obligó a modificar y adaptar el modelo educativo para hacer uso de la tecnología, aunque se tuviera falta de experiencia en el tema.

Las herramientas que se nombran a continuación, son algunas de las más utilizadas y conocidas en la enseñanza de la programación para niños y jóvenes. Además, han sido objeto de estudio en investigaciones asociadas al área de la educación en programación y fueron utilizadas en algunos talleres de *Mi Superpoder es la Programación*, estas herramientas son: 1) Scratch, 2) Pilas Bloques, 3) Codemonkey, 4) Code.org, 5) Tynker, y 6) Rabbids Coding

1) Scratch:

Lenguaje de programación desarrollado por el MIT Media Lab, el cual permite por medio de componentes visuales como bloques, manipular escenarios, dar comportamientos a personajes y modificar sonidos o videos. Cuenta con su propia herramienta de edición de código, y está diseñado para ser intuitivo y de fácil uso, permitiendo a personas sin experiencia en programación utilizarla. Pertenece a la categoría de software libre y es ampliamente reconocido entre los niños y jóvenes de todo el mundo [MIT 2007].

2) Pilas Bloques:

Es una herramienta para la enseñanza de la programación por medio de bloques, nace a partir del programa educativo argentino Program.AR, el cual busca que todos los niños de Argentina aprendan sobre programación en sus escuelas y hogares, debido a todas las ventajas que proporciona. El programa está enfocado en niños que se encuentran cursando grados de primaria.

3) CodeMonkey:

Es una herramienta web para el aprendizaje de la programación basado en juegos para niños y jóvenes. Esta herramienta promete que los usuarios podrán desenvolverse en el mundo de la programación sin problemas al finalizar todos los niveles que se ofrecen. Se pueden encontrar diversos cursos en los niveles de principiante, intermedio y avanzado. Es de pago y se basa en los lenguajes de programación por bloques, CoffeeScript o Python.

Otras de las herramientas analizadas fueron: 4) Code.org, organización sin ánimo de lucro, enfocada en llevar la programación a todas las escuelas del mundo. Ofrece por medio de su sitio web cursos basados en videojuegos por Bloques [Code.org 2013], es de libre acceso y es financiada por grandes empresas como Amazon, Facebook y Google; 5) Tynker, herramienta de pago, la cual ofrece un plan de estudio completo para niños y jóvenes, brindando la posibilidad de aprender por bloques y lenguajes más avanzados como Javascript, HTML, CSS y Python [Tynker 2012] y 6) Rabbids Coding, videojuego creado por Ubisoft, enfocado en la enseñanza de la programación basado en bloques [Sapura et al 2020].

A partir del análisis, se realizó una tabla comparativa con las herramientas más utilizadas y analizadas en los inicios de *Mi Superpoder es la Programación* como proyecto social, para identificar las debilidades de las herramientas existentes y considerar las fortalezas como elementos a implementar y utilizar en la nueva herramienta. En la Tabla 1, se presenta un comparativo de las herramientas, incluyendo la desarrollada, en función de portabilidad, adaptabilidad, idioma, niveles y licenciamiento.

Tabla 1: Análisis de las herramientas más utilizadas, para la extracción de las características que aportaron a la construcción y definición de la nueva herramienta

Herramienta	**Características**							
	Ambiente web	Portabilidad (app móvil)	Responsive	Idioma Español	Ejercicios previos a la codificación	Incrementar nivel y dificultad	Código diferente a bloques	Gratuita
Scratch	✔	✔	✔/X	✔/X	X	✔/X	X	✔
Pilas Bloques	✔	X	✔	✔	X	X	X	✔
Codemonkey	✔	X	✔/X	✔/X	✔/X	✔	✔	X
Code.org	✔	X	✔	✔/X	X	✔/X	✔/X	✔

Tynker	✔	✔	✔ / X	✔/X	X	✔	✔	X
Rabbids Coding	X	✔	X	X	✔/X	X	X	✔
Mi Superpoder es la Programación	✔	X	✔	✔	✔	✔	✔	✔

Como se observa en la tabla de análisis, la mayoría de herramientas están diseñadas para ser accedidas desde un navegador web pero a través de un computador. Sin embargo, algunas tienen traducciones deficientes al español y no cuentan con un módulo de entrenamiento en las bases de la computación, que permitan aprender sobre diagramas de flujo, pseudocódigo y partes de un computador. Las aplicaciones móviles analizadas tienen diferencias significativas de la versión de escritorio o web con respecto a los ejercicios y alcance.

La mayoría de estas herramientas son gratuitas, lo que facilita el intercambio entre ellas cuando se requiere adquirir nuevos conocimientos o incrementar el nivel. Sin embargo, las que no cuentan con capacidad de ajuste a la pantalla del usuario, limitan y bloquean el proceso de los niños y jóvenes por la falta de adaptabilidad a sus dispositivos, a lo que se suma textos en un idioma no conocido.

En la enseñanza de la programación en niños y jóvenes, se ha demostrado que el uso de herramientas web y aplicaciones mejora el interés de los niños en los contenidos académicos, y facilita la transmisión del conocimiento, si se compara con la enseñanza tradicional de los principios de la programación y algoritmia [García 2017].

En el trabajo "La enseñanza-aprendizaje del pensamiento computacional en edades tempranas: una revisión del estado del arte", se nombran otras herramientas didácticas para la enseñanza de la programación, las cuales no hacen uso de un computador, como por ejemplo los ejercicios disponibles en los libros de Hello Ruby, donde se tienen actividades asociadas principalmente al desarrollo de la lógica computacional [González 2018].

En sus inicios, la enseñanza de la programación empezó impartiéndose de manera presencial, pero con la transformación digital acelerada por la pandemia, la educación virtual pasó de ser algo lejano a una alternativa, ya que facilita el acceso al conocimiento, mitigando obstáculos para aprender, debido a que la educación de manera presencial no puede llegar fácilmente a todos los lugares. El internet ha permitido que el ser humano rompa el esquema tradicional de comunicación, el cual le permite mantenerse en constante aprendizaje [Ossa 2002].

Los nuevos conceptos que aparecen en la enseñanza de la programación tienen gran importancia, como el caso del "aprendizaje significativo", donde se señala que los nuevos conocimientos aprendidos se relacionan con los previamente adquiridos, particularmente en la práctica de la programación. Este concepto es estudiado por tres universidades de Chile en el trabajo "Experiencias prácticas con el uso del lenguaje de programación Scratch para desarrollar el pensamiento algorítmico de estudiantes en Chile" [Vidal et al 2015], resaltando que las personas aprenden mejor y disfrutan más cuando trabajan en proyectos con significado y propósito personal [Lead 2012].

4. Desarrollo

El desarrollo y construcción de la herramienta, se definió a través de un esquema de arquitectura basado en Serverless, ya que no se requiere la asignación de tareas en administración de la infraestructura, escalamiento y elasticidad [AWS 2022]. La definición de la arquitectura puede observarse a través de la Figura 1.

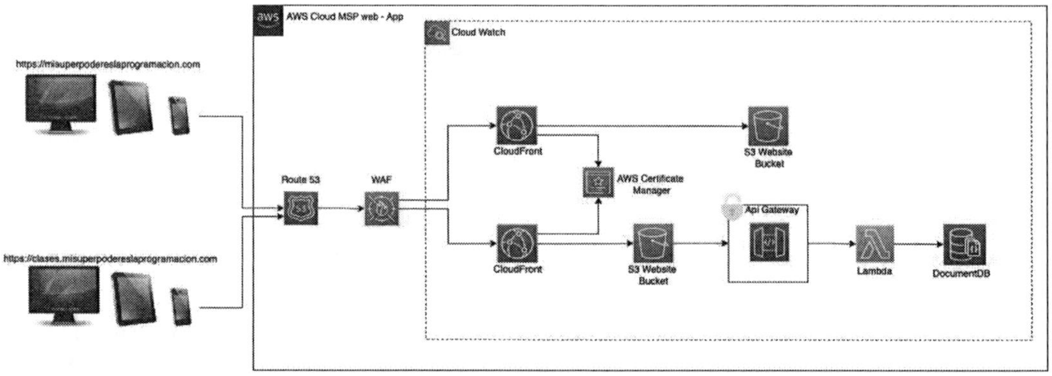

Figura 1. Diseño de arquitectura final para el sitio web estático e informativo y la herramienta para la enseñanza de la programación

La herramienta web *Mi Superpoder es la Programación*, se desarrolló utilizando metodologías de software como Scrum para el seguimiento del proyecto y planeación de los entregables. Esta herramienta fue creada por los autores, los cuales estuvieron presentes en todas las etapas del proceso (requisitos, diseño, definición, implementación). Se contó con el apoyo de diseñadores e ilustradores para mejorar y validar los diseños, así como de arquitectos de software con experiencia en la industria para validar y mejorar la arquitectura.

La construcción de la herramienta se basó en el enfoque centrado en el usuario, con el fin de garantizar no solo la usabilidad, sino que también las funcionalidades del videojuego respondieran a los objetivos de enseñanza de la programación. Del proceso de análisis surgió el documento de especificación de requisitos con la descripción de cada elemento y se construyó el documento de diseño de juego (GDD)[1], para detallar los escenarios del juego, personajes, historia, componentes de gamificación y recompensa, mecánicas y concepto del arte.

4.1 Mi Superpoder es la Programación, herramienta web

Mi Superpoder es la Programación es una herramienta web desarrollada bajo una arquitectura de tipo Serverless, donde fueron utilizados en su implementación HTML, CSS y la librería de React para la creación de los componentes visuales, mientras que para la creación de los componentes del videojuego se hizo uso de la librería de Javascript P5. La herramienta fue creada en los lenguajes de programación Javascript y Typescript y su infraestructura está soportada por AWS.

[1] Documento de diseño de juego. https://goo.su/80d34

La herramienta cuenta con tres bloques enfocados en fundamentos de programación 1, donde los niños y jóvenes pueden aprender sobre secuencias, patrones, diagramas de flujo y definición de autómatas; fundamentos 2, que hace énfasis en pseudocódigo, variables, condiciones y ciclos, y finalmente, fundamentos 3, para complementar el aprendizaje por medio de funciones, estructuras de datos y programación orientada a objetos (POO).

Los niños y jóvenes podrán acceder a las actividades disponibles para su aprendizaje, por medio del rol del estudiante. En su rol también encontrarán opciones de ayuda para contactarse directamente con el profesor encargado de sus clases. Como estrategia de gamificación, se crea la posibilidad de visualizar el avance de su personaje a través de la apariencia mejorada al superar los módulos exitosamente.

La herramienta web es accesible por medio del enlace *https://misuperpodereslaprogramacion.com/*, y puede ser cargada desde computadores o celulares, dispositivos mayoritariamente utilizados por los niños y jóvenes de Colombia. Las validaciones de la herramienta se hicieron en navegadores como Opera, Firefox y Safari, pero se recomienda hacer uso del navegador Google Chrome.

En la Figura 2, se muestra la estructura principal de la herramienta, distribuida de la siguiente manera. a) Pantalla de acceso a la herramienta, b) Pantalla de visualización de las actividades asignadas, pendientes por realizar, c) Pantalla informativa del nivel, características del contenido a aprender, d) Pantalla de realización de la actividad a través de un nivel del videojuego, e) Pantalla de progreso y visualización de mejoras del personaje según el nivel de avance y f) Pantalla de ayuda y soporte.

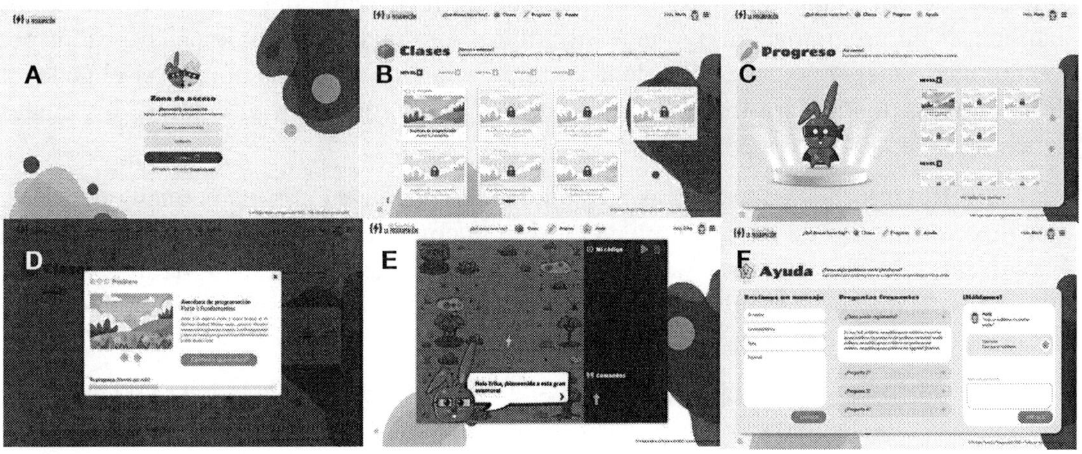

Figura 2. Interfaz de la aplicación Mi Superpoder es la Programación en el rol de estudiante

En el rol del profesor, como es posible observar en la Figura 3, se encuentran las pantallas de: a) Inicio de sesión, b) Visualización de opciones o menú de inicio principal, c) Creación de estudiantes e inscripción a una clase para, así, asignar módulos según el nivel y conocimientos que poseen los niños y jóvenes, d) Visualización de estudiantes creados y opciones para su edición, e) Modal de chat para comunicación y soporte con el estudiante y f) Actividades por niveles disponibles para la capacitación del profesor.

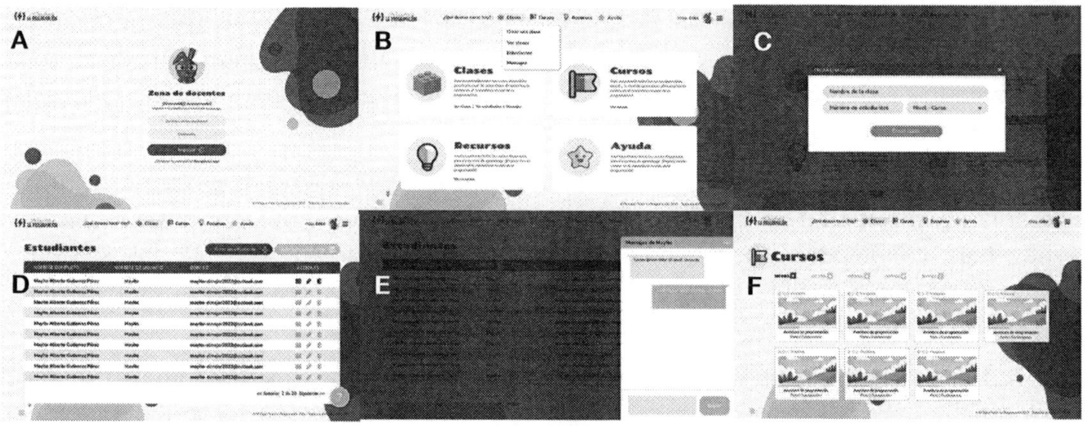

Figura 3. Interfaz de la aplicación Mi Superpoder es la Programación en el rol de profesor

La herramienta web se basa en un videojuego, donde se deberán superar obstáculos mientras se completan niveles y se aprende lógica y programación. El videojuego está compuesto de una historia, dinámicas y recompensas que están dirigidas a niños de 6 a 12 años con capacidades lectores y conocimientos básicos en operaciones matemáticas. El lenguaje es el español y cuenta con videos, imágenes y sonidos de apoyo.

4.2 El videojuego

La historia del videojuego de la herramienta para la enseñanza de la programación, gira alrededor de una competencia de carreras, donde Mayito, un conejo que a través de sus habilidades en programación ayuda a sus amigos a salir de los problemas causados por Rocco, otro conejo que hace parte de la competencia y que además quiere ser el ganador de la carrera, donde para lograrlo dejará diversos obstáculos en el camino, los cuales deberán ser superados por Mayito.

A lo largo de sus aventuras, el jugador se encontrará con retos que deberán ser resueltos por medio de código y elementos de la computación, los cuales permitarán a Mayito rescatar a sus amigos y objetos de valor, para llegar a la meta de la carrera, lo que otorgará nuevas habilidades y poderes siempre y cuando se culminen con éxito todos los ejercicios de lógica y programación.

La historia del videojuego se basa en la conocida fábula de la liebre y la tortuga, con algunas adaptaciones. En este caso, se introduce la alianza entre un conejo y una tortuga, para alcanzar la meta de una competencia de carreras. La idea de la historia del videojuego, módulos y concepto surge a partir de la experiencia adquirida en los talleres de programación que han sido dictados desde el año 2017 y también desde las necesidades identificadas en cada una de las sesiones de clase.

A continuación, se describe cada uno de los módulos con los que cuenta el videojuego y se resaltan los niveles disponibles para esta primera versión. En esta etapa inicial, se han completado la mayoría de los niveles. Sin embargo, se debe tener en cuenta que cada módulo debe estar conformado por un total de 10 niveles, a excepción del módulo de autómatas, conformado solo por la mitad.

4.2.1 Partes del Computador

Partes del computador, es un módulo encargado de proporcionar conocimientos sobre cada uno de los elementos que conforman un computador y su respectivo funcionamiento. Los niños y jóvenes aprenderán sobre las diferencias existentes entre dispositivos de entrada y salida, hardware y software y componentes internos utilizados que permiten su funcionamiento. En la Figura 4, se muestra uno de los niveles del módulo.

Figura 4. Nivel perteneciente al módulo partes del computador

Figura 5. Nivel perteneciente al módulo autómatas

4.2.2 Autómatas

Autómatas, es el módulo encargado de enseñar a los niños y jóvenes sobre la definición de esta palabra. Aquí se aprenderá que los dispositivos considerados como autómatas son aquellos capaces de seguir instrucciones a partir de una serie de pasos, secuencias y operaciones dadas. Uno de los niveles puede ser visualizado en la Figura 5. En este módulo se encuentran solo 5 niveles de práctica.

4.2.3 Secuencias y Patrones

Secuencias y patrones, es un módulo encargado de fortalecer los conocimientos en lógica computacional, por lo que la gran mayoría de los ejercicios están conformados en la resolución de secuencias que deben ser ordenadas para dar una instrucción y la identificación de patrones repetitivos para llegar a un objetivo. En la figura 6 se muestra un nivel correspondiente a este módulo.

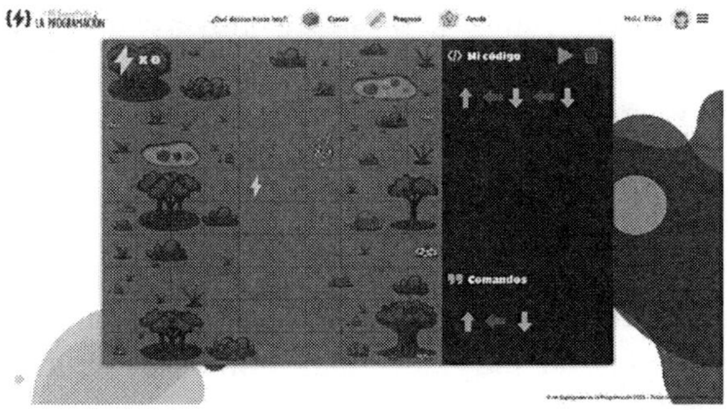

Figura 6. Nivel perteneciente al módulo de secuencias y patrones

4.2.4 Diagramas de Flujo

Diagramas de flujo, es un módulo en donde los niños y jóvenes deberán estructurar las instrucciones haciendo uso de símbolos que permiten indicar las acciones y decisiones a tomar, según el camino a seguir para alcanzar un objetivo. En la figura 7 se muestra un ejemplo de un nivel perteneciente a este módulo.

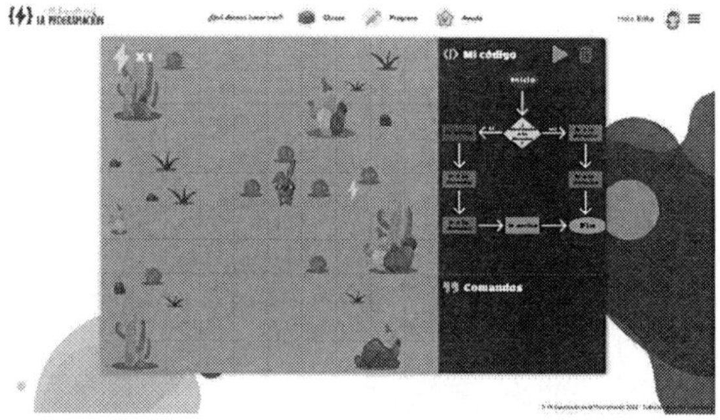

Figura 7. Nivel perteneciente al módulo de diagramas de flujo

4.2.5 Codificación

Codificación, es el módulo donde los niños y jóvenes colocan en práctica todo lo aprendido anteriormente y pasan a utilizar pseudocódigo para dar instrucciones basándose en lenguaje natural. Luego de superados los desafíos, los ejercicios deberán resolverse utilizando código real del lenguaje de programación basado en Javascript. Este módulo está en proceso de construcción, por lo tanto, no fue evaluado en esta primera versión.

5. Evaluación de la herramienta

Con el propósito de identificar la efectividad de la herramienta con relación a su funcionamiento, motivación que generaba en el uso, experiencia de usuario y adaptabilidad, se llevó a cabo un taller virtual con duración de 10 horas, distribuidos en 1 hora semanal. Para esta primera etapa se consideraron 13 niños de edades entre los 6 y los 12 años, de diferentes departamentos de Colombia, como Valle del Cauca, Antioquia, Guajira y Cundinamarca, la distribución de edades fue la siguiente: 2 niños de 6 años, 1 de 9 años, 4 de 8 años, 2 de 10 años, 2 de 7 años y 2 niños de 11 años.

Todos los niños estuvieron presentes en las 10 horas del taller, haciendo uso de un computador o celular, conectándose desde sus hogares o desde bibliotecas públicas. En caso de que alguno de los niños tuviera problemas para participar en el horario establecido, se crearon espacios adicionales con el fin de asegurar que todos los niños vieran las clases del taller y realizaran sus actividades.

La convocatoria para las pruebas fue abierta y se utilizaron redes sociales como medio de difusión, el proyecto social cuenta con página de Instagram, Facebook y página web. También se difundió la invitación a los niños para participar de las pruebas a través de LinkedIn, donde además se sumaron niños asistentes a la biblioteca Rafael Pombo de la ciudad de Cali. De todos los niños inscritos, 20 en total, se le dio prioridad a todos aquellos que podían asistir todos los días.

Para las pruebas se seleccionaron los módulos de secuencia y diagramas de flujo, con el fin de identificar si los ejercicios disponibles aportan a los conocimientos básicos de la lógica computacional. Los resultados de las pruebas fueron divididos en dos secciones y se presentan a continuación:

5.1 Análisis cualitativo

Para la captura de esta información, se realizó un formulario[2] [3] con una evaluación que contenía preguntas que facilitaban identificar el estado actual en conocimientos sobre tecnología y programación por parte de los niños, para así garantizar posterior al uso de la herramienta, la efectividad en la transmisión de conocimientos básicos en lógica computacional.

A la mayoría de niños se les dificultaron las actividades asociadas al uso de algoritmos en lenguaje natural. Sin embargo, al utilizar la herramienta, no se presentaron complicaciones en la interacción, a esto se le atribuye el contacto previo con dispositivos electrónicos como celular, tablet o computador. Además del conocimiento en el uso de internet para consultas.

En el proceso de evaluación, se observó que los niños comprendieron la mecánica del juego fácilmente y no fue necesario recibir apoyo para la solución de los ejercicios, e hicieron gran uso de las instrucciones proporcionadas por el avatar de la herramienta. En los módulos más avanzados, los niños más pequeños tuvieron dificultades para comprender algunos elementos como las decisiones de los diagramas de flujo, por lo que fue necesario repetir los niveles enfocados en este tema al menos por una segunda vez.

El análisis cualitativo sugiere que los niños comprendieron el funcionamiento de la herramienta y que además consideraron los ejercicios divertidos y entretenidos. Al finalizar el uso de la herramienta, los niños se enfrentaron a ejercicios sobre temas asociados a los diagramas de flujo y secuencia, los cuales fueron superados exitosamente.

En la Figura 8, se muestra el uso de la herramienta por parte de una de las niñas participantes. La fotografía cuenta con autorización por escrito para ser publicada.

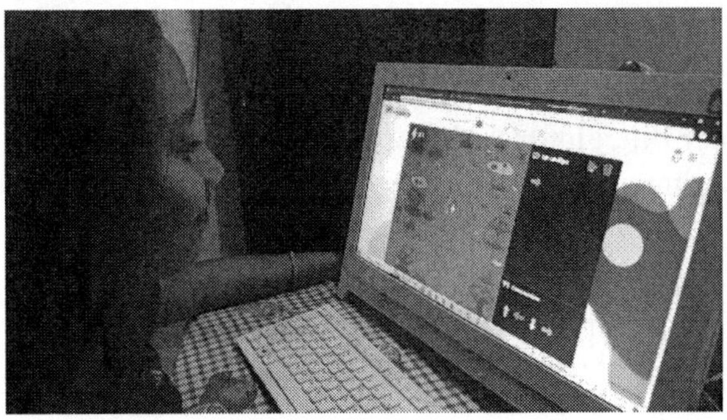

Figura 8. Niña haciendo uso de la herramienta web Mi Superpoder es la Programación

[2] Planeación taller - Mi superpoder es la programación. https://goo.su/ZQaJ7w7

[3] Cuestionario habilidades. https://goo.su/5TzipQQ

5.2 Análisis cuantitativo

Para esta evaluación, se entregó a los niños al final del uso de la herramienta, un formulario[4] con el fin de obtener información que sería utilizada en el análisis técnico e interpretación de los datos. El 15.4%, lo que corresponde a 2 niños de 13 evaluados, dieron una calificación de 4 en facilidad de uso, mientras que el 84.6% asignó una calificación de 5. Se manejó como rango de evaluación una escala de 1 a 5, siendo 5 excelente y la máxima calificación. Se le preguntó a los niños sobre las razones del puntaje asignado por debajo de 5, a lo que indicaron complejidad en el manejo del avatar por no permitir el salto de instrucciones aunque el nivel ya hubiera sido superado.

Respecto a la apariencia visual de la herramienta, 2 niños, lo que corresponde al 15.4% asignaron calificación de 4, mientras que el 84.6% asignaron una calificación de 5, las razones del puntaje por debajo de 5 se enfocaron en la falta de elementos de mayor interacción como videos y sonidos, que servirían de gran complemento para el entendimiento. A pesar de esto, todos los evaluados consideran agradable y acorde los colores, tipografía y estructura de los elementos.

Se consultó a los evaluados si recomendarían la herramienta, a lo que todos respondieron positivamente que sí lo harían. Posterior a esta pregunta se les consultó sobre elementos que agregarían a la herramienta, se obtuvieron respuestas como:

- Incremento en el tamaño elementos, 1 niño (7.7%)
- Agregar más personajes, 2 niños (15.4%)
- Agregar música y sonidos, 1 niño (7.7%)
- Más niveles con mayor dificultad, 4 niños (30.8%)
- Nada nuevo, 5 niños (38.5%)

También, se les consultó a los evaluados si cambiarían algo de lo que observaron en la herramienta, obteniendo como respuesta no cambiarían nada en un 100%.

En las pruebas, los niños no identificaron errores. Sin embargo, proponen mejorar el tiempo para mostrar el mensaje de instrucciones del avatar y posibilidad de contar con un botón para repetir la instrucción, sobre todo en el módulo de diagramas de flujo, que es donde se tiene mayor complejidad y se requiere mayor detalle en la instrucción

Se resalta que dos niños de los 13 evaluados participaron del taller a través de su celular sin presentar dificultades e inconvenientes, también 5 niños reportaron poseer un equipo con requerimientos técnicos regulares, sin embargo, esto no representó un impedimento.

Previo a las pruebas de los niños, se realizaron pruebas de carga y estrés con más de 35 usuarios conectados, sin presentar inconvenientes en el rendimiento de la aplicación, donde 6 de los evaluadores utilizaron su celular y lograron navegar y desarrollar los ejercicios de la herramienta sin inconvenientes.

6. Conclusiones

La herramienta web *Mi Superpoder es la Programación* ha demostrado durante las

[4] Cuestionario habilidades. https://goo.su/5TzipQQ

pruebas ser una opción adecuada en el campo de la enseñanza de la programación, ya que fue posible observar que los niños se adaptaron fácilmente al videojuego comprendiendo rápidamente sus mecánicas. Esta herramienta fue de gran apoyo para el docente encargado de acompañar el taller, gracias al avatar que a través de las descripciones y el paso a paso de la actividad brinda opciones para mejorar la comprensión del reto a realizar.

Es importante destacar que se trabajó con un número limitado de niños en las pruebas, debido a las restricciones de recursos y tiempo para llevar a cabo la investigación. Sin embargo, se espera aumentar el número de niveles de la herramienta para ser utilizada por un número mayor de participantes, con el fin de ampliar la validez de los resultados obtenidos en esta primera etapa.

Mi Superpoder es la Programación, es un herramienta que puede ser utilizada desde lugares remotos con o sin acompañamiento de un profesor, siendo posible de acceder a esta desde un celular con una conexión a internet por medio de datos móviles. En conclusión, la herramienta ha demostrado, en esta primera etapa, ser una opción prometedora en el campo de la enseñanza de la programación.

Como trabajo futuro se tiene la creación de nuevos niveles para los módulos asociados a los autómatas y partes del computador, además de la finalización del módulo de codificación. Se espera incluir más niveles en todos los demás módulos para aumentar la complejidad y agregar ejercicios de práctica que fortalezcan los conocimientos de los niños y jóvenes, los cuales puedan ser evaluados en ambientes escolares y de educación virtual.

Referencias

Dane.gov.co. (2018). "Boletín Técnico Indicadores básicos de tenencia y uso de tecnologías de la información y comunicación en empresas (TIC empresas) 2018". https://www.dane.gov.co/files/investigaciones/boletines/tic/bol_empresas_2018.pdf. Enero 2023

Patiño Montoya, Alex Julián., Hernández Álvarez, Jorge Mario., Espinal Ramos, Hermis. (2016). "Analizar por qué se debe enseñar la lógica de programación a niños y jóvenes en los hogares de la ciudad de Medellín". En Revista CIES Escolme 7.01, páginas 2-14

Pisabarro Marrón, Alma María., Vivaracho Pascual, Carlos Enrique., Manso Martínez, Esperanza., González Díaz, María Luisa. (2018) "Evaluación del uso de un Juego Serio no virtual en Programación". Actas de las Jenui. Barcelona, España., pp. 23-30

MSP. (2017). https://misuperpodereslaprogramacion.com/. Enero 2023

MIT. (2007). "Scratch - Acerca de Scratch". https://scratch.mit.edu/about. Enero 2023

Program.AR. (2016). "Pilas Bloques es una aplicación para enseñar y aprender a programar". https://pilasbloques.program.ar/acerca-de-pilas-bloques/. Enero 2023

Schor, Jonathan. (2014). "CodeMonkey - CODING FOR KIDS". https://www.codemonkey.com/. Enero 2023

MinTIC. (2014). "Puntos Digitales".

https://mintic.gov.co/portal/vivedigital/612/w3-propertyvalue-669.html#:~:text=El%20Punto%20Digital%20es%20un,lugar%2C%20con%20el%20fin%20de, Enero 2023

Liukas, Linda. (2015) Hello Ruby: adventures in coding. Macmillan. Vol. 1

Liukas, Linda (2017). Hello Ruby: Journey inside the computer. Hello Ruby. Vol. 2

Martínez, Juan Carlos et al. (2018) "Using Software Product Lines to Support Language Rehabilitation Therapies: An Experience Report," 2018 ICAI Workshops (ICAIW), Bogota, Colombia., pp. 1-6, doi: 10.1109/ICAIW.2018.8554992.

Martínez, J., Gutiérrez, E., Alvaréz, G., Castillo, Á. D., Portilla., A and Almanza, V. (2019). "Video Games to Support Language Therapies in Children with Hearing Disabilities," International Conference on Virtual Reality and Visualization (ICVRV), Hong Kong, China., pp. 172-175, doi: 10.1109/ICVRV47840.2019.00040

Álvarez, Gloria Inés, et al. (2021). SATReLO: A tool to support language therapies for children with hearing disabilities using video games. Revista Facultad de Ingeniería Universidad de Antioquia, no 99., p. 99-112

Code.org. (2013). "About Us".https://code.org/international/about. Enero 2023

Tynker. (2012). "About Us". https://www.tynker.com/about/. Enero 2023

Sapura, Danny., Oswari, Liniyanti. (2020). "Usability User Experience, Learning Motivation and Learning Rate Characteristic of Learning Programming Using Game Making onUsers with Different Computer Experience". International Conference on Information Technology and Its Application, p. 649-654.

García de los Salmones Gómez, P. (2017). "Desarrollo de un videojuego para enseñar programación a niños"

González, Carina Soledad. (2018) "La enseñanza-aprendizaje del Pensamiento Computacional en edades tempranas: una revisión del estado del arte." Pensamiento computacional., p. 1-37

Ossa, Guillermo. (2002). "Tendencias Educativas para el siglo XXI". Educación virtual, online y @learning. Elementos para la discusión. Edutec, Revista electrónica de tecnología educativa. p. a025-a025

Vidal Cristian et al. (2015). "Experiencias prácticas con el uso del lenguaje de programación Scratch para desarrollar el pensamiento algorítmico de estudiantes en Chile"., Formación universitaria., vol. 8., p. 23-32

The Lead Project. (2012). "Super Scratch Programming Adventure!: Learn to Program by Making Cool Games"

AWS. (2022). "Creación de aplicaciones con arquitecturas sin servidor". https://aws.amazon.com/es/lambda/serverless-architectures-learn-more/#:~:text=What%20is%20a%20serverless%20architecture,management%20is%20done%20by%20AWS. Enero 2023

Advanced Undergraduate Computing Students' Perception of Software Quality Teaching: a Survey in the Brazilian Paraná State

Guilherme N. Ferrari[1], Thais S. Nepomuceno[1], Claudia H. Santana[1], Carlos D. Luz[1], Gislaine C. Leal[1], Aline M. M. M. Amaral[1], Renato Balancieri[2], Edson OliveiraJr[1]

[1]State University of Maringá
Maringá – PR – Brazil

[2]State University of Paraná
Apucarana – PR – Brazil

{guinetoferrari, thais.nepomuceno1, chsantana}@gmail.com

carlos.danilo.luz@gmail.com, {gclleal, ammmamaral}@uem.br

renato.balancieri@unespar.edu.br, edson@din.uem.br

Abstract. *Aspects of software quality (SQ), such as process and product metrics, and assessment techniques, can be taught to computing students during their undergraduate courses, however, there is no consensus on how. In Brazil, computing courses are structured as the Brazilian Computer Society suggests, still, researchers point out that there are few SQ subjects in these courses. This paper aims to analyze the perception of SQ concepts by advanced undergraduate students in the northwest of the Paraná state. We applied a survey and received ninety-nine answers. Our results show that most SQ concepts are taught, but the students feel they did not learn and are not able to apply them. We discuss and suggest guidelines to improve the understanding of SQ concepts.*

1. Introduction

Software quality management incorporates a set of activities to guide and control the organization with a focus on processes, products, and services. Such management is an essential factor for an organization to maintain a competitive position in the market, in addition to ensuring business success, customer satisfaction, and product acceptance [Laporte et al. 2007, Jenkins 2007, Bourque et al. 2014]. The absence of Software Quality (SQ) has impacting consequences, such as delays in the delivery of new applications, high maintenance and support costs for customers, and long learning curves. [Jones and Bonsignour 2011].

For software users, quality is related to the usability and implementation of required functionalities. As for software developers, the most important quality issue is that the software meets the specifications and provides services as previously contracted [Tian 2005, Kokol 2022]. Therefore, quality is subjectively determined by those who interact with the system, whether to solve their problems through software or are responsible for designing, implementing, and testing the solutions, making judgments about the quality of the product [Gillies 2011, Suali et al. 2019]. Therefore, the use of techniques and tools that ensure and guarantee SQ is essential [Page 2008, Chren et al. 2022].

An important piece of graduates has their first contact with the job market in areas that require SQ knowledge, such as testing and maintenance. Usually, they are not deeply involved in undergraduate programs which offer educational content on how to build high-quality software or how to integrate quality activities during the software development process [Hilburn and Towhidnejad 2002, Garousi et al. 2019]. In addition, there is no consensus on how to educate future software engineers on topics of SQ and software improvement [Dingsøyr et al. 2000, Kappelman et al. 2016].

As SQ is becoming increasingly important, both because of educational requirements and the industry, it should be at the center of the undergraduate curriculum of courses that teach software development. Thus, students are introduced to a variety of SQ activities, enabling them to develop technical knowledge and skills [Hilburn and Towhidnejad 2002, Richardson et al. 2011].

According to [Bettin et al. 2022], there is a low number of specific courses on SQ in undergraduate computing courses, as well as differences between the topics covered in the program and what is expected for the graduates' profile. They claim what is taught is not enough for students to have a proper view of SQ, which might imply a deficit of skills in the software development industry. Thus, investigating such claims is an existing demand in the area.

In this context, this paper is aimed at carrying out an exploratory analysis of the perception of undergraduate Computing students in relation to the knowledge acquired in SQ courses.

The analysis was based on nine knowledge axes defined by the Brazilian Computing Society (SBC) in its educational References for Undergraduate Computing Courses. To fulfill this objective, a survey was carried out with 99 students from the last two years of different undergraduate Computing courses from higher education institutions, public or private, in the state of Paraná, southern Brazil.

Our results provide an understanding of the perception of the undergraduate students regarding their knowledge of SQ acquired during the course, and how they perceive themselves regarding their capability in applying what was learned. This way, we can contribute to the discussions of the curricula on computing courses, highlighting the knowledge axes that should be improved in order to improve the learning for future practitioners.

This paper is organized as follows: Section 2 provides essential concepts on the teaching of software quality and the SBC educational references; Section 3 presents the methodology of our study; Section 4 presents general and research question-based data analysis; Section 5 discusses the obtained results; and Section 6 presents the conclusion and directions for future work.

2. Background

To contextualize the research, we will present in this session the fundamental concepts of teaching software quality and the SBC's Software Quality Formation Reference.

2.1. Teaching of Software Quality

Specific subjects in the computing courses are intrinsically challenging for the teaching process. Students complain about excessive theoretical content, with a high-volume demand and short deadlines. On the other side, teachers report issues regarding the short time to teach a large quantity of content and a lack of integration between other subjects. Added to the subject's challenges, the teachers also face diversity in the level of knowledge of students [Lemos et al. 2019].

The teaching of Software Engineering (SE) is present in most of the computing undergraduate courses in Brazil and is considered of great importance to developing qualified professionals. These professionals can contribute to the SQ, as well as contribute to solving traditional issues in the software industry [Gibbs 1994, Prikladnicki et al. 2009].

According to [Moser et al. 2021], computing undergraduate courses provide students with theoretical and practical knowledge to prepare them for professional exercise. However, certain processes are often not properly addressed during software teaching, as is the case with SQ, which is often overlooked by the students who do not see it as a priority. However, according to [Gupta and Goel 2019], once the students are exposed to the software industry and its demands, they must acquire this previously neglected knowledge.

SQ has always been present in the curricula of computing undergraduate courses, often with its concepts showing upon different subjects or in one specific subject in the course dedicated to this topic [Chren et al. 2022, Hilburn and Towhidnejad 2002]. Researchers mention that SQ should be approached since the beginning of the students' graduation to integrate the fundamental concepts as early as possible [Scatalon et al. 2017, Gomes et al. 2021].

SQ teaching should provide knowledge that allows the student to implement, measure, assess, and improve the software product throughout its entire life cycle. SQ is a vast knowledge area, its teaching should follow a structured approach, making the student experience close to the software industry reality [Suryn 2003].

2.2. SBC's Software Quality Formation Reference

SBC is a scientific society that brings together Brazilian students, teachers, researchers, and professionals in the area of Computing and Informatics from all over the country. One of its functions is to define national scientific and technological politics. Its goal is to elaborate and provide the reference for the curriculum building of the computing courses in Brazil, aiming at contributing to the formation of computing professionals with social responsibilities [Ribeiro et al. 2019, Zorzo et al. 2017].

At the end of 2016, SBC provided the document entitled "Formation Reference for Computing Undergraduate Courses" (RF-CC-2017), where they presented the references for the formation of undergraduate courses in the area of computing, such as Computer Science, Informatics, Computing Engineering, Information Systems, and other technical degrees. These references are a result of the contribution between the SBC associates from different universities and are material that is used as a consultation for the preparation of these courses' curricula and should be aligned to other national curricula guidelines [Zorzo et al. 2017].

For the Software Engineering course, the SBC (RF-CC-2017) specifies an expected knowledge related to SQ, demanding: "The student should be able to produce high-quality software that conforms to its requirements and satisfies user needs. The achievement of SQ involves models and techniques of the software product and process quality".

From this specification, the SBC defines nine axes of knowledge for SQ, which are competencies and skills that are expected of the graduates [Zorzo et al. 2017]. These are:

- QA = Quality Attributes: to understand what are the software product quality attributes and their utility;
- PM = Software Product Metrics: To apply software product quality measurements tools;
- AT = Product Assessment Techniques: to apply product assessment techniques;
- RS = Review Techniques and Static Analysis: To apply techniques and procedures of validation and verification (static and dynamic);
- MP = Product Quality Models and Standards: To understand the software product quality models and standards;
- MC = Process Quality Models and Standards: To understand the software process quality models and standards;
- SC = Quality Standardization and Certification: to understand the quality standardization and certification processes;
- CM = Process Metrics: to apply process metrics;
- ST = Software Testing: to apply software testing.

3. Methodology

This section presents the methodology adopted for this study.

3.1. Aim and Research Questions

This paper consists of a characterization of the perception of SQ knowledge of undergraduate students in computing courses, such as Computer Science, Informatics, Production Engineering, Systems Analysis and Development, and Software Engineering. For this, the following research question was elaborated: "***What is the perception of undergraduate advanced computing students in relation to their acquired Software Quality skills?***".

3.2. Audience

The audience of our study is students enrolled in the last two years of undergraduate computing courses from universities in the state of Paraná. Our focus on the last two years of the course is because the first years students may not yet have attended disciplines on SQ.

3.3. Sampling

The data collection was done through the application of an online survey - following the guidelines by [Linåker et al. 2015] - developed on Google Forms. Participation in the survey was optional and anonymous.

The survey was made available for thirty days and sent by email to the undergraduate courses coordinators to be sent to their students. In the end, we collected ninety-nine answers to the survey.

3.4. Design

We decided to perform exploratory research because our aim is to understand the perception of the students regarding SQ concepts.

3.5. Instrument and Evaluation

The structure of the survey is divided into two main sections. The first is a characterization of the participant and its undergraduate course, in which we collect data on the name and duration of the course, the semester in which the student is enrolled, if the university is public or private, the city it is located, and if the respondent has any experience in software development. The universities were not identified because our focus is not to compare the teaching capacities among the institutions, but rather on their students' perception of knowledge.

The second section focuses on the students' perceptions regarding their knowledge and skills on SQ concepts, more specifically the competencies for the SQ knowledge defined by SBC, as we explained previously and discussed by [Bettin et al. 2022].

For each competency, there is a short description of its concepts, followed by three quantitative questions to be answered by a five-point Likert scale [Likert 1932], which aims to verify the level of agreement of the individual with a proposition that expresses something ranging from "totally disagree" to "totally agree" in relation to the SQ. Table 1 presents these questions.

Once we built the survey, it was validated by two professors who specialized in the SQ subject. We applied a pilot version of the survey on a sample of six invited students to refine the instrument and to eliminate any doubts that might arise during the application. The time required for students to answer the survey was an average of seven minutes, as initially foreseen in the pilot version.

3.6. Data Sharing

All data from our research is available at `https://doi.org/10.5281/zenodo.7429490`.

4. Data Analysis

As we discussed before, the participants of our survey answered six questions aiming at characterizing them, and twenty-seven questions about their skills regarding the nine SQ competencies as presented in Table 1. This subsection is divided into two parts, one for the characterization of the participant and one for illustrating the specific answers of each of the competencies.

4.1. Demographics

Table 2 presents the quantitative and percentage distribution of responses regarding the first six questions characterizing the participants.

The majority of participants are in Software Engineering (32.32%) and Computer Science (20.20%) courses. Most participants are from private institutions (60.61%) and 77.78% of respondents are from Maringá. About 23.23% of the total do not have any experience in software development, while almost half of the participants have about 1 to 3 years of experience.

4.2. Software Quality Competencies

In this section, we present the distribution of the scores given by the participants to each of the competencies. Figure 1 presents the bar graphs for each competency and their scores according to the scale we used. Following, we are going to discuss each graph.

Table 1. Questions regarding the knowledge axis competencies

Competency	Questions
AXIS 1 - QA	QA1 - My course contemplates or addresses concepts of software quality attributes.
	QA2 - I learned about concepts of software quality attributes.
	QA3 - I feel able to apply aspects of software quality attributes.
AXIS 2 - PM	PM1 - My course contemplates or addresses the software product metrics.
	PM2 - I learned about concepts of software product metrics.
	PM3 - I feel able to apply software product metrics.
AXIS 3 - AT	AT1 - My course contemplates or addresses product assessment techniques.
	AT2 - I learned about product assessment techniques.
	AT3 - I feel able to apply product assessment techniques.
AXIS 4 - RS	RS1 - My course contemplates or addresses review techniques and static analysis.
	RS2 - I learned about aspects of review techniques and static analysis.
	RS3 - I feel able to apply review techniques and static analysis.
AXIS 5 - MP	MP1 - My course contemplates or addresses product quality models and standards.
	MP2 - I learned about product quality models and standards.
	MP3 - I feel able to apply product quality models and standards.
AXIS 6 - MC	MC1 - My course contemplates or addresses process quality models and standards.
	MC2 - I learned about process quality models and standards.
	MC3 - I feel able to apply process quality models and standards.
AXIS 7 - SC	SC1 - My course contemplates or addresses quality standardization and certification.
	SC2 - I learned about aspects of quality standardization and certification.
	SC3 - I feel able to apply quality standardization and certification.
AXIS 8 - CM	CM1 - My course contemplates or addresses the process metrics.
	CM2 - I learned about process metrics.
	CM3 - I feel able to apply process metrics.
AXIS 9 - ST	ST1 - My course contemplates or addresses software testing.
	ST2 - I learned about software testing.
	ST3 - I feel able to apply software testing.

***QA** = Quality Attributes, **PM** = Software Product Metrics, **AT** = Product Assessment Techniques*
***RS** = Review Techniques and Static Analysis, **MP** = Product Quality Models and Standards*
***MC** = Process Quality Models and Standards, **SC** = Quality Standardization and Certification*
***CM** = Process Metrics, **ST** = Software Testing*

QA - Quality Attributes

Approximately 76.7% of the participants are positive that the content is seen during the undergraduate course. The majority, about 75.7%, considered having learned the content, but even so, a significant portion, 34.4% feels neutral about being able to apply SQ attributes. The results can be seen in graph (a) of Figure 1.

PM - Software Product Metrics

Table 2. Characterization of the participants of the survey

Participant Characteristic	Count	Percentage
Course		
Software Engineering	32	32.32%
Computer Science	20	20.20%
Analysis and System Development	18	18.18%
Informatics	10	10.10%
Industrial Engineering with an Emphasis in Software	8	8.08%
Information Systems	7	7.07%
Computer Engineering	3	3.03%
Major in Computing	1	1.01%
Institution		
Public	39	39.39%
Private	60	60.61%
City of the Institution		
Maringá	77	77.78%
Apucarana	12	12.12%
Campo Mourão	8	8.08%
Londrina	1	1.01%
Jandaia do Sul	1	1.01%
Software Development Experience		
No experience	23	23.23%
Less than 1 year of experience	20	20.20%
Between 1 and 3 years of experience	47	47.47%
Between 3 and 6 years of experience	9	9.09%
More than 6 years of experience	0	0.00%

We can visualize in graph (b) of Figure 1 that the majority of the participants, about 63.3%, are positive that they have seen the content of this competency, 57.5% agree they have learned it, however, about 65.6%, are neutral or negative about feeling able to apply software product metrics.

AT - Product Assessment Techniques

About 54.5% are positive that the content is seen. About 45.4% consider that they have learned it, but only 22.2% feel able to use product assessment techniques. These results can be seen in graph (c) of Figure 1.

RS - Review Techniques and Static Analysis

56.5% of the participants are positive about having seen the content. About 34.3% felt neutral regarding having learned, hence, just 26.2% feel able to apply review techniques and static analysis. These results can be seen in graph (d) of Figure 1.

MP - Product Quality Models and Standards

In graph (e) of Figure 1 about 72.1%, are positive about having seen the content. About 56.7% are positive about learning it. Even so, the majority of the answers regarding being able to apply the knowledge remained neutral.

MC - Process Quality Models and Standards

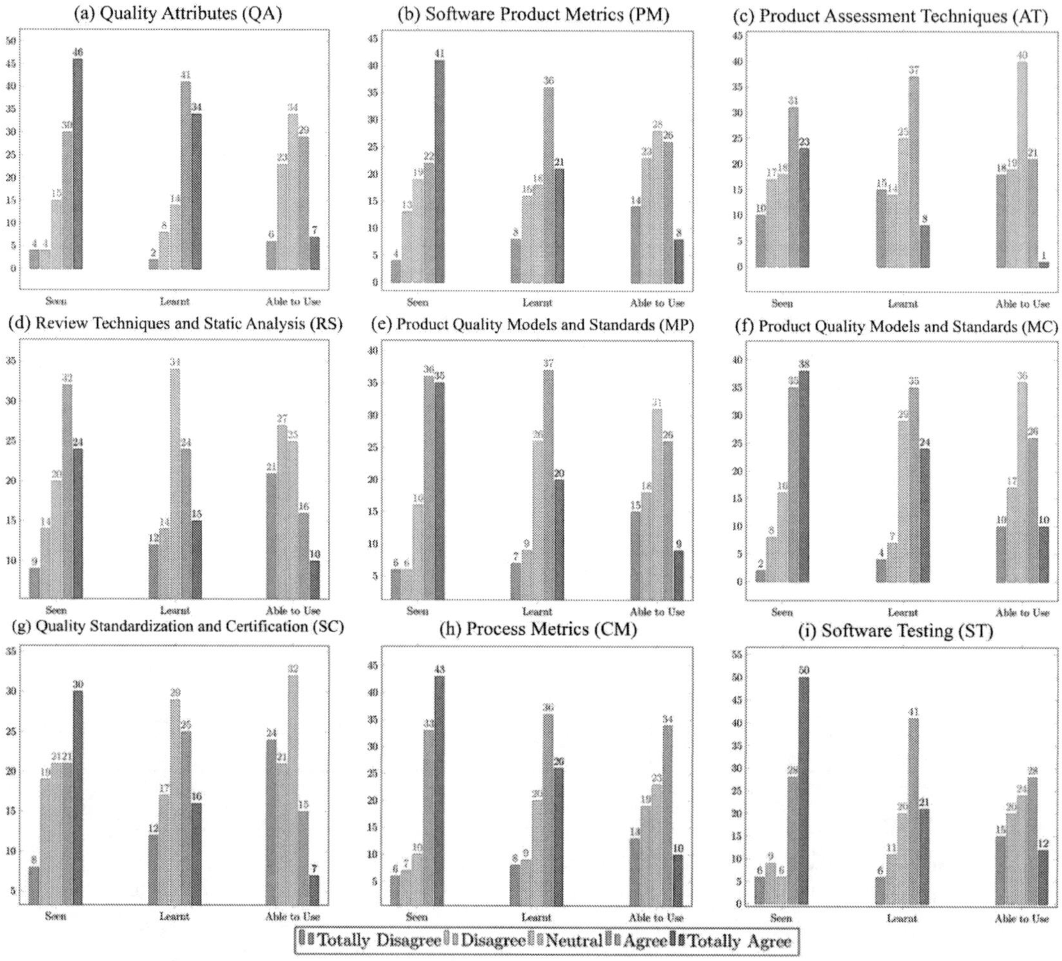

Figure 1. Scores given to the nine software quality competencies

Most participants stated that they had seen the content. Similarly, about 35.4% agreed, and 24.2% strongly agreed about learning it. However, when it comes to feeling able to use it, the response that most prevailed was neutral, about 36.4%, as can be seen in graph (f) of Figure 1.

SC - Quality Standardization and Certification

30.3% totally agreed and 21.2% both agreed and were neutral about having seen the content. Around 29.3%, remained neutral about having learned it, as shown in graph (g) of Figure 1. Almost half of the participants, about 45.4%, do not feel able to apply this knowledge, while about 32.3% remained neutral.

CM - Process Metrics

About 43.5% totally agreed that the content was seen. About 36.4% and 26.3% agreed and totally agreed, respectively, about having learned it. As seen in graph (h) of Figure 1, 34.3% agreed that they feel able to apply the knowledge, while 32% partially or totally disagreed.

ST - Software Testing

In graph (i) of Figure 1 about 78.8% are positive about having seen it. About 41.4% agreed to have learned the content. However, only 12.1% feel totally able to apply it, while about 20% disagree with the affirmation, and 24% remained neutral.

5. Discussion of Results

According to the data analysis, for each knowledge axis, few students disagreed about having seen the content during their courses.

The Software Testing axis draws our attention due to its level of agreement being higher than 50% of the participants regarding having seen its content. This may have happened due to its content being frequently approached during Software Engineering subjects.

About the data presented in Table 2 regarding the characterization of the participants, we can focus on the level of software development experience to further discuss our findings. We did not specify the type of experience asked, thus we can consider software development in different contexts, such as professional activities or even development from study or research.

We can check that about 23.2% do not have any experience with software development. While around 76.77% of the participants have some level of experience. Of the ninety-nine participants, none said having more than six years of experience in software development.

Aiming at better understanding how this difference in the experience level can influence the student perception, the survey answers were grouped according to the level of experience to be analyzed. Thus, we can calculate the average of the scores given by the students to the twenty-seven questions regarding the nine competencies.

Figure 2 presents three radar charts, one for each question that repeats along the survey. The axes of the chart represent the nine competencies and its scale follows the Likert scale used in our survey. The plotted data on the chart are the average score given by the students grouped by their level of experience, creating four overlapping polygons.

By comparing the three charts in Figure 2 we can see that the level of agreement decreases across the three questions. This can indicate that even though the students agree that the content was seen during their course, they disagree regarding having learned it and feeling able to apply this knowledge. This shows a problem that goes beyond the curriculum structure of the computing courses, it points out that these contents need to be understood and absorbed by the students.

In chart (b) we can see that the green line, representing the higher level of experience, often has higher average scores on competencies like PM, AT, RS, MP, and ST, and, on the other competencies, has lower scores than the other levels of experience. In the SC competence, for example, green and blue lines, representing the two highest levels of experience, is lower than the others, while the red one, which represents no experience, has the highest scores.

Similarly, in chart (c), the green line showed the highest scores on competencies like ST, MP, PM, and QA, while the yellow line, which represents students with less than one year of experience, has the lowest average values.

We can discuss that these high average scores from the more experienced stu-

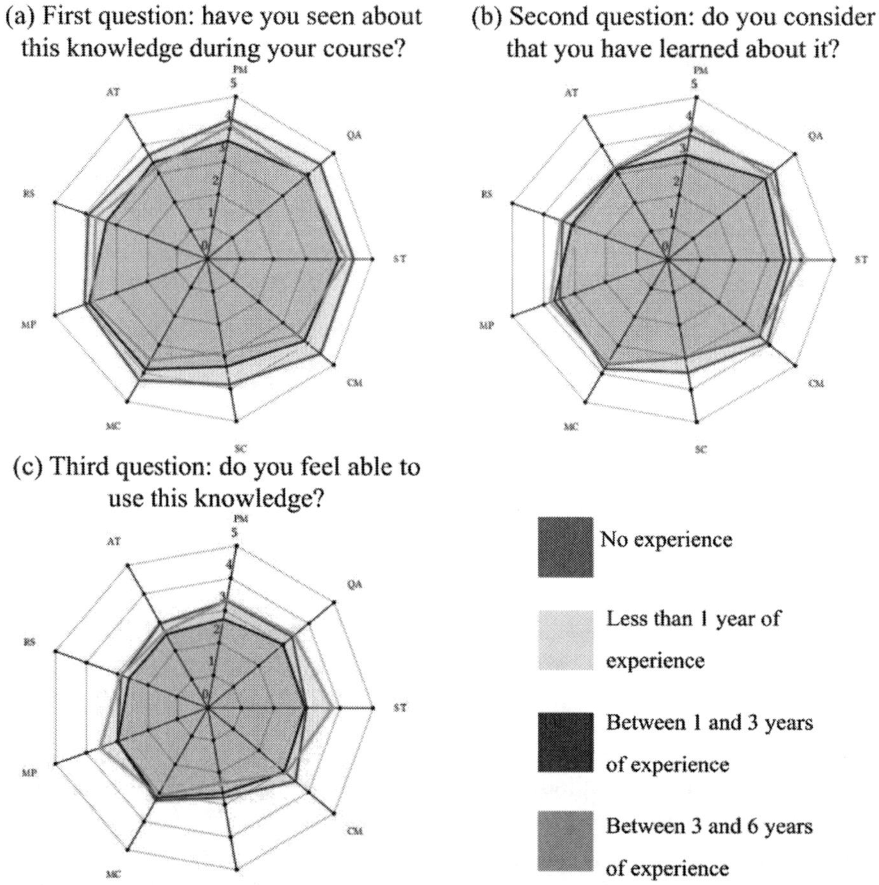

Figure 2. Average scores of the questions according to experience level

dents to competencies like PM, AT, RS, MP, and ST, could indicate that having experience with development practices can contribute to learning. While competencies like SC, where higher experience had lower scores than the rest, can indicate that the practice was different than what was learned or was not enough for them to feel able to apply their knowledge, something that has not yet happened to students with little to no experience.

Therefore, competencies like QA, PM, AT, RS, MP, and ST showed better performance among experienced students. These competencies can be enhanced when the student is practicing software development. While the SC competency showed opposite results, which can signify that what was taught is different or outdated from what is applied in the practice.

To visualize even better the difference of scores given to the three questions for each group of the level of experience, we built Figure 3, which presents four radar charts for the four categories of experience levels. In this case, the data plotted creates three polygons for the three asked questions for each of the nine competencies.

Comparing the three charts, we can notice how the lines representing the scores for each question behave. Figure 3 shows that the lines are more spaced in the first charts and this distance between them is reduced along the charts. It is possible to notice that the more experience in software development the student has, the more they can affirm they have learned what was seen during the course.

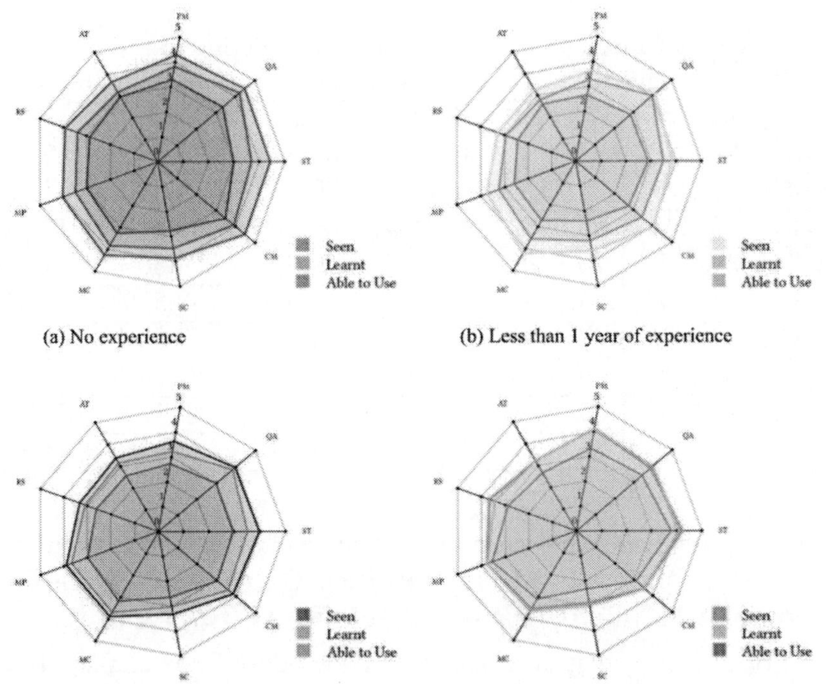

(a) No experience (b) Less than 1 year of experience

(c) Between 1 and 3 years of experience (d) Between 3 and 6 years of experience

Figure 3. Graphs for the averages for each of the respondent's experience levels

Also, in some competencies, such as MP and TS, experienced students can affirm that they feel able to apply the knowledge almost on the same level that they affirm that they have seen and learned about it during their course. Thus, the experience with software development can contribute to the student's perception regarding their level of understanding and capacity in applying the knowledge of the competencies in SQ.

Another point that we can discuss is regarding the high number of neutral answers to the survey. Some examples are shown in the previous section, like graph (c) of Figure 1, where around 40% of the participants remained neutral regarding knowing how to apply product assessment techniques, or in graph (g) of Figure 1, where both the answers to "learnt" and "able to use" were mostly neutral to the Quality Standardization and Certification competency.

Aiming at analyzing the answers on the extreme ends of the scale, we built Table 3, presenting the percentage of answers regarding each knowledge axis not considering the option "neutral". The answers "agree" and "totally agree" were grouped, as well as "disagree" and "totally disagree". Thus, it is possible to summarize the student's perceptions into positive or negative values.

Regarding having their content addressed during the course, the axis with the most positive scores were QA (93.08%), MC (87.95%), and MP (85.55%). While the ones with the most negative scores were SC (34.62%), AT (33.33%), and RS (29.11%).

Regarding having learned its content, the QA showed the better positive score (88.23%), followed by MC (84.29%), and, third, CM and ST tied (78.48%). On the other hand, the ones with the most negative score was SC (41.43%), RS (40%), and AT (39.18%).

Table 3. Participants answers for each axis not considering the "neutral" option

Axis	Seen		Learnt		Able to Use	
	Disagree	Agree	Disagree	Agree	Disagree	Agree
1 - QA	6.92%	93.08%	11.77%	88.23%	44.61%	55.38%
2 - PM	21.25%	78.75%	29.63%	70.37%	44.61%	47.88%
3 - AT	33.33%	66.67%	39.18%	60.82%	62.71%	37.29%
4 - RS	29.11%	70.89%	40.00%	60.00%	64.86%	35.14%
5 - MP	14.45%	85.55%	21.91%	78.09%	48.52%	51.48%
6 - MC	12.05%	87.95%	15.71%	84.29%	42.86%	57.14%
7 - SC	34.62%	65.38%	41.43%	58.57%	67.16%	32.84%
8 - CM	14.61%	85.39%	21.52%	78.48%	42.10%	57.90%
9 - ST	16.13%	83.87%	21.52%	78.48%	46.67%	53.33%

Lastly, regarding being able to apply the knowledge, the higher positive score was seen in CM (57.90%), followed by MC (57.14%), and QA (55.38%). While the axis with the lowest scores were SC (67.16%), RS (64.86%), and AT (62.71%).

The majority agreed that the content was seen during the course. However, according to [Richardson et al. 2011], the presence of a topic in a curriculum does not provide any guidance on how it should be taught. Therefore, we created three guidelines to help and improve the teaching of SQ, allowing students to understand the concepts and also develop the social and emotional skills - soft skills - that are desired in the software industry.

G.1: Integrate the content of the Software Quality competencies.

We noticed a difference between students with little experience in software development to those with some years of practice. We believe that aiming at relating what is taught in the classroom to what is applied during software development practices can help students who do not yet have experience also acquire adequate knowledge about these concepts. Also, all the contents of the SQ axis could be addressed together, since one complements the other.

G.2: Promote learning through practice based on case studies, problems, experiences, and real or fictional projects.

By developing activities that relate what is taught to what is practiced in the software industry, we hope that the student can develop leadership, good communication skills, and strategic thinking, among other skills desired.

G.3: Review the content of the curriculum of the computing undergraduate courses regarding SQ.

It is necessary to guarantee that what is offered in the curriculum of undergraduate courses is updated, following the orientations of the Ministry of Education and the guidelines of SBC.

5.1. Validity Evaluation

Some limitations and threats to validity regard the application of the survey. We noticed a low volume of participation by universities and students. This may have happened due to the limited time that the questionnaire was available. We understand that the number of participants can influence the results, however, we had to work with these values due to a limited time for the research. Hence, we suggest a replication with a larger sample of students. Moreover, there were a lot of neutral answers, which may indicate uncertainty in how to respond or fear of giving an opinion. We suggest the use of a scale with an even value of answers, which can contribute to reducing this neutrality and mitigating the threat.

6. Conclusion

Our paper presents the results acquired through an exploratory analysis of the perception of undergraduate students of computing courses in the universities of Paraná regarding the knowledge of SQ competencies.

Our results allowed us to understand that, even when the students are presented with the content of the SQ competencies, they often still say that did not learn it and do not feel able of applying it. This condition could be a reflection of the teaching method during the undergraduate course. Thus, the present study fills a gap discussed by [Bettin et al. 2022] and identifies the need to check whether the content defined in the course curriculum is actually being addressed.

Thinking about this issue, we created some guidelines to improve the teaching of SQ in universities, aiming to support a better understanding of these concepts so that the students can develop the skills and capabilities expected in industry practitioners.

With our paper, one is able to analyze how these competencies of SQ, defined by SBC, are being approached and how learning of them is being perceived by advanced undergraduate students. We hope to point to viable paths to improve the teaching and development of the students, and to provide capable professionals for the market.

For future work, we believe that the results could benefit from a larger sample of students, which could allow a deeper and more insightful analysis of the difference between the perception of understanding for each experience level. Also, we believe that this work can be expanded with more detailed questions regarding the students' perception of learning, elaborating even further for each subject on what are the topics that they feel positive about having learned, narrowing in order to identify the most critical lessons for the competencies.

We also suggest (i) the application of this research to universities of other states in Brazil; (ii) developing research about the method of teaching SQ beyond the student perception; and (iii) analyzing the graduated student regarding their skills acquired during the course.

Acknowledgements

Edson OliveiraJr thanks CNPq/Brazil (Grant #311503/2022-5). Authors thank CAPES/PROAP/Brazil, support Grant #88881.753469/2022-01.

References

Bettin, G., Herculani, J., Shigenaga, M., Leal, G., Balancieri, R., OliveiraJr, E., Colanzi, T., and Amaral, A. (2022). Teaching of software quality in public higher-level universities of paraná-brasil: an exploratory study. In *Proceedings of the 30th Workshop on Computing Education*, pages 286–297, Porto Alegre, RS, Brasil. SBC. in Portuguese.

Bourque, P., Fairley, R. E., and Society, I. C. (2014). *Guide to the Software Engineering Body of Knowledge (SWEBOK(R)): Version 3.0.* IEEE Computer Society Press, Washington, DC, USA, 3rd edition.

Chren, S., Macák, M., Rossi, B., and Buhnova, B. (2022). Evaluating code improvements in software quality course projects. In *Proceedings of the International Conference on Evaluation and Assessment in Software Engineering 2022*, EASE '22, page 160–169, New York, NY, USA. Association for Computing Machinery.

Dingsøyr, T., Jaccheri, M. L., and Wang, A. I. (2000). Teaching software process improvement through a case study. *Computer Applications in Engineering Education*, 8(3-4):229–234.

Garousi, V., Giray, G., Tuzun, E., Catal, C., and Felderer, M. (2019). Closing the gap between software engineering education and industrial needs. *IEEE software*, 37(2):68–77.

Gibbs, W. W. (1994). Software's chronic crisis. *Scientific american*, 271(3):86–95.

Gillies, A. (2011). *Software quality: theory and management.* Lulu. com.

Gomes, P. H., Garcia, R. E., Eler, D. M., Correia, R. C., and Junior, C. O. (2021). Software quality as a subsidy for teaching programming. In *2021 IEEE Frontiers in Education Conference (FIE)*, pages 1–9.

Gupta, R. and Goel, S. (2019). Infusing software quality concepts in computer science engineering courses. *2019 Twelfth International Conference on Contemporary Computing (IC3)*, pages 1–7.

Hilburn, Y. and Towhidnejad, M. (2002). Software quality across the curriculum. In *32nd Annual Frontiers in Education*, volume 3, pages S1G–S1G. IEEE.

Jenkins, M. (2007). Experience in teaching software quality management at the graduate level. In *2007 Annual Conference & Exposition*, pages 12–711.

Jones, C. and Bonsignour, O. (2011). *The economics of software quality.* Addison-Wesley Professional.

Kappelman, L., Jones, M. C., Johnson, V., McLean, E. R., and Boonme, K. (2016). Skills for success at different stages of an it professional's career. *Commun. ACM*, 59(8):64–70.

Kokol, P. (2022). Software quality: How much does it matter? *Electronics*, 11(16).

Laporte, C. Y., April, A., and Bencherif, K. (2007). Teaching software quality assurance in an undergraduate software engineering program. *Software Quality Professional*, 9(3):4.

Lemos, W., Cunha, J., and Saraiva, J. (2019). Teaching software engineering in an information systems course: An analysis of problems and solutions in the perspective of teachers and students. In *Proceedings of the 27th Workshop on Computing Education*, pages 305–318, Porto Alegre, RS, Brasil. SBC. in Portuguese.

Likert, R. (1932). A technique for the measurement of attitudes. *Archives of psychology*.

Linåker, J., Sulaman, S., Höst, M., and de Mello, R. (2015). Guidelines for conducting surveys in software engineering. Technical Report 1.1, Lund University, Sweden.

Moser, G., Vallon, R., Bernhart, M., and Grechenig, T. (2021). Teaching software quality assurance with gamification and continuous feedback techniques. In *2021 IEEE Global Engineering Education Conference (EDUCON)*, pages 505–509.

Page, T. (2008). Ensuring software quality in engineering environments. *i-Manager's Journal on Software Engineering*, 2(4):1.

Prikladnicki, R., Albuquerque, A. B., von Wangenheim, C. G., and Cabral, R. (2009). Teaching software engineering: challenges, teaching strategies and lessons learned. In *Software Engineering Education Forum*, pages 1–8. in Portuguese.

Ribeiro, K., Azevedo, J., Maciel, C., and Bim, S. (2019). A gender analysis based on data from brazilian computer society. In *Proceedings of the 13th Women in Information Technology*, pages 159–163, Porto Alegre, RS, Brasil. SBC. in Portuguese.

Richardson, I., Reid, L., Seidman, S. B., Pattinson, B., and Delaney, Y. (2011). Educating software engineers of the future: Software quality research through problem-based learning. In *2011 24th IEEE-CS Conference on Software Engineering Education and Training (CSEE&T)*, pages 91–100. IEEE.

Scatalon, L. P., Barbosa, E. F., and Garcia, R. E. (2017). Challenges to integrate software testing into introductory programming courses. In *2017 IEEE Frontiers in Education Conference (FIE)*, pages 1–9.

Suali, A., Fauzi, S., Nasir, M., Sobri, W., and Raharjana, I. (2019). Software quality measurement in software engineering project: A systematic literature review. *Journal of Theoretical and Applied Information Technology*, 97(3):918–929.

Suryn, W. (2003). Thoughts on teaching software quality engineering. In *Proceedings of 8th Annual INSPIRE Conference*.

Tian, J. (2005). *Software quality engineering: testing, quality assurance, and quantifiable improvement.* John Wiley & Sons.

Zorzo, A., Nunes, D., Matos, E., Steinmacher, I., Leite, J., Araujo, R., Correia, R., and Martins, S. (2017). *References for Formation of Computing Undergraduate Courses*. Brazilian Computing Society (SBC). in Portuguese.

Using Team Topologies in Model-Driven Strategic Alignment

Rene Noel[1,2], **Jose Ignacio Panach** [3], **Oscar Pastor** [1]

[1]Valencian Research Institute for Artificial Intelligence - Universitat Politècnica de València
Valencia, Spain

[2]Escuela de Ingeniería Informática - Universidad de Valparaíso
Valparaíso, Chile

[3]Escola Tècnica Superior d'Enginyeria - Universitat de València
Valencia, Spain

rnoe@vrain.upv.es, j.ignacio.panach@uv.es, opastor@dsic.upv.es

Abstract. *Model-driven techniques for designing strategically aligned information systems usually map the goals of multiple and competing actors to business process models through automatic model-to-model transformations and analysis. In previous work, we designed Stra2Bis, a method for designing strategically aligned business processes based on a different approach: mapping the business strategy and organisation structure into the business process model. Stra2Bis and goal-based techniques share an issue: only some organisational level elements actors directly affect the business domain and, thus, the business processes. In this article, we propose to extend Stra2Bis by adding concepts from Team Topologies, an approach for organising business and technology teams. Team Topologies help distinguish the business-relevant organisation units from other supporting units; we exploit these concepts to constrain the model-to-model mappings, avoiding unnecessary analysis and modelling outside the business domain. We formalise the approach by specifying the method's metamodel extension and redefining the model-to-model transformation guidelines. We also discuss how existing goal-based alignment frameworks can exploit this approach.*

1. Introduction

In the past two decades, model-driven initiatives have helped business analysts design business processes aligned with their stakeholders' strategic intentions to design strategically aligned information systems to support those processes. By using goal modelling frameworks such as i* [Yu 2011] and GRL [Amyot et al. 2022], business analysts have addressed the organisational complexity of multiple stakeholders having competing goals, which will drive the design of business processes. Goal models have been used as inputs for different model-to-model mapping techniques, which aim for generating elements of the business process models to ensure its alignment [Ruiz et al. 2015], for the automatic validation of inconsistencies [Gröner et al. 2014], and analysing the impact of business process activities in goal achievement [Guizzardi and Reis 2015], among others.

Recently, organisations that need to accelerate their software delivery, especially software-centric companies, have adopted a different strategic alignment approach. Organisational complexity has been identified as a key factor hindering software development efficiency [Forsgren et al. 2018]. Instead of modelling and analysing organisational complexity, it is reduced by designing a loosely-coupled organisational structure to drive the design of loosely-coupled business processes and thus, loosely-coupled systems[1]. Hence, organisation units and dependencies are relevant for strategic alignment, setting a challenge for model-driven alignment initiatives, mainly focused on modelling system actors' goals and mapping them to business processes' activities. To tackle this challenge, in previous works, we designed Stra2Bis [Noel et al. 2022], a lightweight, situational modelling method for aligning business process models with business strategy and organisational structure. Stra2Bis proposes modelling the strategic scenario that drives a software development endeavour in terms of the organisational structure and strategic actions and intentions. This model is transformed into loosely-coupled business process models, preserving the organisational structure and dependencies.

Model-driven alignment techniques and Stra2Bis share a common concern: organisational models might describe actors, roles, and intentions which are not relevant for business process re-engineering, though they are needed for analysing the strategy elements to achieve business goals. For instance, a goal for a successful software development endeavour could be to diminish the time needed to hire new developers; since hiring developers does not affect the business domain or the design of business processes, mapping this goal to the business process level might be useless. Even though undesired model-elements can be filtered using model transformation features, models should provide semantically relevant marks to apply such filters.

Identifying organisational actors critical for business domain has been addressed in the industry by a novel approach: Team Topologies (TT) [Skelton and Pais 2019]. TT distinguishes Stream Aligned Teams from other teams for helping to overcome difficulties (Enabling Teams), for developing internal products for improving efficiency (Platform Teams), and from highly specialised teams (Complicated subsystem Teams). TT also define (and constrain) the relationships between teams, fostering them to serve their business value "as a service" to other teams, supporting the design of a loosely-coupled organisational structure.

This paper presents an extension of the Stra2Bis method that integrates TT concepts to scope model-to-model mappings to business-relevant organisational actors. We present extensions for the method's metamodel and transformation guidelines for including TT and discuss how other model-driven alignment methods can exploit this approach. The rest of the article continues as follows: Section 2 presents the related work, and Section 3 presents the Stra2Bis method. In Section 4 we describe the proposal, and in Section 5 we discuss the implications of the approach, while Section 6 presents the conclusions and future work.

2. Related Work

Aligning business strategy and technology has been recognised as a key enabler for organisational agility. On the one hand, model-driven initiatives have supported modelling the relationship of high-level business definitions and technological components through enterprise architecture frameworks [The Open Group 2022]. On the other hand, goal-oriented models have been mapped to business process models in order to ensure that both are aligned with stakeholders' strategic intentions. Among the latter approaches, we distinguish between *generative* initiatives, which take as input goal models and generate business process elements to ensure alignment, and *analytical* initiatives, which check consistence between goal models and business process models. Regarding generative initiatives, in [Kraiem et al. 2014], goals and strategies modelled in MAPs are transformed into activities and sequences in the Business

[1]Conway's law. https://martinfowler.com/bliki/ ConwaysLaw.html

Process Modelling Notation (BPMN). In [Ruiz et al. 2015], strategic dependencies in i* models are mapped as communicative events at the business process level, modelled in Communication Analysis [España et al. 2009], a communication-centred modelling method.

Concerning analytical initiatives, in [Sousa and Prado Leite 2014], i* models are aligned with BPMN models introducing key-performance indicators and an intermediate model to specify roles' activities to achieve goals. Validation rules for the URN method [Amyot et al. 2022] have been proposed to check if traceability links are modelled to connect goal and process models expressed in the Use Case Maps (UCM) notation. In [Gröner et al. 2014], a mapping is proposed to validate the consistency between GRL models and processes modelled in BPMN, while in [Li et al. 2015], BPMN models consistency is validated against UCM models. Other analytical initiatives help analysing the purpose of BPMN activities by mapping them to MAP models [de la Vara et al. 2008]. In [Guizzardi and Reis 2015], a method to reason about the impact of plans in achieving goals is presented, consisting of assigning weights to goals and propagating them to process activities. In [Nagel et al. 2013], a method to check consistency between goals and business processes is proposed for designing systems in a service-oriented architecture.

All the above initiatives rely on goal modelling methods for representing business process relevant goals and actors. However, such methods do not provide modelling guidance or semantics for stating that an organisational actor is relevant for business process alignment, hindering their practical implementation.

3. Background: The Stra2Bis Mehtod

Stra2Bis [Noel et al. 2022] is a modelling method for designing strategically aligned business processes. Stra2Bis proposes 1. To model the strategic scenario and organisational structure that drives the software development endeavour, and 2. Transformation guidelines for generating the initial structure of the business process model from the organisational structure.

The **strategic scenario modelling** is performed with LiteStrat [Noel et al. 2021], a business strategy modelling method designed from assembling concepts from goal modelling and enterprise architecture frameworks to represent business strategy and organisational structure jointly. LiteStrat concepts consider strategic actions and intentions (*strategy* and *tactic*, *goal* and *objective*), and *refinement* relationships to connect them. The organisational structure is modelled through *roles* and *organisation units*, to which the strategic actions and intentions can be *assigned*, and can contain other units and roles. The organisation units are connected by the *influence* relationships, representing that the behaviour of a unit influences another unit. Entities external to the organisation are modelled as *actors* and can influence or be influenced by organisation units.

Figure 1.A presents a model for PetCare, a fictional software-centric company that allows pet owners to hire pet sitters through a web application. PetCare needs to react to a competitor, PetSitting Co., which offers a similar service but with certified pet sitters. Under this scenario, PetCare's goal is to make the pet owners confident about the pet sitters. The primary strategy is to implement a reputation system for pet sitters based on scores given by pet owners. To implement the strategy, the Reputation Team will be created to implement the reputation system in the PetCare app. The Connections Team, responsible for the features for searching and hiring pet sitters, must integrate the reputation information as part of their process. Also, the Recruitment Team must hire an experienced UX professional for the Reputation Team. The expected outcome is to offer reputation-based pet sitters to pet owners.

Stra2Bis proposes **three model-to-model transformation guidelines** to map business

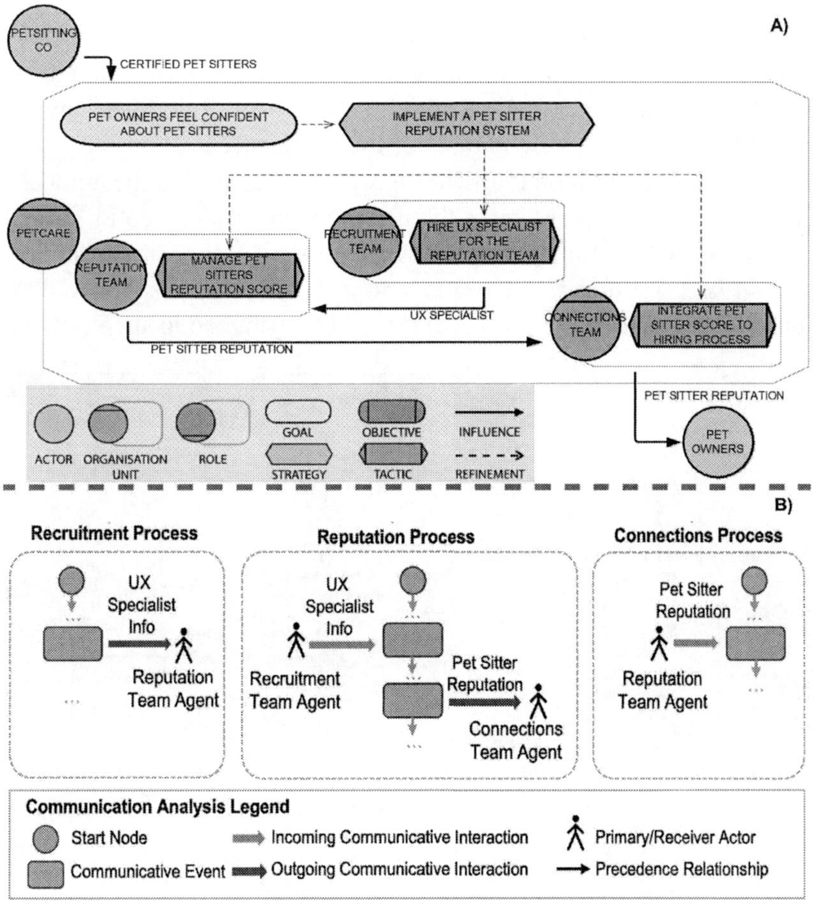

Figure 1. A) Business strategy model and B) Generated business process structure.

strategy models to Communication Analysis (CA) models, a communication-centred business process modelling method. CA shares its focus on events with BPMN's choreography diagrams, but allows specifying the information being shared by process' actors [España et al. 2009]. CA models can be transformed into information system models [España 2011], completing a model-driven development method from requirements to code.

Stra2Bis' transformation Guideline 1 states that each organisation unit is mapped into a business process start node, i.e., units have independent business processes. Guideline 2 proposes mapping the relationships between organisation units into interactions in the business process models, representing external processes as actors and the interactions as events. Finally, Guideline 3 proposes to map objectives to data collection events in the process models to measure the achievement of the objectives. Business analysts are expected to complete process models according to business logic but preserving the elements generated by the guidelines. Figure 1.B depicts the application of the two first guidelines to the model in Figure 1.A. As seen, it would produce three business processes: one for the Connections Team, one for the Reputation Team, and one for the Recruitment Team. However, the recruitment process (including searching, and on-boarding new developers, for instance) is not a business process. In order to distinguish between different types of organisation units, additional concepts are needed.

4. Extending Stra2Bis with Team Topologies

We propose to extend the Litestrat modelling language by applying Team Topologies types as extensions of LiteStrat's organisation units. Also, Team Topologies' interaction modes between teams are considered for extending LiteStrat's influence relationship to specify different dependencies between organisation units. In Figure 2, we propose a metamodel extension for LiteStrat. The definition and notation for the new concepts is detailed in Table 1. It is worth noting that we kept the "stream-aligned" concept to name units since a stream is *a flow of work aligned to a business domain or organisational capability* [Skelton and Pais 2019] and a stream-aligned team (in our case, unit) is expected to be aligned to such flow of work.

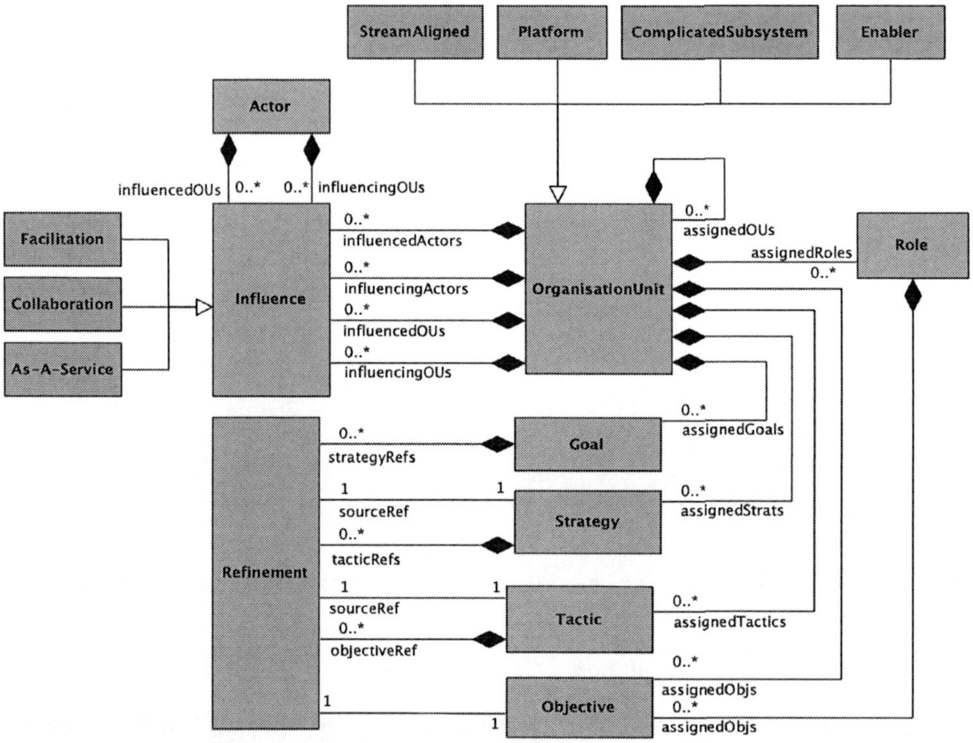

Figure 2. LiteStrat metamodel extension for Team Topologies.

Encompassing the modelling extensions, two extensions for the transformation guidelines are introduced, to constrain the transformations to the stream-aligned units and services, so elements outside the business domain are not generated in the business process model. Below we re-define the guidelines, marking the differences from the original definition.

Guideline 1: For each ***stream aligned*** organisation unit belonging to the overall organisation in the business strategy model, create a new process in the business process model. Add a start event with the unit's name to the new process to make the process visible in the model.

Guideline 2: For each ***X-as-a-Service*** influence between ***stream-aligned*** organisation units in the business strategy model, add events to units' processes to handle the dependency. For the process associated with the influencing unit, add process elements to provide the service to an actor representing the influenced units' process. Similarly, add elements to the influenced unit's process to consume the service from an actor representing the influencing unit's process.

Table 1. Concepts and notation for the Team Topologies extension.

Construct Extension	Definition	Notation
Stream-Aligned Unit (extends Organisation Unit)	Organisational units performing a work of flow that handles a business domain or a part of the business domain.	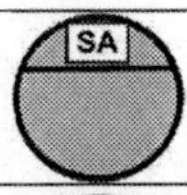
Complicated Subsystem Unit (extends Organisation Unit)	Organisational units that concentrate significant technical capabilities (e.g., mathematical models, pattern recognition algorithms, etc.) which are useful for adding business value	
Platform Unit (extends Organisation Unit)	Organisational units that develop internal products to improve the performance of Stream-Aligned Units.	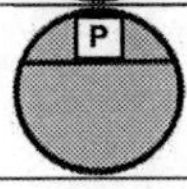
Enabling Unit (extends Organisation Unit)	Organisational units that help Stream-Aligned Units to improve their performance by researching, testing, and transferring new techniques, tools, methods or anything that helps bridge Stream-Aligned Units' capability gaps.	
Relationship Extension	**Definition**	**Notation**
X-as-a-service (extends influence)	Type of influence between two organisation units where the influencing unit provides something with minimal collaboration to the influenced unit.	
Collaboration (extends influence)	Type of influence between two organisations that temporarily work closely for a specific goal.	
Facilitating (extends Influence)	Type of influence where the influencing organisational unit helps the influenced organisational unit to overcome an obstacle.	

Figure 3 presents the example from Figure 1.A using the extensions. The Reputation Team is characterised as a stream-aligned unit that serves the Pet Sitter Reputation as a service to the Connections Team, another stream-aligned unit. The Recruitment Team is modelled as an enabling unit that facilitates Reputation Team's work. Following the extended transformation rules, the Recruitment Process in Figure 1 will not be mapped, nor is the Recruitment Team Agent and the UX Specialist Info interaction in the Reputation Process. We extended the example including two teams for implementing tactics for analysing customer engagement: the Analytics Team design the engagement research study, modelled as Complicated Subsystem unit, and the Cloud Team, marked as Platform unit for providing the infrastructure for collecting engagement data.

5. Discussion

Extending business strategy modelling with Team Topologies' team types and interaction modes allows to better scope the generation of business process models from business strategy model. The main implication for Stra2Bis is that the model-to-model transformation can now be automatically executed, without needing additional analysis during the process. A limitation of the approach is that it could be hard to apply in traditional organisations since it is expected that stream-aligned teams are cross functional and autonomous [Skelton and Pais 2019].

On the other hand, we think that having TT's types of interactions, particularly the "x-as-a-service", helps analysts to model the strategic scenario under the mindset of *what an unit is serving to others*, which contributes to reduce the coupling between the units. This might help the organisation to from the scientifically demonstrated benefits of low organisational structure coupling [Forsgren et al. 2018]. Other unit types not considered in the current proposal could be exploited through through model-driven techniques, such as eliciting requirements for developing of hiring platform-as-a-service from Platform units, identifying capabilities for

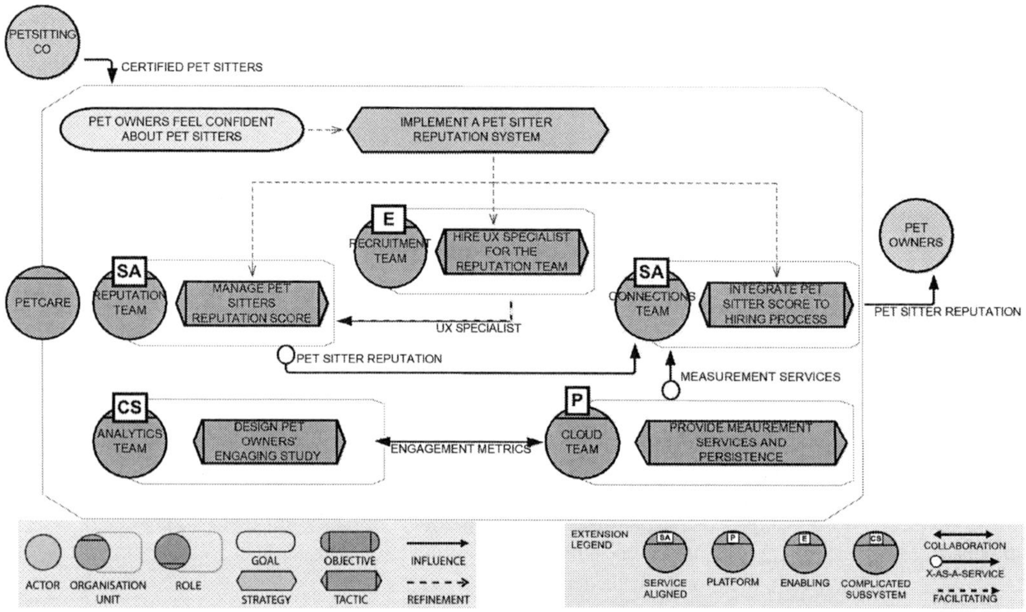

Figure 3. LiteStrat model with the Team Topologies extensions.

Complicates Subsystem units, or scheduling the tasks of Enabling units.

While the formal definition of the proposal is focused to Stra2Bis and its associated notations, a similar approach could be exploited by the alignment approaches discussed in Section 2. In particular, analytical approaches could benefit, since non-business process elements that hinder their practical application, can now be filtered using the TTs marks. TTs can be added to existing goal modelling languages through well defined processes [Goncalves et al. 2020].

6. Conclusions and Future Work

In this article, we presented an extension for Stra2Bis [Noel et al. 2022], a model-driven method for designing strategically aligned business processes. By including a taxonomy of organisation units based on the team types and interaction modes from Team Topologies [Skelton and Pais 2019], we aim to scope the automatic generation of business processes to organisational elements which are business relevant. We proposed an extension for the business strategy modelling language and transformation guidelines. We discussed how other model-driven alignment techniques could benefit from characterising organisational actors through Team Topologies. Future work will focus on applying for the proposed extension in a real-world context to assess the effects and limitations of the proposal empirically.

Acknowledgement

This work was supported by the Valencian Innovation Agency and Innovation through the OGMIOS project (INNEST/2021/57), the Generalitat Valenciana through the CoMoDiD project (CIPROM/2021/023), and the Spanish State Research Agency through the DELFOS (PDC2021-121243-I00) and SREC (PID2021-123824OB-I00) projects, MICIN/AEI/10.13039/501 100011033 and co-financed with ERDF and the European Union Next Generation EU/PRTR.

References

Amyot, D., Akhigbe, O., Baslyman, M., Ghanavati, S., Ghasemi, M., Hassine, J., Lessard, L., Mussbacher, G., Shen, K., and Yu, E. (2022). Combining goal modelling with business process modelling. *Enterprise Modelling and Information Systems Architectures (EMISAJ).*

de la Vara, J. L., Sánchez, J., and Pastor, Ó. (2008). Business process modelling and purpose analysis for requirements analysis of information systems. In *Advanced Information Systems Engineering*, pages 213–227, Berlin, Heidelberg. Springer.

España, S., González, A., and Pastor, Ó. (2009). Communication analysis: a requirements engineering method for information systems. In *International Conference on Advanced Information Systems Engineering*, pages 530–545, Berlin, Heidelberg. Springer.

España, S. (2011). *Methodological Integration of Communication Analysis into a Model-Driven Software Development Framework*. PhD thesis, Universitat Politècnica de València, Spain.

Forsgren, N., Humbpotifle, J., and Kim, G. (2018). *Accelerate: The Science of Lean Software and DevOps Building and Scaling High Performing Technology Organizations*. IT Revolution Press.

Goncalves, E., Araujo, J., and Castro, J. (2020). Prise: A process to support istar extensions. *Journal of Systems and Software*, 168:110649.

Gröner, G., Asadi, M., Mohabbati, B., Gašević, D., and Parreiras, F. S. (2014). Validation of user intentions in process orchestration and choreography. *Information Systems*, 43:83–99.

Guizzardi, R. and Reis, A. N. (2015). A method to align goals and business processes. In *International Conference on Conceptual Modeling*, pages 79–93, Cham. Springer.

Kraiem, N., Kaffela, H., Dimassi, J., and Al Khanjari, Z. (2014). Mapping from map models to bpmn processes. *Journal of Software Engineering*, 8(4):252–264.

Li, Z., Zhou, X., Gu, A., and Li, Q. (2015). A complete approach for cim modelling and model formalising. *Information and Software Technology*, 65:39–55.

Nagel, B., Gerth, C., Engels, G., and Post, J. (2013). Ensuring consistency among business goals and business process models. In *2013 17th IEEE International Enterprise Distributed Object Computing Conference*, pages 17–26, Vancouver. IEEE.

Noel, R., Panach, J. I., Ruiz, M., and Pastor, O. (2022). Stra2bis: A model-driven method for aligning business strategy and business processes. In *In Proceedings of the 41st International Conference on Conceptual Modeling (ER'22)*, Cham. Springer.

Noel, R., Panach Navarrete, J. I., Ruiz, M., and Pastor Lopez, O. (2021). The litestrat method: Towards strategic model-driven development. In *Procedings of the International Conference on Information Systems Development*. AIS Electronic Library.

Ruiz, M., Costal, D., España, S., Franch, X., and Pastor, O. (2015). Gobis: An integrated framework to analyse the goal and business process perspectives in information systems. *Information Systems*, 53:330–345.

Skelton, M. and Pais, M. (2019). *Team topologies: organizing business and technology teams for fast flow*. It Revolution.

Sousa, H. P. and Prado Leite, J. C. S. d. (2014). Modeling organizational alignment. In *International Conference on Conceptual Modeling*, pages 407–414, Cham. Springer.

The Open Group (2022). The archimate® enterprise architecture modeling language. `https://www.opengroup.org/archimate-home`. (Accessed on 04/20/2022).

Yu, E. (2011). Modeling strategic relationships for process reengineering. *Social Modeling for Requirements Engineering*, 11(2011):66–87.

Estudios de casos realizados en PyMES de Argentina para validar DepProMod

Marisa Panizzi[1], Marcela Genero[2], Rodolfo Bertone[3]

[1]Departamento de Ingeniería en Sistemas de Información - Universidad Tecnológica Nacional -Regional Buenos Aires, Argentina

[2]Departamento de Tecnologías y Sistemas de Información, Universidad de Castilla-La Mancha, Ciudad Real, España

[3]Facultad de Informática -Instituto de Investigación en Informática LIDI (III-LIDI) - Universidad Nacional de La Plata, La Plata, Argentina

marisadanielapanizzi@gmail.com, marcela.genero@uclm.es, pbertone@lidi.unlp.edu.ar

Resumen. *DepProMod es un modelo de proceso de despliegue de sistemas de software que se desarrolló para realizar el despliegue de sistemas software desarrollados a medida, de manera sistematizada y controlada. En este artículo se presentan 3 estudios de casos realizados en PyMES de Argentina con el propósito de evaluar las percepciones de los usuarios sobre el modelo. Los resultados constataron que el modelo impacta en la mejora de la calidad de los despliegues de las PyMES, y que su flexibilidad, debido a que permite su aplicación de manera escalonada por niveles, es muy apreciada por los usuarios. Todos los elementos del modelo fueron muy bien valorados, excepto las plantillas, entradas y salidas. Aspectos que se tendrán en cuenta para refinar el modelo.*

1. Introducción

El despliegue de sistemas de software es un proceso crucial del ciclo de vida de desarrollo de software porque después de un despliegue exitoso, el sistema de software finalmente está operativo para que el cliente pueda beneficiarse económicamente de su uso [Subramanian 2017]. En el despliegue se presentan inconvenientes como por ejemplo la falta de componentes (externos), descargas incompletas, la infraestructura heterogénea e incompatible, incumplimiento de calendarios, retrabajo por falta de pocas capacidades y competencias tecnológicas, capacitación y preparación inadecuadas de los usuarios finales entre otros puntualmente en Pequeñas y Medianas Empresas (PyMES) [Subramanian 2017], [Jansen *et al.* 2006], [Reascos *et al.* 2019], [Paredes *et al.* 2017].

En Argentina, la industria del software se compone mayoritariamente por PyMES, representando casi el 80% del sector, lo que constituye un eslabón fundamental, en el sector, para el país y refuerza la necesidad de llevar adelante iniciativas que contribuyan con el desarrollo y mejora de competitividad de dichas empresas [Ministerio de Producción y Trabajo 2018].

A nivel internacional se refleja la misma realidad respecto a que las PyMES ocupan una gran porción de la industria del software [Abushama 2016]. La industria del software es uno de los sectores que ha crecido rápidamente y se la considera de gran aporte a la economía de los países [Mishra *et al.* 2009]. La aparición de un mayor número de empresas de software transformó a la industria del software más competitiva. La mejora en la calidad del software se ha convertido en un factor clave de éxito que permite a las empresas lograr una ventaja competitiva y es esencial para la calidad del producto, la sostenibilidad comercial y el crecimiento [Abushama 2016]. El porcentaje de representatividad de las PyMES en el sector de la industria del software se mantiene desde las últimas dos décadas [Mishra *et al.* 2009], [Felderer et al. 2016], [Sharma *et al.* 2019], [Pino *et al.* 2008]. Las PyMES representan una gran porción de la industria del software en muchos países en todo el mundo [MarketLine 2015].

En consecuencia, dada la relevancia del proceso de despliegue, los inconvenientes que conlleva un despliegue inadecuado más la necesidad de las PyMES de disponer de procesos estabilizados y controlados para la entrega de sistemas de software que satisfagan las necesidades de sus clientes, decidimos definir un modelo de proceso de despliegue de sistemas de software. Este modelo, denominado DepProMod (en inglés, *Deployment Process Model*), ha sido propuesto para realizar el despliegue de sistemas software desarrollados a medida de manera sistematizada y controlada en PyMES de Argentina.

Para el diseño de DepProMod se siguieron los siguientes pasos: el estado del arte mediante un mapeo sistemático de la literatura [Panizzi *et al.* 2020], una encuesta para realizar un estudio exploratorio sobre el estado actual de la práctica del proceso de despliegue de sistemas de software en PyMES de Argentina [Panizzi *et al.* 2021] y dos estudios empíricos para obtener retroalimentación del modelo, por parte de los expertos, con el fin de refinarlo y completarlo [Panizzi *et al.* 2022].

En este artículo se presentan los resultados de la validación de DepProMod realizada mediante tres estudios de casos que permitieron evaluar la percepción de los usuarios del modelo en PyMES desarrolladoras de software de Argentina para detectar las fortalezas y debilidades del modelo. Las tres variables de percepción tomadas del *Technology Acceptance Model* (TAM) [Davis 1989] son: "Facilidad de Uso Percibida" (en inglés, *Perceived Ease of Use* o PEOU), "Utilidad Percibida" (en inglés, *Perceived Usefulness* o PU) e "Intención de Uso" (en inglés, *Intention to Use* o ITU).

2. Descripción general de DepProMod

DepProMod tiene un modelo de ciclo de vida que adopta los 5 grupos de procesos del PMBOK [Institute Project Management 2013]: Planificación, Ejecución, Seguimiento y Control y Cierre. Cada uno de estos procesos en DepProMod se denominan "subprocesos". Para la definición de las actividades de DepProMod se consideraron un conjunto de procesos del estándar ISO/IEC/IEEE 12207 [IEEE ISO/IEC/IEEE 2017]. A nivel de "tareas", el modelo adopta un grupo de tareas propuestas en la metodología Metrica v3 [Ministerio de Administraciones Públicas de España 2001]. Además, se consideraron una serie de actividades propuestas en el proceso técnico de "transición" de la norma ISO/IEC/IEEE 12207 [IEEE ISO/IEC/IEEE 2017]. En la Figura 1 se presentan las relaciones entre los subprocesos de DepProMod y se detallan las actividades de cada subproceso. La justificación de las decisiones tomadas para el diseño de DepProMod así como también un mayor grado de detalle de los subprocesos, actividades y tareas se encuentra en [Panizzi *et al.* 2022], [Panizzi 2022].

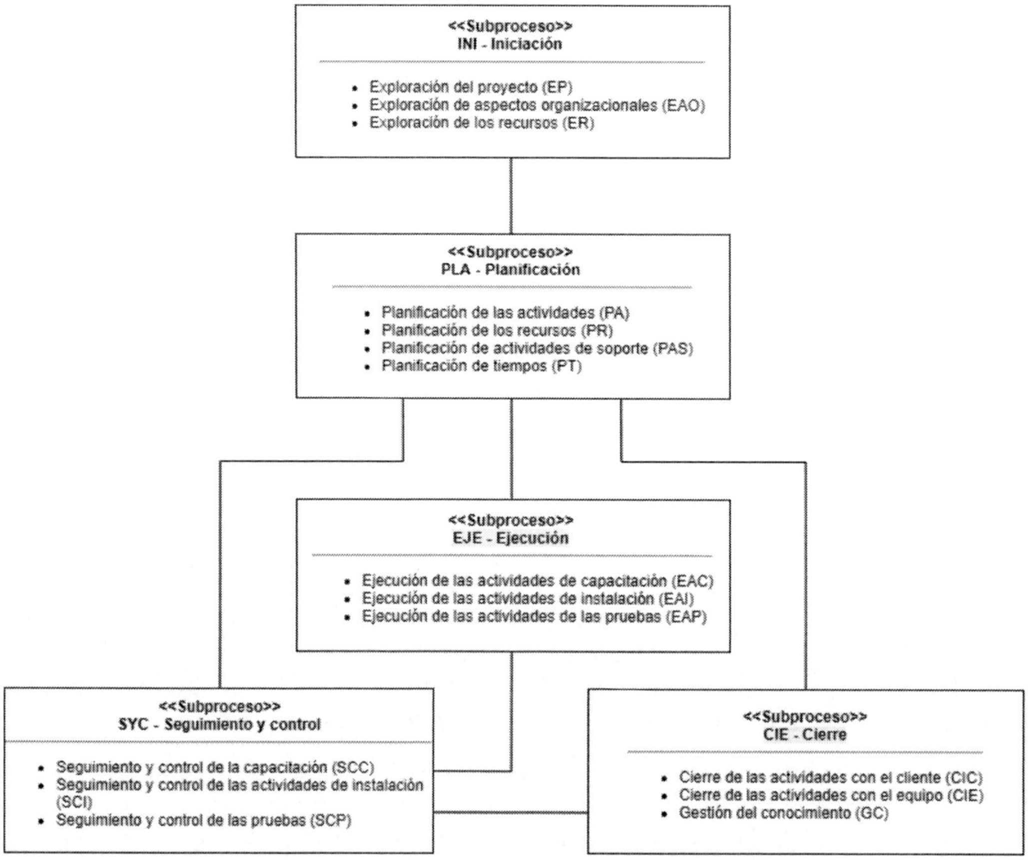

Figura 1. Relación entre los subprocesos de DepProMod.

Para que una PyME pueda implementar el modelo paso a paso, y en la medida que logre estabilizar el proceso en un determinado nivel de aplicación y que alcance los conocimientos necesarios para escalarlo al siguiente nivel, se define una arquitectura por niveles adoptando tres de los niveles de capacidad del estándar CMMI-DEV [CMMI Institute 2010]. Estos niveles son: nivel 1 = Realizado (representado en color amarillo), nivel 2 = Gestionado (representado en color azul) y nivel 3 = Definido (representado en color verde). Estos niveles fueron analizados y definidos a nivel de granularidad de las tareas consideradas en el modelo. La manera de implementación de DepProMod se encuentra en el apéndice [Panizzi *et al.* 2023].

El patrón de procesos utilizado para la representación del modelo es el propuesto en el modelo Competisoft [Competisoft 2008]. DepProMod tiene un total de 16 actividades distribuidas en 5 subprocesos y propone 6 roles para la ejecución del despliegue que se describen en [Panizzi 2022].

DeproMod define las herramientas que se utilizarán en las tareas, que incluyen la gestión de la configuración, la instalación, la documentación, la gestión del plan de despliegue, la formación y las herramientas de diseño. Las herramientas se proponen en función de su utilidad, y las PYMES pueden utilizar las herramientas que tienen. Además, define 27 plantillas en total para los 5 subprocesos que componen el modelo [Panizzi 2022].

3. Estudios de casos

En esta sección, se presentan tres estudios de casos (EC1, EC2, EC3) realizados en PyMES desarrolladoras de software de Argentina con el propósito de validar DepProMod para detectar sus fortalezas y debilidades. En estos estudios se evaluaron las percepciones de las variables PEOU, PU e ITU tomadas como se mencionó anteriormente del *Technology Acceptance Model* (TAM) [Davis 1989]. Para la realización y reporte de los estudios de casos se siguieron las directrices propuestas por en [Runeson *et al.* 2012].

3.1. Objetivos y preguntas de investigacion (PI) de los estudios de casos

En la Tabla 1 se presenta el objetivo de los estudios de casos siguiendo el paradigma *Goal-Question-Metric* [Basili *et al.* 1988].

Tabla 1. Objetivo de los estudios de casos.

Analizar	el proceso de despliegue de sistemas de software utilizando DepProMod,
con el propósito de	evaluar la percepción de los usuarios,
con respecto a	la "Facilidad de Uso Percibida", "Utilidad Percibida" e "Intención de Uso",
desde el punto de vista	de profesionales de la industria del software,
en el contexto de	de PyMES de Argentina.

Para lograr este objetivo se plantearon las siguientes preguntas de investigación (PI):

PI1: ¿Cuál ha sido la percepción de los profesionales de la industria del software al aplicar DepProMod?

Para dar respuesta a esta pregunta, como se comentó anteriormente, se evaluaron tres variables de percepción tomadas del *Technology Acceptance Model* (TAM) [Davis 1989].

PI2: ¿Cuáles son las fortalezas y debilidades informadas por la empresa al aplicar DepProMod?

Con esta pregunta se buscó indagar las fortalezas y debilidades del uso de DepProMod, y así detectar qué aspectos sería necesario mejorar.

3.2. Contexto, caso y unidad de análisis

De acuerdo con la clasificación de Yin [Yin 2014] los tres estudios de casos son holísticos y de casos únicos caracterizados por los elementos que se presentan en la Tabla 2. Se utilizó la clasificación de PyMES en Argentina según la cantidad de empleados [Ministerio de Desarrollo Productivo 2018].

Tabla 2. Contexto, caso y unidad de análisis de los estudios de casos (EC1, EC2, EC3).

Estudios de casos	Contexto	Caso	Unidad de análisis
EC1	**Micro PyME** de 3 empleados, ubicada en Argentina, que ofrece productos y servicios de consultoría.	Despliegue de un sistema web del tipo "Tienda Virtual", dedicado al comercio en el rubro de los repuestos y accesorios para motos y afines.	Aplicación del nivel 1 de DepProMod.
EC2	**PyME Mediana de tramo 1**, de 45 empleados aproximadamente, ubicada en Argentina, que ofrece productos y servicios de consultoría de desarrollo web y consultoría de marketing digital.	Despliegue de un sistema web del tipo catálogo de software de mantenimiento que ofrece el cliente final para diferentes industrias.	Aplicación del nivel 2 de DepProMod.
EC3	**PyME Mediana de tramo 2** de aproximadamente 430 empleados, ubicada en Argentina. La empresa desarrolla sistemas de software a medida para clientes de diversos rubros.	Despliegue de funcionalidades de un Portal de Recursos Humanos realizado para una entidad bancaria de Argentina.	Aplicación del nivel 3 de DepProMod.

3.3. Preparación para la recolección de los datos

En los estudios de casos participaron en total 11 profesionales de la industria del software, 2 en EC1, 5 en EC2 y 4 en EC3 respectivamente. La correspondencia entre los roles propuestos en DepProMod, los perfiles de la PyME que utilizaron el modelo y el número de usuario asignado en cada caso, la estrategia de despliegue empleada en cada despliegue y las plantillas utilizadas se describen en el apéndice [Panizzi *et al.* 2023].

Las actividades de formación de los usuarios de DepProMod se realizaron de manera virtual vía la plataforma *Meet*. El material utilizado en esta formación se encuentra en [Panizzi 2021].

La duración de la formación en cada empresa ha sido de 3 sesiones de 3 horas y a todos los usuarios se los entrenó en el modelo completo Una vez finalizada la formación se mantuvo contacto permanente con la empresa vía telefónica, *WhatsApp* y por videoconferencia para la resolución de dudas que surgieron durante el despliegue durante un mes aproximadamente.

La recolección de los datos se realizó en dos etapas:

1. La primera etapa consistió en la realización del cuestionario TAM, para evaluar la percepción de los usuarios una vez aplicado DepProMod, con el propósito de dar respuesta a la primera pregunta de investigación (PI1). Al mes de la finalización del despliegue en cada una de las empresas, se envió vía correo electrónico el cuestionario a los usuarios del modelo. El cuestionario TAM se encuentra disponible en el apéndice [Panizzi *et al.* 2023]. Este cuestionario contiene 20 ítems definidos para medir las variables PEOU, PU e ITU. Cada ítem se evalúa con una escala Likert de 5 puntos utilizando etiquetas lingüísticas. Las etiquetas lingüísticas utilizadas son: "Totalmente de acuerdo", "De acuerdo", "Parcialmente de acuerdo", "En desacuerdo" y "Totalmente en desacuerdo". La

estructura del cuestionario cuenta con un primer nivel que se refiere a cada uno de los elementos de DepProMod en general (fases, actividades y tareas, roles, entradas y salidas, plantillas y recursos). Cada uno de estos elementos del modelo cuenta con un segundo nivel para cada una de las variables de percepción a medir (PEOU, PU y ITU). La variable PEOU se mide utilizando diez ítems de la encuesta (P1, P3, P5, P7, P9, P10, P13, P15, P17 y P20). La variable PU se mide con cinco ítems de la encuesta (P2, P6, P11, P16 y P19). Y la variable ITU se mide con cinco ítems (P4, P8, P12, P14 y P18). Además, para asegurar el balanceo de los ítems, en el cuestionario se plantearon algunos ítems de manera positiva y algunos ítems de manera negativa y así evitar respuestas monótonas. Los resultados obtenidos del cuestionario TAM se volcaron en una hoja de cálculo para su posterior análisis.

2. La segunda etapa consistió en la realización de una entrevista semi estructurada a cada uno de los usuarios de DepProMod con el objetivo de indagar sobre las fortalezas y debilidades de DepProMod para dar respuesta a la segunda pregunta de investigación (PI2). El cuestionario empleado en la entrevista se divide en siete categorías de preguntas. Para las preguntas de la primera categoría respecto a las preguntas demográficas (PE1 y PE2) se consideraron las preguntas del estudio HELENA [Kurmann *et al.* 2018], por tratarse de un estudio internacionalmente reconocido y otra pregunta respecto a si la empresa dispone o no de un proceso de despliegue (PE3). Las otras seis categorías se corresponden a los elementos de DepProMod; las Fases/actividades y tareas (PE4, PE5 y PE6), los roles (PE7 y PE8), las entradas y salidas (PE9 y PE10), las plantillas (PE11 y PE12), los recursos (PE13 y PE14) y la experiencia general de DepProMod (PE15, PE16 y PE17). En la Tabla 3 se presentan las preguntas del cuestionario utilizado en la entrevista.

Tabla 3. Cuestionario utilizado en las entrevistas.

Categoría 1: Preguntas demográficas.
PE1.- ¿Cuál es su rol actual en la empresa?
PE2.- ¿Cuánto tiempo hace que trabaja en la industria del software?
PE3.- ¿Su empresa cuenta con un modelo de proceso para el despliegue?
Categoría 2: Preguntas sobre fases/actividades y tareas.
PE4.¿Qué ventajas encontró al utilizar las fases, actividades y tareas de DepProMod?
PE5.-¿Le sirvieron de guía para realizar el proceso de despliegue?
PE6.-¿Qué dificultades encontró en la aplicación de las fases, actividades y tareas?
Categoría 3: Preguntas sobre roles.
PE7.-¿Pudo desempeñar su rol sin inconvenientes?
PE8.-¿Le pareció adecuado el rol para las tareas que realizó en el despliegue?
Categoría 4: Preguntas sobre entradas y salidas.
PE9.-¿Pudo aplicar las entradas y salidas DepProMod de manera correcta?
PE10.- ¿Considera las entradas y salidas para las actividades de DepProMod son adecuadas?
Categoría 5: Preguntas sobre Plantillas.
PE11.- ¿Utilizó todas las plantillas definidas para el nivel de DepProMod que utilizó?
PE12.- ¿Cuál es su opinión respecto a las plantillas de DepProMod?
Categoría 6: Preguntas sobre recursos.
PE13.- ¿Considera que los recursos propuestos en DepProMod son los adecuados?

PE14.- Podría mencionar cuáles son las recursos que utilizó para realizar cada una de las tareas.	
Categoría 7: Preguntas sobre DepProMod en general .	
PE15.- ¿Qué agregaría o quitaría a DepProMod?	
PE16.-¿Cuál es su valoración sobre su experiencia del uso de DepProMod? (Muy buena/Buena/Parcialmente buena/Regular/Mala).	
PE17.- ¿Cómo valora el impacto de usar DeProMod en la calidad de sus futuros despliegues?(Alto/Medio/Bajo).	

Las entrevistas se desarrollaron de la siguiente manera:

- Fase 1: explicación del objetivo de la entrevista. En esta etapa se solicitó permiso para la grabación.
- Fase 2: en esta etapa se realizaron preguntas relacionadas a la experiencia profesional en la industria del software, rol que desempeña en la empresa y que desempeñó en el proceso de despliegue y si la empresa dispone o no de un proceso de despliegue.
- Fase 3: en esta etapa se realizaron las preguntas relacionadas a los elementos de DepProMod.
- Fase 4: en esta etapa se realizaron preguntas relacionadas con la experiencia general del uso de DepProMod.

Una vez realizadas las entrevistas se realizó su transcripción manual para su posterior análisis.

3.4. Análisis e interpretación de los datos de EC1, EC2 y EC3

En esta sección, en primer lugar, se presentan los resultados obtenidos del cuestionario TAM sobre las percepciones de los usuarios de DepProMod para dar respuesta a la PI1. En segundo lugar, se describen los resultados de las entrevistas realizadas a cada uno de los usuarios con el propósito de dar respuesta a la PI2 respecto a las fortalezas y debilidades de DepProMod. A continuación, se presentan los cálculos realizados para dar respuesta a la PI1, así como también el análisis e interpretación de los datos.

PI1: ¿Cuál ha sido la percepción de los profesionales de la industria del software al aplicar DepProMod?

En la Tabla 4 se presentan los resultados obtenidos de las variables de percepción de cada uno de los usuarios de DepProMod que participaron en los estudios de casos.

Tabla 4. Variables de percepción por usuario de DepProMod (EC1, EC2 y EC3).

Usuarios (EC1)	**PEOU**	**PU**	**ITU**
Usuario1	92%	96%	76%
Usuario2	84%	76%	68%
Usuarios (EC2)	**PEOU**	**PU**	**ITU**
Usuario1	82%	76%	76%
Usuario2	80%	88%	72%
Usuario3	78%	76%	72%
Usuario4	84%	84%	72%
Usuario5	86%	88%	72%
Usuarios (EC3)	**PEOU**	**PU**	**ITU**
Usuario1	92%	96%	92%
Usuario2	88%	92%	92%

Usuario3	80%	92%	80%
Usuario4	88%	84%	80%

Para calcular cada una de las variables de percepción para cada uno de los usuarios se realizaron los siguientes pasos:

1. Se convirtieron todas las respuestas dentro de la escala de Likert (0..5) dado que en el cuestionario había ítems que se planteaban de manera positiva y otros de manera negativa.
2. Se realizó la sumatoria de los ítems para cada una de las categorías (Elementos de DepProMod).
3. Cada una de las variables de percepción fue calculada de acuerdo con el total de respuestas que corresponden a dicha variable, por ejemplo, en la Tabla 5 se presenta el cálculo de la variable PEOU. Los cálculos de las variables PU e ITU se encuentran en el apéndice [Panizzi *et al.* 2023]. La percepción total de cada variable se calcula de la siguiente manera:
   Puntuación total en la escala /Puntuación máxima posible

Tabla 5. Cálculo de la variable PEOU.

Cálculo de PEOU					
Total de preguntas	**Total de respuestas**	**Puntuación minima posible**	**Puntuación máxima posible**	**Puntuación total en la escala**	**% Percepción**
10	10	10	50	Valor obtenido	Porcentaje de percepción resultante

Con el propósito de conocer para cada una de las variables de percepción su composición porcentual respecto a cada uno de los elementos de DepProMod para cada uno de los usuarios y de esta manera descubrir en cuál de los elementos debíamos realizar mejoras (en caso de que fuese necesario) se realizaron los siguientes pasos:

1. Para cada variable se calculó la percepción parcial por elemento de la misma manera que se calcula la percepción total de la variable. Los valores para emplear en los cálculos se presentan en la Tabla 6.

Tabla 6. Cálculo de la variable ITU.

Cálculo de variable de percepción – Elemento					
Total de preguntas	Total de respuestas	Puntuación minima posible	Puntuación máxima posible	Puntuación total en la escala	% Percepción por elemento

2. Una vez obtenidos los porcentajes para cada uno de los elementos de una determinada variable de percepción, se realiza la sumatoria.
3. Para cada elemento de una determinada variable de percepción se realiza el siguiente cálculo:
   Porcentaje del elemento/Sumatoria de los porcentajes de todos los elementos

De esta manera, se obtiene la descomposición porcentual de la variable para cada uno de los elementos de DepProMod. Por restricciones de espacio, los resultados de los cálculos se detallan en el apéndice [Panizzi *et al.* 2023].

A continuación, se describe el análisis e interpretación de los datos para cada uno de los estudios de casos.

En EC1 en relación con las variables de percepción obtenidas del cuestionario realizado a los usuarios del nivel 1 de DepProMod en la micro PyME, se observa que los valores de percepción son mayores para el Usuario1 (PEOU=92%, PU=96% y ITU=76%) que para el Usuario2 (PEOU=84%, PU=76% e ITU=68%). Si bien el Usuario 1 desempeñó varios roles propuestos en el modelo, es el dueño de la empresa y ha sido su decisión experimentar con DepProMod a diferencia del Usuario2 que el uso de DepProMod no ha sido su decisión, sino que se le ha impuesto su uso.

Respecto a los elementos fases/actividades/tareas, roles y recursos, para el Usuario1, la variable PEOU presentan un mayor valor de percepción (21,74%) respecto al Usuario2. El mayor valor de percepción de la variable PEOU para los dos usuarios está representado por el elemento recursos. Y el menor valor de percepción de la variable PEOU para los dos usuarios está representado por los elementos entradas y salidas y plantillas.

La variable PU para los elementos fases/actividades/tareas, roles, plantillas y recursos presentan el mismo porcentaje de representación (20,83%) siendo el valor más alto, mientras que para el Usuario2 el valor más alto está dado por los recursos (26,32%). En el caso del Usuario1, el valor más bajo para esta variable se presenta en las entradas y salidas (16,68%) mientras que, en el Usuario2, se presenta en las entradas y salidas y las plantillas (15,79%) para cada elemento. Los elementos fases/actividades/tareas y roles cuentan con un valor de representatividad intermedia (21,05%) respecto al valor total de la variable.

El porcentaje de representación del elemento recursos para la variable ITU es alta para ambos usuarios respecto al valor total de la variable (25,10% y 23,53% respectivamente). Las fases/actividades/tareas y roles cuentan con el valor intermedio de representatividad (20,30%) del valor total de la variable para el Usuario1. El valor de representación más bajo que compone la variable ITU se presenta en las entradas y salidas y en las plantillas para ambos usuarios a excepción que en el Usuario2, el elemento fases/actividades/tareas presenta un valor bajo de porcentaje en la composición de la percepción total de la variable.

En relación con las variables de percepción (PEOU, PU e ITU), los elementos entradas y salidas representan el menor porcentaje de representación respecto al valor total de cada una de las variables para los dos usuarios. El mayor porcentaje de representación para las variables de percepción (PEOU, PU e ITU) corresponde a los elementos recursos y roles.

En EC2, en los resultados de las variables de percepción obtenidas del cuestionario realizado a los usuarios del nivel 2 de DepProMod en la PyME (aproximadamente 45 empleados) se observa que las variables de percepción (PEOU y PU) demuestran un alto grado de valoración de DepProMod por parte de los usuarios en relación con su facilidad y utilidad. No obstante, se observa que con relación a la intención de uso de DepProMod en futuros despliegues de sistemas de software, es menor la valoración expresada por los usuarios.

Los elementos entradas y salidas y plantillas para las variables de percepción (PEOU, PU e ITU) representan el menor valor de porcentaje en la composición de las variables. El mayor valor de porcentaje en la composición para las variables de percepción (PEOU, PU e ITU) corresponde a los elementos fases/actividades/tareas y los roles.

Para el elemento recursos, se observa un porcentaje alto de representación para la variable ITU, un valor de porcentaje medio en la composición de la variable de percepción PEOU y el menor porcentaje de representación para la variable de percepción PU exceptuando los Usuario3 y Usuario4.

En EC3, en relación con las variables de percepción obtenidas del cuestionario realizado a los usuarios del nivel 3 de DepProMod en la PyME se observa que la variable de percepción PU demuestran una mayor valoración de DepProMod por parte de los usuarios en relación con su utilidad. En segundo lugar, se encuentra la variable PEOU relacionada con la facilidad de uso del modelo. En tercer lugar, se observa que con relación a la intención de uso (variable ITU) de DepProMod en futuros despliegues de sistemas de software, es menor la valoración expresada por los usuarios.

Las plantillas de DepProMod representan el menor porcentaje de composición para las tres variables de percepción (PEOU, PU e ITU). El mayor porcentaje de composición para las variables de percepción (PEOU, PU e ITU) corresponde a los elementos roles y recursos

Con relación al elemento fases/actividades/tareas, se observan diferentes porcentajes de composición de la variable PEOU, dos de los usuarios (Usuario2 y Usuario4) presentan un porcentaje bajo, otro de los usuarios (Usuario3), un porcentaje intermedio y otro usuario (Usuario1), un porcentaje más alto. En relación con la variable de percepción PU, los cuatro usuarios coinciden con un valor de porcentaje alto en la composición de la variable. En relación con la variable de percepción ITU, dos usuarios (Usuario1 y Usuario2) coinciden con un valor de porcentaje alto del elemento fases/actividades/tareas en la composición de la variable y los otros dos usuarios (Usuario3 y Usuario4) coinciden con un valor de porcentaje intermedio en la composición de la variable ITU.

En relación con las variables PU e ITU, las entradas y salidas y las plantillas de DepProMod representan un porcentaje bajo en la composición de las variables para los cuatro usuarios de EC3. En el caso de la variable de percepción PEOU, para la mayoría de los usuarios coinciden con un porcentaje de composición bajo.

A continuación, se presentan los resultados de las entrevistas realizadas a cada uno de los usuarios de DepProMod que permitieron dar respuesta a la PI2.

PI2: ¿Cuáles son las fortalezas y debilidades informadas por la empresa al aplicar DepProMod?

En EC1, los dos usuarios de DepProMod entrevistados cuentan con una experiencia de más de 10 años en la industria del software. La empresa no posee un modelo para la ejecución del despliegue. Ambos usuarios consideran que la experiencia general con DepProMod ha sido buena y que el impacto en la calidad de los futuros despliegues de sistemas de software de la empresa es indistinto. Ambos usuarios coinciden en que las fases/actividades/tareas les permite sistematizar el proceso de despliegue y que no han tenido inconveniente con el rol que han desempeñado en DepProMod. Ambos usuarios mencionan que el modelo presenta demasiadas plantillas y que su seguimiento requiere más esfuerzo de trabajo. Ambos usuarios consideran adecuado que los recursos a emplear para la realización de las tareas se proponen de forma genérica, es decir que no exige una marca en especial pudiendo ser gratuitos o adquiridos.

En EC2, de los cinco usuarios de DepProMod entrevistados, tres de ellos cuentan con una experiencia comprendida entre 6 y 10 años en la industria del software y los otros dos cuentan con una experiencia de más de 10 años en la industria del software. La empresa no disponía de un modelo de proceso para el despliegue de sistemas de software.

Todos los usuarios consideran que la experiencia general con DepProMod ha sido buena y cuatro de ellos consideran que el impacto de DepProMod en la calidad de los futuros despliegues de sistemas de software de la empresa es alto. Respecto a las plantillas, todos los usuarios coinciden en la necesidad de eliminar o simplificar plantillas de DepProMod.

Los cinco usuarios consideran que las fases/actividades/tareas les sirvieron de guía para llevar a cabo el proceso de despliegue. Además, coincidieron que el rol que se les asignó para el despliegue es el indicado y que las tareas se encuentran con relación a ese rol.

En relación con las entradas y salidas, tres de los usuarios consideran que son adecuadas, uno de los usuarios planteo la necesidad de simplificar salidas y otro mencionó que por el tipo de despliegue no se generaron algunas salidas propuestas en el modelo.

En relación con las plantillas, los usuarios valoran de manera positiva la documentación para la gestión de los proyectos, aunque reconocen que requiere tiempo y esfuerzo su seguimiento y control y que en perfiles más técnicos no se encuentran motivados para realizar su seguimiento.

Respecto a los recursos a utilizar en las tareas definidas en DepProMod, todos los usuarios que participaron en EC2 coinciden que las herramientas propuestas son las indicadas y resaltan que al sugerirla de acuerdo con la función que ofrece la herramienta y no indicando la marca, permite libertad de selección de acuerdo con el tipo de despliegue y además de utilizar las herramientas que han sido definidas para todo el proyecto.

En EC3, de los cuatro usuarios de DepProMod entrevistados, tres de ellos cuentan con una experiencia de más de 10 años en la industria del software y solo uno cuenta con una mediana experiencia comprendida entre los 6 y 10 años en la industria del software. La empresa no cuenta con un modelo para el despliegue de sistemas de software solo posee documentación que permite registrar algunas cuestiones del despliegue.

Tres de los usuarios consideran que la experiencia general con DepProMod ha sido muy buena y solo uno informó que ha sido buena. Todos los usuarios que participaron en EC3 coinciden que DepProMod tiene un alto impacto en la calidad de los futuros despliegues de sistemas de software que gestione la PyME.

Con respecto a las fortalezas de DepProMod, los usuarios informaron que las fases/actividades/tareas presentan un nivel de detalle que les sirve de guía para llevar a cabo el proceso de despliegue y de esta manera no omitir ninguna tarea, además destacaron la posibilidad de ejecutar el despliegue en distintos niveles de aplicación del modelo. Además, los usuarios encontraron adecuados los roles propuestos en DepProMod y que tuvieron que desempeñar.

Con relación a las entradas y salidas de DepProMod, los usuarios expresaron que eran bastantes y contaban con un alto nivel de detalle generando una gran carga de trabajo, el seguimiento de estas. Además, los usuarios sugirieron su revisión con el propósito de simplificación y eliminación.

En relación con las plantillas, uno de los usuarios expresó que son importantes porque permiten consolidar el conocimiento, los otros tres usuarios informaron que se deberían simplificar y que algunas de las plantillas no deberían estar tan estandarizadas y que algunas actividades deberían documentarse de acuerdo con el tipo de despliegue y al tipo de cliente. Otra de las debilidades respecto a las plantillas expresada por los usuarios es el esfuerzo de trabajo y su impacto en la agilidad del proceso de despliegue de sistemas de software.

Respecto a los recursos a utilizar en las tareas definidas en DepProMod, todos los usuarios que participaron en EC3 coincidieron que las herramientas propuestas son las correctas y resaltan que DepProMod ofrece libertad en la elección de estas.

4. Amenazas a la validez (EC1, EC2 y EC3)

Para analizar las amenazas a la validez de EC1, EC2 y EC3 se tuvieron en cuenta los factores propuestos en [Runeson *et al.* 2012]:

- Validez del constructo. Este aspecto refleja hasta qué punto las medidas operativas que se han realizado se adecuan a lo que el investigador tiene en mente y a lo que se está investigando en función de las preguntas de investigación. El cuestionario basado en TAM permitió evaluar la percepción de las tres variables y de todos los elementos que componen el modelo. Las entrevistas realizadas de manera personalizada permitieron comprender las preguntas por los usuarios. La formación impartida ha sido adecuada y el soporte facilitado a los usuarios de DepProMod permitió resolver las dudas de estos de manera ágil. Todas estas acciones realizadas nos permitieron mitigar este aspecto.
- Validez interna. Este aspecto se basa en estudiar las relaciones causales que hacen que distintos factores afecten al factor investigado pero que no se tenga constancia de todos ellos. Si bien la información obtenida a través del cuestionario basado en TAM y las entrevistas proviene de solo 3 PyMES desarrolladoras de software en Argentina es importante resaltar que el modelo ha sido aplicado y evaluado en el contexto real y que se lograron responder las preguntas de investigación.
- Validez externa. Este aspecto refleja la capacidad de generalización de los resultados del estudio de caso y el interés que puedan suscitar en personas ajenas al propio caso. Aunque, la generalización es limitada debido a que se presentan 3 casos (no aleatorios); los 3 casos son de diferente envergadura y esto ofrece hallazgos valiosos respecto a la percepción de los aspectos estudiados del modelo en esos ámbitos. Encontramos que la mayoría de los profesionales coinciden en que el modelo les sirve de guía para realizar el proceso de

despliegue en particular por sus fases/actividades/tareas, sus roles y la libre elección de herramientas para realizar las tareas.

- Fiabilidad. Los datos de EC1, EC2 y EC3 fueron recopilados por un solo investigador (la primera autora). Aunque fueron analizados con los autores restantes, esto puede considerarse una amenaza para la investigación. Para agregar un mayor grado de confiabilidad, sería recomendable que otro investigador aplicara la estrategia del caso (cuestionario TAM y entrevistas) en otros estudios de casos.

5. Conclusiones y trabajos futuros

En este artículo se han presentado tres estudios de casos en los que se aplicó DepProMod en tres PyMES de Argentina, permitiendo obtener *feedback* de sus usuarios. A continuación, se detallan las principales conclusiones obtenidas:

- Se constató, que los profesionales que participaron en los estudios de casos en su mayoría con más de 10 años de experiencia en la industria del software consideran que el modelo impacta en la mejora de la calidad de los despliegues de los sistemas de software de sus PyMES.
- Dentro de las fortalezas de DepProMod se encuentra la flexibilidad que aporta al poder aplicarse por niveles, permitiendo a las PyMES llevar a cabo sus despliegues de sistemas de software desarrollados a medida de manera sistematizada y controlada, adecuándose a sus recursos y necesidades.
- Los usuarios de DepProMod, en los tres estudios de casos resaltan que las fases/actividades/tareas que ofrece el modelo les sirva de guía para realizar el proceso de despliegue y de esta manera no omitir ninguna tarea, así como también la ventaja de la libre elección de las herramientas para utilizar en las tareas.
- Además, los usuarios encontraron adecuados los roles propuestos en DepProMod y que tuvieron que desempeñar y que no han tenido inconveniente con el rol que han desempeñado en DepProMod.
- Si bien los participantes de los estudios resaltaron la importancia de la gestión de los despliegues, percibieron de manera desfavorable las entradas, salidas y las plantillas por el esfuerzo que conlleva la documentación siendo más acentuado en la micro PyME.

Teniendo en cuenta los resultados obtenidos en los estudios de casos, nuestro próximo paso en esta investigación será modificar el modelo específicamente revisando, simplificando y en algún caso, eliminando entradas, salidas y plantillas o rediseñar las plantillas de manera que se completen automáticamente podría facilitar su uso. Otra iniciativa para introducir agilidad al modelo es la construcción de una herramienta tecnológica para su aplicación.

Otras posibles líneas de trabajo futuro son: a) extender la evaluación de DepProMod a un contexto internacional, más allá de su aplicación en PyMES de Argentina, b) aplicar el modelo en otros tipos de empresas, como por ejemplo empresas emergentes (*Startups*) o empresas de mayor tamaño para contrastarlo con los resultados obtenidos en PyMES y c) aplicar DepProMod en el despliegue de otro tipo de sistemas de software, por ejemplo, los sistemas de software configurables.

Agradecimientos. La investigación presentada en este artículo forma parte de los siguientes proyectos: ADAGIO (Consejería de Educación, Cultura y Deportes de la JCCM, SBLPY/21/180501/000061) y AETHER-UCLM (MICINN, PID2020-112540RB-C42).

Referencias

Abushama, H. (2016). PAM-SMEs: process assessment method for small to medium enterprises. *Software: Evolution and Process*, 28(8):689 –711.

Basili, V. and Rombach, D. (1988). The TAME project: towards improvement-oriented software environments. *IEEE Transactions on Software Engineering*, 14(6):758-773.

CMMI® Institute. (2010). CMMI Development V1.3.

Competisoft. (2008). Mejora de Procesos para Fomentar la Competitividad de la Pequeña y Mediana Industria del Software de Iberoamérica, https://alarcos.esi.uclm.es/competisoft/web/completo/index.htm.

Davis, F. (1989). Perceived Usefulness, Perceived Ease of Use and User Acceptance of Information Technology. *MIS Quarterly,* 13(3):319-340.

Felderer, M. and Ramler, R. (2016). Risk orientation in software testing processes of small and medium enterprises: an exploratory and comparative study. *Software Qual J* 24, 519–548.

IEEE ISO/IEC/IEEE 12207:2017(E). (2017). Systems and software engineering - Software life cycle processes.

Institute Project Management. (2013). A guide to the project management body of knowledge. (PMBOK® Guide) – Fifth Edition. Project Management Institute.

Jansen, S. and Brinkkemper, S. (2006). Definition and validation of the key process of release, delivery and deployment for product software vendors: Turning the ugly duckling into a swan. In *Proceedings of 22nd IEEE International Conference on Software Maintenance*, ICSM '06, pages 166-175, Philadelphia, Pennsylvania, USA.

Kurmann, M., Tell, P., Klünder, J., Hebig, R., Licorish, S. and MacDonell S. (2018). Complementing materials for the HELENA study.

MarketLine. (2015), "Global software and services industry profile: Industry report", https://www.marketline.com

Ministerio de Desarrollo Productivo. (2018), "Nuevas categorías para ser PyMES". https://www.argentina.gob.ar/noticias/nuevas-categorias-para-ser-pyme

Ministerio de Producción y Trabajo. (2018), "Informe Argentina Productiva", Presidencia de la Nación Argentina. Secretaría de la Transformación Productiva. - Economía del Conocimiento, https://biblioteca.produccion.gob.ar/buscar/?fid=16

Mishra, D. and Mishra, A. (2009). Software process improvement in SMEs. *Computer Science and Information Systems*, 16(2):111-140.

Panizzi, M., Genero, M. and Bertone, R. (2020). Software system deployment process: A systematic mapping study. In *Proceedings of the XXIII Iberoamerican Conference on Software Engineering*, CIbSE '20, pages 138-151, Curitiba, Paraná, Brazil.

Panizzi, M., Genero, M. y Bertone, R. (2021). Encuesta para analizar las necesidades con respecto al proceso de despliegue de las PyMES en Argentina. In *Proceedings of the XXIV Iberoamerican Conference on Software Engineering*, CIbSE '21, pages 84-91, San Jose, Costa Rica.

Panizzi, M. (2021). Material para la formacion de DepProMod. https://drive.google.com/uc?export=download&id=1N2TvQBC2PHZNoydtE-iWAPTexsCW8U_I

Panizzi, M., Genero, M. and Bertone, R. (2022). Refining a Software System Deployment Process Model through Empirical Studies. *Journal of Computer Science and Technology* 23(1) https://journal.info.unlp.edu.ar/JCST/in-press_articles

Panizzi, M. (2022). *DepProMod:* Modelo de Proceso de Despliegue de Sistemas de Software. Tesis doctoral en Ciencias Informáticas, Universidad Nacional de La Plata http://sedici.unlp.edu.ar/handle/10915/139509

Panizzi, M., Genero, M. y Bertone, R. (2023). Apéndice. Estudios de casos realizados en PyMES de Argentina para validar DepProMod https://doi.org/10.6084/m9.figshare.22341259.v1

Paredes, I. and Carvalho, J. (2017). Research in Progress: Understanding the process of implantation IT Enterprise Applications in Small and Medium Enterprises (SMEs). In *Proceedings of the 17ª Conferência da Associação Portuguesa de Sistemas de Informação*, CAPSI '17, pages 270-283 Universidade do Minho, Guimarães – Portugal.

Pino, F., García, F. and Piattini, M. (2008). Software process improvement in small and medium software enterprises: A systematic review. *Software Quality Journal*, 16(2): 237–261.

Portal de administración electrónica. Gobierno de España. (2001). Métrica versión.3, https://administracionelectronica.gob.es/pae_Home.

Reascos, I., Carvalho, J. A. and Bossano, S. (2019). Implanting IT applications in government institutions: A process memerging from a case study in a medium-sized municipality. In *Proceedings of the 12th International Conference on Theory and Practice of Electronic Governance,* ICEGOV '19, pages 80-85, Melbourne, VIC, Australia.

Runeson, P., Höst, M., Rainer A. and Regnell, B. (2012), Case study research in software engineering: Guidelines and examples, John Wiley & Sons Inc., Hoboken, New Yersey.

Sharma, P. and Sangal, A. (2019). Building a hierarchical structure model of enablers that affect software process improvement in software SMEs-A mixed method approach. *Computer Standards & Interfaces*, 66(C): 1–23.

Subramanian, N. (2017). The software deployment process and automation. *CrossTalk*, 30(2):28-34.

Yin, R. (2014), Case study research: design and methods, Sage Publications, 5th edition.

Impact of remote work on Portuguese software professionals during the COVID-19 pandemic

Ana J. Almeida[1*] **Jácome Cunha**[2†] **João M. Fernandes**[1‡]

[1]ALGORITMI Research Centre / LASI, Universidade do Minho
Braga, Portugal
a83916@alunos.uminho.pt jmf@di.uminho.pt

[2]Faculdade de Engenharia da Universidade do Porto & HASLab/INESC TEC
Porto, Portugal
jacome@fe.up.pt

Abstract. *Although remote work was already possible and used in some contexts, the COVID-19 pandemic made it normal and, in some situations, even mandatory. This was the case in Portugal and in particular in its software industry. Given this abrupt change in how we work, it became pressing to investigate the impacts of this profound change to remote work, so that we can cope with the potential negative consequences (professional, personal, etc.). Thus, the goal of this work is to study the impact of the referred change to remote work, due to the COVID-19 pandemic, on software professionals in Portugal.*
To achieve this goal, a survey was prepared and distributed via email, LinkedIn, and Instagram. In total, 176 valid answers were collected from software professionals working in Portugal from 38 different companies. After the performed statistical analysis on the targeted population and focusing on the 10 elaborated research questions, two major findings can be concluded with certainty: (i) having worked in a remote regime before the pandemic period has a strong relationship with a higher frequency of use of teleconference tools after this period, and (ii) participants who do not feel safe about coming back to a fully on-site regime are more likely to prefer a fully remote regime than the ones who feel safe, while the latter group is more likely to prefer a hybrid regime.

1. Introduction

Remote work is a type of flexible working arrangement that allows an employee to work from a remote location outside of the corporate offices. This concept dates back to the '70s when many countries worried about their oil and the impact that home-work commuting had on their reservoirs. In that same decade, Jack Nilles, a NASA engineer, laid the foundation for modern remote work when he invented the term "telecommuting" (Hill and Fellows, 2014).

In this century, remote work was somewhat used, often through a Wi-Fi equipped laptop or tablet or even a smartphone, to work from home, public libraries, coffee shops, or other places. The COVID-19 pandemic led multiple world leaders to decide to lockdown their population for several months. Even after that measure was eased, and since

*ORCiD: 0009-0001-7701-7527
†ORCiD: 0000-0002-4713-3834
‡ORCiD: 0000-0003-1174-1966

many restrictions were still mandatory (and, in some cases, still are), some companies decided to continue to embrace remote work.

Thus, this study intends to analyze and understand the impact that the change to remote work, due to the COVID-19 pandemic, caused to software professionals.

The literature is rich in discussing this same problem. For example, some authors focused their effort on understanding the impact on productivity (Bao et al., 2022; Bezerra et al., 2020; Guler et al., 2021; Russo et al., 2021b; Šmite et al., 2022), while others studied the impact of remote work on employees' family members (Chinnaiah and Smt.Chythra, 2021; Ford et al., 2021). Nevertheless, several of the questions analyzed in this work (see Section 3.3 and Section 3.4) were not found in the current literature. In particular, this is the case of the questions for which statistical significance was found.

Since this theme is somewhat extensive, only some parameters (such as dependents, home-work dislocations, productivity, etc.) were chosen (see Section 2 for more details). To achieve this goal, an online survey was created and distributed to which 195 individuals answered. From those answers, at the end, a total of 176 were considered valid.

From the collected data, it can be concluded that having worked in a remote regime before the pandemic period is correlated with a higher frequency of use of teleconference tools after this period. One can also conclude that people who do not feel safe about coming back to a fully on-site regime are more likely to prefer a fully remote regime, while the ones who do feel safe are more likely to prefer a hybrid regime. Both these conclusions are supported by statistical significance. Additionally, although not statistically significant, it was also found that (i) having dependents and someone's support in their care could possibly negatively affect participants' work; (ii) having dependents could possibly show a relation to a preference for a mainly on-site hybrid regime; and (iii) company employee dimension could show a relation to participants' feel of support to maintain productivity.

2. Methodology

To study the impact of COVID-19 on software professionals, a survey was conducted with a significant number of participants from 38 different companies in Portugal.

A survey is an interesting empirical tool that uses the same questionnaire for all respondents and allows statistical handling of the collected answers. Another important advantage of surveys over other mechanisms is that they do not demand too much effort from those that answer the questions (if those are well built, most of the times, the answer is simply "yes" or "no"), which can lead to having a larger number of participants. On the other hand, surveys are limited, since one has to believe that participants answered truthfully, risking getting answers that do not reflect what individuals really think.

Objectives. The main objective of this work is to *study the impact that the change to remote work, due to the COVID-19 pandemic, caused (on multiple levels) to software professionals*. Since answers were collected between December 2021 and May 2022, the results report to that period (although participants' answers may consider events prior to that).

Research questions. The elaborated research questions (RQs), based on the survey objectives, are:

RQ1 Does participants' gender relate to having no support from someone in their household?
RQ2 Do participants who have dependents suffer a negative impact on productivity?
RQ3 Are participants who have dependents and no support from someone in their household more negatively affected at work than those who do?
RQ4 Does having to work more hours than the regular work schedule relate to a change in productivity?
RQ5 Does adopting strategies to maintain productivity have a positive impact on said productivity?
RQ6 Do longer commuting home-work times (i.e., over 30 minutes) relate to a preference for remote work?
RQ7 Does having worked in a remote regime before the pandemic period relate to the frequency of use of teleconference tools?
RQ8 Are participants that do not feel safe about coming back to a fully on-site regime more likely to prefer another regime (i.e., fully remote or hybrid) than those who feel safe?
RQ9 When it comes to the hybrid regime, do participants that have dependents in their household prefer a mainly remote regime?
RQ10 Does company employee dimension relate to the participants' feel of support to maintain productivity?

Population and inclusion criteria. This study target population is software professionals that work in Portugal and switched from an on-site regime to a remote regime during the COVID-19 pandemic.

The questionnaire (and, consequently, the survey) is anonymous and analyzes multiple domains, containing two questions that filter irrelevant answers:

1. To exclude participants who do not consent that their data is used for research purposes;
2. To exclude participants who, during the pandemic period, did not change from an on-site regime to a remote regime.

Questionnaire structure. Based on the RQs, the questionnaire is divided into several sections, namely:

- personal data;
- academic and professional data;
- ascendents/descendents (dependents);
- household (for participants who have dependents);
- caregiver support (for participants who had support from household members);
- aid measures from the company;
- working hours;
- extra hours;
- commuting to work and housing;

- moving from your house;
- productivity;
- productivity strategies;
- remote regime;
- necessary equipment;
- future work regime, with three possible subsections: fully on-site regime, fully remote regime, and hybrid regime.

The conceived questionnaire consists of 20 sections and 40 questions, not all mandatory, since a certain answer may skip some sections and questions. As mentioned, the first two questions are used to exclude irrelevant answers. The next three questions are then used to characterize the participants' personal data and five more to characterize the participants' professional data, although only four were used in the analysis and one of these (company name) was turned into a category. The remaining questions intend to analyze the multiple studied domains, such as dependents, work hours, productivity, and preferred work regime. It should be noted that questions that involve writing and some regarding *housing* and *necessary equipment*, for example, were not considered for the statistical analysis, since most answers were not related to the pandemic and to the change to remote work. These concrete questions can be found in the first author's previous work (Almeida, 2022).

Survey validation. Before the survey was widely distributed, five answers from two different companies were collected so that both the questionnaire accuracy and the survey viability could be validated.

Survey distribution. The questionnaire was originally written in Portuguese, however, to not exclude foreign workers, it was translated into English. Both were shared and data was collected from both. For this study, the chosen platform was Google Forms, one of the most widely-used survey platforms. The two links for the Portuguese and the English versions of the survey were sent to software professionals via email and LinkedIn (via direct messages and posts) and shared through Instagram stories. They were encouraged to share the survey with their colleagues who might also take it. Since the survey is anonymous, an email address was provided so that participants who wanted to know the study results could ask to be contacted. The survey was available between 2021/12/13 and 2022/05/02. In total, 195 answers were collected, from which 176 were considered valid.

Statistical analysis. All the analyzed variables are categorical, that is, they have two or more categories (e.g., "Yes" or "No"), but there is no intrinsic ordering to the referred categories (Watt and Collins, 2019). Therefore, the chi-squared test (χ^2) was used for all RQs in order to assess the existence of statistically significant differences between groups, regarding said categorical variables. *Pearson's* χ^2 *test* was used whenever the percentage of cell count expected to be less than five was inferior to 20%. When the referred percentage was equal or superior to 20%, *Fisher's exact test* was used instead. For measuring the effect size, the value of ϕ was used for variables that only include two categories each and the value of ϕ_c was used when at least one of the variables included more than two categories. All the values of p that are lower than 0.05 were considered statistically significant.

3. Results and Analysis

In this section, the results of this study are presented and analyzed, starting with the participants (Section 3.1) and then the RQs (Section 3.2).

3.1. Participants

The Portuguese version of the survey has 165 answers and the English one has 30. There are two answers from individuals who did not work in Portugal and 17 answers from participants who did not change from an on-site regime to a remote regime during the pandemic period. Thus, the valid answers are **176** (90.3% valid answers). To ease the analysis, a Python script was created to automatically translate the answers in Portuguese to English. Both surveys were then merged to analyze all the answers together.

Regarding the 176 valid answers, 40 of them are from females, 135 from males, and one is from another gender. Most participants (127; 72%) are between 18 and 35 years old, 45 participants are between 35 and 50, and 5 are between 51 and 65. Most participants were born in Portugal (159), six in Brazil, four in France, two in Angola, and several other countries (Canada, Germany, Netherlands, South Africa, and USA) have one participant each. Regarding the academic background, 93 completed a M.Sc., 62 have Bachelor's degree, 10 a Ph.D., nine a professional course, and two concluded high school. As can be seen in Table 1, participants have a range of 41 different job positions, including back-end developers (17), chief executive officers (7), and project managers (14).

3.2. Research Questions

In this section, an overview of the results for each RQ are introduced and studied. Tables 2–11 summarize the referred results and each data cell presents the number of answers and its percentage (within parenthesis) in the corresponding line. For example, in Table 2, the number of female participants that answered *yes* to the *support from someone in household* was eight, representing 61.5% of the total females that answered (13). Each table also presents the statistical test used and the p value. For the RQs for which statistical significance was found, the *effect size* is also presented.

RQ1. Results for the RQ "*Does participants' gender relate to having no support from someone in their household?*" can be regarded in Table 2. In total, 38.5% of the female and 36.4% of the male participants did not have support from someone in their household, which means the difference between them is only 2.1%. Nonetheless, there were 50% fewer answers from female participants, which could mean that, if there had been more answers from this group, this percentage variation could be different. Despite this fact, this data still seems to indicate that **gender could possibly show a relation to having no support from someone in the household**.

Table 1. Frequency of participants' job position.

Job position	Count	Job position	Count
Back-End Developer	17	Product Manager	1
Business Analyst	2	Product Owner	3
Chief Executive Officer (CEO)	7	Professional Services Operations Team	1
Chief Product Officer (CPO)	1	Project Manager	14
Chief Technology Officer (CTO)	5	Quality Engineer	4
Cloud Automation Engineer	1	Quality Manager	1
Commercial	3	Research and Development Director	1
Data Engineer	8	Researcher	2
Data Scientist	3	Security Engineer	1
Database Administrator	1	Senior Consultant	1
Deep Learning Engineer	1	Site Reliability Engineer	1
DevOps Engineer	5	Software Engineer	5
Embedded Systems Developer	10	System Administrator	3
Engineering Director	1	System Analyst	4
Engineering Manager	2	Systems Architect	2
Full-Stack Developer	26	Team Manager	1
Integration Developer	3	Tech Leader	1
Knowledge Manager	1	Technical Consultant	1
Mobile Developer	3	Test Engineer	9
Network Engineer	1	Web Developer	14
Product Designer	5		

Table 2. Overview of RQ1 results.

	Support from someone in household		
Gender	No	Yes	Count
Female	5 (38.5%)	8 (61.5%)	13*
Male	12 (36.4%)	21 (63.6%)	33*

Stats.	*Fisher's exact test* $p = 1.000$

*The number of answers is just 46, since not all participants have dependents and therefore did not answer.

RQ2. Table 3 presents the results for the RQ "*Do participants who have dependents suffer a negative impact on productivity?*". This study shows that 17.3% of participants with dependents had a negative impact on their productivity, while only 12.3% of participants without dependents had a negative impact[1]. Additionally, 54.4% of participants with dependents considered their productivity increased, whilst only 48.4% without dependents answered their productivity increased. Thus, it seems that **having dependents could possibly relate to an impact on productivity, not only negative, but also positive**.

RQ3. Data from Table 4 can be used to answer the RQ "*Are participants who have dependents and no support from someone in their household more negatively affected at work than those who do?*". One third (33.3%) of the participants who have dependents and no support and two thirds (66.7%) of the participants who have both dependents and

[1]The answers "Decreased significantly" and "Decreased slightly" are considered a negative impact on productivity while "Increased slightly" and "Increased significantly" are considered positive.

Table 3. Overview of RQ2 results.

Dependents	Productivity variation: Decreased significantly	Decreased slightly	Stayed the same	Increased slightly	Increased significantly	Count
No	2 (1.5%)	14 (10.8%)	51 (39.2%)	44 (33.8%)	19 (14.6%)	130
Yes	2 (4.3%)	6 (13.0%)	13 (28.3%)	20 (43.5%)	5 (10.9%)	46

Stats.	*Fisher's exact test* $p = 0.404$

support were negatively affected at work. In this case, and since the total number of answers is similar, it seems that **those who have dependents and support could possibly be more negatively affected at work** (contradicting the RQ), which can imply that perhaps the referred support was not sufficient or that other factors may be contributing to said negative impact.

Table 4. Overview of RQ3 results.

Negatively affected at work	Support from someone in household: No	Yes	Count
No	10 (40.0%)	15 (60.0%)	25*
Yes	7 (33.3%)	14 (66.7%)	21*

Stats.	*Pearson's χ^2 test* $p = 0.762$

*The number of answers is just 46, since only participants who have dependents answered these questions.

RQ4. Table 5 shows the results for the RQ "*Does having to work more hours than the regular work schedule relate to a change in productivity?*". This question, as all the others, is only related to working extra hours in the pandemic period (due to the change to remote work). Even though there were about 50% fewer answers from participants that did not comply with their work hours, the percentage of variations of "Decreased significantly" and "Decreased slightly" was around 50% higher compared to the other group, which reveals a **tendency for a decrease in productivity when work hours were not respected**, although the lack of statistical significance does not allow the attainment of certainty.

Table 5. Overview of RQ4 results.

Comply with work hours	Productivity variation: Decreased significantly	Decreased slightly	Stayed the same	Increased slightly	Increased significantly	Count
No	2 (3.4%)	10 (17.2%)	18 (31.0%)	19 (32.8%)	9 (15.5%)	58
Yes	2 (1.7%)	10 (8.5%)	46 (39.0%)	45 (38.1%)	15 (12.7%)	118

Stats.	*Fisher's exact test* $p = 0.324$

RQ5. The results for RQ "*Does adopting strategies to maintain productivity have a positive impact on said productivity?*" are presented in Table 6. A total of 53.6% of the participants that adopted strategies had some positive impact on their productivity, whilst only 46.7% of the ones that did not adopt strategies had an increase in their productivity[2]. In this case and since the answer count is similar, it seems that **adopting strategies does have some positive impact on productivity**. Even though with the presented data no certainty can be obtained, the fact that different groups may consider distinct types of strategies might have affected the results.

Table 6. Overview of RQ5 results.

	Productivity variation					
Adopt strategies	Decreased significantly	Decreased slightly	Stayed the same	Increased slightly	Increased significantly	Count
No	-	10 (10.9%)	39 (42.4%)	31 (33.7%)	12 (13.0%)	92
Yes	4 (4.8%)	10 (11.9%)	25 (29.8%)	33 (39.3%)	12 (14.3%)	84

Stats.	*Fisher's exact test* $p = 0.158$

RQ6. Table 7 illustrates the results for the RQ "*Do longer commuting home-work times (i.e., over 30 minutes) relate to a preference for remote work?*". A total of 15.1% of the participants that take under 30 minutes to get to work, 20% that take 30 minutes to one hour, and 20% that take over one hour to commute to work answered that they preferred a "fully remote" regime, which is a somewhat even distribution. Only two participants (2.5%) preferred a "fully on-site" regime. Thus, the "hybrid" regime is the most preferred option for all kinds of participants, accounting for about 80% in all groups of commuting times. These facts seem to indicate that **commuting times may not be the primary factor for preferring remote/hybrid work**, although statistical significance could not be found.

Table 7. Overview of RQ6 results.

	Preferred work regime			
Commuting home-work times	Fully on-site	Hybrid	Fully remote	Count
Under 30 minutes	1 (1.2%)	72 (83.7%)	13 (15.1%)	86
30 minutes to one hour	1 (1.3%)	63 (78.8%)	16 (20.0%)	80
Over one hour	-	8 (80.0%)	2 (20.0%)	10

Stats.	*Fisher's exact test* $p = 0.841$

RQ7. The results for the RQ "*Does having worked in a remote regime before the pandemic period relate to the frequency of use of teleconference tools?*" are presented in Table 8 and, unlike the previous RQs, these are statistically significant. A total of 52.9% of participants who did work in a past remote regime used teleconference tools with the

[2]The answers "Increased slightly" and "Increased significantly" are considered a positive impact on productivity.

same frequency as before the pandemic period whilst only 33.6% of the participants who did not work in a remote regime in the past used said tools with the same frequency. With this data, it can be affirmed that **having worked in a remote regime before the pandemic period has a correlation with a higher frequency of use of teleconference tools during the pandemic**. In this case, the effect size was computed, and, since ϕ is greater than 0.15, the aforementioned correlation is strong (Akoglu, 2018).

Effectively, participants that have worked in a remote regime before the pandemic period had to use teleconference tools to communicate with their team members or attend meetings. Essentially, their job was exactly the same, only the time period when it occurred changed. Thus, the frequency of use of those tools is somewhat expected to be similar in both periods (i.e., before and after the pandemic). On the other hand, participants that did not work in a remote regime in the past probably rarely used teleconference tools in their tasks, which confirms the smaller frequency of use of those tools.

Table 8. Overview of RQ7 results.

	Same frequency of use of teleconference tools		
Past remote regime	No	Yes	Count
No	83 (66.4%)	42 (33.6%)	125
Yes	24 (47.1%)	27 (52.9%)	51

Stats.	*Pearson's* χ^2 *test* $p = 0.019$ $\phi = 0.180$

RQ8. As in the previous RQ, the results for the question "*Are participants that do not feel safe about coming back to a fully on-site regime more likely to prefer another regime (i.e., fully remote or hybrid) than those who feel safe?*" are statistically significant (Table 9). 38.9% of participants who feel "Significantly insecure" prefer a fully remote regime, whereas 61.1% prefer a hybrid regime; 14.3% and 85.7% of participants who feel "Slightly insecure" prefer a fully remote or a hybrid regime, respectively. In fact, no participants in the referred groups prefer a fully on-site regime. Moreover, 16.7% of participants who feel "Significantly secure" prefer a fully remote regime, while 79.2% prefer a hybrid regime and only 4.2% prefer a fully on-site regime; 3.3% and 96.7% of participants that feel "Slightly secure" prefer a fully remote or a hybrid regime, respectively. Thus, with the present data, it can be affirmed that **participants are more likely to prefer a fully remote regime if they do not feel secure** and that **participants who feel safe about coming back to a fully on-site regime would still prefer to switch to a hybrid one**. Here, the value of ϕ_c (*effect size*) is greater than 0.15, which means that the relation between both analyzed variables is strong (Akoglu, 2018).

It is somewhat expected that participants who do not feel safe about coming back to a fully on-site regime would more likely prefer a fully remote regime when compared to the ones who do feel safe. This regime allows them to avoid being in their physical workplace and possibly being infected with viruses. In this case, for example, a mainly remote hybrid regime would always imply that part of the work hours had to be spent on-site, which could still be another viable alternative if their company did not allow a fully remote regime. On the other hand, participants who feel safe to come back to a fully on-site regime tend to prefer a hybrid regime, which may seem peculiar, but such regime can provide an on-site portion and, at the same time, the comfort of working remotely, reducing commuting times and costs, thus allowing better schedule management.

Table 9. Overview of RQ8 results.

Safe about fully on-site	Preferred work regime: Fully on-site	Hybrid	Fully remote	Count
Significantly insecure	-	11 (61.1%)	7 (38.9%)	18
Slightly insecure	-	24 (85.7%)	4 (14.3%)	28
Neutral	-	41 (78.8%)	11 (21.2%)	52
Slightly secure	-	29 (96.7%)	1 (3.3%)	30
Significantly secure	2 (4.2%)	38 (79.2%)	8 (16.7%)	48

Stats.	*Fisher's exact test* $p = 0.032$ $\phi_c = 0.213$

RQ9. The results for the RQ "*When it comes to the hybrid regime, do participants who have dependents in their household prefer a mainly remote regime?*" are illustrated in Table 10 and show that 47.1%, 35.3%, and 17.6% of participants who have dependents prefer a mainly remote, balanced hybrid, or a mainly on-site regime, respectively. When comparing to participants who do not have dependents, there are over 50% more participants that prefer a mainly on-site regime. Thus, even though this data is not statistically significant, it seems that **having dependents could possibly show a relation to a preference for a hybrid mainly on-site regime**, contradicting the RQ. This can be explained in part due to the fact that taking care of their dependents for long periods may have had a negative impact on participants' personal and professional lives.

Table 10. Overview of RQ9 results.

Dependents	Preferred hybrid regime: Mainly on-site	Balanced hybrid	Mainly remote	Count
No	9 (8.3%)	30 (27.5%)	70 (64.2%)	109*
Yes	6 (17.6%)	12 (35.3%)	16 (47.1%)	34*

Stats.	*Pearson's* χ^2 *test* $p = 0.135$

*The number of answers is just 143, since not every participant prefers a hybrid regime.

RQ10. Table 11 illustrates the results for the RQ "*Does company employee dimension relate to the participants' feel of support to maintain productivity?*". A total of 68.8% of participants from small enterprises, 75.6% from medium-sized enterprises, and 80.2% from large enterprises felt support to maintain productivity. Even though with the presented data no certainty can be achieved, it seems that **company employee dimension could possibly show a relation to professionals' feel of support to maintain productivity**. The fact that there are more answers from participants who work in large enterprises can explain this, which could mean that results could differ if there had been more answers from the other groups.

Table 11. Overview of RQ10 results.

	Company support (productivity)		
Company dimension	No	Yes	Count
Small enterprises (up to 49 employees)	15 (31.3%)	33 (68.8%)	48*
Medium-sized enterprises (50 to 249 employees)	10 (24.4%)	31 (75.6%)	41*
Large enterprises (250+ employees)	16 (19.8%)	65 (80.2%)	81*

Stats.	*Pearson's* χ^2 *test* $p = 0.334$

*The number of answers is just 170, since some participants preferred not to say which company they work for.

3.3. Literature Parallelism

RQ1 hinted that gender could possibly show a relation to having no aid in caregiving of dependents. Even though there were less 50% female answers, they still had a slightly bigger percentage of not getting support when compared to male ones. Previous work (Russo et al., 2021b) states that gender does not reveal any differences in their considered variables, which, in this study case, is not entirely true. On the other hand, Machado et al. (2021) reached a similar conclusion to this study regarding gender *vs.* the lack of support and childcare.

Following the findings in RQ2, RQ4, and RQ5, productivity possibly suffered both positive and negative impacts (depending on the question), agreeing with what has been found (Bao et al., 2022). However, the referred conclusion is not in line with:

- Bezerra et al. (2020) who claim that productivity mostly did not suffer a negative impact;
- Russo et al. (2021b) who state that productivity did not change;
- Guler et al. (2021) who declare that productivity increased in general;
- Šmite et al. (2022) who affirm that productivity did not change significantly.

By analyzing RQ3 results, it can be concluded that having dependents and support from someone in participants' household seems to impact their productivity more negatively than those who do not have support. Ford et al. (2021) reached a similar conclusion on productivity impact when considering proximity to family members, claiming that it is beneficial for some and detrimental for others.

In the revised literature no similar or different conclusions were made that can relate to RQ6, RQ7, RQ8, RQ9, and RQ10.

3.4. Results Overview

Statistical significance could not be obtained for several of the RQs. Nonetheless, some ideas can be formulated:

- having dependents and support in their care from someone in participants' household could possibly negatively affect their work;

- having dependents could possibly show a relation to a preference for a mainly on-site hybrid regime;
- company employee dimension could show a relation to participants' feel of support to maintain productivity.

However, the results for two of the research questions, namely RQ7 and RQ8, show statistical significance:

- the results for RQ7 indicate that having worked in a remote regime before the pandemic period has a strong correlation with a higher frequency of use of teleconference tools after this period, which is reasonable since these participants were already familiarized with the use of such tools;
- for RQ8, the results demonstrate that participants who do not feel safe about coming back to a fully on-site regime are more likely to prefer a fully remote regime than the ones who feel safe and the latter are more likely to prefer a hybrid regime. This seems coherent, since a fully remote regime allows them to avoid being in a "public" workplace and a hybrid regime implies that, on some days, the job has to be done on-site. Like in the previous RQ, this relation is strong.

4. Threats to Validity

In this section, the possible threats to the validity of this work are presented and divided into four categories (Wohlin et al., 2012).

Conclusion Validity. One of the possible issues is the *low statistical power*. Indeed, for some RQs, no statistical significance was found. Nevertheless, the number of valid answers (176) provides a certain amount of confidence in the findings, which are mostly in line with the state of the art. Different statistical tests were used to not *violate assumptions of statistical tests*. Different RQs use distinct datasets, which were validated beforehand. More details about test considerations can be found in (Almeida, 2022).

Internal Validity. If the *instrumentation* (in this case, the survey) is badly designed, it may affect the experiment. To mitigate this threat, a few answers were collected before releasing the survey widely. These answers confirmed that the survey did not raise any issues with the participants and thus confidence was achieved in order to send it to a wider audience. Regarding the *selection* of participants, Wohlin et al. (2012) say that volunteers are generally more motivated for this kind of study, which was the case for all the collected answers.

Construct Validity. A possible issue is participants trying to *guess the hypothesis*. This is always a possibility, being quite difficult to validate. Nevertheless, although some questions have been posed in a negative/positive form, the answers were in the opposite direction. This provides some confidence that participants were trying to give real answers, instead of trying to make the answer "fit" the question.

External Validity. This kind of threat may limit the generalization of the results. In this study, all participants work in Portugal. This was a choice as it was intended to study the effects of COVID-19 on the Portuguese software industry. Nonetheless, almost 10% of the answers came from foreigners working in Portugal. Although this is not sufficient to make the results generic for those outside of our country, the obtained results are generally in line with the current literature, which is mostly international.

5. Related Work

Several other authors have studied the impact of the pandemic on the software industry. As in this work, productivity is one of the variables that has been studied. Bao et al. (2022) conclude that productivity possibly suffered both positive and negative impacts, results that are in line with this work. However, others have achieved different conclusions: Bezerra et al. (2020) claim that productivity mostly did not suffer a negative impact; Russo et al. (2021b) state that productivity did not change; Guler et al. (2021) declare that productivity increased in general; and Šmite et al. (2022) affirm that productivity did not change significantly.

Having dependents and the possible impact of their care was also addressed by Ford et al. (2021), reaching similar conclusions as in this study, that is, proximity to family members is beneficial for some and detrimental for others. When it comes to gender, Russo et al. (2021b) state that it does not reveal any differences in their considered variables, which in this study's case is not entirely accurate. On the other hand, Machado et al. (2021) reach a similar conclusion to the present work regarding gender *vs.* lack of support and childcare, with the proviso that, in this study, dependents refer to both children and elderly (e.g., parents or parents-in-law).

Many other articles were analyzed to better define the scope of this work, although their conclusions are not entirely related to the ones achieved in this study, since the considered variables are not the same. For example, Oz and Crooks (2020) state that communication between different teams increased more than within them and extra work-hour messaging became much more frequent. Russo et al. (2021a) claim that time distribution of working activities before and during the pandemic is very similar and working in a remote regime is not a challenge by itself. Guler et al. (2021) indicate that back pain increased significantly, revealing a decrease in employee health. Miller et al. (2021) conclude that reaching milestones was challenging, and Šmite et al. (2023) claim that workers adapt to their work condition with time. Chinnaiah and Smt.Chythra (2021) found that challenges faced by married and unmarried employees and employees with different educational backgrounds are significantly different and, lastly, Nguyen-Duc et al. (2022) affirm that startups did not perceive the impact of remote work differently.

A more detailed analysis of each of these works can be found in the first author's previous work (Almeida, 2022).

6. Conclusions

The COVID-19 pandemic has been devastating in multiple domains, and its impact cannot be fully calculated and most certainly will never be forgotten. With that in mind, the main objective of this work is to study one of the impacts that the COVID-19 pandemic caused, that is, the impact that the change to remote work caused (on multiple levels) on software professionals.

From analyzing the related work and from the presented work, it can concluded that there is an abundance of different approaches, but the results are somewhat similar – overall, software professionals that worked remotely during the pandemic period did not suffer the severe negative impact many would expect.

Additionally, companies should work on strategies to help their employees, however, those must be done for each and every single one of them individually, since different people have different needs.

One possible increment to this study would be to broaden its participants, for example, by conducting the survey in other countries and possibly finding a relation between them and their policies. Another possibility is to conduct the same survey again and try to obtain more answers in order to make some research questions statistically significant. To expand this study, one could also elaborate another questionnaire and conduct another survey on these same 38 companies in order to understand if there were some changes and how did they adapt, now that the effects of the COVID-19 pandemic have a different nature.

Acknowledgments

This work has been supported by FCT (Fundação para a Ciência e a Tecnologia) within the R&D Units Project Scope: UIDB/00319/2020.

References

Akoglu, H. (2018). User's guide to correlation coefficients. *Turkish Journal of Emergency Medicine*, 18(3):91–93. DOI 10.1016/j.tjem.2018.08.001.

Almeida, A. J. (2022). Analysis of the impact of remote work on portuguese software professionals during the COVID-19 pandemic. Master's thesis, University of Minho, Braga, Portugal. https://hdl.handle.net/1822/83355.

Bao, L., Li, T., Xia, X., Zhu, K., Li, H., and Yang, X. (2022). How does working from home affect developer productivity? — A case study of Baidu during the COVID-19 pandemic. *Science China Information Sciences*, 65(4):142102. DOI 10.1007/s11432-020-3278-4.

Bezerra, C. I. M., de Souza Filho, J. C., Coutinho, E. F., Gama, A., Ferreira, A. L., de Andrade, G. L. a., and Feitosa, C. E. (2020). How human and organizational factors influence software teams productivity in COVID-19 pandemic: A Brazilian survey. In *XXXIV Brazilian Symposium on Software Engineering (SBES 2020)*, p. 606–615. ACM. DOI 10.1145/3422392.3422417.

Chinnaiah, P. and Smt.Chythra, P. (2021). Challenges of working from home in persistent Covid-19 environment. *International Research Journal of Business Studies*, 14(1):85–97.

Ford, D., Storey, M.-A., Zimmermann, T., Bird, C., Jaffe, S., Maddila, C., Butler, J. L., Houck, B., and Nagappan, N. (2021). A tale of two cities: Software developers working from home during the COVID-19 pandemic. *ACM Transaction on Software Engineering Methodology*, 31(2). DOI 10.1145/3487567.

Guler, M. A., Guler, K., Guneser Gulec, M., and Ozdoglar, E. (2021). Working from home during a pandemic: Investigation of the impact of COVID-19 on employee health and productivity. *Journal of Occupational and Environmental Medicine*, 63(9):731–741. DOI 10.1097/JOM.0000000000002277.

Hill, E. J. and Fellows, K. J. (2014). *Encyclopedia of Quality of Life and Well-Being Research*, chapter " "Telecommuting"", pp. 6599–6600. Springer. DOI 10.1007/978-94-007-0753-5_2985.

Machado, L. S., Caldeira, C., Gattermann Perin, M., and de Souza, C. R. (2021). Gendered experiences of software engineers during the COVID-19 crisis. *IEEE Software*, 38(2):38–44. DOI 10.1109/MS.2020.3040135.

Miller, C., Rodeghero, P., Storey, M.-A., Ford, D., and Zimmermann, T. (2021). How was your weekend? Software development teams working from home during COVID-19. In *43rd International Conference on Software Engineering (ICSE 2021)*, p. 624–636. IEEE Press. DOI 10.1109/ICSE43902.2021.00064.

Nguyen-Duc, A., Khanna, D., Greer, D., Wang, X., Zaina, L. M., Matturro, G., Melegati, J., Guerra, E., Le, G. H., Kettunen, P., Hyrynsalmi, S., Edison, H., Sales, A., Rutitis, D., Kemell, K.-K., Aldaeej, A., Mikkonen, T., Garbajosa, J., and Abrahamsson, P. (2022). Work-from-home and its implication for project management, resilience and innovation: A global survey on software companies. *arXiv*. https://arxiv.org/pdf/2202.04950.pdf.

Oz, T. and Crooks, A. (2020). Exploring the impact of mandatory remote work during the COVID-19 pandemic. *SocArXiv*. https://osf.io/preprints/socarxiv/hjre6/.

Russo, D., Hanel, P. H. P., Altnickel, S., and van Berkel, N. (2021). The daily life of software engineers during the COVID-19 pandemic. In *43rd International Conference on Software Engineering: Software Engineering in Practice ICSE-SEIP 2021*, p. 364–373. IEEE Press. DOI 10.1109/ICSE-SEIP52600.2021.00048.

Russo, D., Hanel, P. H. P., and van Berkel, N. (2021). Understanding developers well-being and productivity: A longitudinal analysis of the COVID-19 pandemic. *arXiv*. https://arxiv.org/pdf/2111.10349.pdf.

Šmite, D., Moe, N. B., Klotins, E., and Gonzalez-Huerta, J. (2023). From forced working-from-home to voluntary working-from-anywhere: Two revolutions in telework. *Journal of Systems and Software*, 195:111509. DOI 10.1016/j.jss.2022.111509.

Šmite, D., Tkalich, A., Moe, N. B., Papatheocharous, E., Klotins, E., and Buvik, M. P. (2022). Changes in perceived productivity of software engineers during COVID-19 pandemic: The voice of evidence. *Journal of Systems and Software*, 186:111197. DOI 10.1016/j.jss.2021.111197.

Watt, R. and Collins, E. (2019). *Statistics for psychology: A guide for beginners (and everyone else)*. SAGE Publications.

Wohlin, C., Runeson, P., Höst, M., Ohlsson, M. C., Regnell, B., and Wesslén, A. (2012). *Experimentation in software engineering*. Springer. DOI 10.1007/978-3-642-29044-2.

Um checklist para inspeção de privacidade e proteção de dados pessoais em artefatos de software

Diego André Cerqueira[1], Rafael Maiani de Mello[2], Guilherme Horta Travassos[1]

[1]PESC/COPPE - Universidade Federal do Rio de Janeiro (UFRJ), Rio de Janeiro, RJ - Brasil

[2]Instituto de Computação - Universidade Federal do Rio de Janeiro (UFRJ), Rio de Janeiro, RJ - Brasil

{dc,ght}@cos.ufrj.br, rafaelmello@ic.ufrj.br

Resumo. *A evolução da percepção sobre a privacidade e proteção de dados pessoais requer novas tecnologias para garantir a qualidade do software. Neste cenário, leis recentes para garantir a proteção de dados pessoais estabelecem novos requisitos para o software. Entretanto, a falta de tecnologias adequadas tem desafiado desenvolvedores de diferentes países em garantir a ausência de defeitos em seus produtos de software tendo em vista os princípios estabelecidos por estas leis. Assim, este artigo apresenta a concepção e elaboração inicial da LGPDCheck, uma técnica de inspeção baseada em checklist para identificar defeitos nos artefatos de sistemas de software com base nos princípios estabelecidos pela Lei Geral de Proteção de Dados Pessoais (LGPD).*

Abstract. *The evolution of the perception of privacy and protection of personal data requires new technologies to guarantee software quality. In this scenario, recent laws to ensure the security of personal data establish new software requirements. However, a lack of adequate technologies jeopardizes the developers in different countries to guarantee the absence of defects in their software products, given the principles established by these laws. Thus, this article presents the initial conception and organization of LGPDCheck, a checklist-based inspection technique to support the identification of defects in the artifacts of software systems under development or evolution based on the principles established by the Brazilian General Data Protection Law (LGPD).*

1. Introdução

A produção massiva de dados causada pela popularização de dispositivos móveis, aparelhos inteligentes e uso de redes sociais nas últimas décadas tem desafiado constantemente o direito à privacidade e proteção de dados pessoais na era digital [UN 2017]. Para acompanhar estes desafios, em 2016, foi aprovada a *General Data Protection Regulation* (GDPR). Em seguida, presenciamos em 2018 o ordenamento jurídico no Brasil sobre a temática de Privacidade e Proteção de Dados (PPD) por meio da aprovação da Lei Geral de Proteção de Dados Pessoais (LGPD) [BRASIL 2018].

Embora tanto a *GDPR* como a LGPD não abordem diretamente produtos de software, podemos observar que regulamentos de PPD impactam diversos setores e atividades que influenciam o ciclo de desenvolvimento do software [Dias et al. 2022]. Neste sentido, empresas e profissionais necessitam que seus produtos e processos de software atendam aos requisitos legais previstos nestas leis. Porém, ainda há pouco ou nenhum suporte para isto na prática [Gürses et al. 2011].

Considerando as condições e restrições impostas pela LGPD desde 2020, torna-se necessário garantir a qualidade e a conformidade de produtos de software em construção e existentes frente aos novos requisitos de PPD, evitando possíveis penalidades para as organizações. Neste sentido, observamos uma lacuna persistente nas práticas de implementação dos direitos, deveres e responsabilidades previstos na LGPD em sistemas de software. Esta lacuna pode ser parcialmente explicada pela linguagem jurídica envolvida e seu distanciamento de situações concretas e objetivamente verificáveis. Assim, torna-se necessário reduzir este distanciamento através de tecnologias que organizem, instrumentalizem e integrem arcabouços legais de PPD à prática [Shapiro 2010].

Apesar deste distanciamento persistir, a aplicação da LGPD já faz parte do cotidiano dos diferentes times desenvolvimento brasileiros e sua aplicação tem sido investigada na área. No contexto organizacional, a técnica LGPD4BP (*LGPD for Business Process*) de Araújo et al. (2021) visa avaliar conformidade de um processo de negócio com a LGPD. O questionário de avaliação de e o processo foram construídos com base nos direitos dos titulares e trechos da própria LGPD. Já Mendes et al. (2021) propuseram a versão inicial de um *checklist* voltado para a verificação da adequação do produto de software a alguns atributos extraídos da LGPD e GDPR. Este checklist foi então estendido por Pereira et al., (2022) para apoiar a verificação de sistemas baseados em Internet das coisas (IoT). Apesar da relevância da técnica e dos atributos tratados nestas tecnologias, não foi possível identificar material de apoio à interpretação/aplicação das leis, principalmente à LGPD, no contexto do desenvolvimento de software. Ademais, os *checklists* propostos são voltados para a verificação de sistemas de software em produção, limitando sua utilização, *a priori*, na construção de novos produtos de software. Neste sentido, a investigação de Dias et al. (2022) revelou que os times de desenvolvimento sentem maior impacto da LGPD nas atividades de especificação de requisitos e construção de software.

Com base nestes trabalhos, vislumbramos a oportunidade de promover o desenvolvimento de uma tecnologia de software baseada em evidência que permita a verificação dos princípios da LGPD em artefatos de software e oriente a comunidade da prática a interpretar estes princípios no contexto de atividades de desenvolvimento e evolução de software [Shapiro 2010]. Desta forma, a pesquisa em andamento apresentada neste artigo visa responder à seguinte pergunta de pesquisa: *"Como apoiar profissionais de software a verificar a conformidade de sistemas de software com os princípios estabelecidos pela Lei Geral de Proteção de Dados Pessoais?"*.

Portanto, o objetivo deste trabalho consiste em desenvolver uma técnica de inspeção baseada em checklist (*LGPDCheck*) para apoiar a identificação de defeitos em artefatos produzidos nas diferentes etapas do ciclo de desenvolvimento de software com base nas restrições e condições estabelecidas pela LGPD. Para alcançar tal objetivo, entendemos que a *LGPDCheck* deverá oferecer, além do checklist, instrumentos adicionais que orientem os inspetores a contextualizar os princípios da LGPD na prática de desenvolvimento e evolução do software.

O desenvolvimento da *LGPDCheck* segue uma metodologia de pesquisa inspirada em Design Science (DS) [March and Smith 1995]. O objetivo da DS é resolver problemas do mundo real através da instrumentalização de conhecimentos específicos de um campo ou área e, assim, auxiliar profissionais especialistas a criar soluções para problemas a partir das experiências ou vivências na área [Engström et al. 2020]. Desta forma, os seguintes estágios de trabalho foram executados (1,2,3), estão em execução (4) ou planejados (5): (1) condução de entrevistas com especialistas que atuam na verificação da conformidade sistemas de software com a LGPD;(2) levantamento bibliográfico de aplicação de PPD em Engenharia de Software (ES); (3) análise do conteúdo da LGPD; (4) construção dos artefatos que compõem a *LGPDCheck*; (5) avaliação experimental da *LGPDCheck*. No momento, estamos no quarto estágio, finalizando os instrumentos da técnica de inspeção.

Este artigo, portanto, descreve o estágio atual do desenvolvimento da *LGPDCheck*, a primeira técnica de inspeção aplicada a artefatos de software durante seu desenvolvimento ou evolução.

2. Práticas de Privacidade e Proteção de dados

A Lei Geral de Proteção de Dados Pessoais (LGPD) - 13.709/2018, aprovada em 2018, apresenta definições importantes sobre privacidade e proteção de dados à sociedade brasileira. Em seu Art. 5º são definidos os principais conceitos de PPD utilizados para o desenvolvimento deste trabalho, como *tratamento*, *operação de tratamento*, *agentes de tratamento*, *consentimento* e *titular* [BRASIL 2018].

A LGPD é fundamentada em dez princípios (*finalidade, adequação, necessidade, livre acesso, qualidade dos dados, transparência, segurança, prevenção, não-discriminação,* e *responsabilização e prestação de contas*) que são a base para qualquer operação de tratamento de dados pessoais [BRASIL 2018]. Entretanto, apesar de estabelecer tais princípios, a LGPD não apresenta como tais princípios e práticas de PPD se refletem concretamente em qualquer outro contexto prático, incluindo o desenvolvimento ou evolução de sistemas de software.

Desta forma, a implantação das práticas de PPD segue desafiando a comunidade de software. Gürses *et al.* (2011) destacam as dificuldades causadas por ambiguidade ou imprecisão de tais documentos nas definições de seus conceitos. Outra dificuldade relatada pelos autores consiste em estabelecer objetivamente o que significa estar em conformidade com determinado princípio. Além disto, [Hadar et al. 2018] destacam o risco de confusão conceitual entre os conceitos de PPD e segurança da informação, agravados pela falta de metodologias que suportem a implementação destes conceitos nos diferentes estágios do ciclo de vida de software [Morales-Trujillo et al. 2018].

Ao investigar a literatura sobre PPD, identificamos que o conceito de *Privacidade por Concepção* (PbD) é consideravelmente disseminado. PbD visa estabelecer um conjunto de sete princípios fundamentais que guiam a implementação da privacidade desde os primeiros passos da construção de um produto, podendo estes serem aplicados desde tecnologias digitais à negócios físicos. Assim, os autores de PbD propõe elevar a privacidade a um objetivo principal a ser alcançado [Cavoukian 2009].

Neste sentido, Shapiro (2010) sugere a concepção de tecnologias que ofereçam: (1) uma tradução efetiva de princípios abstratos de privacidade, modelos de risco de privacidade e mecanismos de privacidade em requisitos implementáveis; (2) a integração destes requisitos em um processo apropriado; e (3) a incorporação deste processo no ciclo de vida de desenvolvimento. Isso motiva e justifica disponibilizar uma tecnologia de software que mitigue estas questões, no caso, inspeção de software.

3 Inspeção de Software

O método de inspeção de software representa uma tecnologia para verificação visual de um artefato de software buscando identificar defeitos (anomalias, faltas, erros e desvios em padrões e especificações) [IEEE 2008]. A inspeção de software é considerada uma tecnologia de baixo custo que promove a qualidade dos artefatos de software desde as etapas iniciais do processo de desenvolvimento, aumentando a produtividade devido a redução do retrabalho [Fagan 1976]. Assim, as inspeções auxiliam não apenas na detecção, mas também na promoção da remoção de defeitos potencialmente negligenciados nas diversas etapas do processo de desenvolvimento e evolução do software [Shull et al. 2000]. A utilização de inspeção de software pode ocorrer em diversas etapas do processo de desenvolvimento de software, desde os requisitos [Fagan 1976], [Porter et al. 1995], até as etapas de testes [Boehm and Basili 2001].

De Mello et al. (2011) afirmam que um dos fatores decisivos no planejamento e resultados da inspeção de produtos e projetos de software é a escolha da técnica de inspeção a ser utilizada. É possível encontrar na literatura diferentes tipos de técnicas, tais como *ad-hoc*, *checklists* e baseadas em perspectiva (SHULL et al., 1999). Dentre elas, as técnicas de inspeção baseadas em *checklist* são compostas por perguntas com repostas "Sim/Não", que direcionam o inspetor para a perspectiva de qualidade esperada durante o processo de inspeção de determinado artefato de software [Laitenberger et al. 2001]. Neste sentido, *checklists* podem ser calibrados para direcionar os inspetores para a perspectiva de qualidade pretendida em determinada inspeção. Por exemplo, os princípios de PPD podem servir como perspectiva de qualidade para um *checklist*.

4. Desenvolvendo a *LGPDCheck*

Após estudar os princípios de PPD e da LGPD, identificamos a necessidade prover apoio para a verificação da conformidade de sistemas de software com estes princípios. Para tal, entendemos que o desenvolvimento de uma técnica de inspeção baseada em *checklist* se demonstra adequado. Entretanto, também percebemos a necessidade de melhor compreender como a verificação dos princípios da LGPD tem sido realizada na prática. Neste sentido, conduzimos entrevistas com dois especialistas em LGPD visando caracterizar sua prática quanto à verificação dos princípios da LGPD em sistemas de software. Os especialistas entrevistados possuem experiência prática na aplicação da LGPD durante o ciclo de desenvolvimento de software. Foram conduzidas entrevistas semiestruturadas, via videoconferência, cada uma com duração média de 60 minutos.

Através destas entrevistas, foi possível evidenciar, de forma anedótica, a aplicação *ad-hoc* da LGPD e de práticas de PPD dentro do ciclo de desenvolvimento de software por profissionais experientes e especialistas da área. Estes achados possibilitaram revelar alguns detalhes sobre o processo de aplicação da LGPD na prática, essencialmente fundamentado na experiência e conhecimento dos especialistas entrevistados. Dentre os principais achados, destacamos: (1) tentativa de implementar os princípios de PPD desde o desenho das funcionalidades do sistema; (2) desconhecimento de guias específicos para implementação da LGPD no desenvolvimento de software; (3) adoção de casos de uso para especificação dos dados a serem manipulados na implementação de funcionalidades do sistema; (4) emprego de estruturas adicionais chamadas de *mapa de dados* para o registro de informações relevantes dos dados, tais como origem e tipo; (5) percepção de que os desenvolvedores relevam os princípios da PPD em seus projetos de software. Os achados destas entrevistas influenciaram o desenvolvimento da LGPDCheck[1].

[1] Informações adicionais sobre o perfil dos entrevistados, roteiro e achados das entrevistas estão disponíveis em http://bit.ly/40ooGoT

A partir destes achados, entendemos a necessidade de expandir o escopo inicialmente previsto da inspeção, cobrindo diferentes artefatos e momentos do processo de desenvolvimento. Além disto, a característica genérica dos princípios da LGPD nos levou a optar por desenvolver primeiramente um material de apoio para associar os princípios da LGPD a defeitos em sistemas de software. Ao longo desta experiência, entendemos que seria mais pertinente desenvolvermos uma técnica de inspeção baseada em *checklist* para apoiar a verificação dos princípios da LGPD, uma vez que os itens de verificação de um *checklist* podem guiar os revisores a refletir sobre possíveis defeitos ao invés de determiná-los[Mello et al. 2011].

Assim, iniciamos o desenvolvimento da *LGPDCheck*, uma técnica de inspeção baseada em *checklist* visando a identificação de defeitos (*omissão, fato incorreto, ambiguidade, inconsistência e informação estranha*) em sistemas de software com foco nos princípios estabelecidos pela LGPD. A técnica busca contribuir para a construção de um referencial para os artefatos produzidos em diferentes etapas do ciclo de desenvolvimento de software [Travassos et al. 1999] com base na LGPD.

Em nossos estudos iniciais, identificamos que a verificação dos dez princípios da LGPD pode requerer informações oriundas não somente das especificações de requisitos do sistema, mas também do próprio sistema em execução. Assim, a primeira versão da *LGPDCheck* considera uma abordagem de inspeção em múltiplos níveis. Esta abordagem multinível visa oferecer cobertura à verificação dos seguintes artefatos:

- *Nível I - Requisitos do Sistema*: a verificação ocorre no documento de requisitos do sistema a ser construído ou em construção. Seu objetivo é identificar se dados e seus tratamentos respeitam as definições dos princípios de PPD;
- *Nível II – Sistemas em execução*: a verificação ocorre em nível de funcionalidade do sistema em execução. Seu objetivo é verificar a presença de funcionalidades capazes de garantir que os princípios de PPD sejam implementados;
- *Nível III – Requisitos Organizacionais*: a verificação ocorre em nível organizacional. Seu objetivo é verificar a existência de normas, práticas organizacionais diretrizes da organização detentora do sistema em inspeção capazes de garantir que os princípios de PPD sejam implementados.

A definição destes três níveis promoveu a sua priorização considerando cada um dos dez princípios estabelecidos na LGPD, guiando a construção dos recursos e instrumentos que irão compor a *LGPDCheck*. Esperamos que um inspetor, ao focar no nível de inspeção primário para determinado princípio, consiga otimizar seu esforço de avaliação nos artefatos, aplicando os itens de verificação mais pertinentes.

Para realizar esta priorização, foi considerada a relação entre os princípios da LGPD a partir de suas definições [Brasil, 2018]. Deste modo, os princípios a serem priorizados para o Nível I (requisitos do sistema) são *Finalidade, Adequação e Necessidade.* Para o Nível II (sistemas em execução) são *Livre acesso, Qualidade dos dados e Transparência.* Finalmente, os princípios priorizados para o Nível III (Práticas Organizacionais) são os de *Segurança, Prevenção, Não discriminação e Responsabilização e Prestação de contas.*

4.1. Instrumentos da *LGPDCheck*

Conforme previamente indicado, a *LGPDCheck* oferecerá um conjunto de instrumentos além do *checklist* propriamente dito. Primeiramente, está sendo organizado um *material de apoio*, que visa oferecer ao inspetor um conjunto de recursos que introduz e exemplifica cada princípio da LGPD no contexto de sistemas de software, além de um glossário de termos da LGPD adaptado ao contexto de sistemas de software[2]. Tais cenários são compostos por informações como a *definição do princípio*, a *interpretação do princípio para sistemas de software* e *exemplos de violação do princípio* para estimular a reflexão dos inspetores. Além disto, cada cenário apresenta a *ação esperada pela organização responsável pelo sistema*, indicando o que deveria acontecer em cada tratamento de dados para que o princípio correspondente seja atendido. A Tabela 1 apresenta um dos cenários do material de apoio relacionado ao princípio *necessidade* previsto na LGPD. Por questões de limitação de espaço, apenas um dos dez quadros referentes ao princípio *necessidade* será apresentado no artigo.

Tabela 1 – Cenário do material de apoio referente ao princípio necessidade da LGPD

III – NECESSIDADE		
1.Definição da lei: limitação do tratamento ao mínimo necessário para a realização de suas finalidades, com abrangência dos dados pertinentes, proporcionais e não excessivos em relação às finalidades do tratamento de dados;		
2. Interpretação do princípio para sistemas de software: Em sistemas de software é recomendável coletar apenas dados necessários e específicos para alcançar o objetivo desenhado e disponibilizado como funcionalidade no sistema. Ao desenhar funcionalidades, organizações devem focar em ter sob seu domínio **apenas** o conjunto de dados considerado essencial para alcançar o objetivo da funcionalidade projetada.		
3. Ação esperada pelo agente: espera-se que o agente de tratamento, ao coletar dados pessoais do usuário/titular, leve em consideração a proporcionalidade e a necessidade da coleta dos dados para determinada operação de tratamento, com objetivo de reduzir a quantidade de dados coletados de forma abusiva e desnecessária por parte do agente de tratamento.		
4. Exemplos de violação ao princípio: O princípio é violado quando há uma coletada baseada na máxima de "coletar o que posso, apenas porque posso", ao coletar e armazenar dados não sem nenhuma utilidade. Para realização de uma avaliação de crédito (finalidade), não é **correto** e **necessário** a coleta de dados relacionados à orientação sexual ou gênero, que além de **dados sensíveis**, são desnecessários e desproporcionais à(s) finalidade(s) do tratamento.		
5. Perguntas de inspeção ao Especialista/Inspetor	**(5.A) Resposta esperada**	**(5.B) Classificação defeito**
(7) Ao tratar os dados para disponibilização de uma funcionalidade são coletados apenas o necessário para cumprir com o serviço ou funcionalidade (finalidade) desejada?	Não	Informação Estranha
(8) Foram realizadas tentativas de reduzir ou excluir algum dos dados coletados do conjunto de dados para tornar o conjunto mais enxuto?	Não	Omissão

Para cada um dos dez princípios, existem *itens de verificação* compondo o *checklist* da *LGPDCheck*. A seção 5 do cenário (Tabela 1) exemplifica os dois itens de verificação previstos para o princípio de *necessidade*. Para cada item de verificação, indicamos a resposta esperada (Sim/Não) e qual seria a classificação do possível defeito identificado

[2]Informações adicionais sobre componentes da técnica encontram-se disponíveis em: http://bit.ly/40ooGoT

conforme categorização apresentada em [Mello et al. 2011]: *omissão, fato incorreto, inconsistência, ambiguidade* e *informação estranha.*

O desenvolvimento dos demais instrumentos da *LGPDCheck* encontram-se em fase final de organização. Dentre eles, temos um modelo de *relatório de inspeção* adaptado de [Mello et al. 2011], para o registro de todos os possíveis defeitos encontrados durante a tarefa de inspeção, incluindo informações do nível de inspeção em que o defeito foi identificado, o artefato, a descrição do defeito e sua localização no artefato.

5. Conclusões e Próximos Passos

Este artigo apresentou a concepção e elaboração inicial da técnica de inspeção *LGPDCheck*, tecnologia emergente para a verificação dos princípios de PPD em artefatos de software. Para isso, contamos com o conhecimento prático de juristas especialistas, que permitiu revelar alguns dos desafios, práticas e experiência adquirida durante o período de vigência da LGPD, que disponibiliza um arcabouço legal para incentivar a garantia do direito fundamental à Proteção de Dados Pessoais, fortalecido por meio da EC-115 de 2022 na Constituição Federal Brasileira [Guzzo Pinto 2022].

A *LGPDCheck* se fundamenta na interdisciplinaridade entre as áreas técnicas e jurídicas, permitindo operacionalizar os princípios estabelecidos na LGPD por meio de uma tecnologia de software. Esperamos que a *LGPDCheck* seja uma das responsáveis em promover a cultura de PPD no ciclo de desenvolvimento e evolução do software ao aproximar requisitos legais, práticas organizacionais e sistemas de software.

As próximas atividades envolvem o planejamento e execução de um estudo experimental para avaliar a eficácia e eficiência de *LGDPCheck* em comparação com inspeções *ad hoc.* Adicionalmente, observar os níveis de aceitação dos diferentes instrumentos oferecidos pela LGPDCheck, visando identificar possíveis oportunidades de melhoria. Esperamos que a técnica auxilie na construção e evolução de produtos de software alinhados com as preocupações globais de PPD e os princípios estabelecidos pela LGPD, auxiliando as organizações a verificar sua capacidade de adequação à lei, revelar obstáculos a serem superados e estar disponível para sua aplicação em contextos semelhantes.

Referências

Araújo, E., Vilela, J., Silva, C. and Alves, C. (7 jun 2021). Are My Business Process Models Compliant With LGPD? The LGPD4BP Method to Evaluate and to Model LGPD aware Business Processes. In *XVII Brazilian Symposium on Information Systems*. ACM. https://dl.acm.org/doi/10.1145/3466933.3466982.

Boehm, B. and Basili, V. R. (2001). Software Defect Reduction Top 10 List. Computer, v. 34, n. 1, p. 135–137.

BRASIL (2018). LEI No 13.709, DE 14 DE AGOSTO DE 2018:Lei Geral de Proteção de Dados Pessoais (LGPD). http://www.planalto.gov.br/ccivil_03/_ato2015-2018/2018/lei/L13709.htm, [accessed on Feb 13].

Cavoukian, A. (2009). Privacy by Design - The 7 foundational principles. Information and Privacy Commissioner of Ontario, Canada, p. 5.

Dias, E., Angelica, C., Seidel, T., et al. (2022). Guidelines adopted by agile teams in privacy requirements elicitation after the Brazilian general data protection law (LGPD) implementation. Requirements Engineering, n. 0123456789.

Engström, E., Storey, M. A., Runeson, P., Höst, M. and Baldassarre, M. T. (2020). How software engineering research aligns with design science: a review. Empirical Software Engineering, v. 25, n. 4, p. 2630–2660.

Fagan, M. E. (1976). Design and code inspections to reduce errors in program development. IBM Systems Journal, v. 15, n. 3, p. 182–211.

Gürses, S., Troncoso, C. and Diaz, C. (2011). Engineering: Privacy by design. Computers, Privacy & Data Protection, v. 317, n. 5842, p. 1178–1179.

Guzzo Pinto, D. (2022). A proteção de dados alçada a direito fundamental na Constituição brasileira. https://www.conjur.com.br/2022-fev-27/almeida-protecao-dados-pessoais-constituicao-ec-115.

Hadar, I., Hasson, T., Ayalon, O., et al. (feb 2018). Privacy by designers: software developers' privacy mindset. Empirical Software Engineering, v. 23, n. 1, p. 259–289.

IEEE (2008). 1028-2008 - IEEE Standard for Software Reviews and Audits. IEEE Std 1028-2008, v. 2008, n. August, p. 1–53.

Laitenberger, O., Emam, K. El and Harbich, T. G. (2001). An internally replicated quasi-experimental comparison of checklist and perspective-based reading of code documents. IEEE Transactions on Software Engineering, v. 27, n. 5, p. 387–421.

March, S. T. and Smith, G. F. (dec 1995). Design and natural science research on information technology. Decision Support Systems, v. 15, n. 4, p. 251–266.

Mello, R. M. De, Massollar, J. L. and Travassos, G. H. (6 jun 2011). Técnica de Inspeção Baseada em Checklist para Identificação de Defeitos em Diagramas de Atividades. In Anais do X Simpósio Brasileiro de Qualidade de Software (SBQS 2011).

Morales-Trujillo, M. E., Matla-Cruz, E. O., García-Mireles, G. A. and Piattini, M. (2018). A systematic mapping study of Privacy by Design. Avances en Ingenieria de Software a Nivel Iberoamericano, CIbSE 2018, v. 22, n. 1, p. 107–120.

Pereira, I., Mendes, J., Viana, D., et al. (2022). Extending an LGPD Compliance Inspection Checklist to Assess IoT Solutions: An Initial Proposal. n. 13, p. 28–31.

Porter, A. A., Votta, L. G. and Basili, V. R. (jun 1995). Comparing detection methods for software requirements inspections: a replicated experiment. IEEE Transactions on Software Engineering, v. 21, n. 6, p. 563–575.

Shapiro, S. S. (jun 2010). Privacy by design:Moving from Art to Practice. Communications of the ACM, v. 53, n. 6, p. 27–29.

Shull, F., Rus, I. and Basili, V. (jul 2000). How perspective-based reading can improve requirements inspections. Computer, v. 33, n. 7, p. 73–79.

Shull, F., Travassos, G. H., Carver, J. and Basili, V. R. (1999). Evolving a Set of Techniques for OO Inspections. p. 1–36.

Travassos, G., Shull, F., Fredericks, M. and Basili, V. R. V. R. V. R. (oct 1999). Detecting defects in object-oriented designs. ACM SIGPLAN Notices, v. 34, n. 10, p. 47–56.

UN (2017). The right to privacy in the digital age. . https://documents-dds-ny.un.org/doc/UNDOC/GEN/G17/086/31/PDF/G1708631.pdf?OpenElement.

Refinamiento de un proceso de elicitación de requisitos basado en Design Thinking

Ezequiel Kahan[1], Marcela Genero[2], Alejandro Oliveros[1]

[1]Universidad Nacional de 3 de Febrero - Buenos aires, Argentina
[2]Universidad de Castilla-La Mancha - Ciudad Real, Spain

{ezequiel.kahan@untref.edu.ar, marcela.genero@uclm.es, Alejandro.oliveros@untref.edu.ar}

Abstract. *Los procesos de elicitación de requisitos tienen una serie de desafíos y limitaciones en cuanto al foco en el proceso del negocio, la transparencia del sistema y el lidiar con la complejidad producto de la interdependencia. El enfoque de Design Thinking, centrado en las personas y en comprender el contexto de los problemas, puede aportar a resolverlos. En este artículo se presenta el estado actual de un proceso de elicitación de requisitos basado en Design Thinking propuesto para resolver algunos de los desafíos de los procesos existentes. Está compuesto por tres actividades: empatizar, sintetizar e idear. También se presentan los resultados de un focus group que se realizó con el objetivo de obtener feedback de expertos sobre el proceso, concretamente sobre el rol de la empatía en el proceso, su dominio de aplicación y actividades. Los resultados confirman vla utilidad del proceso y también generan una serie de enseñanzas que permitirán continuar refinándolo.*

Keywords. Elicitación de requisitos, design thinking, focus group

1. Introducción

A pesar de su amplio desarrollo y uso generalizado, las técnicas y procesos de la ingeniería de los requisitos (IR) siguen presentando desafíos y limitaciones [Jarke et al. 2010]. Algunos de estos desafíos están directamente relacionados con la evolución de la Ingeniería de Software (IS), como por ejemplo, que los requisitos se centran en los artefactos tecnológicos en lugar de considerar simultáneamente el proceso de negocio, que no satisfacen la demanda de una experiencia de usuario sin fricciones o fisuras a lo largo de las aplicaciones o que no reflejan que la complejidad global se ha incrementado [Lyytinen et al. 2009]. Del análisis de estos desafíos, surge que muchos se relacionan con la actividad de elicitación de requisitos. Design Thinking (DT) es un enfoque para la innovación potente, eficaz y ampliamente accesible, que puede integrarse en todos los aspectos de los negocios y la sociedad, y que se puede utilizar para generar ideas disruptivas que pueden implementarse y, por lo tanto, generar impacto [Brown 2008]. Es un enfoque que ha generado creciente interés y demostrado tener potencial de aplicación en la IR [Ferreira et al. 2019; Hehn et al. 2020]. Tomando como punto de partida nuestros trabajos anteriores [Kahan et al. 2019; Kahan et al. 2022] y de la experiencia del primer autor aplicando DT en proyectos para distintas organizaciones, vimos la posibilidad de resolver algunos de estos desafíos utilizando DT. Por eso, definimos una versión preliminar de un proceso para la elicitación de requisitos basado en DT [Kahan et al. 2022], cuyo objetivo central es: *Adquirir conocimiento sobre un problema de naturaleza socio-técnica. Esto incluye el problema en sí, su contexto, los actores afectados por el mismo y sus relaciones.* En este artículo se introduce este proceso y además se presenta un *focus group* cuyo objetivo es obtener *feedback* de expertos sobre el proceso, concretamente sobre el rol de la empatía en el proceso, su dominio de aplicación y actividades.

El resto del artículo está estructurado de la siguiente manera: en la sección 2 se presentan trabajos relacionados a procesos de elicitación basados en DT, en la sección 3 se describe el proceso de elicitación propuesto. La planificación y ejecución del *focus group* se presenta en la sección 4, la discusión sobre los resultados se describe en la sección 5 y el análisis de las amenazas a la validez en sección 6. Para finalizar, en la sección 7 se presentan las principales conclusiones obtenidas y los posibles trabajos futuros.

2. Trabajos relacionados

El interés por el empleo de las técnicas y enfoques de DT en la IR ha crecido en los últimos años. Buscando en *Scopus* artículos que relacionen la elicitación de requisitos con DT, se encontraron 5 resultados de interés. Dos de ellos, revisiones de la literatura de grupos de investigación con trayectoria en la temática:

- Canedo et al. [Canedo et al. 2022] realizaron una revisión sistemática de la literatura y una encuesta regional en Brasil, con el objetivo de identificar cuáles de las técnicas de DT se aplican en la práctica a la elicitación de requisitos. Entre las técnicas más utilizadas identificaron: entrevistas, *brainstorming*, casos de uso, análisis de actividades, historias de usuario y prototipos rápidos. Los autores concluyen que, a pesar de existir un gran número de técnicas, la falta de conocimiento sobre las mismas hace que no se usen. Aun así, en los casos que sí se usan, ayudaron a que la elicitación de requerimientos fuera más efectiva.
- Meireles et al. [Meireles et al. 2021] realizaron una revisión sistemática de la literatura para identificar técnicas de DT que pudieran ser utilizadas en la elicitación de requisitos. A partir del análisis de las mismas, presentaron una tabla comparativa para ayudar a los ingenieros de software a seleccionarlas. Los resultados evidencian que esta comparativa ayuda al proceso de selección de las técnicas.

Los otros trabajos encontrados sobre sobre procesos de elicitación basados en DT son:

- En de Souza Filho et al. [Souza Filho et al. 2021] se presenta un estudio exploratorio de cómo DT beneficia el desarrollo de una herramienta de elicitación de requisitos basada en datos. Para eso, aplicaron un proceso de DT basado en el proceso de doble diamante [*Framework for Innovation* 2019] y las técnicas Mapa de *stakeholders,* entrevistas, Mapa conceptual, *personas*, mapa de empatía, *bodystorming* y prototipado. El resultado indica que DT puede ser integrado al desarrollo de un proceso ingeniería de requisitos basado en datos, ayudando a desarrollar un mejor entendimiento del problema y a desarrollar soluciones centradas en los usuarios.

- En Hehn et al. [Hehn et al. 2020] se presenta un análisis de las posibilidades de integración de DT con la IR. Además de comparar DT e IR como enfoques sugieren 3 modalidades de integración de DT e IR: usar DT para guiar la elicitación de requisitos, usar DT como una caja de herramienta para enriquecer IR y usar elementos de ambos de manera continua, tomando DT como un modo de pensar guía. Los autores proponen además un modelo de artefactos que combina DT y IR.
- En Levy y Huli [Levy y Huli 2019] se presenta un workshop de DT para facilitar la elicitación de requisitos en el proceso de negocio de una compañía. El estudio del caso reveló que la aplicación de los métodos y técnicas de DT promovían discusiones entre los *stakeholders* y habilitaban que nuevas voces fueran escuchadas, llevando a nuevos requerimientos, tanto desde la perspectiva humana como de la técnica. A partir de estos resultados, propusieron un Workshop general de DT que ayude a dar dirección los requerimientos de negocio.

Los primeros tres trabajos mencionados más arriba están enfocados principalmente en analizar y seleccionar técnicas de DT. Nuestro trabajo busca desarrollar un proceso de elicitación para resolver desafíos de la IR. El trabajo de Hehn et al. [Hehn et al. 2020] no está puesto específicamente en el desarrollo de un proceso de elicitación que utilice elementos de DT, sino en utilizar DT directamente como un proceso de IR completo. El trabajo de Levy y Huli [Levy y Huli 2019] es más limitado ya que propone la realización de workshops que utilizan técnicas de DT para la elicitación de requisitos, pero no define un proceso en sí.

En conclusión, no existe un proceso para elicitación de requisitos basado en DT. Por ello nuestro aporte es el desarrollo de este proceso y la realización de un focus group cuyo objetivo es validar el proceso, el rol de la empatía en el mismo, su dominio de aplicación y sus actividades y obtener información basándonos en la perspectiva de expertos con interés, habilidad y conocimiento en la temática, para continuar refinándolo.

3. Un proceso de elicitación de requisitos basado en DT

Nuestra propuesta para un proceso de elicitación de requisitos basados en DT, toma el enfoque de DT de Stanford University D.School [Institute of Design at Stanford 2010]. En la definición del proceso utilizamos la estructura propuesta por Loucopoulos y Karakostas [Loucopoulos y Karakostas 1995], la cual establece que un proceso tiene que tener: propósito, entradas u orígenes, actividades, técnicas, y entregables intermedios y finales, e interacción con otras actividades del proceso. De las cinco actividades de este enfoque (empatizar, definir, idear, prototipar y validar) consideramos solo las tres primeras, por ser las que están más relacionadas con la fase de elicitación de requisitos [Kahan et al. 2022]. Las restantes actividades (prototipar y validar), están más orientadas a proponer soluciones que a la adquisición de conocimiento. Si consideramos los prototipos generados como elementos intermedios cuyo propósito es validar la completitud y cohesión del conocimiento adquirido, podemos ver que, en cierto modo, están contenidas en las otras actividades. La Figura 1 muestra el proceso definido. Las actividades seleccionadas están superpuestas e interrelacionadas, y no existe un límite claro entre las mismas. El proceso es iterativo, por ese motivo hay conexiones de cada actividad con la anterior. La empatía es un elemento clave de la elicitación de requisitos, es una de las características más relevantes del proceso propuesto y puede ser vista como una forma de construcción de conocimiento [Köppen & Meinel 2015], el aspecto central de la elicitación de requisitos [Loucopoulos & Karakostas 1995]. Por eso, la figura distingue la actividad del proceso de empatizar del constructo más general empatía, el cual se construye a lo largo de todas las actividades de DT.

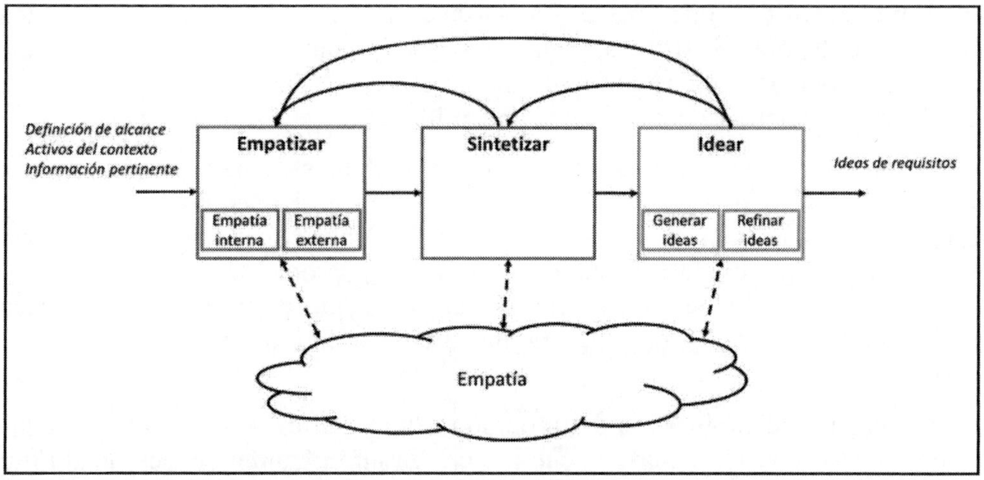

Figura 1. Un proceso de elicitación de requisitos basado en DT

Las principales características del proceso propuesto son:

- Su objetivo central es la adquisición de conocimiento.
- Pone el foco en la exploración del espacio del problema, principalmente a través de la empatía. En otros enfoques, el énfasis está en la generación de ideas innovadoras.
- Se basa en los principios de DT: exploración en el espacio de problema y solución y alternancia entre modalidad de pensamiento convergente y divergente.
- Se distingue entre empatía interna y externa [Koppen y Meinel 2015]. La primera busca desarrollar la identidad de equipo y la colaboración entre ellos, lo que incluye la construcción y clarificación del propósito del proyecto a llevar adelante, la segunda se centra en averiguar las necesidades de los *stakeholders*. El desarrollo de lo fundamental de la empatía interna debe preceder a la externa.
- La actividad idear está constituida por dos sub-actividades, de manera que la ideación sea lo más "divergente" posible y no se condicione de manera anticipada por limitaciones o restricciones. En la sub-actividad de refinamiento, se busca que las ideas que aparecieron en la ideación sean enriquecidas, agrupadas y/o filtradas, usando como base del refinamiento el conocimiento adquirido durante las actividades previas.

Como se mencionó más arriba, este es un proceso en construcción, por lo que no están cerrados en su totalidad los artefactos a utilizar. Una descripción detallada de los principales elementos del proceso propuesto se encuentra en el siguiente enlace https://tinyurl.com/4dpumjny.

Este proceso de elicitación se enmarca en una etapa de los proyectos donde hay un alto nivel de ambigüedad sobre el problema y su contexto. Desde ese punto de vista, la expresión del conocimiento adquirido por los analistas tendrá el formato de "ideas de requisito". Decidimos llamarlo ideas de requisito por considerarlo un antecesor del requisito, que intenta representar los modelos iniciales y difusos que tiene tanto el analista, cómo el *stakeholder*, sobre el problema, sobre los *stakeholders*, y sobre el entorno en el cuál este se desarrolla. Las ideas de requisitos no sólo incluyen ideas de funciones que tendrá el sistema, sino también no-funcionales (asociados con los requisitos no funcionales), que expresan limitaciones y/o restricciones a considerar en el diseño de una solución, así como también necesidades de los *stakeholders*.

El proceso propuesto está pensado para problemas de naturaleza socio-técnica. Si bien algunas actividades como la empatía interna probablemente enriquecerían la conformación de cualquier equipo, la empatía externa busca incorporar una perspectiva humano-céntrica, que es de particular importancia en problemas donde hay un fuerte componente social. Por otro lado, también creemos que es utilizable en situaciones donde el producto a construir es para un cliente definido (interno o externo a la organización).

Un ejemplo de aplicación del proceso es la identificación de ideas de requisitos para una nueva aplicación de uso en entorno empresarial. Durante la actividad Empatía, se trabajará en construir identidad del equipo de proyecto, generando una visión común sobre el problema a resolver, y recabando información sobre el contexto y quienes tienen el problema. Se utilizarán a este fin técnicas como el *Canvas* de visión, Estructura P2P y Mapas de empatía. En la actividad Sintetizar se acordará y definirá el problema a resolver, utilizando técnicas como *Personas* y mapas de la experiencia del usuario. En la actividad de Idear se generarán ideas de requisitos posibles, usando técnicas como el *Brainstoming*. Al completar el proceso, el equipo de proyecto habrá incrementado su conocimiento sobre el problema en sí, su contexto, los actores afectados por el mismo y sus relaciones, y obtenido además una lista inicial de ideas requisitos sobre las cuales avanzar en el diseño de una solución.

4. Planificación y ejecución del *focus group*

En esta sección se presenta el *focus group* que se realizó con el objetivo de obtener feedback de expertos sobre el proceso, en particular sobre el rol de la empatía en el proceso, su dominio de aplicación y actividades. Para realizar el *focus group*, seguimos las actividades propuestas en [Kontio et al. 2008]: Definición del problema a investigar, Selección de participantes, Recolección de datos, Ejecución de *focus group*, Análisis de los datos y Reporte de resultados.

4.1 Definición del problema a investigar

Los *focus group* son un método de investigación que permite recolectar datos e información cualitativa, principalmente a través de la interacción de un grupo de participantes sobre un tema propuesta por los investigadores [Kontio et al. 2008]. Pueden ser utilizados con diferentes propósitos, en función de la etapa de investigación en que se encuentre. El desarrollo de nuestro proceso está en una fase preliminar, por eso entendemos que el *feedback* de expertos será relevante para poder refinarlo y completar su definición, y que el *focus group* es un método adecuado para obtenerlo.

4.2 Selección de participantes

Un *focus group* es muy sensible a la experiencia y perspectiva de los participantes. Por esta razón, el proceso de selección de participantes es crítico para el éxito del mismo. Establecimos los siguientes criterios de selección de participantes:

- Que tuvieran formación académica universitaria en Ingeniería de Software.
- Que tuvieran al menos 15 años de experiencia en desarrollo de software, incluyendo procesos de elicitación de requisitos.

Los tres autores de este trabajo propusieron posibles participantes, acordando una lista de nueve candidatos. A los mismos se les hizo llegar una invitación por correo electrónico, con dos semanas de anticipación a la ejecución del *focus group.* Esta invitación fue aceptada por 5 de ellos. De ellos, 4 tenían además de experiencia práctica y formación, trayectoria docente y como investigadores. Además, uno de ellos poseía título de doctorado y los otros 3 títulos de maestría.

4.3 Recolección de los datos

Para la recolección de datos se utilizó un cuestionario electrónico. El mismo contenía preguntas cerradas, las cuales se evaluaban usando una escala Likert de 5 puntos, siendo uno el peor valor y 5 el mejor, y otras abiertas. El cuestionario se dividió en 4 secciones (ver Tabla 2): la primera dedicada al proceso en global y las otras tres a cada una de las actividades del mismo.

Tabla 2. Cuestionario utilizado en el *focus group*

Sección	Pregunta	Tipo de respuesta
Sección 1: Evaluación del proceso	El objetivo del proceso está bien definido	Likert
	El proceso satisface su objetivo	Likert
	En caso de que no esté satisfecho el objetivo ¿es porque tiene omisiones o gaps? ¿cuáles? ¿otras razones?	Abierta
	El proceso aporta a los siguientes desafíos / problemáticas de la Ingeniería de los requisitos [FOCO EN EL PROCESO DEL NEGOCIO] [TRANSPARENCIA DEL SISTEMA] [COMPLEJIDAD INTERDEPENDIENTE]	Likert
	¿En qué dominios se puede aplicar el proceso? (Por ejemplo: socio – técnicos, sistemas tiempo real, sistemas embebidos, etc.).	Abierta
Sección 2: Evaluación de la actividad Empatizar	El objetivo de la actividad está bien definido	Likert
	La actividad satisface su objetivo	Likert
	En caso de que no esté satisfecho el objetivo ¿es porque tiene omisiones o gaps? ¿cuáles? ¿otras razones?	Likert
	Las entradas de la actividad permiten obtener las salidas propuestas	Likert
	La división de la actividad empatía (interna / externa) es adecuada	Likert
Sección 3: Evaluación de la actividad Sintetizar	El objetivo de la actividad está bien definido	Likert
	La actividad satisface su objetivo	Likert
	En caso de que no esté satisfecho el objetivo ¿es porque tiene omisiones o gaps? ¿cuáles? ¿otras razones?	Abierta
	Las entradas de la actividad permiten obtener las salidas propuestas	Likert

Sección 4: Evaluación de la actividad Idear	El objetivo de la actividad está bien definido	Likert
	La actividad satisface su objetivo	Likert
	En caso de que no esté satisfecho el objetivo ¿es porque tiene omisiones o gaps? ¿cuáles? ¿otras razones?	Abierta
	Las entradas de la actividad permiten obtener las salidas propuestas	Likert

4.4 Desarrollo del *focus group*

Como paso previo al *focus group*, se presentó el material de soporte con la descripción del proceso a un primer experto, y luego se lo entrevistó en profundidad. Su *feedback* proveyó valiosa información sobre el proceso y llevó a realizar ajustes al material de soporte que se entregó a los participantes. Este material, compuesto por un documento con la descripción del proceso y un vídeo de 15 minutos de duración en el que el primer autor del artículo resumió el proceso, se les envió a los participantes unos días antes de realizar el *focus groups*. Se puede acceder al mismo a través del siguiente enlace https://tinyurl.com/4dpumjny.

El *focus group* se realizó en una sesión virtual de 2 horas. Además de los 5 participantes, estuvo presente el primer autor de este artículo, con la función de realizar aclaraciones si fuera necesario y un moderador, que se encargó de facilitar y moderar la sesión y controlar los tiempos dedicados a cada sección. La sesión se grabó con autorización de los participantes. La estructura de la sesión fue la siguiente:

1. Inicio: La sesión se inició con un repaso del plan de la sesión.
2. Sección 1 del cuestionario: Se repasó la presentación ya enviada y se destinó tiempo para preguntas y respuestas. Luego se solicitó que se respondieran las preguntas de la sección 1 del cuestionario electrónico. Se estableció un tiempo para que respondieran (con la posibilidad de extenderlo a pedido de los participantes). Luego, se pidió a los participantes que hicieran los comentarios y observaciones que consideraran pertinentes, haciendo foco en las respuestas que habían obtenido 3 puntos o menos (respuesta neutral o en desacuerdo).
3. Secciones 2, 3 y 4 del cuestionario: Habiéndose dedicado unos 30 minutos a comentarios y observaciones, se continuó con la presentación de cada una de las actividades del proceso. En las restantes secciones se repitió la misma dinámica que en la primera.
4. Cierre: Completadas las 4 secciones, se agradeció la participación de los expertos y se dio por finalizada la sesión.

4.5 Análisis de los datos y reporte de resultados

A continuación, se presentan los principales resultados que surgieron del *focus group,* siguiendo la estructura del cuestionario.

4.5.1 Sección 1: Proceso de elicitación de requisitos

En la Figura 2 se observa que se consideró adecuada la definición del proceso y que satisface el objetivo para el que se lo desarrolló. La mayoría de los participantes consideró dificultoso evaluar el objetivo en sí y en qué medida estaba satisfecho sin utilizar el proceso ellos mismos. Por ejemplo, uno de los participantes comento que: *"Con la información recibida me queda alguna duda con respecto, por ejemplo, a los mecanismos de validación de la información o consciencia desarrollada como parte del*

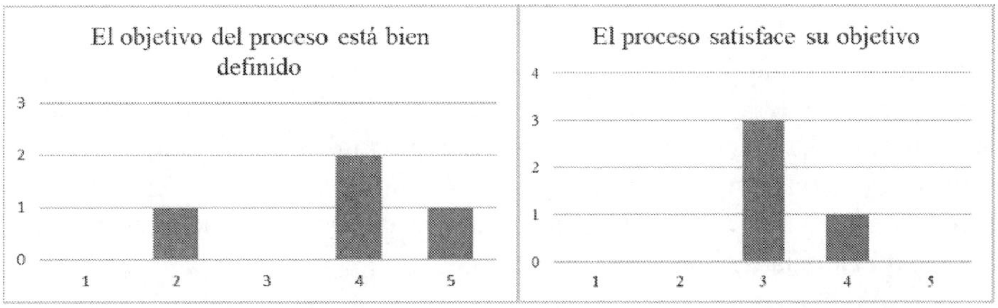

Figura 2. Histogramas de las preguntas 1 y 2 (sección 1)

proceso. [también] cómo trata los posibles modos de fallo en términos de confusión, recorte, sesgo, etc., por parte de los protagonistas (quienes conducen el proceso). Con esto me refiero a que el conocimiento desarrollado no se ajuste o sea virtuoso en relación al problema sociotécnico". En cuanto a la vinculación con sus experiencias en desarrollo, uno de los participantes refirió que para el tipo de proyectos en que él trabajó, el proceso implicaría mucho trabajo y otro manifestó que en muchos de los proyectos que trabaja no hay un proceso de elicitación, sino más bien hipótesis y codificación para validarla. En ese tipo de proyectos hay un único *stakeholder* quién ya formaliza los requerimientos para que el equipo los codifique.

En cuanto al aporte del proceso a los 3 desafíos de la IR que se le presentaron a los participantes, tal como muestra la Figura 3, la mayor valoración la tuvo *transparencia del Sistema,* luego *foco en el proceso de negocio* y por último *complejidad interdependiente.* Sobre este último punto se debatió si el proceso permitía realmente reducir esa complejidad. De acuerdo con alguno de los participantes, al tener el proceso en sí cierta complejidad, no necesariamente ayudaba a reducirla. En sus palabras, *dependiendo de cuan iterativo o lineal sea el proceso, podrá aportar o no a la reducción de esa complejidad.*

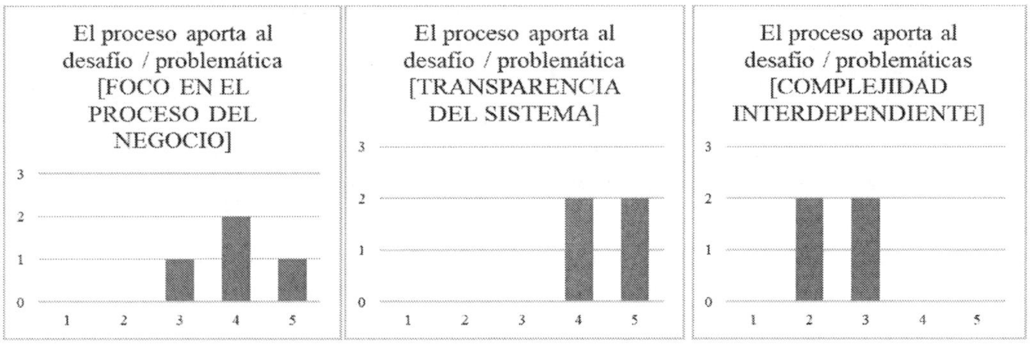

Figura 3. Histograma sobre la pregunta 4 (sección 1)

Sobre el dominio de aplicación, los participantes mencionaron los sistemas de naturaleza principalmente socio-técnica (por ejemplo, sistemas de información empresarial). Un participante añadió la aplicación en procesos de "descubrimiento de producto" (*product discovery*) y en actividades consultivas. En la discusión surgió que su aplicación posiblemente sería más limitada en proyectos de carácter principalmente técnico, uno de los participantes manifestó que podría usarse en el desarrollo de sistemas embebidos y de tiempo real, con alguna adaptación.

Respecto a la incorporación de empatía al proceso, en general se consideró que es un aporte valioso del proceso. Uno de los participantes mencionó que, de los tres desafíos de la IR, el mayor aporte de la empatía es a la *transparencia de los sistemas* sobre todo porque que mucha de la complejidad y de los problemas de tener una experiencia única provienen de la coexistencia de múltiples sistemas. Algunos de los participantes mencionaron que, si bien la empatía es un aporte en esa dirección, en muchos equipos de desarrollo está cubierto con la inclusión de perfiles vinculados a las interfaces y experiencia de usuarios.

4.5.2 Sección 2: Actividad empatizar

La Figura 4 muestra los histogramas de las 2 primeras preguntas de la actividad empatizar. La mayoría de los participantes coincidió en que el objetivo estaba bien definido. Nuevamente, la evaluación sobre la medida en que se satisface el objetivo es menos precisa porque, según lo manifestado por los participantes, no tienen suficiente conocimiento sobre algunas de las técnicas, así como experiencia práctica aplicando el proceso en situaciones reales.

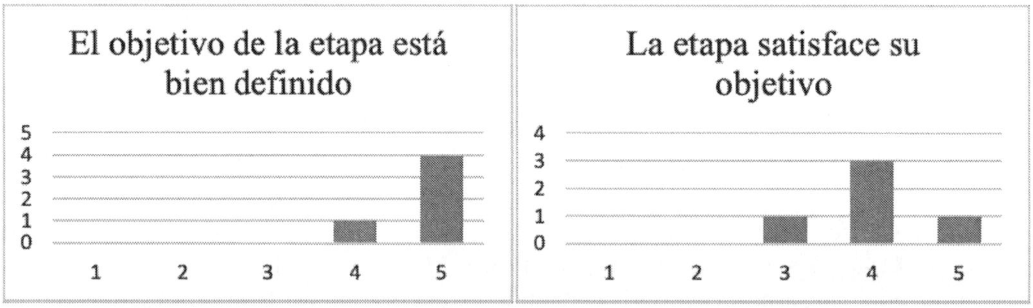

Figura 4. Histograma sobre las preguntas 1 y 2 (sección 2)

Uno de los participantes mencionó que consideraba que había una diferencia en el alcance de la sub-actividad empatía interna y externa, considerando que la segunda es más amplia. En sus palabras: "*Me parece que el objetivo de la sub-actividad Empatía externa es muy desafiante, en el sentido de que apropiarse de la perspectiva parece requerir más que ponerse en los zapatos de las personas, más como caminar muchos kilómetros en sus zapatos. En general, me parece muy positiva y acertada la propuesta, lo único que destaco es que como salidas están cosas más intelectuales, más formales, como hipótesis, cuyo valor de verdad es aún incierto. En ese sentido, la palabra captura de perspectiva siento que puede ser ambiciosa*". Uno de los participantes mencionó que le resultaba sólida la idea de que la empatía ayuda a construir visión compartida y alineamiento.

Respecto a la empatía externa e interna la evaluación, tal como muestra la Figura 5, del cuestionario permite entender que es vista como positiva, con una valoración promedio de 4.

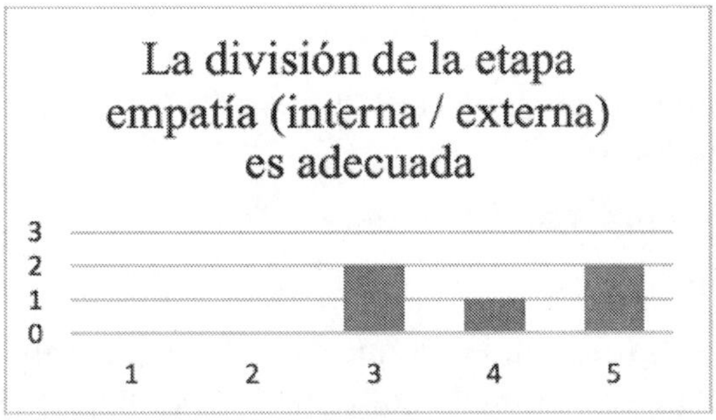

Figura 5. Histograma sobre la pregunta 4 (sección 2)

4.5.3 Sección 3: Actividad sintetizar

Como muestra la Figura 6, la evaluación de la definición del objetivo fue muy alta. La evaluación de la medida en que la actividad satisface el objetivo fue menor, con la misma consideración que la actividad anterior.

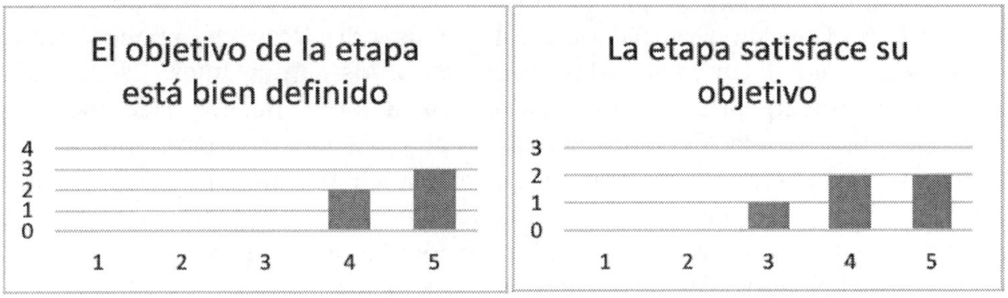

Figura 6. Histograma sobre las preguntas 1 y 2 (sección 3)

Los comentarios formulados se relacionaron con evaluar en qué medida se busca que esta síntesis ayude o no a la priorización de los distintos emergentes del problema, y también a la percepción de que la síntesis algunos de ellos la encuentran vinculada a solución, por lo que les costaba asociarla a un elemento más del espacio del problema. No hubo comentarios respecto a las entradas o salidas de la actividad.

4.5.4 Sección 4: Actividad idear

La evaluación de la definición del objetivo fue muy alta. La evaluación de la medida en que la actividad satisface el objetivo fue menor, siendo los valores obtenidos iguales a los de la actividad sintetizar. Uno de los participantes expresó, con respecto al objetivo de que las ideas estén refinadas, que le costaba entender cómo se evaluaría refinamiento. Otro dudaba respecto al objetivo de "asegurar que las ideas generadas estén alineadas". Su comentario fue "*aunque entiendo que el proceso divergir-converger es poderoso, me falta detalles en términos de validación*". Un participante mencionó la importancia de clarificar el concepto de *modelo mental,* para evitar diversas interpretaciones. La necesidad de clarificar el modo en que se validará la salida de la actividad idear, en términos de un artefacto concreto o de una actividad de *feedback* a los *stakeholders,* fue mencionado por varios participantes. Uno comentó: "*Respecto a la validación no me queda claro que esté validado. Ninguna de las técnicas expuestas parecería adecuada para validar. Alguna de las salidas debería ayudar a integrar el problema con la solución*".

5. Discusión

En esta sección presentamos el análisis de los resultados del *focus group*, siguiendo la estructura del cuestionario.

5.1. Resultados sobre el proceso

Dominio de aplicación

Los resultados del *focus group* sugieren que el proceso descripto es sensible al tipo de proyecto en que se lo aplique, si bien alguno de los participantes se refirió al tamaño o esfuerzo del proyecto, entendemos que la aplicabilidad está más vinculada al momento del proceso de desarrollo de producto en que se encuentra la organización. Esto es, si está en el camino de entender el espacio del problema o el de llevar adelante la solución. Nuestra visión es que el proceso es particularmente útil para el primer tipo de proyectos, en particular en sistemas socio-técnicos.

Aportes a las problemáticas de la IR

De los participantes surge que el mayor aporte del proceso está en lograr mayor *"transparencia del sistema"*. Esta respuesta conecta con uno de los aspectos centrales de DT, como es el centrarse en la experiencia del usuario. Respecto a poder "*Lidiar con la complejidad*" fue el que más dudas generó entre los participantes. La discusión, en ese sentido, es si la empatía ayuda o no a reducir la complejidad. Desde nuestro punto de vista, empatizar ayuda a visibilizar esa complejidad y, por lo tanto, puede ayudar a vehiculizar una solución: entender que la problemática es compleja ayuda a evitar caer en simplificación y reduccionismo. Tenemos en cuenta que hay que distinguir entre la complejidad social y la técnica. Es probable que el aporte de DT ayude principalmente a reducir la complejidad social, pero que los participantes hayan esperado algún aporte sobre la complejidad técnica.

5.2. Resultados sobre la actividad empatizar

Empatía interna: un punto a considerar es que, en los procesos de desarrollo ágiles la empatía interna vendrá dada en muchos casos por el propio proceso de desarrollo: Scrum, por ejemplo, propone que los *stakeholders* tengan representatividad permanente en el ciclo de desarrollo. Además, la propia naturaleza iterativo-incremental, y la propuesta de equipos dedicados a un producto a lo largo del tiempo, permite que esta empatía se vaya consolidando. En el desarrollo ágil de software la forma de conectar con el espacio del problema es construir iterativamente hasta reconocer que el problema fue resuelto (en especial porque es difícil conocer las necesidades a priori). De todos modos, lo anterior no implica que el proceso no pueda aportar valor, sobre todo en las instancias iniciales del proyecto.

Empatía externa: Creemos que hay un aporte concreto de DT a los procesos de desarrollo ágiles Ahí donde Agile tiene una mirada de "prueba y error", la empatía, al ayudar a tener un mayor acercamiento a los *stakeholders*, puede ayudar a reducir la prueba y error.

Si bien algunos de los participantes mencionaron que la empatía y el centrarse en la experiencia de las personas está implícita por la participación de perfiles de Experiencia de Usuario (UX / UI) en los proyectos, entendemos que el proceso propuesto permite incorporar esa visión no sólo a estos perfiles sino al equipo de desarrollo como un todo. Lo que se busca es que todo el equipo tenga una mirada más empática y no sólo algunos perfiles, porque que el proceso es de construcción colaborativa de conocimiento, para reducir los sesgos individuales, y para ayudar a que el proceso de diseño tenga más cohesión. DT permite desarrollar una perspectiva compartida, incorporando la mirada del problematizado, e incorporar información. Establecer la naturaleza de un problema y construir *awareness* sobre el mismo son dos cosas distintas. Probablemente al pensar en las salidas del proceso sea necesario establecer ambos.

5.4. Resultados de la actividad síntetizar

En la actividad sintetizar creemos por algunos de los comentarios que los participantes lo interpretaron como un espacio de proposición de soluciones, más de que síntesis del problema. En ese sentido interpretaron la salida "Costos / Beneficios" como una evaluación de la posible solución. En nuestra propuesta, la síntesis es una actividad de convergencia del problema, que permite encuadrarlo adecuadamente, y habilitar un ejercicio de ideación más efectivo. Entendemos que hay que reflejar mejor esto al momento de establecer las salidas.

5.5. Resultados de la actividad idear

Uno de los puntos que surgió es la necesidad de clarificar el objetivo de esta actividad. En particular "*Generar y proponer posibles respuestas a la problemática antes definida*", puede llevar a la idea de que se está en una instancia de formulación de soluciones, cuando el propósito es la adquisición de conocimiento. Además, dado que se plantea como objetivo el "*Asegurar que las ideas generadas estén alineadas con las actividades anteriores del proceso*", lleva a incorporar alguna validación como parte de las acciones de la actividad Idear. Entendemos que esa validación podría llevarse cabo mediante actividades de revisión de la salida con los *stakeholders* identificados inicialmente en la actividad empatizar, eso permitiría evaluar que el conocimiento obtenido esté alineado con quienes tienen el problema.

5.6 Oportunidades de mejora del proceso

Del *focus group* surgieron algunas posibles mejoras al proceso, que se resumen en la Tabla 3.

Tabla 3. Resumen de posibles impactos al proceso

Actividad	Elemento	Comentarios	Impacto en el proceso
Proceso	Actores	Se percibe que el proceso será aplicado solo por equipos de desarrollo.	Especificar más claramente los actores, resaltar que en el proceso participa el equipo completo (desarrolladores, analistas, especialistas en experiencia de usuarios y personas del negocio y/o vinculadas al problema a resolver).
Proceso	Dominio	En ciertos proyectos, por cuestiones de tamaño, especificidad, *stakeholders*, etc. no se lleva adelante un proceso de elicitación.	El proceso se orienta a proyectos donde es necesario obtener conocimiento relevante del problema y de sus *stakeholders*. Introducir esta noción junto con los objetivos

Proceso	Complejidad interdependiente	No resulta evidente si el proceso aporta para gestionar la complejidad.	El proceso se enfoca en la complejidad social, esto es la complejidad generada por las interacciones sociales y humanas. Justamente este es el rol de la empatía en el proceso, como forma de centrarse en las personas. Esto se explicita en los objetivos de la empatía interna y externa.
Empatía	Objetivo	Se expresaron dudas respecto a la viabilidad de "apropiarse de la perspectiva de quienes tienen el problema" y la dificultad de validar esa apropiación.	Reemplazar el concepto de "apropiación" por "adquirir, analizar y sintetizar la perspectiva" (Bloom) y eliminar ambigüedades en la definición de empatía.
Actividad	**Elemento**	**Comentarios**	**Impacto en el proceso**
Síntesis	Objetivo y Salidas	Se expresaron dudas respecto a la parte del objetivo referida a "Definir el problema", en cuanto a la dificultad de asegurar que el problema quede "definido" en esa instancia	El proceso propuesto para la elicitación acompaña a todo el proceso de requerimientos, que a su vez acompaña a todo el proceso de desarrollo. Se modificará el objetivo a "avanzar en la definición del problema", parar reforzar la idea de recurrencia de las actividades. Modificar las salidas de la actividad considerando que en las mismas habrá "avances en la información relevante a considerar" y "avances en la lista de *stakeholders* identificados" en lugar de "información más estructurada" y "*staholders* refinados".
Idear	Salidas	Necesidad de incorporar una actividad de validación de las ideas generadas en la actividad ideación.	La validación se produce sobre los requisitos una vez que han sido especificados. Incorporar como salida de la actividad actividades de revisión con el usuario para asegurar la fidelidad del conocimiento adquirido.

7. Conclusiones y trabajos futuros

En este artículo se ha presentado una versión preliminar de un proceso de elicitación de requisitos basado en DT y los resultados de un *focus group* realizado con el objetivo de obtener *feedback* de expertos sobre este proceso, en particular sobre el rol de la empatía en esteproceso, su dominio de aplicación y actividades. El análisis de los datos obtenidos en el *focus group* refleja una valoración global positiva sobre el proceso. En general, los expertos reconocieron que el proceso hace un aporte valioso a la elicitación, especialmente en iniciativas que intentan resolver problemas de naturaleza socio-técnica. De los desafíos de la IR que DT permite abordar, el aporte principal del proceso es a la Transparencia del sistema y un aporte parcial a poner Foco en el proceso de negocio. Hay oportunidades de mejora para clarificar el aporte al desafío de

Complejidad interdependiente, lo que podría ser abordado en una futura versión del proceso, y en instancias de experimentación de su aplicabilidad.

En cuanto a las actividades del proceso, todos sus objetivos fueron evaluados como bien definidos, siendo la actividad Empatizar la que tuvo la valoración más alta. En general, los comentarios sobre la relevancia de esta actividad fueron muy positivos. Respecto a la separación de las actividades en una instancia de empatía interna y externa, también fue evaluada como adecuada.

Aunque el número de expertos que participaron en el *focus group* fue limitado, consideramos valioso obtener un primer *feedback* para refinar el modelo, e ideas para completar la definición del proceso. Como línea de trabajo futura, se realizarán ajustes al proceso, usando las mejoras mencionadas en la Tabla 3 con énfasis en los actores, dominio de aplicación y definición de objetivos del proceso y de las etapas, entre otros. Una vez completado el proceso se continuará con su aplicación a través de estudios de casos para validar su utilidad en la adquisición de conocimiento sobre problemas de naturaleza socio-técnica, en contextos empresariales reales.

Agradecimientos. La investigación presentada en este artículo forma parte de los siguientes proyectos: ADAGIO (Consejería de Educación, Cultura y Deportes de la JCCM, SBLPY/21/180501/000061), AETHER-UCLM (MICINN, PID2020-112540RB-C42) y Proyecto de investigación en Procesos de desarrollo de Software (línea de investigación en Ingeniería de requisitos, UNTREF, Argentina).

Referencias

Brown, T. (2008, June 1). *Design Thinking*. Harvard Business Review. https://hbr.org/2008/06/design-thinking

Canedo, E. D., Calazans, A. T. S., Silva, G. R. S., Costa, P. H. T., De Mesquita, R. P., & Masson, E. T. S. (2022). Creativity and Design Thinking as Facilitators in Requirements Elicitation. *International Journal of Software Engineering and Knowledge Engineering*, *32*(10), 1527–1558. Scopus. https://doi.org/10.1142/S0218194022500607

de Souza Filho, J. C., Nakamura, W. T., Teixeira, L. M., da Silva, R. P., Gadelha, B. F., & Conte, T. U. (2021). *Towards a Data-Driven Requirements Elicitation Tool through the Lens of Design Thinking*. *2*, 283–290. Scopus.

Ferreira Martins, H., Carvalho de Oliveira Junior, A., Dias Canedo, E., Dias Kosloski, R. A., Ávila Paldês, R., & Costa Oliveira, E. (2019). Design Thinking: Challenges for Software Requirements Elicitation. *Information*, *10*(12), Article 12. https://doi.org/10.3390/info10120371

Framework for Innovation: Design Council's evolved Double Diamond. (2019). Framework for Innovation: Design Council's Evolved Double Diamond. https://www.designcouncil.org.uk/our-work/skills-learning/tools-frameworks/framework-for-innovation-design-councils-evolved-double-diamond/

Hehn, J., Mendez, D., Uebernickel, F., Brenner, W., & Broy, M. (2020). On Integrating Design Thinking for Human-Centered Requirements Engineering. *IEEE Software*, *37*(2), 25–31. https://doi.org/10.1109/MS.2019.2957715

Hehn, J., Uebernickel, F., Stoeckli, E., & Brenner, W. (n.d.). *Designing Human-Centric Information Systems: Towards an Understanding of Challenges in Specifying Requirements within Design Thinking Projects*. 12.

Institute of Design at Stanford. (2010). *An Introduction to Design Thinking PROCESS*

GUIDE. Stanford. https://dschool-old.stanford.edu/sandbox/groups/designresources/wiki/36873/attachments/74b3d/ModeGuideBOOTCAMP2010L.pdf

Jarke, M., Loucopoulos, P., Lyytinen, K., Mylopoulos, J., & Robinson, W. (2010). The brave new world of design requirements: Four key principles. *International Conference on Advanced Information Systems Engineering*, 470–482. http://link.springer.com/10.1007/978-3-642-13094-6_36

Kahan, E., Genero, M., & Oliveros, A. (2019). Challenges in Requirement Engineering: Could Design Thinking Help? In M. Piattini, P. Rupino da Cunha, I. García Rodríguez de Guzmán, & R. Pérez-Castillo (Eds.), *Quality of Information and Communications Technology* (pp. 79–86). Springer International Publishing. https://doi.org/10.1007/978-3-030-29238-6_6

Kahan, E., Insfran, E., Genero, M., & Oliveros, A. (2022). Studying the Influence of Empathy Maps on Brainstorming for Requirements Elicitation: A Quasi-Experiment. In E. Insfran, F. González, S. Abrahão, M. Fernández, C. Barry, M. Lang, H. Linger, & C. Schneider (Eds.), *Advances in Information Systems Development* (pp. 199–217). Springer International Publishing. https://doi.org/10.1007/978-3-030-95354-6_12

Kahan, Ezequiel, Oliveros, Alejandro, & Genero, Marcela. (2021). A systematic mapping study on the application of design thinking in requirement engineering. *Computación y Sistemas*.

Kontio, J., Bragge, J., & Lehtola, L. (2008). The Focus Group Method as an Empirical Tool in Software Engineering. In F. Shull, J. Singer, & D. I. K. Sjøberg (Eds.), *Guide to Advanced Empirical Software Engineering* (pp. 93–116). Springer London. https://doi.org/10.1007/978-1-84800-044-5_4

Köppen, E., & Meinel, C. (2015). Empathy via Design Thinking: Creation of Sense and Knowledge. In H. Plattner, C. Meinel, & L. Leifer (Eds.), *Design Thinking Research: Building Innovators* (pp. 15–28). Springer International Publishing. https://doi.org/10.1007/978-3-319-06823-7_2

Levy, M., & Huli, C. (2019). *Design thinking in a nutshell for eliciting requirements of a business process: A case study of a design thinking workshop. 2019-September*, 351–356. Scopus. https://doi.org/10.1109/RE.2019.00044

Loucopoulos, P., & Karakostas, V. (1995). *System Requirements Engineering*. McGraw-Hill, Inc.

Lyytinen, K., Loucopoulos, P., Mylopoulos, J., & Robinson, W. N. (Eds.). (2009). *Design Requirements Engineering: A Ten-Year Perspective: Design Requirements Workshop, Cleveland, OH, USA, June 3-6, 2007, Revised and Invited Papers*. Springer-Verlag. https://www.springer.com/la/book/9783540929659

Meireles, M., Souza, A., Conte, T., & Maldonado, J. (2021). *Organizing the Design Thinking Toolbox: Supporting the Requirements Elicitation Decision Making*. 285–290. Scopus. https://doi.org/10.1145/3474624.3477064

Using Metamodel Composition to Unify User Story and Use Case Metamodels

Larissa Mangolim Amaral[1], **Anarosa Alves Franco Brandão**[1], **Fábio Levy Siqueira**[1]

[1]Escola Politécnica – Universidade de São Paulo (USP)
São Paulo – SP – Brazil

{larissa.mangolim.amaral,anarosa.brandao,levy.siqueira}@usp.br

Abstract. *Requirements languages are often defined as metamodels for the standardization of a system's requirements specification. The unification of these metamodels benefits general analysis and interoperability between requirements models. Even tough some authors already discuss systematic composition approaches, this application for requirements languages' metamodels is still little explored. Therefore, we applied non-domain-specific composition frameworks to create a unified metamodel for User Story and Use Case diagram by assessing common points in related work. This application enabled reducing the subjectivity of the requirements languages composition process but still strongly depended on human curation.*

1. Introduction

One of the first activities executed in a software project is speaking to stakeholders in order to understand their requirements, i.e., needs, and associated constraints and conditions for the system [IEEE 2017]. The requirements are then documented to establish a contract as a specification of what has to be fulfilled by the system [IEEE 1990], usually expressed in requirements languages.

Requirements languages determine a set of constructs and verification protocols that are used to shape requirements documentation [IEEE 2017]. There is a wide range of different requirements languages that vary in their aspects and purposes, like expressiveness, visualization, and formality. Formal languages are composed of a syntactical and a semantic definition, the latter being responsible for defining the domain of information supported by the language and for mapping the meaning of expressions validated by the former [Harel and Rumpe 2003]. These definitions for requirements languages are often expressed by taking advantage of metamodeling techniques [Amaral et al. 2022], if not by their original authors, by later authors.

Every model is fundamentally focused on a specific purpose [Bézivin 2005], which justifies the existence of multiple requirements languages - or even versions of the same language - for different perspectives, contexts, or domains. The unification of requirements languages metamodels is approached by some authors, each of them indicating various benefits coming from the unification result and the consequent interoperability of metamodels. Saidi et al. (2013), who proposed a metamodel unifying the semantics of i*, CREWS, and PREview from different requirements approaches (goals, scenarios, and points of view, respectively), focus on the benefit of the translation of information between models written in different languages. Patricio et al. (2011), who unified i* and KAOS requirements languages, indicate that the creation of tools that interoperate with both popular and unpopular notations disseminates the usage of the unpopular one among industry practitioners. Rauh, Golubski and Queins (2017) emphasize two other benefits: (1) the identification of inconsistencies and redundancy in system specifications; and (2) the creation of more complete specifications through the identification of missing information in models.

Although there are some studies that propose a unified metamodel for requirements languages, the majority of them do not use a generic iterative method for this composition — one such as those examined by Abouzahra et al. (2020) that could be systematically used to unify other metamodels. In general, their unification process is composed by the analysis and abstraction of each term that appears in the languages' definition and the identification of any correspondence between them [Kaindl and Wagner 2009, Patricio et al. 2011], always focused on the languages being unified or on a specific domain. Rauh, Golubski and Queins (2017) connected the main concepts from use case description and UML diagrams through their relations to system services, which is a service-specific strategy. Saidi et al. (2013) apply an extension of the Lesk algorithm that calculates the distance between concepts' synonyms using definitions from the lexical database WordNet, which characterizes one of the common heuristics used for the matching operation.

Our research question is related to the evidenced gap for a composition method in the context of requirements languages, and how their matching is usually subjectively done: Does the application of existing non-domain-specific model composition methods for the unification of multiple requirements languages metamodels reduce process subjectivity? In addressing this question, we select a method assessed by Abouzahra et al. (2020) and apply the selected heuristics to two existing requirements languages' metamodels: User Story (US) and Use Case diagram. We were able to create an unification of these metamodels and discuss the process execution and results. In the future, we hope to develop a unified metamodel that takes into account a variety of requirements languages.

This paper is organized as follows. In Section 2, we define the strategies for each step of the requirements metamodels' composition. In Section 3 we apply a combination of existing composition methods in an example, unifying two existing requirements languages' metamodels. In Section 4 we discuss how the method was carried out and its the results, and the identified limitations of our study. Finally, Section 5 presents the conclusions and future work directions.

2. Metamodel Composition

Abouzahra et al. (2020) did a systematic review of studies that propose frameworks and tools for model composition. They vary mainly in their strategies defined by their purposes, but they mostly converge on a structure based on four steps, which are presented in Figure 1. The first step is the *matching operation*, that produces a *matching model* by searching for equivalences between elements from two input models. The matching model contains the links between the input models and can be used for automatic processing depending on how formally it is defined [Abouzahra et al. 2020] - for example, Del Fabro and Valduriez (2007) and Di Ruscio et al. (2012) use weaving models for that. The second step is a *composition operation* that uses the *matching model* together with the input models to produce the resulting composed model. Boronat et al. (2007), Kolovos et al. (2006) and Anwar et al. (2013) also have a step for *conflict resolution* between elements that considered equivalent but with structural differences that conflict, and there must be a defined strategy for determining which structure will be retained in the resulting metamodel - for example, Boronat et al. (2007) choose one input model whose structure will be prioritized. Another step that is considered is a *revision and manual update* of inconsistent links by a domain specialist. Considering the partial or complete automation of the previous steps, this revision can help reduce the loss of information from the adopted heuristics. In Figure 1, *revision* and *conflict resolution* were considered to be executed together as the designer would analyse the resulted matching model.

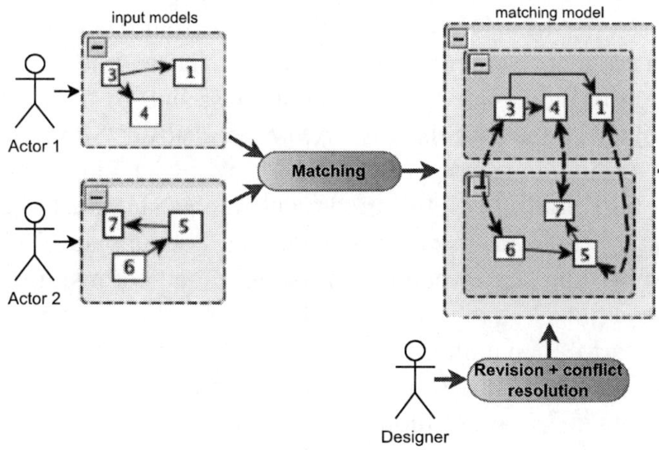

Figure 1. Model composition flow - adapted from Anwar et al. (2013). The different models' elements are represented by boxes with identification numbers, their relationships being the arrows between them. The steps inputs and outputs are indicated by the blue arrows.

Anwar et al. (2013) and Del Fabro and Valduriez (2007) are the model-related works best ranked by Abouzahra et al. (2020). Del Fabro and Valduriez (2007) propose a very complete set of heuristics for calculating matching elements between two input metamodels and building a weaving model as the matching model. Nevertheless, their composition operation bypasses the unified metamodel and uses the matching model to directly generate a transformation for merging two models that each conform to their respective input metamodel - meaning their process actually aims at a composed model instead of a composed metamodel like we intend to have.

3. Composing Requirements Metamodels

A challenge for the systematic model composition we intend to apply is that requirements metamodels usually contemplate abstract concepts whose semantics are not always completely clear. In this paper we merge two requirements metamodels: a metamodel of the unification of UML diagrams (class, use case, activity, and state machine diagrams) [Rauh et al. 2017] (M_1) and a user story (US) metamodel [Wautelet et al. 2014] (M_2). The choice of which requirements languages to unify considered the most popular languages among Software Engineering (SWE) researchers [Amaral et al. 2022]. The metamodels' elements are shown in Figure 2. The choice of what metamodel to use considered only that the metamodel should not be domain-specific, since our intention for future work is to apply this method for the unification of other non-domain-specific requirements languages. M_1 was a strong candidate because it addresses many of the most common requirements languages and is already a work of language unification, therefore it could bring more insight to the analysis of possible problems during the composition process. Similarly, M_2 is an extended version of an US metamodel. M_1 was restricted to restricted to the metaclasses that compose the Use Case diagram, which contemplates the metamodel's static structure partition and the state-related concepts.

3.1. Composition Method Used

To compose the metamodels, we used steps from different metamodel composition methods. The **matching operation** was based on Del Fabro and Valduriez (2007), which consists of: (1) applying a cartesian product between every element from each input metamodel; (2) calculating elements' similarity using predefined heuristics; and (3) filtering links below the determined threshold. For that, we used the AMW tool[1] itself, SimMetrics API[2] and the JAWJAW API[3] - which is a wrapper for WS4J (WordNet Similarity for Java). We did **manual revision and conflict resolution** altogether, choosing the links and structures that made more sense in requirements context. This stage contemplates Del Fabro and Valduriez (2007)'s link rewriting step, when it is possible to transform simple links of equivalence into non-obvious links like inheritance and nesting that are more directly related to the application scenario. The authors do not define an explicit strategy for either of these steps, leading to a more customizable analysis. Anwar et al. (2013) suggest that conflict resolution and the definition of more complex relationships may be done manually by a designer in some cases. For the **composition operation**, we used Anwar et al. (2013)'s out-target merging strategy, which keeps input models unchanged, computes elements' links from the matching model, and translates every element that has no correspondence links into the resulting new metamodel. Merging is a composition strategy that considers that all the information from the input models will be present in the composed metamodel, ideally with no duplication [Abouzahra et al. 2020]. Table 1 summarizes strategies for each step of the execution.

Step	Strategy
Matching operation	Cartesian product; matching heuristics (Levenshtein distance for name similarity, cardinality, type and conformance, Lesk (WordNet)); and threshold filtering [Del Fabro and Valduriez 2007]
Revision	Manual filtering and link rewriting [Del Fabro and Valduriez 2007]
Conflict Resolution	Case by case analysis [Del Fabro and Valduriez 2007]
Composition Operation	Out-target merging strategy and translation [Anwar et al. 2013]

Table 1. Strategies for each step of the composition method.

3.2. Matching Operation

First, both metamodels were represented on Ecore[4] so they could be used as input for the AMW tool. For an initial run of the matching operation, we executed the following

[1] Available at https://www.inf.ufpr.br/didonet/amw/
[2] Available at https://sourceforge.net/projects/simmetrics/
[3] Available at https://code.google.com/archive/p/jawjaw/
[4] Available at https://wiki.eclipse.org/Ecore_Tools

methods with configured weights with the values suggested in the Match Configuration Menu section of the AMW's User Guide[5]: 0.7 for name similarity, 0.2 for cardinality, 0.1 for type and conformance, and 0.4 as threshold. This execution resulted in an empty-link weaving model, shown in Figure 2. That makes sense since the elements had very little name, type, and cardinality similarity. We also tried running the separate methods, and neither one had a higher similarity than the determined threshold.

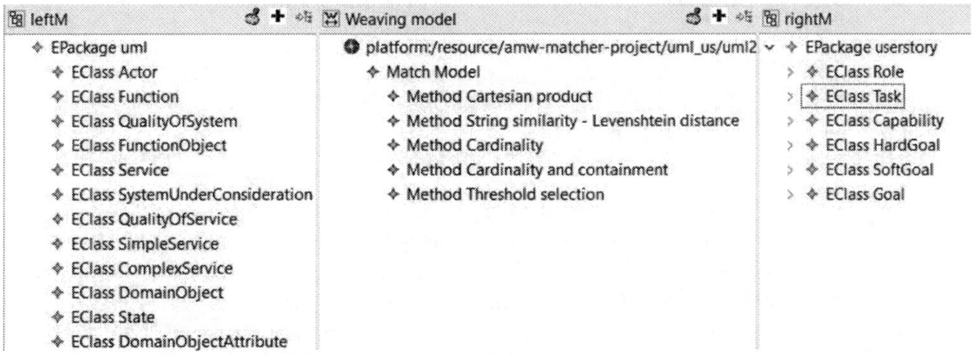

Figure 2. Weaving model after the automatic run of the model matching methods from the AMW tool.

We then applied the Lesk method, which is another heuristic considered by Del Fabro and Valduriez (2007), but not present in the AMW tool version we had access. For that, we implemented a Java matcher using the JAWJAW API[6]. Since the authors of M_2 detailed the history of elements that were unified to each metaclass, we also included this history for the Lesk execution. The similarity score results were filtered with a threshold value of 30, which seemed like a low enough value for us not to lose any meaningful links but also high enough to filter irrelevant ones. The links shown in Figure 3 were inserted manually into the weaving model in the AMW tool.

3.3. Revision and Conflict Resolution

We followed the matching operation with a revision of every link it produced. We kept the equality link for `Actor` and `Role` because it had a very high similarity score since `Role` had previously been unified with `Actor` in M_2 so they would represent the same concept.

`Function`, `Service`, `System` and `State` matched with a lot of elements, probably due to the wideness of their meanings (even inside the requirements context). As a result, equivalences to `System` were all ignored as none of the elements in M_2 had the same level of abstraction as `System`. Equivalences with `State` were discarded as well, since M_2 does not contemplate elements with a requirements' dynamic component. `Function` and `Role` link was rejected, because, even though their general meanings might be similar, they relate to different objects (function refers to the service, and role refers to the actor). `Function` and `Task` link was considered to make more sense and was maintained, as both concepts are about a process that is executed by the system. We considered the comparison between `Service` and `Task`, which had the highest similarity scores. Looking at the semantics given by the authors of the metamodels for these

[5]Available at https://www.inf.ufpr.br/didonet/amw/userguide/index.html
[6]Available at https://github.com/uneluneravie/matching-metamodels

elements, both concepts are focused on achieving a goal: "a 'Service' can provide the 'Actor' a value by supporting to reach a goal of the 'Actor'" [Rauh et al. 2017, p. 2], and "a task specifies a particular way of attaining a goal" [Yu et al. 2011, p. 57]. The main difference, which led us *not* to unify these concepts, was that the `Service` is a more complex entity that *supports* the achievement of a goal through functionality definition, whereas `Task` is a more direct means to this achievement. To make this relationship explicit, we changed their equality link to a relationship between these ununified metaclasses.

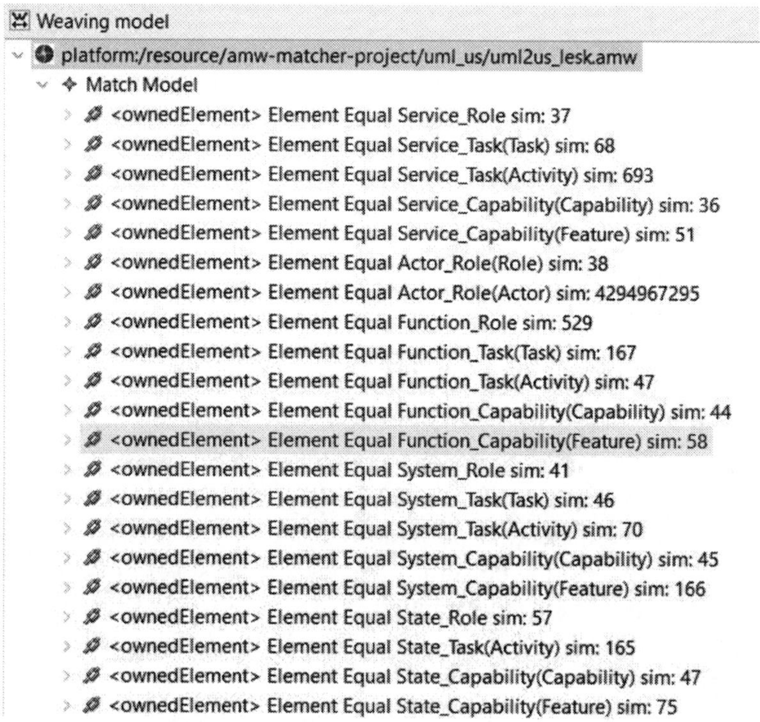

Figure 3. Weaving model after manual insertion of links with similarity generated by the Lesk (WordNet) heuristic.

Afterwards, in conflict resolution, we chose to keep M_2's properties for both unified metaclasses because M_1 does not declare attributes for its elements. The only other conflict happened when unifying `Function` and `Task`, since `Function` already defined a relationship with `Service` and we had declared a special link between the latter and `Task`. We therefore opted for keeping the original relationship and discarding the new link. We also checked for consistency as there would be defined a relationship between `Function` and `Actor`, since it already existed with `Task`. The cardinality did make sense, as the `Actor` can use many `Services` and each `Service` is defined by `Task`, so one or more `Actors` could want many `Tasks`.

For the merging operation, we added `NotFound` links to track the elements in both input models that had no match and would be translated to the composed metamodel. We then resolved every link manually, resulting in the metamodel presented in Figure 4.

4. Discussion

Regarding the composition execution process, it was easier to identify conflicts while composing the final metamodel, raising suspicion that the automation of these steps would

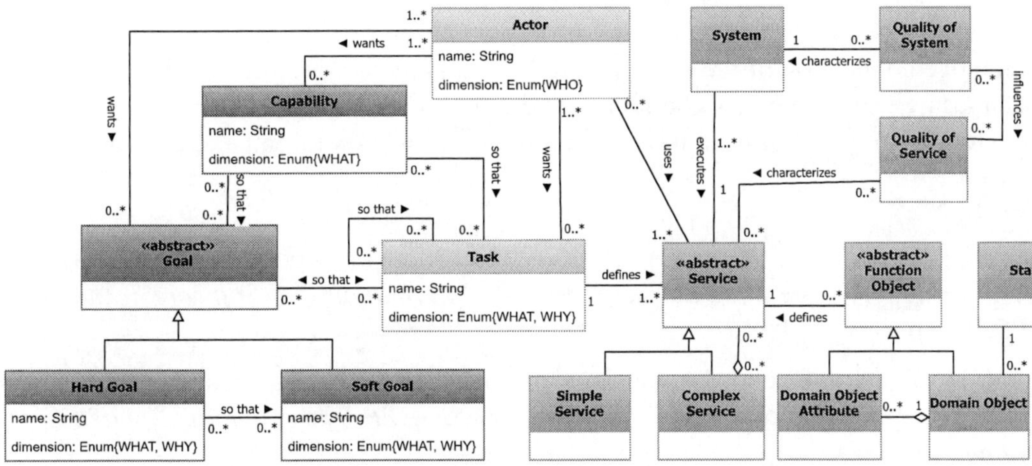

Figure 4. Resulting composed metamodel. Metaclasses from M_1 are in green, from M_2 are in red, and the ones that were a unification of concepts from both models are in yellow.

possibly lead to information loss or inconsistency. Another noteworthy aspect is that the history tracked from M_2 assisted in the recovery of concepts' meanings and links that could have been lost. It would be interesting that in future iterations on the integration of new models, the previous matching models were considered as concepts' history.

Addressing our research question, application of heuristics (especially the Lesk algorithm) removed subjectivity for the matching operation. The matching model also facilitates composition automation and tracking. Even tough, the results we obtained in every step of the process, considering the final metamodel, showed that the requirements domain contains multiple words with wide meaning that are present in a diversity of domains, like actor and role, or even worse, service and system. The fact that composition heuristics do not consider the semantics of these concepts applied to the specific domain endangers the precision of the results and demands more manual revision. Link types are also not able to capture the domain complexity and they too need human intervention to be able to express the proper meaning of relationships other than equality.

5. Conclusion

In this paper, we present an application of general-purpose composition methods for metamodels in the requirements domain and assess its results. We were able to build a composed metamodel for US and UML (from a requirements engineering viewpoint) with cautious manual filtering of the automatically-generated matching links.

The most evident threat to our study is that the application is still inherently dependent on the characteristics of the metamodels being composed; thus, the conclusion validity of our evaluation example is biased on these metamodel selection choices. For example, M_2 lacked any class attributes, making matching and conflict resolution easier. Also, the input models did not have many concepts in common that were matched - that was probably due to their being from different viewpoints (goal and service-oriented). In future work, we intend to systematize these choices to delineate the characteristics of the metamodels that are a better fit for the composition. Another threat is that WordNet does not work well with composed words, which we had to some extent. The matching heuristics could be improved to better consider composed words and domain semantics. The iterative application of the same methods to aggregate more metamodels, each with its peculiarities, can bring new challenges to the composition process, which we expect to do in a future study that aims at the unification of multiple requirements languages.

References

Abouzahra, A., Sabraoui, A., and Afdel, K. (2020). Model composition in Model Driven Engineering: A systematic literature review. *Information and Software Technology*, 125:106316.

Amaral, L., Siqueira, F., and Brandão, A. (2022). A survey on requirements notations in software engineering research. *The 37th ACM/SIGAPP Symposium on Applied Computing (SAC '22)*.

Anwar, A., Benelallam, A., Nassar, M., and Coulette, B. (2013). A Graphical Specification of Model Composition with Triple Graph Grammars. In *Model-Based Methodologies for Pervasive and Embedded Software*, volume 7706, pages 1–18. Springer Berlin Heidelberg, Berlin, Heidelberg.

Bézivin, J. (2005). On the unification power of models. *Software and System Modeling*, 4:171–188.

Del Fabro, M. D. and Valduriez, P. (2007). Semi-automatic model integration using matching transformations and weaving models. In *Proceedings of the 2007 ACM symposium on Applied computing - SAC '07*, page 963, Seoul, Korea. ACM Press.

Harel, D. and Rumpe, B. (2003). Modeling Languages: Syntax, Semantics and all that stuff. Technical report.

IEEE (1990). IEEE Standard Glossary of Software Engineering Terminology. pages 1–84. Conference Name: IEEE Std 610.12-1990.

IEEE (2017). ISO/IEC/IEEE International Standard - Systems and software engineering–Vocabulary. Technical report, IEEE.

Kaindl, H. and Wagner, P. (2009). A Unification of the Essence of Goal-Oriented Requirements Engineering. In *2009 Fourth International Conference on Software Engineering Advances*, pages 45–50, Porto, Portugal. IEEE.

Patricio, P., Amaral, V., Araujo, J., and Monteiro, R. (2011). Towards a Unified Goal-Oriented Language. In *2011 IEEE 35th Annual Computer Software and Applications Conference*, pages 596–601, Munich, Germany. IEEE.

Rauh, A., Golubski, W., and Queins, S. (2017). A Requirements Meta-Model to Integrate Information for the Definition of System Services. In *2017 IEEE Symposium on Service-Oriented System Engineering (SOSE)*, pages 96–101, San Francisco, CA, USA. IEEE.

Wautelet, Y., Heng, S., Kolp, M., and Mirbel, I. (2014). Unifying and Extending User Story Models. In *Advanced Information Systems Engineering*, volume 8484, pages 211–225. Springer International Publishing, Cham.

Yu, E., Giorgini, P., Maiden, N., Mylopoulos, J., and Fickas, S. (2011). Social modeling for requirements engineering.

Towards a Framework Based on Open Science Practices for Promoting Reproducibility of Software Engineering Controlled Experiments

André F. R. Cordeiro [1]

[1]Informatics Department
State University of Maringá – Maringá, PR, Brazil

cordeiroandrefelipe@gmail.com

Abstract. *Experimentation in Software Engineering has increased in the last decades as a way to provide evidence on theories and technologies. In a controlled experiment life cycle, several artifacts are used/reused and even produced. Such artifacts are mostly in the form of data, which should favor the reproducibility of such experiments. In this context, reproducibility can be defined as the ability to reproduce a study. Different benefits, such as methodology and data reuse, can be achieved from this ability. Despite the recognized benefits, several challenges have been faced by researchers regarding the experiments' reproducibility capability. To overcome them, we understand that Open Science practices, related to provenance, preservation, and curation, might aid in improving such a capability. Therefore, in this paper, we present the proposal for an open science-based Framework to deal with controlled experiment research artifacts towards making such experiments de facto reproducible. To do so, different models associated with open science practices are planned to be integrated into the Framework.*

1. Introduction

Experimental Software Engineering (ESE) studies and investigates practices that can be applied in experiments carried out in Software Engineering (SE) [Wohlin et al. 2012, Shull et al. 2007]. Experiments can be represented from processes and stages. A process is presented in [Wohlin et al. 2012], with the stages of scoping, planning, operating, analyzing and interpreting, presenting and packaging, and recording. Figure 1 illustrates this process.

In Figure 1, it is possible to observe all stages of the experimental process. In the definition of scope, the experiment is evaluated, considering the problem under investigation and objectives. In planning, the context, hypotheses, variables, participating subjects (when applicable), experimental design, instrumentation, and assessment of threats to validity are defined. In the operation, data preparation, execution, and validation take place. During analysis and interpretation, data collected in the experiment are evaluated and hypothesis tests are performed.

In presenting and packaging, artifacts are organized for publishing and sharing. An artifact can be defined as every result used or generated during the experiment [Standard 2017]. Different artifacts are generated or manipulated during the experimental life cycle [Wohlin et al. 2012]. In the registration stage, the exposition of the results of

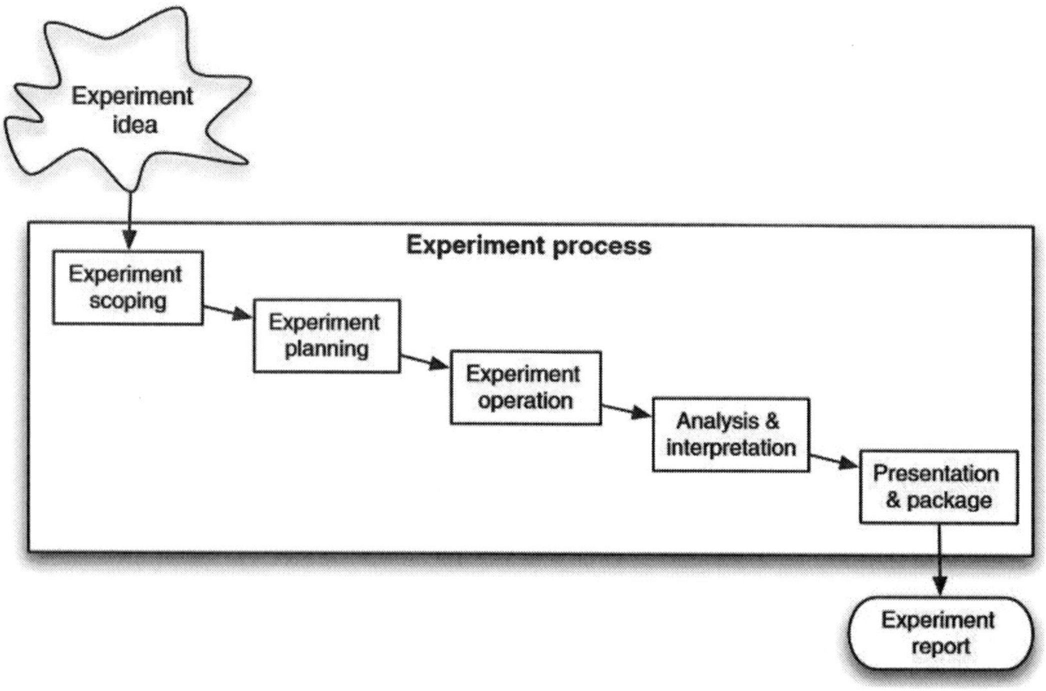

Figure 1. Experiment process [Wohlin et al. 2012].

the experiment is considered. Different means of dissemination can be considered, such as scientific articles and technical reports.

In addition to the experimental process, other subjects are investigated in ESE. Possible subjects include artifact management [Krishnamurthi 2013, Basili et al. 2007] and reproducibility [Li 2021, Liu et al. 2021, González-Barahona and Robles 2012]. Reproducibility is one of the basic rules of the scientific method and can be defined as the ability to reproduce a study, in full or in part, by different researchers [González-Barahona and Robles 2012]. The reuse of research artifacts and the advancement of scientific knowledge are examples of benefits directly related to reproducibility [Mendez et al. 2020, González-Barahona and Robles 2012].

Despite the importance of reproducibility for scientific advancement, different studies have reported the existence of reproducibility problems in SE, under different contexts, such as in Deep Learning (DL) models [Liu et al. 2021], secondary studies [Li 2021] and families of experiments [Kitchenham et al. 2020]. The sharing of artifacts used in experiments [Liu et al. 2021], the difficulty in adopting tools and practices in experiments [Anchundia et al. 2020], and the adoption of experimental packages [Shull et al. 2004] are examples of reported problems.

Problems observed in the reproduction of experiments carried out in SE motivated the proposal of a Framework. A Framework can be defined as a structure that can be refined and extended to support a set of functionalities [Standard 2017]. In the context of this study, a Framework is composed of data, metadata, and practices, focusing on reproducibility. The hypothesis considered is that data sets and metadata can favor reproducibility. Practices associated with Open Science (OS) can be considered in the development of the Framework. OS can be defined as a movement that defends the reuse and sharing of all artifacts produced in scientific research [Mendez et al. 2020]. Different OS subareas have been established. A taxonomy with the main ones is presented in [Pontika et al. 2015]. Among the main subareas is Open Data (OD), defined as the ability to use, share and distribute one or more data sets, free of charge and with respect to defined licenses [Enríquez-Reyes et al. 2021, Osorio-Sanabria et al. 2020, Immonen et al. 2018, Pontika et al. 2015].

The next sections of this study describe the goals and research questions (Section 2), the problem domain (Section 3), the methodology (Section 4), the proposal of solution (Section 5), the research agenda (Section 6) and the final remarks (Section 7).

2. Goals and Research Questions

The objective of this study is to develop a Framework that favors the reproducibility of experiments carried out in SE. The Framework is based on data sets, metadata, and OS practices. In this context, the following research questions were established:

- Which data and metadata can be considered by the Framework?
- What practices associated with OS can be considered by the Framework?
- Is reproducibility favored when different data sets, metadata, and practices associated with OS about the experiment are available?

3. Problem Domain

During the planning, operation, and presentation of experiments, different data sets are constructed. Examples of data sets associated with the experimental process can be seen at [Wohlin et al. 2012]. Considering the knowledge of the experimental process and the problem of reproducibility (Section 1), it is observed that the experimental data sets have not been sufficient to favor the reproducibility of experiments carried out in SE. Difficulties observed with the adoption of experimental packages represent an example of this scenario [Shull et al. 2004].

The issue of reproducibility in SE can be studied and investigated from different perspectives. A study carried out with the aim of identifying tools that maximize reproducibility in SE experiments is presented in [Anchundia et al. 2020]. In [Liu et al. 2021], an investigation is presented on aspects of reproducibility and replicability in SE studies that consider the application of DL techniques. Problems with the reproducibility of secondary studies in Evidence-Based Software Engineering (EBSE) are presented in [Li 2021]. Investigations on the identification of families of experiments that used meta-analysis and evaluation of the reproducibility and validity of the results are presented in [Kitchenham et al. 2020].

In order to improve experimental replications, specific guidelines are presented in [Carver 2010]. The guidelines are proposed and organized into sets. To elaborate on these guidelines, different published replications were reviewed. An assessment, associated with reproducibility in software development, is presented in [Anda et al. 2008]. Among the results of the study is the finding that reproducibility in SE remains a major challenge, observed in research, education, and industry.

An initiative based on collaborative effort is proposed in [Neto et al. 2015], to favor the reproducibility of experiments related to the evaluation of software testing techniques. The development of a tool that performs the execution and analysis of experiments is also proposed. This structure was developed with the objective of helping in the creation and reproduction of experiments. The validation of the structure was carried out from the reproduction of a known experiment, with test case selection techniques. Regarding the reproducibility of studies in the software repositories mining area, elements that can be considered in the reproducibility are presented in [González-Barahona and Robles 2012]. Types of reproduction studies are presented, as well as a methodology to assess the reproducibility of studies.

4. Methodology

Initially, two secondary studies were considered. The first study is related to reproducibility in SE. The aim is to understand how reproducibility is represented and investigated. Some of the retrieved studies were described in Section 3.

The second study is related to the use of practices possibly associated with OS in SE. The objective is to understand which practices are used. Among the practices observed so far are OD offered as a software portal platform; definition of the open data model in applications; suggestions for developing open architectures and open software platforms; use of OD portals for software development. In this case, a portal is composed of different data sets; the use of OD clouds that consider linked OD and ontology; suggestions for developing a plan for creating and sharing artifacts, and recommendations to establish a long-term strategy for artifact sharing and evaluation.

Both secondary studies are in their final stages. The knowledge gained from these studies will guide the improvement of the Framework. At first, the Framework to be built will be finalized after two stages of development. In the first stage, conceptual development will take place, which consists of defining data sets, metadata, and practices. Recommendations to be considered by users of the Framework should also be described. In the second stage, the Framework will be implemented as a tool.

After completion of secondary studies, the following steps will be considered: identification of all models that form the Framework; identification of data and metadata associated with all models; evaluation and selection of OS practices to be used in the Framework; development of guidelines for the use of each Framework model; conceptual Framework development; implementation of the Framework as a tool. At the end of the implementation, it is possible to start the evaluation.

To evaluate the Framework, the empirical strategies of Case Study and Survey are considered [Wohlin et al. 2012]. In the Case Study, a scenario will be presented to illustrate the use of the Framework, in terms of data management, metadata, and practices. The management objective should be to favor the reproducibility of experiments in SE. Study participants must have knowledge of ESE. The aim is to enable its use by SE researchers.

In the Survey, the Case Study participants must evaluate the Framework based on a set of questions. Questions should be related to the ease of use and feasibility of adopting the Framework. Specific methodologies can also be considered. This is the case, for example, of Technology Acceptance Model (TAM) [Davis 1985]. Another possibility of evaluation may be to carry out controlled experiments. A possible experiment suggestion is presented in [Cordeiro 2022].

5. Proposal of Solution

Considering the information presented in section 3, it is understood that data sets and metadata could complement the experimental data. Metadata can be defined as data about data [Yuan et al. 2013]. Personal experiences accumulated in previous projects suggest that metadata can be used to record characteristics of experimental data, in order to favor reproducibility. In the proposed Framework, the characteristics of curation, provenance, preservation, and data management are considered. Curation is associated with the description of metadata that describes actions performed with experimental data [Cordeiro et al. 2022]. Provenance makes it possible to record metadata related to the origin of the data. For example, someone can record the data collection location for a set [Yuan et al. 2013]. Preservation considers the registration of metadata related to the safe and complete maintenance of the artifacts considered [Cordeiro and OliveiraJr 2021]. In data management, there is a concern with sharing and reuse [Cordeiro et al. 2022].

To deal with the reproducibility of experiments performed in SE, a Framework was proposed. Previous experiences with experiments motivated the initial development of the Framework, presented in Figure 2.

When analyzing Figure 2, different elements can be noticed, such as conceptual model, recommender systems, ontology, trusted repositories, and model types. The conceptual model, the ontology, and the recommendation system are related to structures developed for recording and using experimental data [Furtado et al. 2021, Vignando et al. 2020]. The model types are related to metadata (curation, data management, provenance, and preservation) and OS practices.

6. Research Agenda

As mentioned in Section 4, two secondary studies are ongoing. At the end of these studies, the following research agenda will be initiated:

- Definition of all data sets that will be considered. For this definition, different experimental structures can be considered [Furtado et al. 2021, Vignando et al. 2020, Jedlitschka et al. 2008];
- Definition of all metadata sets, related to curation, data management, provenance, and preservation;
- Definition of OS practices associated with the Framework;
- Development of the different models shown in Figure 2. For each model, data, metadata, and OS practices will be considered;
- Conceptual development of the Framework, which consists of refining the structure develop in the previous step;
- Implementation of the Framework as a tool;
- Planning, elaboration, and execution of the Case Study;
- Planning, elaboration, and execution of the Survey;
- Availability of the tool for use by SE researchers.

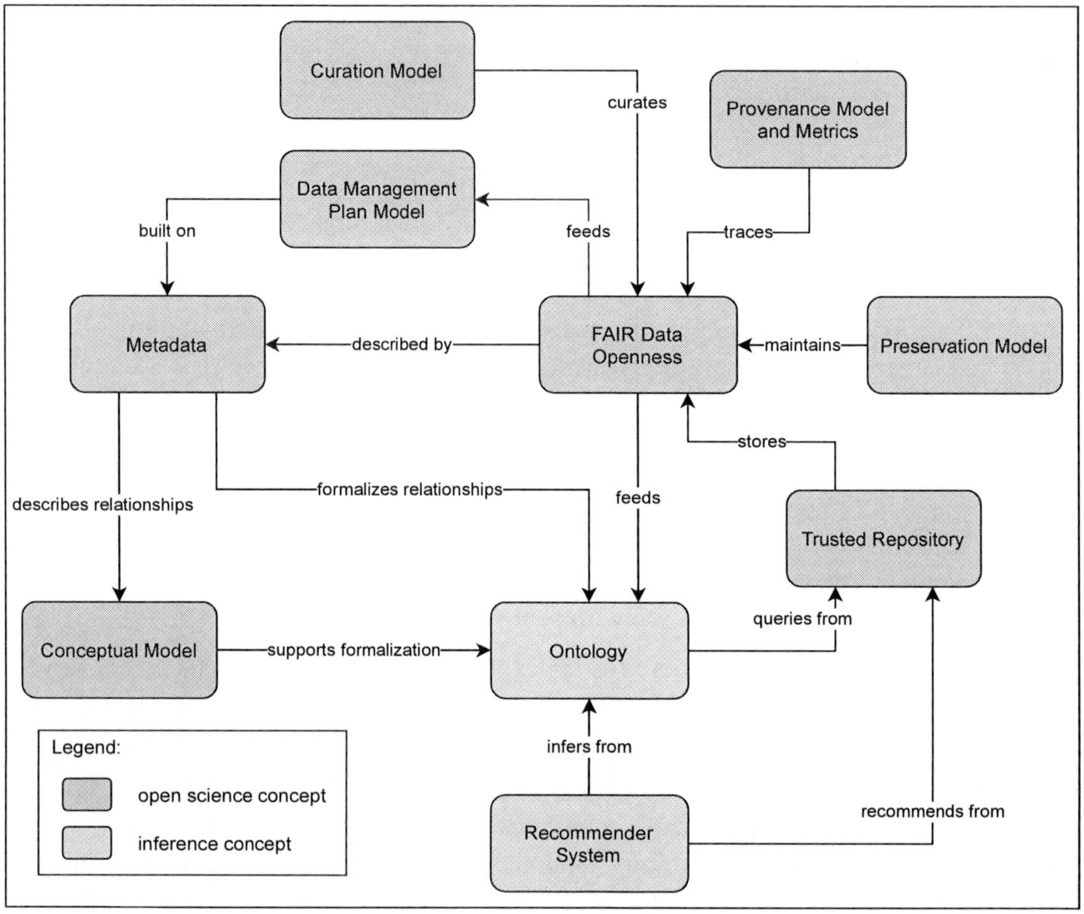

Figure 2. Initial Framework´s Structure [Cordeiro et al. 2022].

7. Final Remarks

This study proposed the development of a Framework to manage data and metadata of experiments performed with SE, focusing on reproducibility. Practices possibly associated with OS and being used in SE will be considered. The core element of the Framework is the data. Different sets of experimental data are from the beginning of the experimental process and represent the input to the Framework. In addition to these data sets, the definition of metadata sets is planned, and related to curation, preservation, provenance, and data management. Practices associated with OS should help organize and manage these sets. It is expected that the different sets of data and metadata can favor reproducibility.

The methodology for developing the research considers carrying out secondary studies, defining data sets and metadata, conceptual construction and implementation of the Framework, as well as carrying out a case study and a survey. In the end, the implemented Framework must be made available for use.

Acknowledgments

I would like to thank my advisor Prof. Dr. Edson OliveiraJr and my colleagues at the Research Group on Systematic Software Reuse and Continuous Experimentation (GREATER) for their support at different moments of the project.

References

Anchundia, C. E. et al. (2020). Resources for reproducibility of experiments in empirical software engineering: Topics derived from a secondary study. *IEEE Access*, 8:8992–9004.

Anda, B. C., Sjøberg, D. I., and Mockus, A. (2008). Variability and reproducibility in software engineering: A study of four companies that developed the same system. *IEEE Transactions on Software Engineering*, 35(3):407–429.

Basili, V. R., Zelkowitz, M. V., Sjøberg, D. I., Johnson, P., and Cowling, A. J. (2007). Protocols in the use of empirical software engineering artifacts. *Empirical Software Engineering*, 12(1):107–119.

Carver, J. C. (2010). Towards reporting guidelines for experimental replications: A proposal. In *1st international workshop on replication in empirical software engineering*, volume 1, pages 1–4.

Cordeiro, A. F. and OliveiraJr, E. (2021). Open science practices for software engineering controlled experiments and quasi-experiments. In *OpenScienSE*, pages 19–21, Brazil. SBC.

Cordeiro, A. F., OliveiraJr, E., and Capretz, L. (2022). Towards an open science-based framework for software engineering controlled (quasi-)experiments. In *Anais do XVI Brazilian e-Science Workshop*, pages 57–64, Porto Alegre, RS, Brasil. SBC.

Cordeiro, A. F. R. (2022). An open science-based framework for managing experimental data in software engineering. In *Proceedings of the International Conference on Evaluation and Assessment in Software Engineering 2022*, pages 342–346.

Davis, F. D. (1985). *A technology acceptance model for empirically testing new end-user information systems: Theory and results*. PhD thesis, Massachusetts Institute of Technology.

Enríquez-Reyes, R., Cadena-Vela, S., Fuster-Guilló, A., Mazón, J.-N., Ibáñez, L. D., and Simperl, E. (2021). Systematic mapping of open data studies: Classification and trends from a technological perspective. *IEEE Access*, 9:12968–12988.

Furtado, V., OliveiraJr, E., and Kalinowski, M. (2021). Guidelines for promoting software product line experiments. In *15th Brazilian Symposium on Software Components, Architectures, and Reuse*, pages 31–40.

González-Barahona, J. M. and Robles, G. (2012). On the reproducibility of empirical software engineering studies based on data retrieved from development repositories. *Empirical Software Engineering*, 17(1):75–89.

Immonen, A., Ovaska, E., and Paaso, T. (2018). Towards certified open data in digital service ecosystems. *Software Quality Journal*, 26(4):1257–1297.

Jedlitschka, A., Ciolkowski, M., and Pfahl, D. (2008). Reporting experiments in software engineering. In *Guide to advanced empirical software engineering*, pages 201–228. Springer, New York.

Kitchenham, B., Madeyski, L., and Brereton, P. (2020). Meta-analysis for families of experiments in software engineering: a systematic review and reproducibility and validity assessment. *Empirical Software Engineering*, 25:353–401.

Krishnamurthi, S. (2013). Artifact evaluation for software conferences. *ACM SIGSOFT Software Engineering Notes*, 38(3):7–10.

Li, Z. (2021). Stop building castles on a swamp! the crisis of reproducing automatic search in evidence-based software engineering. In *2021 IEEE/ACM 43rd International Conference on Software Engineering: New Ideas and Emerging Results (ICSE-NIER)*, pages 16–20. IEEE.

Liu, C., Gao, C., Xia, X., Lo, D., Grundy, J., and Yang, X. (2021). On the reproducibility and replicability of deep learning in software engineering. *ACM Transactions on Software Engineering and Methodology (TOSEM)*, 31(1):1–46.

Mendez, D., Graziotin, D., Wagner, S., and Seibold, H. (2020). Open science in software engineering. In *Contemporary empirical methods in software engineering*, pages 477–501. Springer.

Neto, F. G. D. O., Torkar, R., and Machado, P. D. (2015). An initiative to improve reproducibility and empirical evaluation of software testing techniques. In *2015 IEEE/ACM 37th IEEE International Conference on Software Engineering*, volume 2, pages 575–578. IEEE.

Osorio-Sanabria, M. A., Amaya-Fernández, F., and González-Zabala, M. (2020). Exploring the components of open data ecosystems: A systematic mapping study. In *Proceedings of the 10th Euro-American conference on telematics and information systems*, pages 1–6.

Pontika, N., Knoth, P., Cancellieri, M., and Pearce, S. (2015). Fostering open science to research using a taxonomy and an elearning portal. In *i-KNOW*, pages 1–8, New York. ACM.

Shull, F., Mendoncça, M. G., Basili, V., Carver, J., Maldonado, J. C., Fabbri, S., Travassos, G. H., and Ferreira, M. C. (2004). Knowledge-sharing issues in experimental software engineering. *Empirical Software Engineering*, 9:111–137.

Shull, F., Singer, J., and Sjøberg, D. I. (2007). *Guide to advanced empirical software engineering*. Springer, New York.

Standard, I. I. (2017). International standard - systems and software engineering – vocabulary. *ISO/IEC/IEEE 24765:2017(E)*, pages 1–541.

Vignando, H., Furtado, V. R., Teixeira, L. O., and OliveiraJr, E. (2020). Ontoexper-spl: An ontology for software product line experiments. In *ICEIS (2)*, pages 401–408.

Wohlin, C., Runeson, P., Höst, M., Ohlsson, M. C., Regnell, B., and Wesslén, A. (2012). *Experimentation in software engineering*. Springer Science & Business Media, Germany.

Yuan, D., Yang, Y., and Chen, J. (2013). 2 - literature review. In Yuan, D., Yang, Y., and Chen, J., editors, *Computation and Storage in the Cloud*, pages 5–13. Elsevier.

Framework para desarrollos de robótica educativa en espacios virtuales

Gonzalo Zabala[1]

[1] Centro de Altos Estudios en Tecnología Informática, Facultad de Tecnología Informática, Universidad Abierta Interamericana, CABA, Argentina.

gonzalo.zabala@uai.edu.ar

Abstract. *The presented thesis proposes to build a framework for the development of educational robotics virtual environments based on a 3D simulator that provides features, motivations, and resources similar to those found in the use of physical material, analyzing the impact of its use in comparison with traditional robotics kits.*

Resumen. *La tesis presentada propone construir un framework para el desarrollo de entornos virtuales de robótica educativa basados en un simulador 3D, que aporte características, motivaciones y recursos similares a los encontrados en el uso de material concreto, analizando el impacto de su uso en comparación con kits de robótica tradicionales.*

Keywords: pensamiento computacional, robótica, simulación, laboratorio virtual, programación visual

1. Introducción al campo de la investigación e identificación de los principales desafíos

El uso de robots en las aulas provee a los estudiantes un espacio de aprendizaje reflexivo y experimental. Cuando en equipo diseñan, construyen, programan y documentan el diseño de un robot, no sólo aprenden de tecnología, sino que también ponen en práctica habilidades fundamentales para el mundo que encontrarán cuando salgan de su educación formal. Por otra parte, el mercado laboral requiere cada día más de recursos humanos vinculados al desarrollo de tecnología, en campos como la programación, el diseño y las ingenierías. El estudio de la robótica puede ser un recurso para despertar vocaciones en estas áreas, además de aumentar la retención de estudiantes mujeres que están subrepresentadas en el campo de la tecnología [Miller & Nourbakhsh, 2016].

Por estos motivos, los robots se han convertido en un recurso didáctico valorado por los docentes de nivel primario y secundario. Sin embargo, aún es un recurso costoso para la mayoría de las escuelas y familias, y los docentes presentan algunos temores y rechazos para su incorporación en el aula [Reich-Stiebert & Eyssel, 2016]. Por otro lado, en contextos donde la educación necesariamente debe realizarse en forma remota, como el acaecido por la pandemia del COVID 19, el acceso a laboratorios con material físico se hace imposible.

Asimismo, a partir del aumento de poder de cómputo de las placas gráficas, han surgido con fuerza diferentes ambientes de simulación de robots: CoderZ, Webots, VRT , Gazebo, CoppeliaSim, entre otros. Lamentablemente, los que tienen por detrás un motor físico que representa lo más cabalmente posible al mundo real tienen alguno o algunos de los siguientes inconvenientes:

- Son muy costosos para nuestro país (valor dólar, alrededor de 50U$S por estudiante).
- Necesitan de un equipamiento medianamente sofisticado por el alto nivel de procesamiento para simular la física.
- Son complejos de instalar y operar.

En síntesis, hasta el momento, no existe aún una solución al problema de la robótica educativa sin material concreto, que presente las siguientes características [Hughes, Shimizu, et al., 2019]:

- Acceso gratuito al software de modo que sea totalmente accesible para que lo utilicen los estudiantes.
- Que no posea altos requerimientos de cómputo.
- Facilidad de instalación para que el proceso no sea una barrera de entrada.
- Interfaz de uso intuitivo.
- Versatilidad, de modo que pueda utilizarse tanto para la enseñanza de los fundamentos de la robótica como para la experimentación de temas de mayor complejidad.

Un framework que permita el desarrollo de plataformas de simulación que cumplan con todas estas características, no sólo sería una herramienta fundamental en situaciones donde es necesaria la educación a distancia, sino que se convertiría en un recurso didáctico de gran utilidad por las siguientes razones:

1. Costo bajo o nulo.
2. Permite el trabajo con estudiantes que se encuentran alejados del acceso a los recursos materiales.
3. Permite el trabajo colaborativo entre estudiantes que se encuentran distanciados entre sí.
4. Sirve de entrada al mundo de la robótica educativa de una manera más sencilla que los kits materiales de bajo costo.

En función de lo presentado en el punto anterior, el problema que quiere resolver este trabajo de investigación es la ausencia de un simulador de robots apto para el ámbito educativo, que pueda suplantar el uso de kits físicos por cuestiones de imposibilidad de acceso o por costo.

2. Solución propuesta

Respondiendo a los problemas no resueltos que se describieron en el punto anterior, la solución que se propone es la construcción de un framework para desarrollos online de robótica educativa, basada en un simulador 3D, que permita vivenciar una experiencia lo más similar posible a la realizada con material concreto. Este framework ofrecerá un espacio para la presentación de diferentes propuestas didácticas con diversas situaciones problema en distintos escenarios. Para resolver las situaciones, los estudiantes elegirán la arquitectura de robot adecuada y programarán su comportamiento con un lenguaje de programación visual y/o textual.

Con relación a las características del proyecto, en primer lugar, el uso de un simulador basado en un motor físico 3D se acerca a la experiencia de trabajar con kits físicos. Por otro lado, el costo material es muy bajo comparado con estos recursos. Además, la ejecución en un browser disminuye el requerimiento de equipamiento, lo que baja aún más la necesidad de recursos. Por último, el desarrollo de una interfaz que simplifica el uso del motor 3D, el acompañamiento en la misma plataforma de propuestas didácticas y la incorporación de un lenguaje visual para la programación facilita la enseñanza de robótica en los niveles primario y secundario.

En síntesis, a continuación, se plantea el objetivo general y los específicos del presente proyecto.

Objetivo general

Desarrollar un framework para la creación de plataformas de simulación de robots en ambientes 3D con motor de física, orientado al uso en ámbitos educativos de nivel primario y secundario que permita un aprendizaje similar al de los materiales físicos.

Objetivos específicos

- Establecer los principales aspectos didácticos que debe permitir la implementación del framework.
- Determinar el modelo físico para el desarrollo del simulador.
- Desarrollar espacios virtuales y robots que operan en dichos espacios.
- Especificar un ambiente de programación con diferentes niveles de complejidad asociados a su poder expresivo.
- Determinar el impacto en estudiantes de una implementación del framework.

3. Trabajos relacionados

La robótica ha comenzado a tener cada vez más presencia en las aulas, y existen diversos estudios que analizan su impacto en el aprendizaje de los estudiantes en diversas áreas [Benitti & Spolaôr, 2017; Fagin & Merkle, 2002; García-Peñalvo et al., 2019; Lepuschitz et al., 2018; Merdan et al., 2016; Miller & Nourbakhsh, 2016; Theofanellis et al., 2020]. Sin embargo, el mundo de la simulación presenta otras características que obliga a realizar estudios propios, no sólo con respecto a la mejora en el aprendizaje, sino también en comparación con los laboratorios físicos [Eguchi & Shen, 2012; Fernandes, 2013; Guyot et al., 2011; Hughes, 2016; Infante Jiménez, 2014; Major, 2014].

Para comenzar, uno de los pioneros en esta área fue USARSim, un simulador de búsqueda y rescate en zonas urbanas que se utilizó para la competencia en la categoría Virtual Robots Competition de la Robocup a partir de 2006. Otra plataforma muy popular como base para diferentes proyectos de robótica en educación es Webots, un desarrollo open source de la firma Cyberbotics destinado a la construcción de simulaciones de robots móviles para la investigación. Sobre esta plataforma podemos encontrar diversas propuestas para la educación. Una de ellas es la presentada en [Guyot et al., 2011], donde se introduce un diseño curricular para diferentes niveles de complejidad usando el robot E-puck. En la misma línea surge el proyecto RPN, Robotic Programming Network, con diferentes cursos de robótica usando simuladores construidos sobre Webots [Casañ Núñez & Cervera, 2018; Núñez & Mateu, 2015]. En [Hughes, Aghababa, et al., 2019] se propone la construcción de una plataforma de rescate para Robocup Junior, no sólo sobre Webots, sino que la extienden a Gazebo y V-REP para poder comparar sus características y performance.

Por otra parte, otra plataforma de simulación de física y robótica desarrollada para educación es CoSpaces Edu. Está presente en Robocup Junior en Cospace Rescue

Challenge [Eguchi & Shen, 2012], y existen experiencias de vínculo de la plataforma con espacios curriculares [Hughes, 2016].

También cabe destacar la propuesta de S-Educ, un trabajo similar a la presente tesis, dado que desarrolla su propio espacio de simulación, acompañado de un conjunto de actividades para el aula, y un estudio de impacto en escuelas de Brasil [Fernandes, 2013].

Asimismo, [Hughes, Shimizu, et al., 2019] realiza una revisión de diferentes simuladores de rescate para educación, considerando requerimientos similares a los definidos en este proyecto de investigación.

Con relación al traslado de servidores de los simuladores a la nube, en [Cervera et al., 2017] se presenta un desarrollo en este sentido, que finalmente se tradujo en la creación del sitio The Construct [Learn Robotics from Zero; Robotics & ROS Online Courses, 2020]. Allí se ofrecen diversos cursos de robótica sobre simuladores con estas características.

Con relación a la metodología utilizada para la realización de esta investigación, podemos dividir el análisis en dos. Por un lado, la que se seleccionó para llevar a cabo la plataforma, y por el otro la usada para determinar la efectividad del uso del recurso didáctico en relación con los laboratorios físicos.

Con relación al estudio del impacto del uso de simuladores y laboratorios virtuales en las aulas, [Major, 2014] analiza su efectividad para el aprendizaje en programación. En [Hughes, 2016] se presenta una experiencia realizada con CoSpace en 500 escuelas durante 3 años. Basados en la misma herramienta, en [Eguchi & Shen, 2012] se realiza un estudio entre 78 participantes de la Robocup 2011. En [Casañ Núñez & Cervera, 2018] se analiza el impacto de una herramienta creada en el marco de la iniciativa "The Robot Programming Network", aunque no es un ambiente físico en 3D como el del presente trabajo. Junto con el desarrollo del simulador, en [Fernandes, 2013] se realiza un experimento con 60 usuarios entre profesores, estudiantes y adultos sin conocimientos en robótica. Finalmente, en [Guyot et al., 2011] se desarrolla una propuesta curricular sobre Webots, que es evaluada en 64 estudiantes de escuela media y en la universidad donde se llevó a cabo la investigación.

4. Grado de innovación de la propuesta

La propuesta más innovadora de este trabajo es la de proporcionar un framework que permite combinar en una única plataforma lo que hasta ahora sólo se encontraba de manera parcial en las propuestas anteriores del mismo tipo. Estas características son:

a) Integración de actividades de aula para nivel primario y secundario en la misma plataforma: una interfaz que combine las secuencias didácticas junto con el simulador facilita la tarea del docente y el estudiante. Esta integración la podemos encontrar, implementada de otra manera a la de esta tesis, en S-Educ [Fernandes, 2013] y en la herramienta Robotbenchmark [robotbenchmark, 2020].

b) Simulador 3D con física y de uso sencillo: simuladores como Webots, Gazebo y CoppeliaSim (V-REP) tienen una muy buena representación 3D con física. Sin embargo, no poseen una capa que aísle la complejidad inherente a la riqueza de estos simuladores.

c) Libre, gratuito y de código abierto: la gratuidad permite que el alcance de la herramienta llegue a los que habitualmente no podrían adquirir kits de robótica física. Además, el código abierto abre la oportunidad de trabajos futuros a la comunidad académica.

d) Diferentes tipos de robots y con posibilidad de modificar sensores y actuadores: para acercar la plataforma a los kits del mundo físico, debería tener la posibilidad de ofrecer componentes mecánicos y electrónicos para la construcción del robot, o por lo menos facilitar la importación de construcciones 3D. Esto aumenta la complejidad de la herramienta, esencialmente en los aspectos de detección de colisiones. En el presente proyecto se renunció a esta característica, pero se ofrece un set de robots y la activación o no de diferentes sensores y actuadores. De esta manera, el estudiante debe analizar los requerimientos de los problemas para definir la arquitectura del robot necesaria para su solución.

e) Ejecución en la nube: trasladar el problema de requerimientos a un servidor, ofreciendo acceso al simulador mediante un browser, permite que estudiantes y docentes de todo el mundo puedan acceder al recurso sin necesidad de equipamientos de alto costo. Sobre este mismo principio se construyó Robot Programming Network [Núñez & Mateu, 2015], Constructsim [Cervera et al., 2017] y RobotBenchmark [robotbenchmark, 2020].

f) Concurrencia de robots sobre un mismo escenario: ciertos desafíos de competencia o colaborativos exigen la presencia de más de un robot. Por otro lado, esta característica presenta desafíos de análisis y programación distintos a los ambientes estáticos, dado que el contexto en el que el robot opera cambia permanentemente y de forma impredecible. Los simuladores de base mencionados en el punto b) tienen esta posibilidad. S-Educ [Fernandes, 2013] y USARSim [Carpin et al., 2007] también permiten escenarios con múltiples robots.

g) Programación visual y textual: Las herramientas visuales de programación son de gran utilidad para la introducción de conceptos de pensamiento computacional en los estudiantes de primaria [Sáez-López et al., 2016]. Además, son más motivadoras que las textuales [Tsukamoto et al., 2016]. Al mismo tiempo, los estudiantes perciben que la programación visual es menos poderosa y auténtica que la basada en texto [Weintrop & Wilensky, 2015], además de que la industria utiliza esta última forma de programación. Por este motivo, tener un lenguaje de programación visual que genere el código en texto, al mismo tiempo que pueda programarse completamente en modo textual, permite la combinación de las mejores características de los dos paradigmas.

A continuación, presentamos un cuadro comparativo con las propuestas similares ya existentes, tomando como categorías de comparación las que acabamos de mencionar.

Tabla 1. Comparación entre plataformas de robótica simulada

	Framework propuesto	Virtual Robotics Toolkit	CoderZ	Webots	Gazebo	S-Educ	Robotbenchmark	CoppeliaSim	Eyesim VR
Gratuito	x			x	x	x	x	x	x
Código abierto	x			x	x	?	x	x	
Uso sencillo	x	x	x			x	x		
Bajos requerimientos	x		x						
Orientado a educación	x	x	x			x	x		x
Integración de actividades didácticas	x		x			x	x		
Diferentes robots	x	x	x	x	x		x	x	
Modificación de actuadores y sensor	x			x	x	x		x	
Ejecución en la nube	x		x	x	x		x	x	
Concurrencia de robots	x	x		x	x	x		x	x
Programación visual	x		x	x	x			x	
Programación textual	x		x	x	x	x	x	x	x

5. Esbozo de la metodología y resultados obtenidos hasta la fecha

La metodología seleccionada para el estudio consiste en los siguientes pasos:

a) Desarrollo de un mapeo sistemático para el estado del arte.
b) Selección de motor de física 3D para la elaboración del framework.
c) Construcción de ambientes de simulación en el motor seleccionado.
d) Ensamblaje con el entorno de programación visual y textual.
e) Montaje de la plataforma en servidores.
f) Testeo y evaluación con grupos experimentales y de control.

El mapeo sistemático ya fue realizado, obteniendo información sobre los autores, instituciones, congresos y journals más involucrados con la temática, y una lista de experiencias de robótica con simuladores en diversos niveles educativos con sus resultados y conclusiones. También se analizaron los diversos motores físicos utilizados en educación para la robótica simulada.

A partir de este estudio, y experimentando con los diferentes motores mencionados, se seleccionó a Webots como base para el desarrollo del framework. En colaboración con los institutos de educación técnica, se elaboró un simulador de Sumo robótico en Webots, y adaptamos otro de fútbol. Con ellos organizamos campeonatos virtuales locales y latinoamericanos, analizando mediante encuestas las ventajas y desventajas que encontraron los participantes en relación con la robótica física.

Actualmente se están ampliando los ambientes de simulación para una curva de aprendizaje más suave, trasladando a la virtualidad desafíos clásicos de la robótica educativa.

6. Trabajo futuro

En el primer semestre de 2023, se realizará el ensamble con el entorno de programación visual y textual ya desarrollado. Al mismo tiempo, se comenzará la experiencia en servidores, y el desarrollo de la interfaz web que permita la operación del ambiente de simulación. En forma paralela, se plantearán las características y metodología del estudio de campo que permitirá la comparación entre los logros obtenidos con el uso del simulador desarrollado en comparación con los materiales tradicionales.

En el segundo semestre de 2023 y el primer semestre de 2024 se llevará a cabo dicho estudio de campo con estudiantes de secundaria. Para ello, se dictará un curso cuyo objetivo es que aprendan conceptos básicos de robótica y programación de robots. Durante el estudio, el grupo experimental trabajará con la plataforma desarrollada, mientras que el grupo de control utilizará kits educativos de robótica física.

7. Referencias

Benitti, F. B. V., & Spolaôr, N. (2017). How Have Robots Supported STEM Teaching? En M. S. Khine (Ed.), *Robotics in STEM Education: Redesigning the Learning Experience* (pp. 103–129). Springer International Publishing. https://doi.org/10.1007/978-3-319-57786-9_5

Casañ Núñez, G. A., & Cervera, E. (2018). *The Experience of the Robot Programming Network Initiative*.

Cervera, E., Casañ, G., & Tellez, R. (2017). Cloud Simulations for RoboCup. *Robot World Cup*, 180–189.

Eguchi, A., & Shen, J. (2012). Student learning experience through CoSpace educational robotics. *Society for Information Technology & Teacher Education International Conference*, 19–24.

Fagin, B. S., & Merkle, L. (2002). Quantitative analysis of the effects of robots on introductory Computer Science education. *Journal on Educational Resources in Computing*, *2*(4), 2–es. https://doi.org/10.1145/949257.949259

Fernandes, C. da C. (2013). *S-Educ: Um Simulador de Ambiente de Robótica Educacional em Plataforma Virtual*. https://repositorio.ufrn.br/jspui/handle/123456789/15464

García-Peñalvo, F. J., Conde, M. Á., Gonçalves, J., & Lima, J. (2019). Computational thinking and robotics in education. *Proceedings of the Seventh International Conference on Technological Ecosystems for Enhancing Multiculturality*, 2–5.

Guyot, L., Heiniger, N., Michel, O., & Rohrer, F. (2011). Teaching robotics with an open curriculum based on the e-puck robot, simulations and competitions. *Proceedings of the 2nd International Conference on Robotics in Education. Vienna, Austria.*

Hughes, J. (2016). Robotic rescue simulation for computing teaching in the UK: A case study. *2016 IEEE Global Engineering Education Conference (EDUCON)*, 1051–

1055.

Hughes, J., Aghababa, F. P., Kabiri, A., Shimizu, M., & Visser, A. (2019). *A proposal on more advanced Robot Rescue Simulation challenges for Robotics Education⋆.*

Hughes, J., Shimizu, M., & Visser, A. (2019). A review of robot rescue simulation platforms for robotics education. *Robot World Cup*, 86–98.

Learn Robotics from Zero; Robotics & ROS Online Courses. (2020). The Construct. https://www.theconstructsim.com/

Lepuschitz, W., Merdan, M., Koppensteiner, G., Balogh, R., & Obdržálek, D. (2018). *Robotics in Education: Methods and Applications for Teaching and Learning* (Vol. 829). Springer.

Major, L. (2014). *An empirical investigation into the effectiveness of a robot simulator as a tool to support the learning of introductory programming.* [PhD Thesis]. Keele University.

Merdan, M., Lepuschitz, W., Koppensteiner, G., & Balogh, R. (2016). *Robotics in education: Research and practices for robotics in STEM education* (Vol. 457). Springer.

Miller, D. P., & Nourbakhsh, I. (2016). Robotics for education. En *Springer handbook of robotics* (pp. 2115–2134). Springer.

Núñez, G. A. C., & Mateu, E. C. (2015). RPN: Aprendizaje de la programación de robots mediante bloques en un entorno 3D. *ReVisión*, *8*(3), 8.

Reich-Stiebert, N., & Eyssel, F. (2016). Robots in the classroom: What teachers think about teaching and learning with education robots. *International Conference on Social Robotics*, 671–680.

Robotbenchmark. (2020). https://robotbenchmark.net/

Sáez-López, J.-M., Román-González, M., & Vázquez-Cano, E. (2016). Visual programming languages integrated across the curriculum in elementary school: A two year case study using "Scratch" in five schools. *Computers & Education*, *97*, 129–141.

Theofanellis, T., Voulgari, E., & Tsolakis, S. (2020). Educational Robotics and Computational Thinking Development. En *Handbook of Research on Tools for Teaching Computational Thinking in P-12 Education* (pp. 306–334). IGI Global.

Tsukamoto, H., Takemura, Y., Oomori, Y., Ikeda, I., Nagumo, H., Monden, A., & Matsumoto, K. (2016). Textual vs. Visual programming languages in programming education for primary schoolchildren. *2016 IEEE Frontiers in Education Conference (FIE)*, 1–7.

Weintrop, D., & Wilensky, U. (2015). To block or not to block, that is the question: Students' perceptions of blocks-based programming. *Proceedings of the 14th international conference on interaction design and children*, 199–208.

CollaboraTheories: Construção Colaborativa de Teorias Baseadas em Evidências em Engenharia de Software

Anrafel Fernandes Pereira [1,2]

[1] Departamento de Informática – Pontifícia Universidade Católica do Rio de Janeiro (PUC-Rio)

[2] Coordenação de Ensino Digital – Universidade de Vassouras (UniVassouras)

anrafel.fernandes@gmail.com

Abstract. *This article presents an ongoing doctoral research that aims to develop an approach to support the collaborative construction, by actors from industry and academia, of theories based on evidence in Software Engineering. The research methods devised for this work include conducting a literature review, preparing a proposal for a preliminary solution, feasibility and observational studies, and applying case studies in real contexts involving these actors. It is expected that this study can facilitate the collaborative construction of new theories based on evidence for the area of Software Engineering, involving and bringing benefits to industry and academia.*

Resumo. *Este artigo apresenta uma pesquisa de doutorado em andamento que objetiva elaborar uma abordagem para apoiar a construção colaborativa, por atores da indústria e da academia, de teorias baseadas em evidências em Engenharia de Software. Os métodos de pesquisa pensados para este trabalho incluem a realização de uma revisão da literatura, a elaboração de uma proposta de solução preliminar, estudos de viabilidade e observacionais e ainda a aplicação de estudos de casos em contextos reais envolvendo esses atores. Espera-se que este estudo possa facilitar a construção colaborativa de novas teorias baseadas em evidências para a área de Engenharia de Software, envolvendo e trazendo benefícios para a indústria e a academia.*

1. Introdução

A busca por evidências científicas na área de Engenharia de Software (ES) não é novidade, visto o crescente interesse e esforço da comunidade nesta direção [Dos Santos et al. 2008]. Cada vez mais, pesquisadores da área de ES, tem buscado abordagens que apoiem que o conhecimento científico produzido possa orientar o desenvolvimento de novos estudos e ainda, apoiar decisões tanto na academia quanto na indústria [Kitchenham et al. 2004]. Entretanto, aproximar academia e indústria não é uma atividade trivial.

A colaboração entre estes atores muitas das vezes é prejudicada por diversos fatores. Para este trabalho destacamos alguns, tais como: (i) a dificuldade do uso de linguagens técnicas presentes em estudos e publicações realizadas pela academia; (ii) a dificuldade de transposição do conhecimento gerado pela academia para a indústria de software; (iii) a dificuldade de acesso para a indústria aos artigos, bases de conhecimentos científicos; e (iv) a falta de alinhamento entre os interesses de colaboração por parte da academia e da indústria [Garousi et al., 2016], [Ribeiro e Travassos, 2022].

De maneira geral, a indústria não é vista e não se vê como parte integrante do processo de geração do conhecimento científico, embora esse aspecto venha mudando ao longo dos anos. Em Garousi et al. (2016), os autores apresentam algumas evidências disso, tais como, o crescente número de estudos envolvendo a colaboração entre a indústria e a academia, além do número crescente de *workshops* e painéis com participação da indústria organizados em conferências internacionais da área de ES.

No trabalho de Sjøberg et al. (2008), os autores corroboram a importância da qualidade e da relevância de estudos científicos para a indústria, e apresentam uma discussão sobre o foco na construção de teorias em Engenharia de Software e também na síntese dessas evidências. Os fundamentos providos a partir da construção de teorias podem levar a tecnologia a novos patamares, apoiando times e organizações a entregarem software melhores [Jacobson et al., 2019]. Além disso, as teorias podem gerar oportunidades de apoiarem de fato a indústria, em face a mudanças de requisitos e tecnologias utilizadas, por exemplo [NG, 2015]; [Sjøberg et al. 2008].

Conforme pode ser percebido na literatura, em engenharia de software, há relativamente pouco foco em teorias. Em particular, há pouco uso e desenvolvimento de teorias de base empírica [Hannay et al. 2007], [NG, 2014]. Buscando minimizar os problemas apresentados acima, este estudo propõe o desenvolvimento de uma abordagem denominada *CollaboraTheories*. Para isso, a proposta central é oferecer aos atores envolvidos neste contexto, uma proposta de solução que possa incentivar e apoiar a construção colaborativa de novas teorias em ES tendo como apoio a Engenharia de Software Baseada em Evidências (ESBE). A Figura 1, adaptada de Ribeiro e Travassos (2022), retrata o contexto no qual a abordagem proposta está inserida. Nela é possível perceber que geralmente o conhecimento gerado pela academia é compartilhado em repositórios específicos e com termos e linguagens científicos, dificultando que a indústria vá ao encontro destes artefatos. O mesmo cenário se repete na indústria. Geralmente, o conhecimento prático que é gerado, quando disponibilizado, é feito em bases não científicas ou meios de interesse da indústria, que normalmente não são creditados pela academia. Aumentando ainda mais esse *gap* de colaboração entre ambos os atores.

A abordagem apresentada neste estudo, procura minimizar esse *gap* através de uma proposta que apoia a colaboração entre a indústria e a academia para a construção de novas teorias baseadas em evidências em ES e comunica-las de maneira mais efetiva para a prática. Entende-se por evidências, estudos e experiências compartilhadas e disponibilizadas nas bases científicas e de experiências apresentadas na Figura 1. Como forma de comunicação das teorias geradas a partir da colaboração, espera-se entregar uma visão sucinta da teoria, junto com estudos secundários que sintetizam as evidências empíricas que a sustentam. Tudo isso de maneira visual e mais objetiva para a prática da área de ES. Em *https://anrafel.github.io* é possível obter mais informações sobre como a abordagem está sendo idealizada neste estudo.

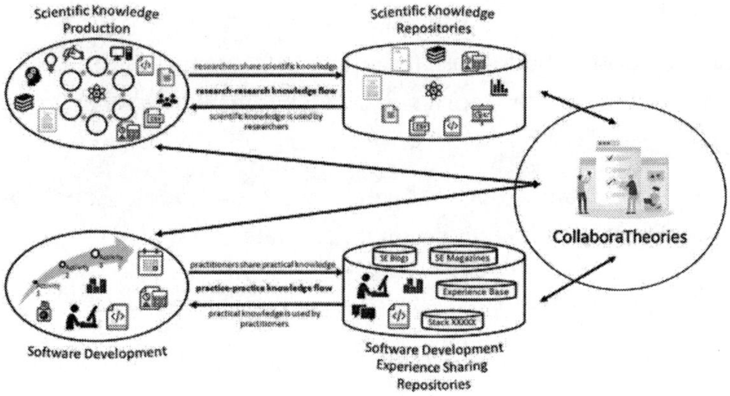

Figura 1. Contexto da Abordagem *CollaboraTheories* (adaptada de Ribeiro e Travassos, 2022)

A Figura 2 ilustra uma visão geral do cenário que envolve a abordagem *CollaboraTheories*. A figura mostra que as teorias podem ser utilizadas para apoiar tanto a academia quanto a indústria. Através dela, fica clara a proposta deste estudo de estimular que a academia e a indústria possam colaborar de maneira que novas teorias para a área de ES possam ser construídas e disponibilizadas, retroalimentando todo o ecossistema.

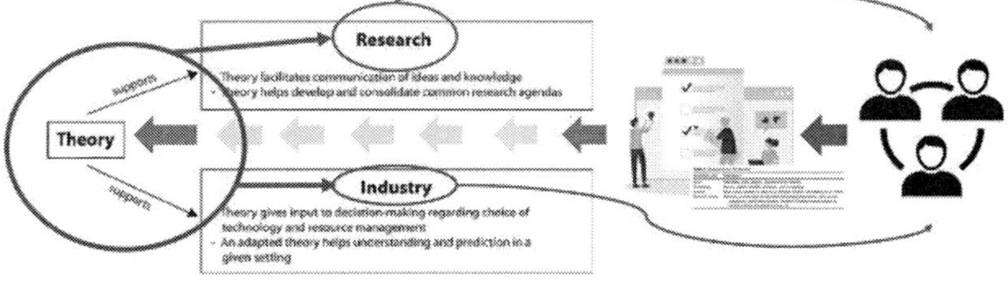

Figura 2. Visão Geral da *CollaboraTheories* (adaptada de Sjøberg et al., 2008)

Vale ressaltar que esta tese se encontra em fase inicial. Entretanto, já é possível compreender sua possível relevância e contribuição para área de ES. Na Seção 2 os objetivos deste estudo são apresentados e algumas questões que se esperam responder são levantadas. A Seção 3 apresenta alguns trabalhos relacionados que são considerados relevantes e que estão servindo como fundamentação para o desenvolvimento desta tese. A Seção 4 mostra a metodologia desenhada para a proposta e em seguida, os resultados iniciais obtidos. Por fim, na Seção 5, as considerações finais são apresentadas.

2. Objetivos

O objetivo principal deste estudo é apoiar a construção colaborativa, por atores da indústria e da academia, de teorias baseadas em evidências em Engenharia de Software (ES), procurando ainda, comunicar melhor os resultados gerados a partir da atividade realizada. Para alcançar este objetivo, esperamos responder as seguintes questões de pesquisa:

Questão 1: Como podemos apoiar a construção colaborativa, por atores da indústria e da academia, de teorias baseadas em evidências em Engenharia de Software (ES)?

Questão 2: Como comunicar os resultados gerados através da *CollaboraTheories* para a indústria de maneira mais efetiva?

3. Trabalhos Relacionados

Nesta seção são apresentados alguns trabalhos relacionados ao tema desta pesquisa.

No trabalho Sjøberg et al. (2008), os autores discutem como, na área de ES, há pouco foco e uso de teorias, especificamente no desenvolvimento de teorias com base empírica. Os autores ressaltam ainda que em outras áreas das ciências a construção de teorias é o principal método de aquisição e acúmulo de conhecimento. Para isso, apresentam uma estrutura inicial para descrever teorias de ES, e orientar sobre como construir e usar essas teorias para apoiar tanto a pesquisa quanto a prática em ES, destacando oportunidades que as teorias podem trazer para a área.

Em Garousi et al. (2016), os autores descrevem sobre os desafios e as melhores práticas que podem ser utilizadas para apoiar a colaboração entre a indústria de software e academia de ES, ressaltando que ambos pertencem a grandes e importantes comunidades. Para isso, através de uma Revisão Sistemática da Literatura (RSL), os autores identificam os principais desafios para evitar riscos à colaboração e evidenciam as melhores práticas para auxiliar esses atores na realização de projetos colaborativos.

O trabalho de Storey et al. (2017) apresenta um *template* visual para servir com uma lente para apoiar e promover a comunicação do Design Science Research (DSR) em ES. Embora este estudo esteja em um contexto diferente, pretende-se explorar e validar a oportunidade de aplicar e/ou adaptar o *template* apresentado pelos autores para promover a comunicação das teorias construídas pela *CollaboraTheories* para os atores envolvidos no contexto da abordagem.

Em Cartaxo et al. (2016), os autores mostram oportunidades de transferência de conhecimentos de estudos secundários, tais como revisões sistemáticas da literatura para a indústria, a partir de *Evidence Briefing*. Este estudo é interessante e segue alinhado com este trabalho, pois mostra que há o interesse em investigar novas maneiras e oportunidades de transferência de conhecimento da academia para a indústria.

Os trabalhos apresentados acima abordam a construção de teorias, a colaboração entre indústria e academia e formas de comunicar resultados científicos para a indústria. Dada a proximidade com os objetivos desta pesquisa, acreditamos que eles podem ajudar a subsidiar a proposta de solução.

4. Métodos de Pesquisa

A metodologia de pesquisa elaborada para este estudo está baseada no paradigma Design Science Research [Wieringa, 2014], [Engström et al. 2020], e é apresentada a seguir: "***Melhorar*** a construção de teorias em Engenharia de Software ***por*** meio da *CollaboraTheories* (abordagem projetada nesse trabalho) ***que satisfaça*** as premissas para uma boa colaboração entre indústria e a academia [Garousi et al., 2016], ***para*** gerar novas teorias baseadas em evidências em ES que sejam úteis e aplicáveis, apoiando concretamente as necessidades da indústria."

Para isso, como primeiro passo para este estudo, foi realizada uma revisão de abordagens que têm sido utilizadas para construir teorias em Engenharia de Software. O trabalho de Sjøberg et al. (2008) nos auxiliou a entender melhor o assunto, identificar as principais abordagens e ainda, as oportunidades que a construção de teorias traz para a área de ES. No trabalho de Hannay et al. (2007), uma Revisão Sistemática da Literatura (RSL) é apresentada com o propósito de discutir o uso de teorias em ES. Através desta RSL foi possível realizar uma imersão no tema e conhecer teorias que foram e têm sido propostas para a ES, além de nos permitir encontrar evidências que mostram a relevância deste tema para a área. Espera-se no futuro realizar uma atualização desta RSL como oportunidade de contribuição para a comunidade nessa temática. O trabalho de Sousa et al. (2018) apresenta um exemplo prático de construção de uma teoria de ES a partir dos resultados obtidos de estudos de casos.

A partir dos passos anteriores, e atendendo a DSR, a proposta começou a ser projetada. A *CollaboraTheories* foi desenhada para ser uma abordagem que, em essência, envolve o desenvolvimento de um workshop colaborativo, trazendo atores da indústria e da academia, visando alinhar o entendimento das suas necessidades e interesses para a construção de novas teorias baseadas em evidências em ES (ver mais em: *https://anrafel.github.io*). A primeira fase da *CollaboraTheories* envolve a aplicação de um *template* que possa apoiar a concepção conjunta de teorias de Engenharia de Software a serem investigadas, a partir da necessidade dos atores da indústria e o alinhamento com atores da academia, em um *workshop* colaborativo.

Este método contempla delinear uma versão preliminar da teoria, envolvendo a identificação dos construtos, que podem ser entendidos como as entidades da teoria, a definição das proposições, as quais estabelecem as relações que descrevem como os construtos interagem, destacando ainda a explicação do porquê se acredita que as relações são verdadeiras, o escopo da teoria, englobando onde, quando e a quem a teoria se aplica, entre outros pontos relevantes a serem considerados. Após a concepção conjunta da teoria preliminar, a segunda fase da *CollaboraTheories* envolve promover a colaboração através de uma cocriação ágil entre a indústria e a academia para o levantamento de evidências e refinamento da teoria construída. Neste momento estamos amadurecendo a abordagem, detalhando, por exemplo, uso e/ou aplicação de *sprints*, definição das melhores maneiras para representação dos conhecimentos gerados a partir dessa colaboração, entre outros pontos.

No trabalho de Shull et al. (2001), os autores mostram um fluxo para orientar a avaliação de tecnologias na área de ES, facilitando levá-las da fase conceitual até a transferência para a indústria. A metodologia proposta pelos autores apresenta algumas questões importantes de serem abordadas, além de orientar os tipos de estudos que melhor abordam essas questões. Baseado neste trabalho, planeja-se primeiro realizar um estudo de viabilidade da *CollaboraTheories*, em seguida um estudo observacional, e posteriormente aplicar estudos de caso. Para a aplicação do estudo de caso estamos levando em consideração aplica-lo em um contexto real, controlado na academia e depois em um contexto de uso na indústria. Ainda estamos definindo os objetivos mais detalhados destes estudos e o foco de qualidade para as avaliações.

5. Estágio Atual

Este trabalho é referente ao desenvolvimento de uma tese de doutorado que se encontra em fase inicial. Entretanto, algumas atividades já foram desenvolvidas como oportunidade de analisar a viabilidade da proposta da tese. Na Tabela 1 são descritas algumas atividades já realizadas.

Tabela 1. Atividades Realizadas.

	Atividades
Imersão no Tema	(i) Investigação sobre os tipos de abordagens para a construção de teorias em ES; (ii) investigação sobre as oportunidades e desafios do uso de teorias em ES; e (iii) identificação de desafios e oportunidades que podem ser geradas ao promover a colaboração entre a indústria e a academia.
Solução	(i) identificação de requisitos para a proposta de solução; (ii) Busca de técnicas, ferramentas e artefatos que possam ser relacionados com a abordagem deste estudo para alcançar os objetivos propostos; e (iii) Prototipação exploratória de propostas de solução para a abordagem *CollaboraTheories*, envolvendo a quebra da abordagem em uma fase de concepção (workshop colaborativo) e uma de cocriação ágil (levantamento de evidências e refinamento).

Validação	(i) Preparação de um estudo de viabilidade da *CollaboraTheories*, e partir dos resultados obtidos avançar com novos estudos que corroborem e tragam a luz novas evidências dos benefícios da abordagem proposta.
Publicação	(i) Preparação deste primeiro artigo e submissão para o Simpósio de Doutorado do CIbSE como oportunidade de obter feedbacks que possam contribuir para o avanço deste estudo e gerar contribuições significativas para a área de ES a serem publicadas em fóruns científicos relacionados com engenharia de software experimental.

Seguimos trabalhando no refinamento de algumas atividades como oportunidade de realiza-las e aplica-las em breve. Entretanto, já é possível compreender, mesmo que de maneira inicial, a possível relevância e contribuição que este estudo pode apresentar para área de ES.

6. Considerações Finais

Este estudo apresenta uma pesquisa de doutorado em fase inicial, cujo objetivo principal é promover a colaboração e aproximação da indústria e da academia para a construção de novas teorias de relevância prática e baseadas em evidências em Engenharia de Software. A abordagem proposta, *CollaboraTheories,* ainda está em fase inicial e precisa ser avaliada e aprimorada a partir de estudos experimentais.

Entre as principais contribuições esperadas desta tese, podemos destacar a *CollaboraTheories* para a construção de novas teorias baseadas em evidências para área de ES, através da colaboração entre a academia e a indústria. Espera-se que esta abordagem possa ajudar a promover a colaboração entre esses atores para construir teorias de relevância prática que promovam o uso de evidências científicas e conhecimentos obtidos de experiências industriais, muitas vezes não conhecidas por profissionais da área. Os próximos passos desta tese contemplam o detalhamento da abordagem e a definição e realização de estudos experimentais para sua avaliação e melhoria.

References

Cartaxo, B., Pinto, G., Vieira, E., and Soares, S. (2016). Evidence briefings: Towards a medium to transfer knowledge from systematic reviews to practitioners. Proceedings of the 10th ACM/IEEE ESEM.

Dos Santos, P. S. M.; Travassos, G. H. (2008). Colaboração entre academia e indústria: oportunidades para utilização da pesquisa-ação em engenharia de software. In: Workshop de Engenharia de Software Experimental (ESELAW).

Engström, E., Storey, M.A., Runeson, P., Höst, M. and Baldassarre, M.T. (2020). How software engineering research aligns with design science: a review. Empirical Software Engineering, 25(4), pp.2630-2660.

Garousi, V; Petersen, K; Ozkan, B. (2016). Challenges and best practices in industry-academia collaborations in software engineering: A systematic literature review. Information and Software Technology, v. 79, p. 106-127.

Hannay, Jo E.; Sjoberg, Dag Ik; Dyba, Tore. (2007). A systematic review of theory use in software engineering experiments. IEEE transactions on Software Engineering, v. 33, n. 2, p. 87-107.

Jacobson, I., Ng, P. W., McMahon, P. E., and Goedicke, M. (2019). The essentials of modern software engineering: free the practices from the method prisons. Morgan & Claypool.

Kitchenham B. A., Dybå T and Jørgensen M. (2004). Evidence-Based Software Engineering. In: ICSE 2004, 273-281, IEEE Computer Society Press.

NG, Pan-Wei. (2014). Theory based software engineering with the SEMAT kernel: preliminary investigation and experiences. In: Proceedings of the 3rd SEMAT Workshop on General Theories of Software Engineering. p. 13-20.

NG, Pan-Wei. (2015) Integrating software engineering theory and practice using essence: A case study. Science of Computer Programming, v. 101, p. 66-78.

Ribeiro, T.V, Travassos, G. H. (2022). Insights on Transferring Software Engineering Scientific Knowledge to Practice, Tese de Doutorado. Disponível em: https://www.cos.ufrj.br/index.php/pt-BR/publicacoes-pesquisa/details/15/3075

Sousa, L., Oliveira, A., Oizumi, W., Barbosa, S., Garcia, A., Lee, J., and Paes, R. (2018). Identifying design problems in the source code: A grounded theory. In Proceedings of the 40th international conference on software engineering (pp. 921-931).

Shull, F., Carver, J., Travassos, G. (2001). An Empirical Methodology for Introducing Software Processes, In: Proc. of the Joint European Software Engineering Conference and SIGSOFT Symposium on the Foundations of Software Engineering, pp. 288-296.

Sjøberg, D. I., Dybå, T., Anda, B. C., and Hannay, J. E. (2008). Building theories in software engineering. In: Guide to advanced empirical software engineering. Springer, London. p. 312-336.

Storey, M. A., Engstrom, E., Höst, M., Runeson, P., and Bjarnason, E. (2017). Using a visual abstract as a lens for communicating and promoting design science research in software engineering. In: 2017 ACM/IEEE International Symposium on Empirical Software Engineering and Measurement (ESEM). IEEE. p. 181-186.

Wieringa, Roel J. (2014). Design science methodology for information systems and software engineering. Springer.

Uma Abordagem de Teste de Integração com Planejamento em Inteligência Artificial

Luis Felipe de Lima[1]

[1]Programa de Pós-Graduação em Informática (PPGInf)
Departamento de Informática (DInf)
Universidade Federal do Paraná (UFPR)
Curitiba - PR - Brasil

lflima@inf.ufpr.br

Abstract. *This paper presents ongoing doctoral research that proposes an approach based on artificial intelligence (AI) planning techniques to support integration testing. AI planning is used in integration testing representations that result in testing plans indicating an order for software systems integration and testing. The approach is structured in an architecture to generate the testing plans and execute the tests from the plan information. The research method includes bibliographic reviews, feasibility studies, case studies, and experiments to evaluate the representation and approach. It is expected to reduce the effort of planning and executing the integration testing.*

Resumo. *Este artigo apresenta uma pesquisa de doutorado em andamento que propõe uma abordagem baseada em técnicas de planejamento em inteligência artificial (IA) para apoiar o teste de integração. O planejamento em IA é utilizado em representações do teste de integração que resultam em planos de teste que indicam uma ordem para integrar e testar sistemas de software. A abordagem é estruturada em uma arquitetura para gerar os planos de teste e executar o teste a partir das informações dos planos. O método de pesquisa inclui revisões bibliográficas, estudos de viabilidade, estudos de caso e experimentos de avaliação da representação e da abordagem. Espera-se contribuir com a redução do esforço do planejamento e da execução do teste de integração.*

1. Introdução

Diante do aumento da complexidade e escala dos sistemas de software, os testes tornaram-se essenciais para garantir produtos mais confiáveis, com maior qualidade e menores custos [Garousi et al. 2020]. Um teste consiste na execução de um software[1] em um ambiente controlado com a intenção de revelar defeitos [Myers 1979]. A literatura de engenharia de software (ES) [Wazlawick 2013, Sommerville 2019, Pressman and Maxim 2021] destaca que esses benefícios são alcançados com a realização dos testes em fases distintas ao longo do desenvolvimento do software.

As fases de teste se iniciam com testes individuais de cada unidade, ou módulo de programação, do software. Após o teste unitário, as unidades são integradas conforme a especificação. Nessa fase, chamada teste de integração, os testes são conduzidos à

[1]Neste trabalho, um sistema de software em teste é chamado de sistema sob teste (SST).

medida que as unidades são gradualmente integradas para revelar defeitos ocasionados pela interação entre as unidades. Com o software totalmente integrado, ocorrem testes de verificação das funcionalidades e validação com usuários [Delamaro et al. 2016].

A integração das unidades é feita geralmente conforme uma ordenação pre-definida e pode ser direcionada por estratégias como a *top-down* e a *bottom-up* [Sommerville 2019]. As estratégias de integração consideram a estrutura hierárquica de controle do software que é dividida em níveis e estabelecida pelas chamadas de operações (ou dependências) entre as unidades. A estratégia *top-down* inicia a integração com as unidades de nível de hierarquia mais alto e a *bottom-up* com unidades de nível mais baixo.

Essas características do teste de integração podem impactar a complexidade do planejamento e, consequentemente, contribuir para o aumento do esforço requerido na execução do teste. Assim, caracteriza-se a necessidade do apoio de técnicas para otimizar recursos e reduzir o esforço durante o planejamento desses testes.

As técnicas de inteligência artificial (IA) têm sido amplamente estudadas e aplicadas na ES [Mashkoor et al. 2022]. Nesse contexto, as técnicas de planejamento em IA são usadas em várias áreas da ES, como teste de segurança [Lima 2020] e alocação de requisitos [Pereira et al. 2022]. Informalmente, o planejamento em IA consiste na geração de um conjunto de ações, ou plano, para a resolução de um problema a partir de uma representação do conhecimento sobre esse problema [Russell and Norvig 2016]. Como o planejamento em IA pode ser custoso no que diz respeito a tempo e recursos, busca-se a geração de planos factíveis e não necessariamente planos ótimos [Ghallab et al. 2004].

As representações com planejamento em IA são formalizadas em linguagens formais e os planos são gerados por ferramentas chamadas planejadores. As técnicas de planejamento em IA não-clássico potencializam a expressividade da representação ao possibilitar o uso de valorações numéricas [Ghallab et al. 2004]. Esses aspectos contribuem para representar problemas configuráveis, flexíveis e com critérios.

A *Planning Domain Definition Language* (PDDL) [McDermott et al. 1998] é a linguagem-padrão em competições de planejamento em IA não-clássico. As representações em PDDL são especificadas por um modelo composto por um domínio e um problema. O domínio contém o conhecimento do problema a ser resolvido e o problema compreende uma instância com definições válidas para um problema específico. O domínio e o problema são descritos em arquivos distintos que são usados como entrada do planejador para a geração dos planos. O Metric-FF[2] [Hoffmann 2003] é um planejador geralmente utilizado para a resolução de problemas de PDDL.

Diante dessas características, o planejamento em IA permite orquestrar atividades e serviços a partir da parametrização de comandos e da definição de condições. Um teste de software, que contém uma situação inicial e objetivos bem definidos, pode ser diretamente representado como um problema de planejamento em IA. Assim, o uso do planejamento em IA no teste de software também é motivado pela possibilidade de associação entre problemas com ênfase em objetivo. [Bozic and Wotawa 2019, Lima et al. 2020]. Dessa forma, o problema de pesquisa que direciona este trabalho é como o planejamento em IA pode contribuir com o planejamento e a execução do teste de integração.

[2]Detalhes sobre o funcionamento do Metric-FF são encontrados em `https://fai.cs.uni-saarland.de/hoffmann/metric-ff.html`

Este artigo apresenta uma pesquisa de doutorado em andamento que propõe uma abordagem que busca contribuir com a redução do esforço do teste de integração usando técnicas de planejamento em IA não-clássico. Os usuários pretendidos são gerentes de teste e testadores. Espera-se que a abordagem possa ser utilizada por leigos em IA, devido a modelagem ser pré-configurada e instanciada dinamicamente. O uso da abordagem é esperado para cenários de desenvolvimento prescritivo ou ágil e com possibilidade de direcionamento para ambientes de integração contínua. Acredita-se que a abordagem não seja limitada a algum tipo de linguagem ou *framework* de desenvolvimento específicos.

O restante do artigo está estruturado nas seguintes seções: a Seção 2 apresenta os objetivos e as questões de pesquisa. A Seção 3 descreve trabalhos relacionados. A Seção 4 relata o método de pesquisa. A Seção 5 destaca os resultados preliminares. Por fim, a Seção 6 conclui o artigo e aponta as próximas etapas da pesquisa.

2. Objetivos e questões de pesquisa

Com base na contextualização apresentada, o objetivo geral desta pesquisa é:

- Propor uma abordagem baseada em técnicas de planejamento em IA não-clássico que gera planos de teste de integração que indicam uma ordem para integrar e testar sistemas de software de acordo com as estratégias *top-down* e *bottom-up*.

Para alcançar o objetivo geral, são propostos os seguintes objetivos específicos:

a) Definir uma arquitetura que associa o planejamento em IA ao teste de integração;
b) Representar características do teste de integração em linguagem de planejamento;
c) Avaliar a representação e a abordagem em estudos experimentais.

Diante desses objetivos, espera-se responder as seguintes questões de pesquisa:

- QP1. Quais são os elementos necessários para gerar planos de teste de integração com planejamento em IA?
- QP2. Quais são os benefícios da aplicação do planejamento em IA no contexto de teste de integração?

3. Trabalhos relacionados

Esta seção apresenta alguns trabalhos relacionados ao tema da presente pesquisa.

Estudos recentes de revisão bibliográfica destacam a aplicação do planejamento em IA no teste de software [Bozic and Wotawa 2019, Lima et al. 2020]. Os trabalhos mencionados nessas revisões incluem propostas para as fases de teste de unidade [Galler et al. 2010] e teste de sistema [Simos et al. 2019, Bozic et al. 2019]. Esta pesquisa se difere ao aplicar o planejamento em IA na fase de teste de integração.

Outras técnicas de IA, como algoritmos de otimização e genéticos, são usadas para apoiar o planejamento do teste de integração [Zhang et al. 2019] [Zhang et al. 2022]. Esses técnicas utilizam características dos grafos que representam os sistemas para realizar a ordenação de unidades. A presente pesquisa se baseia em planejamento em IA para gerar planos que indicam uma ordem para a integração. Nesse sentido, o principal diferencial do planejamento em IA é a possibilidade de representar mais características do ambiente de teste e adaptar a ordenação de acordo com diferentes estratégias de integração.

O trabalho [Silva and Lemos 2011] propõe uma representação com planejamento em IA que gera planos indicando uma ordem de integração e teste de componentes de sistemas auto-adaptativos. Esta pesquisa representa alguns aspectos adicionais associados ao teste, como prioridades, níveis hierárquicos e estratégias de integração.

4. Método de pesquisa

O *Design Science* [Engström et al. 2020] é um paradigma que auxilia a elaborar e apresentar soluções de pesquisas aplicadas e contribui para sumarizar, justificar, avaliar e comunicar suas contribuições, além de indicar o que se espera de sua relevância prática, rigor e inovação. O método de pesquisa é descrito nesta seção a partir dos elementos do *Design Science* apresentados na Figura 1.

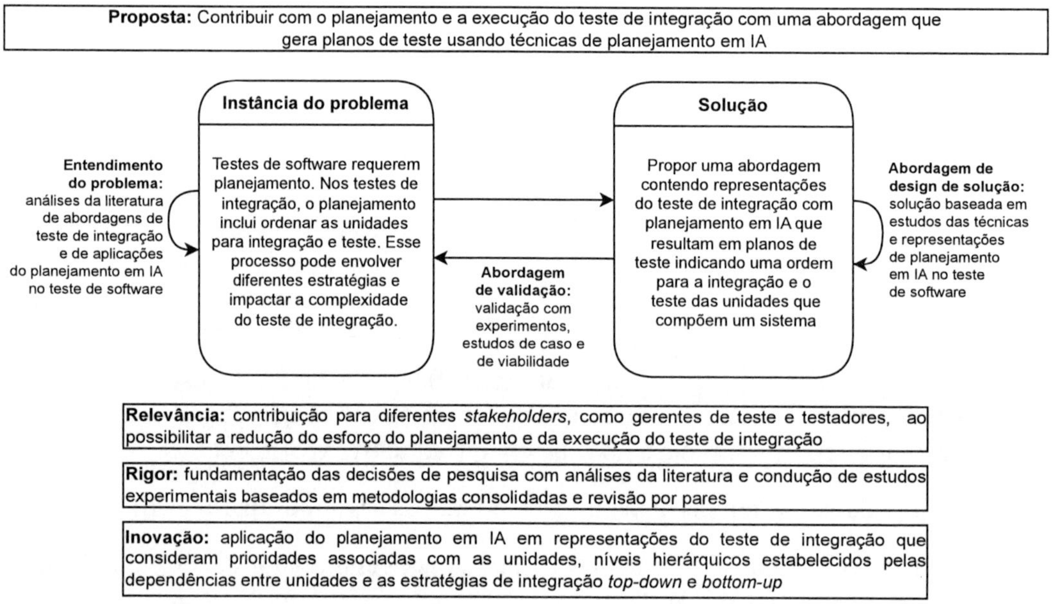

Figura 1. Abordagem proposta estruturada com o paradigma *Design Science*.

A **proposta** é referente ao objetivo geral da pesquisa apresentado na Seção 2. A **instância do problema** são aspectos do planejamento do teste de integração que motivaram o desenvolvimento da solução. O **entendimento do problema** abrange as análises da literatura conduzidas para aprofundar o embasamento teórico do escopo da pesquisa. A **abordagem de design de solução** inclui estudos que contribuíram para a definição da abordagem. Diante desses elementos, foi proposta como **solução** a abordagem usando técnicas de planejamento em IA para gerar planos de teste que auxiliam o planejamento e a execução do teste de integração. A **abordagem de validação** destaca os estudos esperados para validar a abordagem proposta.

A partir desse delineamento, a pesquisa é baseada nas seguintes atividades:

(i) Realizar revisões bibliográficas sobre o teste de integração e o planejamento em IA a fim de identificar lacunas para posicionar a pesquisa na literatura e obter contribuições para fundamentar e complementar a abordagem proposta;
(ii) Definir módulos de planejamento e execução do teste para compor uma arquitetura que que associa o teste de integração ao planejamento em IA com base em procedimentos de teoria de teste de software consolidados na literatura;

(iii) Representar o teste de integração como um problema de planejamento em IA;
(iv) Modelar o problema de planejamento em IA em PDDL;
(v) Conduzir um estudo de viabilidade com simulações de SSTs para verificar evidências da efetividade do planejamento em IA na geração dos planos a partir da representação proposta;
(vi) Realizar revisões na representação e na modelagem com base nos resultados da estudo de viabilidade;
(vii) Conduzir um estudo de caso usando especificações reais de ambientes de teste integração para instanciar a modelagem revisada e gerar planos de teste;
(viii) Implementar os componentes de software e definir as ferramentas de apoio para a arquitetura da abordagem;
(ix) Definir métricas para a medição do esforço da abordagem;
(x) Conduzir experimentos para avaliar a representação e a abordagem. Estudos experimentais podem avaliar as métricas definidas e realizar comparações com trabalhos correlatos. Estudos com usuários podem avaliar aspectos das representações como legibilidade, benefícios observados no teste como transparência e rastreabilidade, além da aplicação da abordagem na prática de desenvolvimento.

5. Resultados preliminares

Esta pesquisa foi iniciada em abril de 2020 com a realização das revisões bibliográficas (atividade i) que contribuíram para as definições da arquitetura do teste de integração (atividade ii), dos elementos contidos na representação do teste (atividade iii) e da linguagem de planejamento e do planejador considerados na atividade (iv).

Na atividade (ii) foi definida uma arquitetura para a abordagem com módulos de planejamento e execução do teste, como ilustra a Figura 2. O módulo de planejamento do teste tem como principal *stakeholder* o gerente de teste. A entrada desse módulo é um arquivo contendo informações obtidas em especificações sobre o SST. As informações desse arquivo são usadas na instanciação dinâmica dos arquivos PDDL que são encaminhadas ao planejador Metric-FF para gerar os planos de teste. O tratamento dos arquivos e a automatização do planejador são realizados por um *framework*.

O módulo de execução do teste contém mecanismos para a execução do teste baseados na teoria de teste de software de [Delamaro et al. 2016]. Para isso, o *framework* mapeia o plano de teste para um *script* que, ao ser executado pelo testador, realiza a integração das unidades e os testes no SST conforme a ordenação indicada. A abordagem prevê uma ferramenta de apoio que gera dados de teste adequados para os testes com base na especificação do SST. A saída desse módulo é um relatório de resultados do teste. A atividade (ii) é associada ao objetivo específico *a*.

Na atividade (iii) foram definidas formalizações considerando um SST representado por um conjunto U de unidades, um conjunto N de níveis hierárquicos e um conjunto P_r de prioridades. Essas formalizações incluem a descrição de como cada unidade $u_i \in U$ está organizada nos níveis $n_j \in N$ e sua respectiva associação com uma prioridade $p_{r_i} \in Pr$ de precedência de integração. Ainda, foi estabelecido como essas definições são usadas na representação das estratégias *top-down* e *bottom-up*.

Na atividade (iv), o problema de planejamento correspondente foi modelado em PDDL seguindo as definições da atividade (iii). Essas atividades contribuem com o obje-

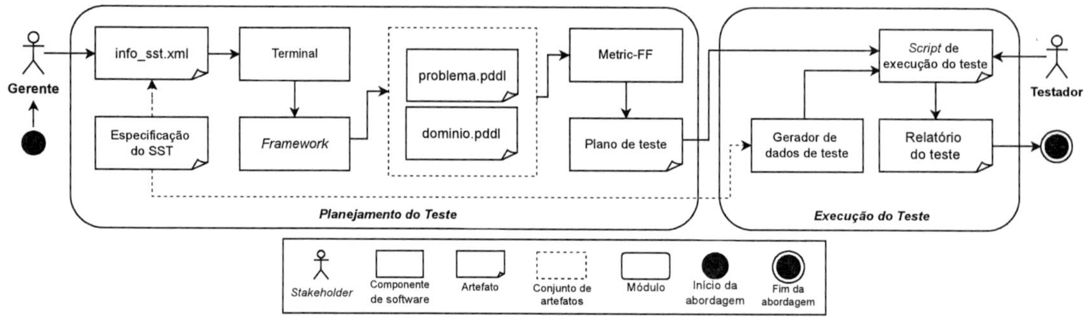

Figura 2. Visão geral da arquitetura da abordagem.

tivo específico *b*. O domínio PDDL foi ajustado para as estratégias *top-down* e *bottom-up* e contém a descrição de quatro ações. A ação **INTEGRA_UNIDADE** representa a integração das unidades, a ação **TESTA_SUBSISTEMA** indica o teste do subsistema gerado após cada integração, a ação **INCREMENTA_PRIORIDADE** realiza o incremento das prioridades e a ação **TROCA_NIVEL** realiza a troca dos níveis hierárquicos.

O problema PDDL representa um cenário de teste estabelecido pelas características do SST e da estratégia de integração. O estado inicial equivale ao momento anterior ao início do teste de integração. O estado final é alcançado após a integração de todas as unidades de U e de pelo menos uma execução do teste no SST a cada integração.

Os planos são compostos por ações que indicam a ordem de integração das unidades e a execução do teste do SST. Após cada execução do teste é indicado o incremento da prioridade. Quando todas as unidades de um determinado nível foram integradas é indicada a troca para o próximo nível. Os planos estabelecem o início da integração pelas unidades do primeiro nível para a estratégia *top-down* e pelas unidades do último nível para a estratégia *bottom-up*.

Exemplos da modelagem PDDL ajustada para as estratégias *top-down* e *bottom-up* estão disponíveis em um repositório [(*link*)]. Esses exemplos foram elaboradas durante um estudo de viabilidade (atividade v) baseado na metodologia de [Wohlin et al. 2000]. Os exemplos consideram uma simulação de SST com cinco unidades (*A, B, C, D, E*), estruturadas em três níveis (*N1, N2, N3*) e associadas a duas prioridades (*P1, P2*). O Código 1 apresenta excertos dos planos de teste gerados pelo Metric-FF para cada exemplo.

Código 1. Planos de teste gerados pelo Metric-FF.

```
Estratégia top-down                 Estratégia bottom-up

INTEGRA_UNIDADE A N1 P1             INTEGRA_UNIDADE E N3 P1
TESTA_SUBSISTEMA                    TESTA_SUBSISTEMA
INCREMENTA_PRIORIDADE               INCREMENTA_PRIORIDADE
INCREMENTA_PRIORIDADE               INTEGRA_UNIDADE D N3 P2
TROCA_NIVEL                         TESTA_SUBSISTEMA
INTEGRA_UNIDADE B N2 P1             INCREMENTA_PRIORIDADE
TESTA_SUBSISTEMA                    TROCA_NIVEL
INCREMENTA_PRIORIDADE               INTEGRA_UNIDADE B N2 P1
INTEGRA_UNIDADE C N2 P2             TESTA_SUBSISTEMA
TESTA_SUBSISTEMA                    INCREMENTA_PRIORIDADE
INCREMENTA_PRIORIDADE               INTEGRA_UNIDADE C N2 P2
```

```
TROCA_NIVEL                          TESTA_SUBSISTEMA
INTEGRA_UNIDADE E N3 P1              INCREMENTA_PRIORIDADE
TESTA_SUBSISTEMA                     TROCA_NIVEL
INCREMENTA_PRIORIDADE                INTEGRA_UNIDADE A N1 P1
INTEGRA_UNIDADE D N3 P2              TESTA_SUBSISTEMA
TESTA_SUBSISTEMA
```

O estudo de viabilidade mostrou que foi possível gerar planos de teste factíveis a partir da modelagem proposta, indicando que a representação do teste de integração com planejamento em IA foi efetiva. O estudo também destacou possíveis atualizações na representação que serão consideradas nas atividades futuras da pesquisa. A atividade (v) contribuiu para o objetivo específico *c*.

6. Considerações finais

Este artigo apresentou uma pesquisa de doutorado em andamento que objetiva contribuir com o teste de integração. A principal contribuição da pesquisa é gerar planos de teste a partir de representações com planejamento em IA. Os planos de teste são artefatos que podem ser usados por diferentes *stakeholders* para auxiliar o gerenciamento e a redução do esforço do teste de integração.

Atualmente estão sendo conduzidas as atividades (vi) e (vii) como parte do objetivo específico *b*. As próximas etapas da pesquisa são as atividades (viii), (ix) e (x) buscando atingir o objetivo específico *c*. Paralelamente, está prevista a produção de artigos com os resultados alcançados para publicação em eventos e revistas das áreas de teste de software, ES e IA para destacar o caráter multidisciplinar da pesquisa.

Agradecimentos

Este artigo foi realizado com o apoio do PPGInf-CAPES/MEC e C3SL-DInf/UFPR.

Referências

Bozic, J., Tazl, O. A., and Wotawa, F. (2019). Chatbot testing using AI planning. In *International Conference On Artificial Intelligence Testing*, pages 37–44.

Bozic, J. and Wotawa, F. (2019). Software testing: According to plan! In *International Conference on Software Testing, Verification and Validation Workshops*, pages 23–31.

Delamaro, M., Jino, M., and Maldonado, J. (2016). *Introdução ao teste de software. 2. ed.* Elsevier.

Engström, E., Storey, M.-A., Runeson, P., Höst, M., and Baldassarre, M. T. (2020). How software engineering research aligns with design science: a review. *Empirical Software Engineering*, 25(4):2630–2660.

Galler, S. J., Zehentner, C., and Wotawa, F. (2010). AIana: An AI planning system for test data generation. In *Workshop on Testing Object-Oriented Systems*, pages 1–8.

Garousi, V., Rainer, A., Lauvås Jr, P., and Arcuri, A. (2020). Software-testing education: A systematic literature mapping. *Journal of Systems and Software*, 165:110570.

Ghallab, M., Nau, D., and Traverso, P. (2004). *Automated Planning: theory and practice*. Elsevier.

Hoffmann, J. (2003). The Metric-FF planning system: translating "ignoring delete lists" to numeric state variables. *Journal of artificial intelligence research*, 20:291–341.

Lima, L. F. (2020). Teste de intrusão para aplicações web: um método com planejamento em inteligência artificial. Dissertação (Mestrado em Informática) - Programa de Pós-graduação em Informática, Universidade Federal do Paraná.

Lima, L. F., Silva, F., Grégio, A. R. A., and Peres, L. M. (2020). A systematic literature mapping of artificial intelligence planning in software testing. In *International Conference on Software Technologies*, pages 152–159.

Mashkoor, A., Menzies, T., Egyed, A., and Ramler, R. (2022). Artificial intelligence and software engineering: Are we ready? *Computer*, 55(3):24–28.

McDermott, D., Ghallab, M., Howe, A., Knoblock, C., Ram, A., Veloso, M., Weld, D., and Wilkins, D. (1998). PDDL - The Planning Domain Definition Language. *Technical Report CVC TR-98-003/DCS TR-1165, Yale Center for Computational.*

Myers, G. J. (1979). The art of software testing. *ISBN: 0-471-04328-1.*

Pereira, F. C., Neto, G. B., Lima, L. F. d., Silva, F., and Peres, L. M. (2022). A tool for software requirement allocation using artificial intelligence planning. In *2022 IEEE 30th International Requirements Engineering Conference (RE)*, pages 257–258.

Pressman, R. S. and Maxim, B. R. (2021). *Engenharia de software - 9ª edição.* AMGH. ISBN: 978-6558040101.

Russell, S. J. and Norvig, P. (2016). *Artificial intelligence: A modern approach.* Malaysia; Pearson Education Limited.

Silva, C. E. d. and Lemos, R. d. (2011). Dynamic plans for integration testing of self-adaptive software systems. In *International Symposium on Software Engineering for Adaptive and Self-managing Systems*, pages 148–157.

Simos, D. E., Bozic, J., Garn, B., Leithner, M., Duan, F., Kleine, K., Lei, Y., and Wotawa, F. (2019). Testing TLS using planning-based combinatorial methods and execution framework. *Software Quality Journal*, 27(2):703–729.

Sommerville, I. (2019). *Engenharia de software. 10ª edição.* Pearson Universidades, ISBN: 978-8543024974.

Wazlawick, R. (2013). *Engenharia de software: Conceitos e práticas*, volume 1. Elsevier Brasil.

Wohlin, C., Runeson, P., Host, M., Ohlsson, M. C., and Regnell, B. (2000). Experimentation in Software Engineering - An Introduction. *Doedrecht the Netherlands.*

Zhang, Y., Jiang, S., Ding, Y., Yuan, G., Liu, J., Lu, D., and Qian, J. (2022). Generating optimal class integration test orders using genetic algorithms. *International Journal of Software Engineering and Knowledge Engineering*, 32(06):871–892.

Zhang, Y., Jiang, S., Wang, X., Chen, R., and Zhang, M. (2019). An optimization algorithm applied to the class integration and test order problem. *Soft Computing*, 23(12):4239–4253.

Capacidad de Negocio y Marco de trabajo para mejorar proyectos basados en BizDevOps

Guillermo Fuentes-Quijada

Instituto de Tecnología y Sistemas de Información – Universidad de Castilla-La Mancha
Ciudad Real, España

gfuentes@uclm.es

Resumen. *BizDevOps es un enfoque de desarrollo de SW que extiende DevOps con un ciclo de negocio en donde incorpora stakeholders ajenos a TI. Este ciclo se centra en el alineamiento TI/Negocio para responder mejor a las necesidades de las empresas, pero, hasta ahora, no considera el reto de la agilidad. Este trabajo doctoral propone dos contribuciones para ayudar a las organizaciones a: i) adoptar BizDevOps, y ii) hacerlo garantizando el alineamiento ágil TI/Negocio. Para lo primero se propone definir una capacidad de negocio que especifique todo lo que la organización necesita para ser capaz de desarrollar SW aplicando el enfoque. Para lo segundo se propone un marco de trabajo que incluye artefactos y prácticas de arquitectura empresarial.*

1. Introducción

BizDevOps (*Business, Development and Operations*) es un enfoque para el desarrollo de software (SW) que considera tres ciclos continuos (negocio, desarrollo y operaciones) e integrados para llevar a cabo los requerimientos SW de la organización [Gruhn & Schäfer, 2015]. Este enfoque extiende a DevOps [IEEE, 2021] con un tercer ciclo con foco en el negocio [Lohrasbinasab, Acharya, & Colomo-Palacios, 2020], que busca reforzar la participación de las áreas de negocio en el desarrollo del SW para que el área de tecnologías de información (TI) proporcione respuestas mejor alineadas a las necesidades de la organización [Sanjurjo, Pedreira, Garcia, & Piattini, 2020]. A pesar de que los ciclos de desarrollo y operaciones, típicos de DevOps, han sido abordados favorablemente con agilidad [Almeida, Simões, & Lopes, 2022; Hemon, Lyonnet, Rowe, & Fitzgerald, 2020; Raj & Sinha, 2020; Snyder & Curtis, 2018], esto no es así en el ciclo de negocio. Hasta ahora, el ciclo asociado al alineamiento TI/Negocio no ha abordado el reto de la agilidad. Esto puede generar un cuello de botella en el ciclo de vida del desarrollo de SW y ocasionar que se pierda la agilidad en general, a pesar de que los ciclos asociados a DevOps sí sean ágiles. Esto es perjudicial para la organización al perderse los beneficios de la agilidad que DevOps aporta, tales como detección temprana de errores, mejoras en la comunicación del equipo, un menor consumo de recursos (tiempo, dinero) y una mejora en la calidad del software [Raj & Sinha, 2020].

Por otra parte, las organizaciones pueden adoptar el uso de la práctica de arquitecturas empresariales (AE) que sirve para facilitar y soportar el alineamiento TI/Negocio [Lankhorst, 2017]. Además de la práctica de AE, pueden adoptar el uso de las descripciones de AE que se consideran una herramienta fundamental tanto para visualizar como para proyectar el estado actual y futuro de las empresas [Moscoso-Zea, Paredes-Gualtor, & Luján-Mora, 2019], permitiendo facilitar el gobierno y gestión de las

TI y con ello conseguir el correcto alineamiento con objetivos del negocio [Lankhorst, 2017; Pérez-Castillo, Ruiz, Piattini, & Ebert, 2019]. Por consiguiente, la reciente versión 10 del framework de arquitectura empresarial TOGAF incorpora una guía para realizar y aplicar la práctica de arquitectura empresarial de forma ágil [The Open Group, 2022c]. Para ello, TOGAF reutiliza prácticas ágiles como los sprints con iteraciones cortas, que resultan útiles para obtener los primeros comentarios y resultados de las partes interesadas [The Open Group, 2022b].

Por otro lado, cuando las organizaciones cuentan con todo lo necesario para realizar alguna función y cumplir un objetivo de negocio, se dice que tienen la capacidad para cumplir ese objetivo. En este contexto nace el término de 'Capacidad de Negocio' (*business capability*), que podemos definir como la habilidad o capacidad que tiene una organización para lograr un propósito o resultado específico [Homann, 2006]. Esta capacidad de la organización puede ser definida como una combinación de personal, procesos, información y recursos que son necesarios para lograr un objetivo establecido [The Open Group, 2022a].

Teniendo presente todo lo anterior, la motivación de este trabajo doctoral es evitar el cuello de botella y facilitar que las organizaciones puedan realizar el alineamiento TI/Negocio durante el desarrollo de SW aplicando BizDevOps y, a la vez, garantizar la agilidad de forma similar a como se hace en DevOps. Para ello se proponen dos artefactos principales. En primer lugar, una capacidad de negocio para BizDevOps en la que se identifica y define todo lo necesario para llevar a cabo con éxito la práctica ágil de BizDevOps. En segundo lugar, un marco de trabajo basado en una arquitectura de referencia, que viene a ser una especie de plantilla arquitectónica para reutilizar conocimiento, donde se especifica en detalle, usando notaciones de arquitectura empresarial estandarizadas, todas esas cosas que se necesitan para hacer BizDevOps ágil.

La estructura de este documento es la siguiente, en la sección 2 se presentan los principales conceptos del trabajo doctoral. La sección 3 platea los objetivos de investigación. En la sección 4 se precisan los trabajos relacionados a este trabajo doctoral. Luego, en la sección 5 se describe la metodología de investigación en uso. Secciones 6 y 7 describen la propuesta de solución y los resultados preliminares. Finalmente, en la sección 8 se presentan las conclusiones y trabajo futuro.

2. Marco Conceptual

En esta sección se presentan los principales fundamentos empleados en el ámbito de esta investigación.

2.1 BizDevOps

BizDevOps defiende la participación activa de equipos conformados por stakeholders de las áreas de negocio, desarrollo y operaciones, en los proyectos de desarrollo de software [Gruhn & Schäfer, 2015]. Este enfoque surge como una extensión de DevOps, y busca integrar a los stakeholders del negocio [Lohrasbinasab et al., 2020]. En Gruhn and Schäfer [2015] este enfoque se justifica desde tres perspectivas, cada una de ellas asociada a uno de los ciclos a los que se vincula el concepto: i) permite a las personas de los departamentos de negocio expresar y revisar los requisitos de forma práctica y, por lo tanto, reduce la transferencia de conocimiento necesaria del negocio a TI y proporciona ciclos de retroalimentación lo más rápidos posibles (el *'Biz'* en BizDevOps); ii) permite a los departamentos de TI gobernar todo el proceso de desarrollo de aplicaciones para garantizar la alta calidad de los artefactos de software (el *'Dev'* en BizDevOps); y iii) proporciona una integración de la cadena de herramientas asociadas a la integración y despliegue de SW para permitir la mayor automatización y, por tanto, un mejor ritmo de desarrollo (el *'Ops'* en BizDevOps).

2.2 Arquitectura Empresarial

La práctica de Arquitectura Empresarial nos permite proteger el núcleo de la organización y, al mismo tiempo, disponer de una gran flexibilidad y adaptabilidad [Lankhorst, 2017]. Los aspectos útiles de la EA para los desarrolladores e investigadores de SW han sido resumidos en [Pérez-Castillo et al., 2019]. Por ejemplo, se puede utilizar como: herramienta para controlar los recursos técnicos y evitar así redundancias, para controlar y compartir conocimientos de forma modular, y, para facilitar la comunicación y entendimiento entre stakeholders diferentes. Uno de los principales estándares *de facto* empleados para la práctica de AE es el marco de trabajo TOGAF (*The Open Group Architecture Framework*) [The Open Group, 2022c]. TOGAF establece que el propósito de la AE *'es optimizar, en toda la organización, los procesos (tanto manuales como automatizados) en un entorno integrado que responda al cambio y apoye la entrega de la estrategia empresarial'*. TOGAF, en su última versión, incorpora directrices y métodos para ayudar a los responsables de arquitecturas empresariales a comprender e integrar prácticas ágiles en el establecimiento de la arquitectura inicial y en su evolución. Esto lo hace aprovechando prácticas ágiles como los sprints con iteraciones cortas, que resultan útiles para obtener los primeros comentarios y resultados de las partes interesadas. Esto permite a los arquitectos empresariales aportar valor antes y de forma iterativa e incremental, ya sea de forma planificada o emergente [The Open Group, 2022c].

2.3 Capacidad de Negocio

TOGAF define capacidad como *'una habilidad para hacer algo'* [The Open Group, 2022a], por lo tanto, una capacidad de negocio representa la habilidad de una empresa para hacer algo. Por otra parte, puede ser algo que existe en la actualidad o algo que se requiere para permitir una nueva dirección o estrategia [The Open Group, 2022a]. Una capacidad de negocio es posible gracias a la combinación de procesos, funciones, información y herramientas. Dicho esto, la especificación de una capacidad de negocio requiere establecer cuatro elementos principales: (i) *Personas*, que representan a actores, roles, stakeholders o unidades de negocio relacionadas con la capacidad de negocio; (ii) *Procesos*, los cuales son las acciones que deben poderse realizar; (iii) *Información*, instanciada por datos, conocimientos que son necesarios para la habilitación de la capacidad; y (iv) *Recursos*, que pueden representar a distintas herramientas, materiales o activos que permiten una correcta ejecución de la capacidad de negocio.

3. Objetivos de la Investigación

Esta tesis tiene como objetivo principal facilitar el gobierno y gestión de proyectos de desarrollo de software basados en BizDevOps, garantizando el alineamiento de las TI con el negocio y la agilidad, mediante la especificación de una capacidad de negocio y un marco de trabajo de arquitectura empresarial.

Los objetivos específicos identificados para lograr el anterior objetivo son los siguientes:

- Conocer estado actual de la literatura científica de BizDevOps en el contexto organizacional y la aplicación de las arquitecturas empresariales en este enfoque.
- Especificar una capacidad de negocio que permita a las organizaciones tener las competencias, técnicas y herramientas necesarias para gestionar los proyectos de desarrollo de software basados en BizDevOps.
- Definir un marco de trabajo que basado en el uso de una AE de referencia facilite la gestión y supervisión de proyectos de desarrollo de software que usen BizDevOps.
- Definir una forma de evaluación de estas propuestas con el objetivo de comprobar su utilidad y validez.
- Validar las propuestas en entornos los más reales posibles.

4. Trabajos Relacionados

No se han identificado propuestas que aborden BizDevOps junto con prácticas ágiles y uso la práctica de AE. Sin embargo, existen propuestas que abordan parte del problema de este trabajo doctoral. Primero, considerando el uso de AE en el contexto de DevOps, Hadar and Hadar [2016] describe una arquitectura de referencia para la reutilización del conocimiento. Austel et al. [2015] propone una descripción de AE que permite la integración del desarrollo en el nivel de las operaciones. En [Shahin, Nasab, & Babar, 2021] se presentan descripciones de AE para orientar el desarrollo con DevOps.

Entre las propuestas que incluyen el desarrollo de SW y el uso de AE se encuentra la de [Alzoubi & Gill, 2020]. En donde se sugiere que la AE ágil tiene efectos positivos sobre la comunicación, la finalización dentro del presupuesto, la funcionalidad y la calidad del desarrollo de software.

En el contexto del alineamiento TI/Negocio y BizDevOps, existen dos propuestas interesantes. Gruhn and Schäfer [2015] describe una propuesta para que los usuarios finales participen en la creación de aplicaciones y en [Forbrig, 2018], se propone una forma de representar el conocimiento utilizando una notación formal basada en BPM, denominada S-BPM, para su uso en entornos BizDevOps.

5. Metodología de Investigación

El método de investigación principal utilizado en este trabajo doctoral es DSR (*Design Science Research*) [Hevner & Chatterjee, 2010], el cual se combinará con otros si fuera necesario para alguna actividad o tarea. DSR es un enfoque de investigación que se centra en el diseño, desarrollo y evaluación de soluciones. DSR utiliza un proceso científico para identificar problemas, desarrollar nuevos artefactos, evaluar su rendimiento y contribuir al conocimiento [Hevner & Chatterjee, 2010]. DSR se define como una actividad de investigación con el objetivo de construir nuevos artefactos para así poder resolver problemas o lograr mejoras a soluciones ya existentes.

En este trabajo doctoral se aplicarán dos ciclos de DSR para la construcción del artefacto que define la capacidad de negocio y el artefacto que especifica un marco de trabajo para gobernar proyectos SW con BizDevOps (ver Figura 1). Estos ciclos implican diseñar, construir y evaluar los artefactos.

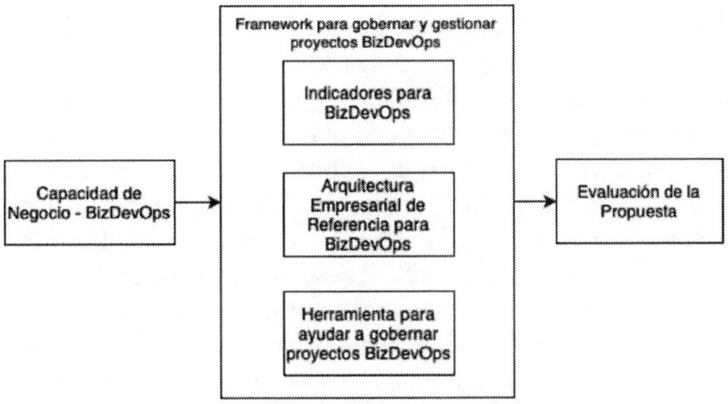

Figura 1. Etapas de la propuesta de solución.

Con el fin de completar el primer objetivo de investigación y, además, establecer de manera inicial la relevancia y rigor del trabajo doctoral, se realizó una revisión de la literatura basada en el método Mapeo Sistemático de la Literatura. El objetivo de este método fue proporcionar una visión general de un tema de interés e identificar la cantidad, el tipo de investigación y los resultados disponibles sobre ese tema [Petersen, Vakkalanka, & Kuzniarz, 2015]. Este método de revisión de la literatura tiene la característica de ser de naturaleza cuantitativa. Por ello, es habitual calcular la frecuencia de las publicaciones a lo largo del tiempo para detectar tendencias o clasificar los artículos encontrados según un esquema de clasificación predefinido [Petersen et al., 2015].

6. Propuesta de Solución

La propuesta de este trabajo doctoral sólo se enfoca en el tercer ciclo incorporado por BizDevOps, siendo una mejora incremental a DevOps. Teniendo en cuenta las directrices de la metodología DSR, este trabajo contempla dos etapas de diseño y una posterior evaluación de las propuestas. Las etapas de la propuesta de solución están representadas en la Figura 1 y cada etapa de diseño tendrá como resultado un artefacto.

La primera etapa tiene como objetivo especificar una capacidad de negocio que permita a las organizaciones desarrollar software utilizando el enfoque de BizDevOps y, al mismo tiempo, ser capaces de realizar el alineamiento TI/Negocio de manera ágil. En particular, esta capacidad de negocio se encargará de establecer lo necesario para ir desde un desarrollo de software con DevOps a no usando el enfoque BizDevOps. La segunda etapa tiene como objetivo diseñar un marco de trabajo para gobernar y gestionar proyectos BizDevOps, teniendo en cuenta la capacidad de negocio adquirida por la organización. Este marco de trabajo estará compuesto por tres elementos o sub-artefactos: a) un catálogo de indicadores (una especie de KPIs, *key performance indicators*) para evaluar el desarrollo adecuado de los proyectos con BizDevOps, especialmente en las vertientes de alineamiento TI/negocio y de agilidad; b) una arquitectura de referencia para BizDevOps, que viene a ser una especie de plantilla arquitectónica para reutilizar conocimiento, donde se especifica en detalle, usando notaciones de arquitectura empresarial estandarizadas, todas esas cosas que se necesitan tener y hacer para hacer BizDevOps con alineamiento ágil con el negocio; y c) una herramienta software para facilitar la gestión y el gobierno de estos proyectos, que sirva de guía y para la toma de decisiones en base a los indicadores y la arquitectura de referencia.

Uno de los principales desafíos del trabajo doctoral está relacionado con la evaluación. Para evaluar la completitud, validez, carencias y mejoras posibles de la propuesta se ha pensado usar los métodos de panel de expertos y caso de estudio. El método de caso de estudio es el que presenta mayores limitaciones debido a la alta dificultad que implica encontrar una organización que desarrolle software con DevOps y quiera desarrollar software con BizDevOps, y, además, tenga experiencia real en la práctica de arquitectura empresarial. A lo último se añade que casi todas las organizaciones que llevan a cabo esta práctica, salvo unos pocos entes públicos de ciertos países, consideran su arquitectura empresarial como algo confidencial y valioso para su competitividad y, por lo tanto, no están dispuestas a compartir la información, y menos aún a colaborar en pruebas o estudios que supondrían tener que cambiar en aspectos relevantes de cómo son, cómo funcionan o cómo compiten, en nuestro caso, haciendo software. Para evaluar algunos sub-artefactos concretos se intentará realizar algún experimento puntual. Puede ser el caso de la validez de la herramienta software.

7. Resultados Preliminares

Uno de los resultados preliminares de este trabajo doctoral es un mapeo sistemático de la literatura (actualmente en revisión en revista indexada) con el objetivo de determinar el uso de la práctica de arquitectura empresarial en el contexto del desarrollo de software con BizDevOps. En esta revisión de la literatura se concluye que la práctica de arquitecturas empresariales podría ser de gran utilidad para el desarrollo de SW con BizDevOps, debido a su capacidad de proporcionar una visión completa y holística de los procesos y actividades involucrados en el desarrollo de software con BizDevOps. Otro de los resultados, es un punto de vista arquitectónico, en notación Archimate, que describe las preocupaciones y necesidades de los desarrolladores y los encargados de las operaciones en el desarrollo de software con el enfoque DevOps [Fuentes-Quijada, Ruiz-González, & Caro, 2022]. Esto fue desarrollado como prueba de concepto para posteriormente especificar un punto de vista arquitectónico específico para el enfoque BizDevOps. Además, se trabajó en un artículo de posición en donde se aborda el problema que motiva este trabajo doctoral y las soluciones que componen la propuesta de la tesis [Fuentes-Quijada, Ruiz-González, & Caro, 2023].

8. Conclusiones y Trabajo Futuro

Este trabajo doctoral ha elegido la metodología de investigación DSR con el propósito de diseñar y evaluar artefactos, de forma iterativa e incremental, que permitan alcanzar los objetivos de investigación definidos. Además, el hecho de que el alcance y objetivos de la tesis se enmarca en un dominio complejo, donde se deben relacionar personas, procesos, información y recursos de la organización, nos lleva a pensar que es una metodología adecuada de investigación, ya que nos facilita iterar y evaluar los artefactos a producir, lo cual nos permite mejorarlos y/o adaptarlos según los resultados que se obtengan.

Hasta el momento, solo se ha cumplido completamente el primer objetivo específico, pero esto ha permitido establecer las bases metodológicas y el alcance preciso de la investigación.

Para el trabajo futuro, se planea especificar la capacidad de negocio para BizDevOps ágil y el marco de trabajo (indicadores, arquitectura de referencia, y herramienta software) para gestionar y gobernar los proyectos con esta metodología.

Además, se buscará establecer inicialmente las habilidades y conocimientos necesarios para el panel de expertos que realizará la evaluación del trabajo doctoral.

Agradecimientos

Este trabajo doctoral está parcialmente soportado por el proyecto OASSIS (PID2021-122554OB-C31, financiado por MCIN/ AEI/10.13039/501100011033 y "FEDER Una manera de hacer Europa") y por la ayuda predoctoral PRE2019-087303, financiada por MCIN/AEI/ 10.13039/501100011033 y por "FSE Invierte en tu futuro".

Referencias

Almeida, F., Simões, J., & Lopes, S. (2022). Exploring the Benefits of Combining DevOps and Agile. *Future Internet, 14*(2). doi:10.3390/fi14020063

Alzoubi, Y. I., & Gill, A. Q. (2020). An Empirical Investigation of Geographically Distributed Agile Development: The Agile Enterprise Architecture is a Communication Enabler. *IEEE Access, 8*, 80269-80289. doi:10.1109/access.2020.2990389

Austel, P., Chen, H., Mikalsen, T., Rouvellou, I., Sharma, U., Silva-Lepe, I., & Subramanian, R. (2015). *Continuous Delivery of Composite Solutions*. Paper presented at the Proceedings of the 2nd International Workshop on Software-Defined Ecosystems, Portland, Oregon, USA. https://dl.acm.org/doi/10.1145/2756594.2756595

Forbrig, P. (2018). *BizDevOps and the Role of S-BPM*. Paper presented at the Proceedings of the 10th International Conference on Subject-Oriented Business Process Management, Linz, Austria. http://dl.acm.org/citation.cfm?doid=3178248.3178250

Fuentes-Quijada, G., Ruiz-González, F., & Caro, A. (2022). *Punto de Vista Arquitectónico para Ecosistemas DevOps*. Paper presented at the XXVI Jornadas de Ingeniería del Software y Bases de Datos (JISBD 2022). http://hdl.handle.net/11705/JISBD/2022/3360

Fuentes-Quijada, G., Ruiz-González, F., & Caro, A. (2023). *Towards Agile IT/Business Alignment at BizDevOps*. Paper presented at the 25th International Conference on Enterprise Information Systems.

Gruhn, V., & Schäfer, C. (2015). *BizDevOps: Because DevOps is Not the End of the Story*. Paper presented at the Intelligent Software Methodologies, Tools and Techniques. SoMeT 2015. Communications in Computer and Information Science.

Hadar, E., & Hadar, I. (2016). *CURA: Complex-system Unified Reference Architecture - Position Paper: A Practitioner View*. Paper presented at the Proceedings of the 11th International Conference on Evaluation of Novel Software Approaches to Software Engineering, Rome, Italy. http://www.scitepress.org/DigitalLibrary/Link.aspx?doi=10.5220/0005894302160221

Hemon, A., Lyonnet, B., Rowe, F., & Fitzgerald, B. (2020). From Agile to DevOps: Smart Skills and Collaborations. *Information Systems Frontiers, 22*(4), 927-945. doi:10.1007/s10796-019-09905-1

Hevner, A., & Chatterjee, S. (2010). Design Science Research in Information Systems. In A. Hevner & S. Chatterjee (Eds.), *Design Research in Information Systems: Theory and Practice* (pp. 9-22). Boston, MA: Springer US.

Homann, U. (2006). *A Business-Oriented Foundation for Service Orientation.*

IEEE. (2021). IEEE 2675: 2021 IEEE Standard for DevOps. *IEEE Standard for DevOps*, 92-92. Retrieved from https://standards.ieee.org/standard/2675-2021.html

Lankhorst, M. (2017). *Enterprise Architecture at Work* (4 ed.). Berlin, Heidelberg: Springer Berlin Heidelberg.

Lohrasbinasab, I., Acharya, P. B., & Colomo-Palacios, R. (2020). *BizDevOps: A Multivocal Literature Review*. Paper presented at the Computational Science and Its Applications -- ICCSA 2020, Cagliari, Italy. https://link.springer.com/10.1007/978-3-030-58817-5_50

Moscoso-Zea, O., Paredes-Gualtor, J., & Luján-Mora, S. (2019). Enterprise Architecture, an enabler of change and knowledge management. *Enfoque UTE, 10*(1), 247-257. Retrieved from http://ingenieria.ute.edu.ec/enfoqueute/

Pérez-Castillo, R., Ruiz, F., Piattini, M., & Ebert, C. (2019). Enterprise Architecture. *IEEE Software, 36*(4), 12-19. doi:10.1109/MS.2019.2909329

Petersen, K., Vakkalanka, S., & Kuzniarz, L. (2015). Guidelines for conducting systematic mapping studies in software engineering: An update. *Information and Software Technology, 64*, 1-18. doi:10.1016/j.infsof.2015.03.007

Raj, P., & Sinha, P. (2020). Project Management In Era Of Agile And Devops Methodlogies. *International Journal of Scientific & Technology Research, 9*, 1-1.

Sanjurjo, E., Pedreira, O., Garcia, F., & Piattini, M. (2020). *Process Reference Model for BizDevOps*. Paper presented at the 15th Iberian Conference on Information Systems and Technologies (CISTI), Seville, Spain.

Shahin, M., Nasab, A. R., & Babar, M. A. (2021). A qualitative study of architectural design issues in DevOps. *Journal of Software: Evolution and Process*, 2047-7473. doi:10.1002/smr.2379

Snyder, B., & Curtis, B. (2018). Using Analytics to Guide Improvement during an Agile–DevOps Transformation. *IEEE Software, 35*(1), 78-83. doi:10.1109/ms.2017.4541032

The Open Group. (2022a). Business Capabilities, Version 2. Retrieved from https://pubs.opengroup.org/togaf-standard/business-architecture/business-capabilities.html

The Open Group. (2022b). *Enabling Enterprise Agility*. Retrieved from https://pubs.opengroup.org/togaf-standard/guides/enabling-enterprise-agility/index.html

The Open Group. (2022c). TOGAF® Standard, Version 10. *TOGAF® Standard, Version 10.* Retrieved from https://www.opengroup.org/togaf/10thedition

Uma Abordagem para Alinhamento de Requisitos de Segurança e Proteção de Sistemas IoT Críticos

Ernesto Fonseca Veiga[1]

[1]Instituto de Informática – Universidade Federal de Goiás (UFG)
Goiânia – GO – Brazil

ernestoveiga@ufg.br

Abstract. *The complexity and heterogeneity of IoT systems have given rise to new challenges in the Requirements Engineering (RE) process, such as the joint treatment of security and protection requirements, essential in most of these systems, especially those considered critical. Given the lack of studies that meet this objective, this work presents a proposal for an approach to align security and protection requirements of critical IoT systems, which aims to reduce the complexity of carrying out the RE process for engineers and developers of these systems.*

Resumo. *A complexidade e heterogeneidade dos sistemas IoT tem dado origem a novos desafios no processo de Engenharia de Requisitos (ER), como o tratamento conjunto de requisitos de segurança e proteção, essenciais em grande parte destes sistemas, principalmente aqueles considerados críticos. Diante da carência de estudos que atendam esse objetivo, este trabalho apresenta uma proposta de abordagem para alinhamento de requisitos de segurança e proteção de sistemas IoT críticos, que visa reduzir a complexidade na realização do processo de ER para engenheiros e desenvolvedores destes sistemas.*

1. Introdução

A crescente integração entre infraestruturas de software, hardware e comunicação atribui novas preocupações e características específicas aos sistemas de Internet das Coisas (IoT) e Ciberfísicos (CPS)[1]. Estes sistemas são considerados complexos em várias dimensões, pois operam em ambientes dinâmicos, com alta heterogeneidade de dispositivos e de comunicação [Nguyen-Duc et al. 2019]. Enquanto essa complexidade dos sistemas IoT está aumentando constantemente, o processo de Engenharia de Requisitos (ER) que compreende a descoberta, análise, documentação e validação dos seus serviços e restrições, torna-se também cada vez mais difícil e desempenha um papel fundamental no projeto e desenvolvimento desses sistemas [Binder et al. 2021, Fritz et al. 2019].

Com o objetivo de exemplificar essas características em um domínio de aplicação, e melhorar o entendimento da problemática que será tratada neste trabalho, adotemos o seguinte cenário ilustrativo no domínio de veículos autônomos (VAs):

[1]Os termos "Internet das Coisas" (IoT) e "Sistemas Ciberfísicos" (CPS) têm origens distintas, mas definições sobrepostas, ambas se referindo a tendências na integração de capacidades digitais, incluindo conectividade de rede e capacidade computacional, com dispositivos e sistemas físicos [Greer et al. 2019]. Neste trabalho consideramos o entendimento de equivalência entre IoT e CPS. Por este motivo, para simplificar o texto, padronizamos a sigla IoT como referência aos dois termos.

VAs possuem grande quantidade de sensores, de diferentes tipos, responsáveis pelas entradas de dados no sistema, tais como radares, sonares, sensores de detecção de luz e alcance, GPS, acelerômetro, câmeras, dentre outros. Esses dados são essenciais, pois é a partir do seu processamento em tempo-real que o VA pode entender o contexto e o ambiente em que se encontra para tomar decisões. Além disso, ele controla uma série de atuadores responsáveis por mecanismos como aceleração, frenagem e direção, usados para realizar ações orquestradas de acordo com os dados lidos e processados (ex.: acelerar, manter-se na faixa correta e parar). Em muitos casos, um VA pode também interagir com outros veículos, sistemas e mesmo com pessoas e o próprio ambiente. Esse sistema atua de maneira intensa durante todo o período que o VA estiver em operação, para simplesmente se deslocar com segurança no trânsito, o que mostra sua complexidade. Qualquer decisão equivocada pode colocar em risco as pessoas e o ambiente, neste caso o trânsito, que é altamente dinâmico. Dessa forma, esses sistemas precisam lidar com a alta heterogeneidade de componentes e ambientes dinâmicos desde a sua concepção, o que reflete diretamente na complexidade do processo de ER.

Neste contexto, como primeiro passo desta pesquisa na investigação do processo de ER para sistemas IoT, foi conduzido um mapeamento sistemático da literatura (MSL), cujos resultados preliminares podem ser analisados em [Veiga and Bulcão-Neto 2022][2]. O estudo realizado seguiu um protocolo desenvolvido juntamente com especialistas em ER com objetivo de permitir a identificação das principais tendências, práticas (métodos e técnicas), nível de maturidade e contribuições dos estudos, além de questões em aberto no estado da arte de ER para sistemas IoT.

Buscando identificar lacunas de pesquisa quanto à ER desses sistemas, uma das informações extraídas foi o tipo de requisito abordado em cada estudo revisado. A análise desses dados revelou uma forte preocupação desses sistemas com requisitos de proteção (*security*[3]) e também a necessidade de que estes sejam projetados e operados sob uma visão de alinhamento com segurança (*safety*) [Wolf and Serpanos 2018]. Neste contexto, segurança é "a capacidade do sistema de operar sem falhas que possam causar danos a pessoas ou ao seu ambiente" enquanto proteção é definida como "a capacidade do sistema em se proteger contra intrusão acidental ou deliberada", destacando a sua relação com as questões de segurança da informação e privacidade [Avizienis et al. 2004].

Complementando o cenário apresentado, podemos citar alguns exemplos de requisitos de segurança e proteção (em alto nível) para os sistemas de VAs:

Requisitos de segurança: *a redundância de sistemas de hardware e software (garantir que, em caso de falha de um componente, o VA continue operando com segurança); e a detecção e prevenção de colisões (sensores devem detectar e prever colisões com outros veículos, objetos ou pedestres).*

Requisitos de proteção: *o controle de acesso (sistemas de VAs devem ter protocolos robustos de autenticação para garantir que apenas pessoas autorizadas possam acessar e controlar o veículo); e proteção contra ataques (tanto de hackers quanto de sistemas maliciosos que possam comprometer a segurança do veículo, passageiros e pedestres).*

Requisito que implica diretamente na segurança e na proteção: *a verificação de integridade (VAs devem monitorar constantemente a integridade do software e dos dados processados de modo a detectar eventuais falhas ou ataques).*

---

[2]Disponível em: `https://bityli.com/hI2mel`

[3]Na literatura também é encontrada a expressão "segurança da informação" como tradução para *security*. Adotaremos o termo "proteção" no intuito de facilitar a separação entre as traduções de *security* e *safety*.

Historicamente, os esforços em segurança e proteção surgiram de comunidades distintas e eram considerados de maneira independente. Entretanto, a integração de software e hardware para criar esses tipos de sistemas abriu uma vasta gama de problemas que exigem o tratamento conjunto desses requisitos [Wolf and Serpanos 2018]. Por exemplo, o ataque que viole a proteção de um sistema IoT pode gerar também ameaças à sua segurança, produzindo ações inesperadas ou fora de controle, que causem danos a pessoas ou ao ambiente com o qual o sistema interage.

Dessa forma, tratar as relações existentes entre segurança e proteção tem se tornando essencial em sistemas IoT complexos, que não podem ser considerados seguros se não forem também protegidos, como é o caso dos automóveis autônomos, veículos aéreos não tripulados, dentre outros [Mailloux et al. 2019]. Além disso, o tratamento desses requisitos é imprescindível em sistemas considerados críticos, que são aqueles cujas falhas podem levar a ferimentos ou morte de pessoas, danos ao ambiente, divulgação de informações não autorizadas e perdas financeiras graves [Sommerville 2015].

1.1. Problema

O estudo de [Kavallieratos et al. 2020] destaca que uma combinação fraca dos requisitos de segurança e proteção pode resultar no projeto e desenvolvimento insatisfatórios de um sistema e, possivelmente, em danos ao ecossistema IoT. Neste sentido, [Sadvandi et al. 2012] citam ainda que diversos problemas metodológicos podem surgir de processos de segurança e proteção desconectados, tais como: i) multiplicidade e inconsistências de concepção e projeto, devido ao tratamento independente dessas disciplinas, muitas vezes realizado por diferentes equipes, para o mesmo sistema; e ii) atividades de análise redundantes, devido ao uso de vocabulários distintos para as mesmas tarefas.

A revisão conduzida por [Lisova et al. 2019] reforça essa visão, identificando que segurança e proteção podem influenciar negativamente uma à outra. Portanto, analisar sua interação de maneira eficiente significa reduzir o esforço que precisa ser investido para alcançar um sistema seguro e protegido. Os resultados da pesquisa também ressaltam a necessidade de mais esforços em abordagens de co-análise desses requisitos em todas as áreas de aplicação e também na sua avaliação.

A análise conjunta de segurança e proteção envolve ainda importantes relações que podem surgir entre estes requisitos e devem ser consideradas. [Piètre-Cambacédès 2010] resume as interações entre segurança e proteção em quatro tipos: i) *dependência condicional*, quando o cumprimento dos requisitos de segurança condiciona o nível de proteção ou vice-versa (proteção condiciona a segurança); ii) *reforço mútuo*, quando medidas tomadas para fins de segurança também contribuem para a proteção ou vice-versa (proteção contribui para a segurança); iii) *antagonismo*, quando os requisitos de segurança e proteção, considerados em conjunto, levam a situações conflitantes; e iv) *independência*, quando não há interação entre os requisitos de segurança e proteção. Por exemplo:

Dependência condicional: *[ameaça à proteção] após explorar com sucesso uma vulnerabilidade do sistema de entretenimento do VA, um usuário não autorizado acessa indevidamente o sistema; [risco à segurança] o atacante pode causar ameaças de interrupção, tornando parte do sistema indisponível, ou de alteração, modificando algum ativo do sistema; [consequência da relação] o ataque a uma vulnerabilidade do VA pode causar o seu mau funcionamento e possíveis riscos aos seus ocupantes e ao trânsito.*

__Reforço mútuo__: [requisito de proteção] o sistema de um VA precisa ser capaz de detectar e registrar ataques realizados por sistemas externos; [requisito de segurança] o VA precisa detectar e registrar possíveis situações de falha para evitar acidentes e se antecipar a situações de perigo; [consequência da relação] o registro e tratamento de eventos e atividades em um VA é um requisito necessário tanto aos componentes de segurança quanto de proteção, reforçando-se entre eles.

__Antagonismo__: [ameaça à proteção e risco à segurança acontecendo simultaneamente] em caso de um ataque externo, o sistema de proteção do VA mantém todas as portas trancadas para evitar um possível furto do veículo ou dos pertences dentro dele; porém, se durante esse ataque o VA estiver se deslocando e for detectada uma colisão, ou outro tipo de acidente com risco aos passageiros, o veículo deve manter as portas destrancadas para facilitar a saída ou resgate dos seus ocupantes; [consequência da relação] há um conflito entre os requisitos de segurança e proteção, ameaçando o funcionamento correto do sistema.

Com base nos desafios identificados por [Piètre-Cambacédès 2010, Lisova et al. 2019], o problema de pesquisa a ser investigado nesta proposta é a *carência de abordagens de ER que auxiliem as atividades de análise e especificação dos requisitos de segurança e proteção para sistemas IoT críticos, e permitam o tratamento das interações existentes entre estes requisitos desde a sua concepção.*

1.2. Questão de Pesquisa e Objetivos

Dado o problema apresentado, este trabalho visa responder a seguinte questão de pesquisa: "é possível definir uma abordagem de ER voltada à análise e especificação das interações de requisitos de segurança e proteção para sistemas IoT críticos?".

Assim, o objetivo geral desta pesquisa de doutorado é produzir uma abordagem de ER que contemple as atividades de análise e especificação das interações entre requisitos de segurança e proteção para sistemas IoT críticos. Para tal, definem-se como objetivos específicos deste trabalho: i) definir técnica e artefato de análise conjunta de requisitos de segurança e proteção, conforme os tipos de interações entre esses requisitos; ii) definir técnica e artefato de especificação de requisitos que documente o alinhamento entre requisitos de segurança e proteção; e iii) experimentar e avaliar a abordagem de análise e especificação elaboradas em i e ii com exemplos de sistemas IoT críticos.

2. Procedimentos Metodológicos

Essa pesquisa de doutorado está dividida em 4 fases subsequentes, que são apresentadas na Figura 1, a saber: 1) informativa, 2) analítica, 3) proposicional e 4) avaliativa.

No intuito de aprofundar a análise dos resultados do MSL conduzido na fase informativa desta pesquisa por [Veiga and Bulcão-Neto 2022], foi aplicado o método de Síntese Temática, com base em [Dixon-Woods et al. 2005], que contribuiu para consolidar as evidências encontradas, por meio de análise qualitativa dos dados extraídos dos estudos mapeados. Foi identificada grande preocupação com requisitos não funcionais (RNFs), onde segurança e proteção predominam como os mais importantes no processo ER de sistemas IoT, mas ainda com poucos trabalhos que os tratam de forma integrada.

No momento desta publicação o trabalho se encontra no estágio final da fase analítica, com o estudo das abordagens existentes para co-análise de requisitos de segurança e proteção. Para compreender o estado da arte sobre ER de segurança e proteção de sistemas IoT e identificar lacunas existentes, encontra-se em andamento uma revisão sistemática da literatura (RSL). Esse trabalho de revisão tem como ponto de partida uma busca empregando a técnica de *snowballing forward* [Wohlin 2014] a partir dos

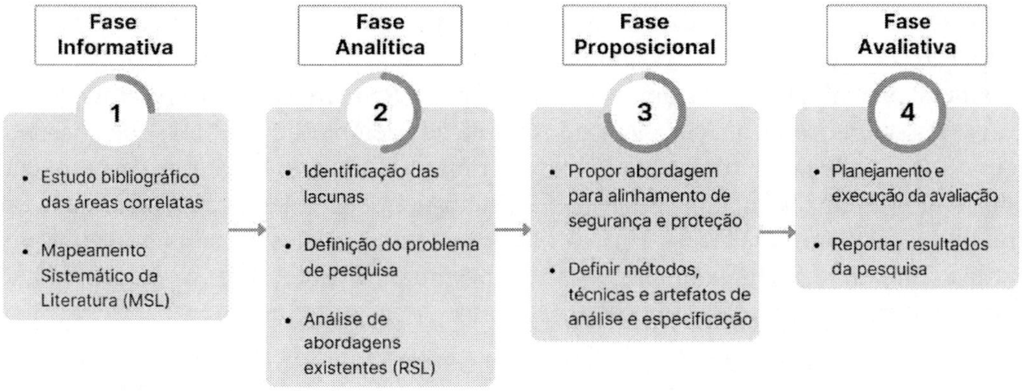

Figura 1. Fases da pesquisa de doutoramento.

14 estudos iniciais (analisados no MSL, que tem como foco principal os requisitos de segurança e/ou proteção). Essa busca identificou 142 novos trabalhos, dos quais 36 foram selecionados como relevantes para a extração de dados, que se encontra em andamento.

A partir dessa RSL serão melhor definidas as atividades de ER a serem tratadas por esta pesquisa, bem como o tipo de abordagem a ser realizada. Até o momento foram identificados gargalos quanto as etapas de análise[4] e especificação destes requisitos. Muitas das abordagens propostas, analisadas até o momento, não realizam um processo de análise abrangente [Japs 2020] ou são dependentes de domínio [Kavallieratos et al. 2020], e ainda trazem poucos resultados práticos em relação à especificação conjunta dos requisitos de segurança e proteção [Japs 2020, Kavallieratos et al. 2020], que servirá como base para o projeto e desenvolvimento de sistemas IoT críticos.

A proposta desse trabalho, a ser detalhada na fase proposicional, deverá cobrir as lacunas identificadas na RSL, de modo a contribuir tanto para a evolução acadêmica da área, como também para os seus praticantes, visando reduzir a complexidade do trabalhos de engenheiros de software e desenvolvedores que precisam lidar com requisitos de segurança e proteção em sistemas IoT críticos. Por fim, as metodologias de experimentação que serão aplicadas na fase avaliativa da pesquisa serão analisadas e definidas posteriormente, de acordo com a abordagem proposta para o processo de ER.

3. Proposta de Solução

De modo geral, os requisitos de segurança enfatizam o desencadeamento acidental de perigos que podem infingir danos às pessoas, enquanto os requisitos de proteção se preocupam com a natureza maliciosa de ataques e ameaças que levam a impactos negativos sobre os ativos de um sistema [Asplund et al. 2019]. A relação entre segurança e proteção vem da sobreposição entre essas perspectivas, por exemplo, quando danos são infligidos a pessoas como parte de um ataque ou como efeito colateral acidental do mesmo. Compreender essas relações é muito importante para sistemas IoT críticos, uma vez que eles permitem a interação com processos físicos por meio de sistemas e software [Wolf and Serpanos 2018, Mailloux et al. 2019]. Entretanto, conforme discutido por meio do cenário da Seção 1, a complexidade destes sistemas torna desafiador o seu processo de ER, exigindo o desenvolvimento e avaliação de novas abordagens.

[4]Alguns dos estudos sobre segurança e proteção incluem elicitação como parte das atividades de análise.

Os resultados do MSL mostraram apenas dois estudos consideraram a integração de requisitos de segurança e proteção para sistemas IoT [Japs 2020, Kavallieratos et al. 2020]. A análise preliminar da RSL mostra um crescimento significativo dessa preocupação, com 9 estudos publicados entre 2021 e 2022, que consideram algum tipo de relação entre estes requisitos. Entretanto, como uma área de pesquisa recente e em desenvolvimento, ainda não existem métodos e técnicas consolidadas para a realização das tarefas necessárias, o que leva muitos destes estudos a adaptarem ou reutilizarem conhecimentos da engenharia de segurança/proteção e novos processos experimentais para as atividades de ER.

A partir da análise de estudos recentes (MSL e RSL em andamento) pudemos identificar lacunas e limitações quanto as atividades de análise e principalmente especificação conjunta de requisitos de segurança e proteção. Grande parte dos estudos ainda não realiza um processo de análise abrangente levando em consideração os diferentes tipos de relações e impacto mútuo entre segurança e proteção destacados por [Piètre-Cambacédès 2010, Lisova et al. 2019]. Esse cenário se agrava quanto à especificação, que é ainda menos explorada por esses estudos.

Buscando avançar o estado da arte e da prática nessa área de pesquisa, a proposta de solução deste trabalho de doutorado consiste na definição e avaliação de uma abordagem sistemática, bem como dos artefatos necessários, para a realização de uma análise abrangente e a produção da especificação de requisitos de segurança e proteção de sistemas IoT críticos, que possa ser aplicada a diferentes subdomínios. No momento atual da pesquisa estão sendo investigados métodos e técnicas que possam contribuir para o desenvolvimento da abordagem proposta. Nesse ponto existe o desafio de alinhamento das diferentes perspectivas relacionadas a este objetivo, uma vez que precisam ser levadas em consideração tanto as preocupações das atividades de ER quanto as necessidades específicas de engenharia de proteção e segurança, no contexto de sistemas IoT críticos.

Diferentes caminhos para condução dessa abordagem tem sido considerados, buscando avaliar os seus benefícios e limitações. Os estudos analisados apontam diferentes tipos de abordagens de especificação para requisitos de proteção, por exemplo, que podem ser adotados de acordo com as necessidades específicas do projeto ou da complexidade sistema, como os modelos formais, amplamente adotados para sistemas críticos.

4. Trabalhos Relacionados

Com foco nos requisitos de proteção, [Hofbauer et al. 2019] apresentam uma abordagem para criação de aplicações seguras onde definem-se os requisitos e controles, que formam um catálogo referente a um caso de uso de acesso remoto da Indústria 4.0. A abordagem, entretanto, não explora a interseção com requisitos de segurança que podem ser afetados neste domínio. Ainda neste contexto, o trabalho de [Hansch et al. 2019] evidencia que a arquitetura de comunicação de sistemas de Internet das Coisas Industrial (IIoT) apresenta sérios desafios de proteção, especialmente na comunicação entre máquinas, locais de produção e produtos inteligentes. Ataques e falhas nestes sistemas mostram que é necessária uma ER de proteção rigorosa para atender ao cenário de ameaças cada vez maior e em rápida evolução, porém, o estudo não aborda a relação com requisitos de segurança.

O trabalho de [Japs 2020], cujo grupo de pesquisa possui estudos correlatos na RSL, cobrem as atividades de elicitação e análise de requisitos de segurança e proteção, com ênfase para a necessidade de uma cooperação eficiente entre *stakeholders* e propondo uma abordagem baseada em modelos para a identificação dos requisitos. Entretanto as contribuições ainda são limitadas quanto a análise das relações entre esses requisitos e não cobrem a sua especificação. A segunda abordagem que trata a segurança e proteção no contexto do MSL realizado, é o método SafeSec Tropos, proposto no estudo de [Kavallieratos et al. 2020], e adotado nos estudos correlatos do grupo, que tem como objetivo facilitar a análise conjunta de requisitos de segurança e proteção, modelando o sistema para ambos os propósitos e identificando potenciais conflitos entre os requisitos. Apesar de propor um método de análise mais robusto, a abordagem é dependente de domínio e não contempla como a especificação destes requisitos pode ser realizada.

A proposta apresentada neste artigo visa explorar as lacunas de pesquisa existentes quanto à análise das diferentes relações entre requisitos de proteção e segurança para diferentes domínios de sistemas IoT críticos e também a sua especificação.

5. Contribuições Esperadas

Ao final dessa pesquisa espera-se alcançar como contribuições: i) uma abordagem de ER para sistemas IoT críticos que permita o alinhamento de requisitos de proteção e segurança; e ii) modelos de artefatos para análise e especificação de segurança e proteção para sistemas IoT críticos, que permitam o tratamento das diferentes relações entre estes requisitos, incluindo a identificação e resolução de conflitos, desde a etapa inicial de projeto destes sistemas. Como contribuição parcial desta pesquisa foi publicado um mapeamento sistemático da literatura que investiga o processo de ER de sistemas IoT/CPS [Veiga and Bulcão-Neto 2022] e apresenta um panorama geral sobre o estado da arte e da prática, identificando tendências, problemas e lacunas de pesquisa. Esse estudo está sendo complementado através de uma RSL (descrita na Seção 2), cujos resultados deverão ser submetidos para publicação em congresso da área ou revista especializada.

6. Conclusões e Trabalhos Futuros

Foi apresentada neste trabalho uma proposta de abordagem para alinhamento de requisitos de segurança e proteção de sistemas IoT críticos com apoio aos diferentes tipos de relações entre estes requisitos. Essa proposta é embasada nos resultados de um MSL conduzido no início do doutoramento e em uma RSL em andamento, cujas lacunas de pesquisa identificadas apontam a necessidade de tratamento conjunto dos requisitos de segurança e proteção, ainda pouco explorada no contexto de sistemas IoT críticos.

O trabalho encontra-se andamento, em fase de investigação de abordagens que contribuam para a co-análise análise e especificação conjunta de requisitos e segurança e proteção para sistemas IoT críticos. Após a definição da abordagem, pretende-se verificar a possibilidade de aplicação desta pesquisa para validação e avaliação em projetos do Centro de Excelência em Inteligência Artificial[5] (CEIA), que atualmente desenvolve projetos voltados para sistemas IoT críticos em diferentes subdomínios de aplicação.

Esta pesquisa está sendo realizada no contexto de um trabalho de doutorado que teve início em março de 2021 e possui data prevista de conclusão para março de 2025.

[5]https://ceia.ufg.br/

Referências

Asplund, F., McDermid, J., Oates, R., and Roberts, J. (2019). Rapid Integration of CPS Security and Safety. *IEEE Embedded Systems Letters*, 11(4):111–114.

Avizienis, A., Laprie, J.-C., Randell, B., and Landwehr, C. (2004). Basic concepts and taxonomy of dependable and secure computing. *IEEE Transactions on Dependable and Secure Computing*, pages 11–33.

Binder, C., Polanec, K., Brankovic, B., Neureiter, C., Lastro, G., and Lüder, A. (2021). Enabling Model-Based Requirements Engineering in a Complex Industrial System of Systems Environment. In *2021 26th IEEE Int. Conf. on Emerging Technologies and Factory Automation (ETFA)*, page 1–6. IEEE Press.

Dixon-Woods, M., Agarwal, S., Jones, D., Young, B., and Sutton, A. (2005). Synthesising qualitative and quantitative evidence: a review of possible methods. *Journal of health services research & policy*, 10(1):45–53.

Fritz, S., Weber, F., and Ovtcharova, J. (2019). A Guideline for the Requirements Engineering Process of SMEs Regarding to the Development of CPS. In *2019 8th International Conference on Industrial Technology and Management (ICITM)*, pages 85–94.

Greer, C., Burns, M., Wollman, D., and Griffor, E. (2019). Cyber-Physical Systems and Internet of Things.

Hansch, G., Schneider, P., Fischer, K., and Böttinger, K. (2019). A Unified Architecture for Industrial IoT Security Requirements in Open Platform Communications. In *2019 24th IEEE International Conference on Emerging Technologies and Factory Automation (ETFA)*, pages 325–332.

Hofbauer, D., Ivkic, I., Maksuti, S., Aldrian, A., and Tauber, M. (2019). On the Cost of Security Compliance in Information Systems. *CoRR*, abs/1905.06122.

Japs, S. (2020). Security & Safety by Model-based Requirements Engineering. In *2020 IEEE 28th International Requirements Engineering Conference (RE)*, pages 422–427.

Kavallieratos, G., Katsikas, S., and Gkioulos, V. (2020). SafeSec Tropos: Joint security and safety requirements elicitation. *Computer Standards & Interfaces*, 70:103429.

Lisova, E., Šljivo, I., and Čaušević, A. (2019). Safety and Security Co-Analyses: A Systematic Literature Review. *IEEE Systems Journal*, 13(3):2189–2200.

Mailloux, L. O., Span, M., Mills, R. F., and Young, W. (2019). A Top Down Approach for Eliciting Systems Security Requirements for a Notional Autonomous Space System. In *2019 IEEE International Systems Conference (SysCon)*, pages 1–7.

Nguyen-Duc, A., Khalid, K., Shahid Bajwa, S., and Lønnestad, T. (2019). Minimum Viable Products for Internet of Things Applications: Common Pitfalls and Practices. *Future Internet*, 11(2).

Piètre-Cambacédès, L. (2010). *Des relations entre sûreté et sécurité*. PhD thesis, Télécom ParisTech.

Sadvandi, S., Chapon, N., and Piètre-Cambacédès, L. (2012). Safety and Security Interdependencies in Complex Systems and SoS: Challenges and Perspectives. In *Complex Systems Design & Management*, pages 229–241, Berlin, Heidelberg. Springer Berlin Heidelberg.

Sommerville, I. (2015). *Software Engineering*. Pearson, 10th edition.

Veiga, E. F. and Bulcão-Neto, R. F. (2022). Engenharia de Requisitos de Sistemas IoT e Ciber-Físicos: Resultados Preliminares. In *Anais do WER22 - Workshop em Engenharia de Requisitos*, page 1–14.

Wohlin, C. (2014). Guidelines for Snowballing in Systematic Literature Studies and a Replication in Software Engineering. In *Proceedings of the 18th International Conference on Evaluation and Assessment in Software Engineering*, EASE '14, New York, NY, USA. Association for Computing Machinery.

Wolf, M. and Serpanos, D. (2018). Safety and Security in Cyber-Physical Systems and Internet-of-Things Systems. *Proceedings of the IEEE*, 106(1):9–20.